Second Edition

ORGANIZATION DEVELOPMENT

Second Edition

ORGANIZATION DEVELOPMENT

The Process of Leading Organizational Change

Donald L. Anderson

University of Denver

Los Angeles | London | New Delhi
Singapore | Washington DC

Los Angeles | London | New Delhi
Singapore | Washington DC

FOR INFORMATION:

SAGE Publications, Inc.
2455 Teller Road
Thousand Oaks, California 91320
E-mail: order@sagepub.com

SAGE Publications Ltd.
1 Oliver's Yard
55 City Road
London EC1Y 1SP
United Kingdom

SAGE Publications India Pvt. Ltd.
B 1/I 1 Mohan Cooperative Industrial Area
Mathura Road, New Delhi 110 044
India

SAGE Publications Asia-Pacific Pte. Ltd.
33 Pekin Street #02-01
Far East Square
Singapore 048763

Acquisitions Editor: Lisa Cuevas Shaw
Associate Editor: Julie Nemer
Editorial Assistant: MaryAnn Vail
Production Editor: Kelle Schillaci
Copy Editor: Trey Thoelcke
Typesetter: C&M Digitals (P) Ltd.
Proofreader: Theresa Kay
Indexer: Maria Sosnowski
Cover Designer: Gail Buschman
Marketing Manager: Helen Salmon

Copyright © 2012 by SAGE Publications, Inc.

Library of Congress Cataloging-in-Publication Data

Anderson, Donald L., 1971-
Organization development : the process of leading organizational change / Donald L. Anderson. — 2nd ed.

p. cm.
Includes bibliographical references and index.

ISBN 978-1-4129-8774-5 (pbk.)

1. Organizational change. I. Title.

HD58.8.A68144 2012
658.4'06—dc22   2011010544

This book is printed on acid-free paper.

11 12 13 14 15 10 9 8 7 6 5 4 3 2 1

Contents

Preface

I n the corporate world today, it may be the prevailing sentiment that organization development (OD) is no longer relevant. There are many reasons for that view, some reasonable based on historical practices (or old beliefs that may not apply today) and some unreasonable based on inaccurate assumptions about what OD is. I do not think that it has to be that way and, after reading this book, I hope you agree.

I wrote this book because I firmly believe that OD as a field of research and practice has much to offer to people in contemporary organizations who are struggling with an incredible amount of change. Old management styles no longer fit the needs of today's workplace and workers. New organizational forms are emerging to cope with the increasing pace of change, globalization, the latest technologies, economic pressures, and the expectations of the contemporary workforce. Managers struggle to engage employees despite ever-present threats of downsizing and outsourcing. In such an environment, many employees find work to be less personally satisfying than they did before.

Skilled OD practitioners understand the dynamics of human systems and can intervene to encourage a healthy, engaging, and productive environment. Unfortunately, it has been challenging for many students to develop these skills. It generally requires "breaking in" to an OD department, finding a (hopefully skilled) mentor, and learning as much as possible through academic courses or self-discovery. While they are regularly tested on the job, managers and executives have few opportunities to develop their skills as change agents as well. My hope is that this book will provide theoretical and practical background in OD to give you an introduction to the basic processes of organization development and change. It will also give you a chance to practice in a safe environment where you can develop your skills.

My thanks to students at the University of Denver's University College, who taught me a great deal about their struggles at work and shared their opinions about how OD is practiced. Practical advice and experiences from consulting colleagues have been invaluable. I have benefited from the support of family, friends, and colleagues, including particularly Karen Tracy and Lola Wilcox (who was a gracious mentor to me). Thanks also to the editors and reviewers at SAGE who provided suggestions and helpful insights and who strongly supported this second edition. Most important, thanks to my wife Jennifer who always encourages me.

—Donald L. Anderson

Ancillaries

Instructor Teaching Site

A password-protected instructor's manual is available at **www.sagepub.com/ andersonod2e** to help instructors plan and teach their courses. These resources have been designed to help instructors make the classes as practical and interesting as possible for students.

- **Overview for the Instructor** offers the author's insights on how to most effectively use this book in a course on organization development.
- **PowerPoint Slides** capture key concepts and terms for each chapter for use in lectures and review.
- **Case Epilogues** provide additional information about the organizations or scenarios featured in the text.
- **Discussion Questions** suggest additional topics to engage students during classroom discussions and activities.
- **Sample Course Syllabus** provides a model for structuring your course.

Student Study Site

An open-access student study site can be found at **www.sagepub.com/anderson od2e.** The site offers videos of the author discussing the major stages of organization development, online quizzes, Web links to additional tools, discussion questions, and **Learning From SAGE Journal Articles**, with access to recent, relevant full-text articles from SAGE's leading research journals. Each article supports and expands on the concepts presented in the book. This feature also provides discussion questions to focus and guide student interpretation.

This text is accompanied by *Cases and Exercises in Organization Development & Change* (ISBN 978–1-4129–8773–8). A bundle of this text with the cases and exercises book is also available (ISBN 978–1-4129–9960–1).

CHAPTER 1

What Is Organization Development?

Think for a moment about the organizations to which you belong. You probably have many to name, such as the company where you work, a school, perhaps a volunteer organization, or a reading group. You are undoubtedly influenced by many other organizations in your life, such as a health care organization like a doctor's office or hospital, a church group, a child's school, a bank, or the local city council or state government. Using an expansive definition of organization, you could name your own family or a group of friends as an organization that you belong to as well. With just a few moments' reflection, you are likely to be able to name dozens of organizations that you belong to or that influence you.

Now consider an organization that you currently do not belong to, but one that you were dissatisfied with at some point in the past. What was it about that organization that made the experience dissatisfying? Perhaps you left a job because you did not have the opportunity to contribute that you would have liked. Maybe it was a dissatisfying team atmosphere, or you were not appreciated or recognized for the time and energy that you dedicated to the job. It could have been a change to your responsibilities, the team, or the organization's processes. Some people report that they did not feel a larger sense of purpose at work, they did not have control or autonomy over their work, or they did not find an acceptable path to growth and career development. Perhaps you've witnessed or been part of an organization that has failed for some reason. Perhaps it went out of business or it disbanded because it could no longer reach its goals.

You've likely had some excellent experiences in organizations, too. You may have had a job that was especially fulfilling or where you learned a great deal and coworkers became good friends. Maybe your local volunteer organization helped a number of people through organized fundraisers or other social services activities.

Perhaps you joined or started a local community group to successfully campaign against the decision of your local city council or school board.

All of this is to demonstrate what you already know intuitively, that we spend a great deal of our lives working in, connected to, and affected by organizations. Some of these organizations function quite well, whereas others struggle. Some are quite rewarding environments in which to work or participate, but in others, organizational members are frustrated, neglected, and disengaged.

The purpose of this book is to introduce you to the field of organization development, an area of academic study and professional practice focused on making organizations better—that is, more effective and productive and at the same time more rewarding, satisfying, and engaging places in which to work and participate. By learning about the field of organization development and the process by which it is conducted, you will be a more effective change agent inside the organizations to which you belong.

Organization Development Defined

Organization development (OD) is an interdisciplinary field with contributions from business, industrial/organizational psychology, human resources management, communication, sociology, and many other disciplines. Not surprisingly, for a field with such diverse intellectual roots, there are many definitions of organization development. Definitions can be illuminating as they point us in a direction and provide a shared context for mutual discussion, but they can also be constraining as certain concepts are inevitably left out with boundaries drawn to exclude some activities. What counts as OD thus depends on the practitioner and the definition, and these definitions have changed over time. In a study of 27 definitions of organization development published since 1969, Egan (2002) found that there were as many as 60 different variables listed in those definitions. Nonetheless, there are some points on which definitions converge.

One of the most frequently cited definitions of OD comes from Richard Beckhard (1969), an early leader in the field of OD:

> Organization development is an effort (1) *planned,* (2) *organizationwide,* and (3) *managed* from the *top,* to (4) increase *organization effectiveness* and *health* through (5) *planned interventions* in the organization's "processes," using *behavioral-science* knowledge. (p. 9)

Beckhard's definition has many points that have survived the test of time, including his emphasis on organizational effectiveness, the use of behavioral science knowledge, and the inclusion of planned interventions in the organization's functions. Some critique this definition, however, for its emphasis on planned change (many organizational changes, and thus OD efforts, are in response to environmental threats that are not so neatly planned) and its emphasis on the need to drive organizational change through top management. Many contemporary OD activities do not necessarily happen at the top management level, as increasingly organizations are developing less hierarchical structures.

A more recent definition comes from Burke and Bradford (2005):

> Based on (1) a set of values, largely humanistic; (2) application of the behavioral sciences; and (3) open systems theory, organization development is a systemwide process of planned change aimed toward improving overall organization effectiveness by way of enhanced congruence of such key organizational dimensions as external environment, mission, strategy, leadership, culture, structure, information and reward systems, and work policies and procedures. (p. 12)

Finally, I offer a third:

> Organization development is the process of increasing organizational effectiveness and facilitating personal and organizational change through the use of interventions driven by social and behavioral science knowledge.

These definitions include a number of consistent themes about what constitutes organization development. They propose that an outcome of OD activities is organizational effectiveness. They also each stress the applicability of knowledge gained through the social and behavioral sciences (such as sociology, business and management, psychology, and more) to organizational settings.

Change Is a Constant Pressure

Perhaps the point on which most definitions agree is that the backdrop and purpose of organization development is change. As you have no doubt personally experienced, large-scale organizational change is rarely simple and met without skepticism. As Peter Senge writes, "Most of us know firsthand that change programs fail. We've seen enough 'flavor of the month' programs 'rolled out' from top management to last a lifetime" (Senge et al., 1999, p. 6). Because of its impact on the organizational culture and potential importance to the organization's success, organizational change has been a frequent topic of interest to both academic and popular management thinkers. With change as the overriding context for OD work, OD practitioners develop interventions so that change can be developed and integrated into the organization's functioning.

To become effective, productive, and satisfying to members, organizations need to change. It will come as no surprise to any observer of today's organizations that change is a significant part of organizational life. Change is required at the organizational level as customers demand more, technologies are developed with a rapidly changing life cycle (especially high-tech products; Wilhelm, Damodaran, & Li, 2003), and investors demand results. This requires that organizations develop new strategies, economic structures, technologies, organizational structures, and processes. As a result, change is also required of individuals. Employees learn new skills as jobs change or are eliminated. Organizational members are expected to quickly and flexibly adapt to the newest direction. Best-selling business books such as *Who Moved My Cheese?* teach lessons in ensuring that one's skills are current and that being comfortable and reluctant to adapt is a fatal flaw. For organizational members, change can be enlightening and exciting, and it can be hurtful, stressful, and frustrating.

Whether or not we agree with the values behind "change as a constant," it is likely to continue for the foreseeable future. Whereas some decry an overabundance of change in organizations (Zorn, Christensen, & Cheney, 1999), others note that it is the defining characteristic of the current era in organizations and that becoming competent at organizational change is a necessary and distinguishing characteristic of successful organizations (Lawler & Worley, 2006). There are, however, more- and less-effective ways to manage change. Creating and managing change in order to create higher performing organizations in which individuals can grow and develop is a central theme of the field of OD. When we speak of organization development, we are referring to the management of certain kinds of these changes, especially how people implement and are affected by them.

What Organization Development Looks Like

It may be easiest to understand what organization development is by understanding what forms it takes and how it is practiced. The following are five examples of published case studies of OD in action.

Example 1: Increasing Employee Participation in a Public Sector Organization (O'Brien, 2002)

Public sector organizations, it has been noted (Coram & Burns, 2001), often face additional special challenges in the management of change. Bureaucratic structures, interfaces with regional governments and legislatures, political pressures, and legislative policies all complicate the implementation of new processes and changes to organizational practices. In the Republic of Ireland, a special initiative launched in the mid-1990s aimed to reduce bureaucracy in the public sector to gain efficiency, improve customer service, and improve interdepartmental coordination. Many programs of this type have been launched in other organizations as top-down mandates from senior management, causing frustration and decreased commitment among staff members who resisted the mandated changes.

One department wanted to do things differently. The offices were in the division of Social Welfare Services (SWS), a community welfare organization of 4,000 employees. Two Dublin offices (50 employees each) became the focus of this case. These offices chose to involve employees in the development of an initiative that would improve working conditions in the department as well as increase the employees' capacity for managing changes. A project steering team was formed, and they began by administering an employee survey to inquire about working relationships, career development, training, technology, and management. Follow-up data gathering occurred in focus groups and individual interviews. The tremendous response rate of more than 90% gave the steering team a positive feeling about the engagement of the population, but the results of the survey indicated that a great deal of improvement was necessary. Many employees felt underappreciated, distrusted, and not included in key decisions or changes. Relationships with management were also a concern as employees indicated few opportunities for communication with management and that jobs had become routine and dull.

The steering team invited volunteers (employees and their management) to work on several of the central problems. One team worked on the problem of communication and proposed many changes that were later implemented, including a redesign of the office layout to improve circulation and contact among employees. As the teams continued discussions, they began to question standard practices and inefficiencies and to suggest improvements, eventually devising a list of almost 30 actions that they could take. Managers listened to employee suggestions, impressed by their insights. As one manager put it, "I have learned that a little encouragement goes a long way and people are capable of much more than given credit for in their normal everyday routine" (O'Brien, 2002, p. 450).

The joint management-employee working teams had begun to increase collaboration and interaction among the two groups, with each reaching new insights about the other. As a result of the increased participation, "There appeared to be an enhanced acceptance of the change process, coupled with demands for better communications, increased involvement in decision making, changed relationships with supervisors and improved access to training and development opportunities" (p. 451).

Example 2: Senior Management Coaching at Vodaphone (Eaton & Brown, 2002)

Vodaphone is a multibillion-dollar global communications technology company headquartered in the United Kingdom and was an early leader in the mobile telephone market. Faced with increasing competition, the company realized that in order to remain innovative and a leader in a challenging market, the culture of the organization would need to adapt accordingly. Specifically, senior management realized that its current "command and control" culture of blame and political games would hinder collaboration and mutual accountability needed to succeed in a competitive environment. Instead, the company wanted to encourage a culture of empowered teams who made their own decisions and shared learning and development, speed, and accountability.

Several culture initiatives were implemented, including the development of shared values, the introduction of IT systems that shared and exchanged information across major divisions that had hindered cross-functional learning, and the establishment of teams and a team-building program.

To support the initiatives and encourage a new, collaborative management style, Vodaphone implemented a leadership coaching program. Through the program, top managers attended a program to learn skills in conducting performance reviews, helping employees set goals, and coaching teams. Following the program, managers had one-on-one coaching sessions with a professional coach who worked with participants to help them set coaching goals and reflect on how successfully they were able to implement the skills learned in the program.

As a result of the program, managers began to delegate more as teams started to solve problems themselves. Teams began to feel more confident in their decisions as managers trusted them. The authors attribute several subsequent company successes to the program, noting that it was critical that the coaching program was integrated with the other culture change initiatives that it supported. "Cultural change takes time," Eaton and Brown (2002, p. 287) note, and "traditional attitudes to management do not die away overnight." However, they point out that a gradual evolution took place and the new cultural values are now the standard.

Example 3: Team Development in a Cancer Center (Black & Westwood, 2004)

Health care workers who have the challenge of caring for critically ill patients experience stress, emotional exhaustion, and burnout at very high rates compared with workers in other fields. Without social support from friends or other coworkers, many workers seek to leave the field or to reduce hours to cope with the emotional exhaustion of a demanding occupation. Consequently, many researchers have found that health care workers in particular need clear roles, professional autonomy, and social support to reduce burnout and turnover.

In one Canadian cancer center, a senior administrator sought to address some of these needs by creating a leadership team that could manage its own work in a multidisciplinary team environment. Team members would have professional autonomy and would provide social support to one another. Leaders volunteered or were chosen from each of the center's main disciplines, such as oncology, surgery, nursing, and more. Organization development consultants were invited to lead workshops in which the team could develop cohesive trusting relationships and agree on working conditions that would reduce the potential for conflict among disciplines.

In a series of three 2-day workshops over 3 months, the team participated in a number of important activities. They did role-play and dramatic exercises in which they took on one another's roles in order to be able to see how others see them. They completed surveys of their personal working styles to understand their own communication and behavior patterns. The team learned problem-solving techniques, they clarified roles, and they established group goals.

Three months after the final workshop was conducted, the facilitators conducted interviews to assess the progress of the group. All of the participants reported a better sense of belonging, a feeling of trust and safety with the team, and a better understanding of themselves and others with whom they worked. One participant said about a coworker, "I felt that [the workshops] connected me far differently to [coworker] than I would have ever had an opportunity to do otherwise, you know in a normal work setting" (Black & Westwood, 2004, p. 584). The consultants noted that participants wanted to continue group development on an ongoing basis.

Example 4: A Future Search
Conference in a Northern California
Community (Blue Sky Productions, 1996)

Santa Cruz County is located in Northern California, about an hour south of San Francisco. In the 1960s, the county had approximately 25,000 residents in an agricultural region and in a small retirement community. In the late 1960s, the University of California, Santa Cruz opened its doors, and in the following years the county began to experience a demographic shift as people began to move to the area and real estate prices skyrocketed. By 1990, the population had reached 250,000 residents, and increasingly expensive real estate prices meant that many residents could no longer afford to live there. Affordable housing was especially a problem for the agricultural community. A local leadership group had convened several conferences but could never agree on an approach to the housing problem.

In the mid-1990s, a consortium of leaders representing different community groups decided to explore the problem further by holding a future search conference. They invited 72 diverse citizens to a 3-day conference not only to explore the problem of affordable housing but also to address other issues that they had in common. The citizen groups represented a cross-section of the community, from young to old, executives to farmworkers, and social services agencies. Attendees were chosen to try to mirror the community as a "vertical slice" of the population. They called the conference "Coming Together as a Community Around Housing: A Search for Our Future in Santa Cruz County."

At the conference, attendees explored their shared past as individuals and residents of the county. They discussed the history of the county and their own place in it. Next, they described the current state of the county and the issues that were currently being addressed by the stakeholder groups in attendance. The process was a collaborative one, as one attendee said, "What one person would raise as an issue, another person would add to, and another person would add to." There were also some surprises as new information was shared. One county social services employee realized that "there were a couple of things that I contributed that I thought everyone in the county knew about, and [I] listen[ed] to people respond to my input, [and say] 'oh, really?'" Finally, the attendees explored what they wanted to work on in their stakeholder groups. They described a future county environment 10 years out and presented scenarios that took a creative form as imaginary TV shows and board of supervisors meetings. Group members committed to action plans, including short- and long-term goals.

Eighteen months later, attendees had reached a number of important goals that had been discussed at the conference. Not only had they been able to increase funding for a farmworkers housing loan program and created a rental assistance fund, but they were on their way to building a $5.5 million low-income housing project. In addition, participants addressed a number of nonhousing issues as well. They embarked on diversity training in their stakeholder groups, created a citizen action corps, invited other community members to participate on additional task force groups, and created a plan to revitalize a local downtown area. "Did the future search conference work?" one participant wondered. "No question about it. It provided a living model of democracy."

Example 5: A Long-Term Strategic Change Engagement (Sackmann, Eggenhofer-Rehart, & Friesl, 2009)

ABA, a German trading company with 15,000 employees, embarked on a major strategic change initiative driven by stiff competition. A global expansion prompted the company to reorganize into a three-division structure. A decentralized shared services model, comprised of 14 new groups, was created for administrative departments that would now support internal divisions. To support the culture of the new organization, executives developed a mission and vision statement that explained the company's new values and asked managers to cascade these messages to their staffs. This effort was kicked off and managed from the top of the organization.

The director of the newly formed shared services centers contacted external consultants, suspecting that a simple communication cascade to employees would not result in the behavioral changes needed in the new structure. The new administrative groups would have significant changes to work processes, and the lead managers of each of the 14 new groups would need assistance to put the new values and beliefs into practice. The consultants proposed an employee survey to gauge the beliefs and feelings of the staff and to provide an upward communication mechanism. Survey results were available to managers of each center, and the external consultants coached the managers through an interpretation of the results to guide self-exploration and personal development. Internal consultants worked with the managers of each of the new centers to facilitate a readout of the survey results with employees and take actions customized to the needs of each group. Consultants conducted workshops for managers to help them further develop personal leadership and communication skills, topics that the survey suggested were common areas of improvement across the management team. Over a period of 4 years, the cycle was repeated, using variations of the employee survey questions, a feedback step, and management development workshops covering new subjects each time.

Interviews and surveys conducted late in the process showed that employees had a positive feeling about change in general. Leaders reported noticing a more trusting relationship between employees and their managers characterized by more open communication. Center managers took the initiative to make regular and ongoing improvements to their units. The authors noted the need for a major change like this one to include multiple intervention targets. This organization experienced "changes in strategy, structure, management instruments, leadership, employee orientation, and the organization's culture context" (p. 537), which required a broad set of surveys, coaching, and workshops to support. "These change supporting activities helped implement the change with lasting effect" (p. 537), they conclude.

As you can see from this and the previous examples, OD is concerned with a diverse variety of issues to address problems involving organizations, teams, and individuals. OD is also conducted in a diverse variety of organizations, including federal, state, and local governments (which are among the largest employers in the United States, according to the U.S. Bureau of Labor Statistics), public sector organizations around the world, health care organizations, educational settings, and nonprofit and private enterprises. Interventions can involve a single individual, a small team (such as the cancer center team described above), multiple teams, or a whole organization. It can also consist of multiple targets of change, such as in the Vodaphone initiative that involved not only large-scale culture change but also the implementation of teams and individual coaching. OD can also deal with multiorganization efforts, such as that described in Santa Cruz County, or it can involve multiple national governments. The target of change can be something as seemingly simple as increasing employee involvement or developing coworker relationships, or it can be as potentially large as creating the vision or strategy of an entire organization or documenting the 10-year future of a large county.

What Organization Development Is Not

Despite this seemingly expansive definition of what organization development is and what issues and problems it addresses, it is also limited. OD is not any of the following.

Management Consulting

OD can be distinguished from management consulting in specific functional areas such as finance, marketing, corporate strategy, or supply chain management. It is also distinguished from information technology applications. Yet, OD is applicable to any of these areas. When organizations attempt conscious changes, whether it involves implementing a new IT system; changes in strategy, goals, or direction; or adapting to a new team leader, OD offers relevant processes and techniques to make the change function effectively. An OD practitioner would not likely use expertise in one of these content areas (for example, best practices in financial structures of supplier relationships or contemporary marketing analysis) to make recommendations about how an organization does this activity. Most management consulting also is not based on OD's set of foundational values (a topic that we will take up in detail in Chapter 3). In Chapter 5 we will discuss OD consulting in particular and differentiate it from management consulting activities with which you may be familiar.

Training and Development

While individual and organization learning is a part of OD and a key value we will discuss in a later chapter, OD work is not confined to training activities. OD is not generally the context in situations in which learning is the sole objective, such as learning a new skill, system, or procedure. OD deals with organizational change efforts that may or may not involve members of the organization needing to learn specific new skills or systems. Many training and development professionals are gravitating toward OD to enhance their skills in identifying the structural elements of organizations that need to be changed or enhanced for training and new skills to be effective. Other aspects of the training and development profession, however, such as needs assessment, course development, the use of technology, or on-the-job training, are not central to the job of the OD practitioner.

In addition, most training programs are developed for a large audience, often independent of how the program would be applied in any given organization. While some OD interventions do incorporate training programs and skill building, OD is more centrally concerned with the context that would make a training program successful, such as management support, job role clarification, process design, and more. As Burke (2008) writes, "Individual development cannot be separated from OD, but to be OD, individual development must be in the service of or leverage for system-wide change, an integral aspect of OD's definition" (p. 23).

Short Term

OD is intended to address long-term change. Even in cases in which the intervention is carried out over a short period (such as the several-day workshops conducted at the cancer center described earlier), the change is intended to be a long-term or permanent one. OD efforts are intended to develop systemic changes that are long lasting. In the contemporary environment in which changes are constantly being made, this can be particularly challenging.

The Application of a Toolkit

Many OD practitioners speak of the OD "toolkit." It is true that OD does occasionally involve the application of an instrumented training or standard models, but it is also more than that. To confuse OD with a toolkit is to deny that it also has values that complement its science. It is more than a rigid procedure for moving an organization, team, or individual from point A to point B. It involves being attuned to the social and personal dynamics of the client organization that usually require flexibility in problem solving, not a standardized set of procedures or tools. In Chapter 3, we will discuss the values that underlie OD to better understand the fundamental concepts that explain how and why OD practitioners make the choices they do.

Who This Book Is For

This book is for students, practitioners, and managers who seek to learn more about the process of organizational change following organization development values and practices. We will use the term *organization development,* as most academic audiences prefer, over the term *organizational development,* which seems to dominate spoken and written practitioner communication. We will also refer to the *organization development practitioner, consultant,* and *change agent* in this book as a single general audience, because these terms emphasize that OD is practiced by a large community that can include more than just internal and external OD consultants.

OD includes (and the book is written for) anyone who must lead organizational change as a part of his or her role. With the magnitude and frequency of organizational change occurring today, this encompasses a wide variety of roles and is an increasingly diverse and growing community. The OD practitioner can include the internal or external organization development consultant, but also managers and executives, human resources and training professionals, quality managers, project managers and information technology specialists, educators, health care administrators, directors of nonprofit organizations, and many more. We will also more frequently discuss *organizational members* than employees, which is a more inclusive term that includes volunteers in nonprofit groups and others who are connected to organizations but who may not have an employment relationship with them. The term also is intended to include not just leaders, executives, and managers but also employees at all levels.

Overview of the Book

This book provides an overview of the content of organization development, including theories and models used by change agents and OD practitioners. It also explores the process by which OD is practiced. The objective of the book is to acquaint you with the field of OD and the process of organization development consulting. The goal is to develop your analytic, consulting, and practitioner skills so that you can apply the concepts of OD to real situations. We will simulate these consulting situations through six detailed case studies, which follow many of the skill development chapters, in which you will be able to immediately practice what you have learned in the chapter.

Chapters 2 through 5 will explore the foundations of the field, including its history, values, and an overview of the key concepts and research in organizational change. In these chapters you will learn how OD began as a field, how it has evolved over the past decades, and how most practitioners think of the field today. In Chapter 3, we will discuss the underlying values and ethical beliefs that influence choices that practitioners must make in working with clients. Chapter 4 provides a foundation in research into organizational change from a systems perspective, a common way of thinking about organizations. We will also discuss a social construction perspective on organizational change. In this chapter you will be exposed to models of organizational systems and organizational change that have influenced the development of many OD interventions. In Chapter 5, we will define the role of the OD consultant, differentiating the OD consultant from other kinds of consultants, and describing the specific advantages and disadvantages to the OD consultant when the consultant is internal or external to the organization.

Beginning with Chapter 6, the book follows an action research and consulting model (entry, contracting, data gathering, data analysis/diagnosis, feedback, interventions, and evaluation). We will discuss the major actions that practitioners take in each of these stages and describe the potential pitfalls to the internal and external consultant. Chapter 6 describes the early stages of the consulting engagement, including entry and contracting. You will learn how a consultant contracts with a client and explores what problems the client is experiencing, how those problems are being managed, and how problems can be (re)defined for a client. In Chapter 7 we will cover how practitioners gather data, as well as assess the advantages and disadvantages of various methods for gathering data about the organization. Chapter 8 describes what OD practitioners do with the data they have gathered by exploring the dynamics of the feedback and joint diagnosis processes. This stage of the consulting process is especially important as it constitutes the point at which the client and consultant define what interventions will best address the problems that have been described.

Chapter 9 begins by describing the most visible aspect of an OD engagement—the intervention. We will discuss the components of interventions and describe the decisions that practitioners must make in grappling with how to structure them for maximum effectiveness. Chapters 10 through 12 address the traditional OD practices with which most practitioners ought to be familiar, including interventions such as organization design, strategic planning, quality interventions, team building, survey feedback, individual instruments, and coaching and mentoring. These chapters also incorporate newer practices being used with increasing frequency, such as appreciative inquiry, future search, and Six Sigma. These interventions are organized according to the target of the intervention, whether it be the whole organization, multiple groups, single groups, or individuals. In Chapter 13 we will conclude our discussion of the OD process by exploring how organization development practitioners separate themselves from client engagements and evaluate the results of their efforts. In Chapter 14 we will discuss the applicability and relevance of OD to contemporary organizations, given trends in demographics, working conditions, and organizational environments.

Many chapters begin with an opening vignette and thought questions to set the stage for the topics covered in those chapters. Some of these vignettes present published case studies of successful and unsuccessful OD efforts. As you read the vignettes and the chapter, consider what factors made the case more or less successful and what lessons the practitioner may have learned from the experience. You may wish to find the published case and read it for additional details not presented in the vignette. Reading published cases can help you develop a deeper appreciation for the complexities of OD work and learn from the successes and struggles that others have experienced.

Following trends in the corporate world, ethical issues in OD are gaining the attention of academics, clients, and practitioners. While we will discuss values and ethics in Chapter 3, rather than leave ethical dilemmas to that chapter alone, we will also discuss ethical issues in organization development at relevant points throughout the book, when appropriate for the stage in the OD process being described.

Analyzing Case Studies

The case studies included in this book are intended to help you learn the role and thought process of an OD consultant or change agent through realistic examples. By reading and analyzing case studies, you will actively participate in applying the theory and concepts of OD to complex, real-life situations that consultants find themselves in every day. These cases are all based in practitioners' real experiences—names and some details have been changed to protect the client's and practitioner's anonymity. By stepping into a practitioner's shoes, you will be challenged to make the tradeoffs and choices that managers and consultants are asked to make. The cases will help you develop the problem-solving and critical-thinking skills that are central to the value that a practitioner brings to a client. Ideally you can discuss these cases with others who have analyzed them as well, and together you can identify the central issues in the cases and debate the most appropriate response. In this way you will be assimilating knowledge that you have about organizations, change, human dynamics, and the concepts and theories of OD. You will learn the logic behind the choices that managers and practitioners make and you will gain practice in making your thought processes explicit. The cases in the book will build on one another in complexity, so you will need to integrate what you have learned from previous chapters as you analyze each case.

The case studies in this book are written as mini-plays or scenes to provide a richly detailed scenario in which you can imagine yourself playing a part, in contrast to many commonly published case studies in which a few short paragraphs provide all of the detail available for analysis. Since a good deal of OD and change management involves noticing and responding to the human and relational dynamics of a situation in addition to the task and content issues, the scenes in this book provide both in order to give you practice in becoming an observer of people during the process of organizational change. The cases in this book also are situated in a number of diverse types of organizations in which OD is practiced, including educational environments, health care and nonprofit organizations, and for-profit businesses. Each of these types of organizations brings with it unique challenges and opportunities for the OD practitioner.

Each case provides a slice of organizational life, constructed as a brief scene in which you can imagine yourself playing a part, but which will require your conscious thinking and reflection. Cases present situations with many options. As Ellet (2007) writes, "A case is a text that refuses to explain itself" (p. 19). It requires you to take an active role to interpret it and discover its meaning. Fortunately, unlike the passage of time in real life, in written cases life is momentarily paused to give you the chance to consider a response. While you do not have the opportunity to gather additional data or ask questions of participants, you do have the ability to flip back a few pages, read the situation again, and contemplate. You can carefully consider alternate courses of action, weigh the pros and cons of each, and clarify why you would choose one option over another.

As a result of having to make these choices, you will hone your ability to communicate your rationale for your decisions. Classmates will make different choices, each with their own well-reasoned rationales. Through discussion you will sharpen your ability to solve problems, understanding the principles behind the decisions that you and your classmates have made. You will learn about how your own experiences shape your assumptions and approaches to problems. You will be challenged to develop your skills to provide evidence for your reasoning, defend your analyses, and explain your thinking in clear and concise ways for fellow practitioners and clients alike. You may find that these discussions prompt you to change your mind about the approach you would take, becoming convinced by a classmate's well-reasoned proposal, or you may find that your reasoning persuades others that your approach has the greater advantages.

Regardless, you will learn that there is no single right answer at the back of the book or to be shared by your instructor after you have struggled. For some of the cases in this book, your instructor may share with you what happened after the case concluded. This information may provide support for the approach you would have taken, or it may make you think that your approach was incorrect. Instead of seeking the right or wrong answer, however, asking yourself whether your proposal was well-reasoned given the circumstances is more important than knowing the exact outcome of the case. While you have the opportunity to do so, use the occasion of the case study and the discussion to play with various alternatives. Here, the process may be more important than the outcome.

The following tips will help you get started with case study analysis.

1. Read the entire case first, and resist the temptation to come to any conclusions the first time you read it. Allow yourself to first gather all of the relevant data about the situation before you propose any solutions or make any judgments about what is happening or what the client needs to do.

2. Use the tools and methods outlined in each chapter to help you think through the issues presented by the case. You will find worksheets, models, and outlines that can assist you in identifying and categorizing problems, selecting and prioritizing interventions, and organizing ideas to respond to the client. Use charts and diagrams to map out organizational structures and underline key phrases and issues. Write questions that come to mind in the margins. Read the case multiple times to ensure that you have not missed a key detail that would indicate to a client that you had not been paying close attention.

3. Realize that like real life, case studies contain many extra details and describe multiple issues. Organizational life is messy and complex, and not all of these details are helpful or necessary to the consultant or change agent. A consultant helping a team redefine roles and responsibilities may be doing so in an environment in which the company has acquired a competitor or quarterly results were disappointing. Part of the practitioner's role is to sort the useful primary information from the unnecessary secondary information (or information that is unnecessary for the immediate problem). This is part of the value of these case exercises and a logic and intuition that you will develop as your skills and experience grow. Ask yourself what the client is trying to achieve, what he or she has asked of you, and what the core issues and central facts are.

4. Similarly, in any response to a client or reaction to a case, resist the temptation to comment on everything. An OD practitioner can help to prioritize the most pressing issues and help the client sort through the complexities of organizational life. It could be that part of the reason the client has asked for help is that the number of possibilities for action are too overwhelming to decide what to do next.

5. When you are prepared to write a response or an analysis, ask yourself whether you have addressed the central questions asked by the case and whether you have clearly stated the issues to the client. Once your response is written, could you send that, in its present form, to the client described in the case? In that regard, is the analysis professionally written and well organized to communicate unambiguously to the client? Will the client understand how and why you reached these conclusions?

6. As you write your analysis, ask yourself how you know any particular fact or interpretation to be true and whether you have sufficiently justified your interpretation with actual data. Instead of boldly stating that "managers are not trained for their roles," you could write, "Only 2 of 10 managers had attended a management training course in the past 5 years, leading me to conclude that management training has not been given a high priority." The latter uses data and makes the interpretation explicit; the former is likely to invite criticism or defensiveness from a client. This does not mean that directness is not appropriate, only that it must follow from the evidence. We will describe the considerations of the feedback process in depth in this book.

7. When you have finished your own thinking and writing about the case, and after you have had the opportunity to discuss the case and options for action with classmates, take the time to write down your reflections from the experience (Ellet, 2007). What did you learn? What principles might apply for the next time you are confronted with these choices?

Summary

Today's organizations are experiencing an incredible amount of change. Organization development is a field of academic study and professional practice that uses social and behavioral science knowledge to develop interventions that help organizations and individuals change successfully. It is a field practiced in almost all kinds of organizations that you can imagine, from education to health care, from government to small and large businesses. Changes that OD practitioners address are diverse as well, addressing organizational structures and strategies, team effectiveness, and much more. OD is not management consulting or training and development, and it is neither short term nor the mere application of a standard procedure or toolkit. OD practitioners can include many kinds of people for whom organizational change is a priority, such as managers and executives, project managers, and organizational members in a variety of roles.

For Further Reading

Beckhard, R. (1969). *Organization development: Strategies and models.* Reading, MA: Addison-Wesley.

Burke, W. W. (2008). A contemporary view of organization development. In T. G. Cummings (Ed.), *Handbook of organization development* (pp. 13–38). Thousand Oaks, CA: Sage.

Egan, T. M. (2002). Organization development: An examination of definitions and dependent variables. *Organization Development Journal, 20*(2), 59–71.

Marshak, R. J. (2006). Organization development as a profession and a field. In B. B. Jones & R. Brazzel (Eds.), *The NTL handbook of organization development and change: Principles, practices, and perspectives* (pp. 13–27). San Francisco: Pfeiffer.

CHAPTER 2

History of Organization Development

I f you have just heard the term *organization development* (OD) used recently, you may be surprised to learn that the practice of OD is now into its seventh decade (even though the term itself first began to be used in the 1960s; see Sashkin & Burke, 1987). Like the business and organizational environments where it is practiced, OD has grown and changed significantly during this time. This chapter highlights different strands of research and practice to illustrate how each of these traditions of OD can be seen, explicitly and implicitly, in how it is practiced today. Eight major traditions of OD research and practice are described here, though these blend together and intersect one another, and the themes in these eight traditions can be seen throughout later chapters. These trends follow one another more or less historically, though there is significant overlap and influence among each of them.

By becoming aware of the history of OD, you will be more aware of how it has been defined throughout its life, as well as the changes that the field has undergone from its historical roots. In addition, you will better understand how today's practice of OD has undergone many years of research and practice to reach its current state.

The eight strands of OD research and practice discussed in this chapter are as follows:

1. Laboratory training and T-groups

2. Action research and survey feedback

3. Management practices

4. Quality and employee involvement

5. Organizational culture

6. Change management, strategic change, and reengineering

The following year, 1947, the first T-group session took place at the National Training Laboratory in Bethel, Maine. T-group sessions were designed to last 3 weeks and were comprised of approximately 10 to 15 participants and one or two trainers. The trainers were not leaders of the group, but facilitators and observers of the group's processes. They posed questions and suggested activities, but remained listeners who encouraged participation and truthfulness rather than directing group activity (Hirsch, 1987). The content and topic of the group's work was developed out of its own chosen goals and objectives; no specific problem-solving tasks were mandated in the T-group's unstructured format. In open and honest sessions in which authenticity and forthright communication were prized, group members spent time analyzing their own and others' contributions, as well as the group's processes. Regardless of whatever process the groups followed, the common objective of each T-group was to create interpersonal change by allowing individuals to learn about their own and others' behavior, so that this education could be translated into more effective behavior when the participants returned home. As the word spread about the effectiveness of the T-group laboratory method, managers and leaders began to attend to learn how to increase their effectiveness in their own organizations. Attendance was aided by a *BusinessWeek* article in 1955 that promoted "unlock[ing] more of the potential" of employees and teams ("What Makes a Small Group Tick," 1955, p. 40). By the mid-1960s, more than 20,000 businesspeople had attended the workshop (which had been reduced to a 2-week session), in what may be considered one of the earliest fads in the field of management (Kleiner, 1996).

The research that Lewin began more than 60 years ago had a significant influence on OD and leadership and management research. His research on leadership styles (such as autocratic, democratic, and laissez-faire) profoundly shaped academic and practitioner thinking about groups and their leaders. His influence on his students Benne, Bradford, and Lippitt in creating the National Training Laboratory has left a legacy that lives on today as NTL continues to offer sessions in interpersonal relationships, group dynamics, and leadership development. The fields of small group research and leadership development owe a great deal to Lewin's pioneering work in these areas. Though the T-group no longer represents mainstream OD practice, we see the roots of this method today in organization development in team-building interventions (a topic addressed in detail in Chapter 11). Lewin's research also influenced another tradition in the history of organization development—action research and survey feedback.

Action Research and Survey Feedback

Recall that Kurt Lewin had founded the Research Center for Group Dynamics in 1945 at MIT to develop research findings and translate them into practical, actionable knowledge that could be used by practitioners to improve groups and solve their problems. Lewin called this model *action research* to capture the idea that the research projects at their core always had both pragmatic and theoretical components, and that rigorous scientific methods could be used to gather data about groups and to intervene in their processes (Cunningham, 1993).

While Lewin and his colleagues were developing the T-group methodology, an effort was taking place at the University of Michigan, where a Survey Research Center was founded in 1946 under the direction of Rensis Likert. In his PhD dissertation at Columbia in 1932, Likert had developed a 5-point scale for measuring attitudes (a scale known today as the Likert scale). One of the first "clients" brought to Michigan was that of the Office of Naval Research, which was "focused on the underlying principles of organizing and managing human activity and on researching techniques to increase productivity and job satisfaction" (Frantilla, 1998, p. 21). The contract with the Office of Naval Research provided needed and important funding for Likert's work on management practices in particular, culminating in a 1961 book, *New Patterns of Management*, which reported the results of his funded research. (These findings are discussed in the next section.)

The Survey Research Center's goal was to create a hub for social science research, specifically with survey research expertise. Sensing an opportunity to improve their organizations, derive economic success, and develop a competitive advantage, some organizations proposed survey research projects to the center but were denied because the center aimed to focus on larger projects of significant importance beyond a single organization and to share the results publicly. These two criteria (addressing questions of larger significance and making the results known to other researchers and practitioners) formed the core of the action research process. One such project that met these criteria was a survey feedback project at Detroit Edison.

Members of the Survey Research Center conducted a 2-year study at Detroit Edison from 1948 to 1950. The survey of 8,000 employees and managers was administered to understand perceptions, opinions, and attitudes about a variety of aspects of the company such as career progression and opportunities for advancement, opinions about managers and colleagues, and the work content and work environment itself. The survey also asked supervisors specifically about their opinions about managing at the company, and invited senior leaders and executives to offer additional perceptions from the perspective of top management. The researchers sought to understand not only how employees at Detroit Edison felt about the organization but also how the results of this project could be used to understand, instigate, and lead change in other organizations. There were four objectives of the research project:

(1) to develop through first-hand experience an understanding of the problems of producing change; (2) to improve relationships; (3) to identify factors which affected the extent of the change; and (4) to develop working hypotheses for later, more directed research. (Mann, 1957, p. 158)

Following the initial data collection, feedback was given to leaders and organizational members about the survey results. Mann (1957) described the process of sharing this feedback as an "interlocking chain of conferences" (p. 158) in which initially the results were shared with the top management, assisted by a member of the research team. At this meeting, participants discussed the results, possible actions, and how the results would be shared with the next level of the organization. Next, each of those participants led a feedback discussion with his or her team about the research results, also conducting action planning and discussing how the results would be shared with the next level. This pattern continued throughout the organization. At each level, the data relevant to that specific group were discussed. Mann noted that the leaders in each case had the responsibility of presenting the data, prioritizing tasks, taking action, and reporting to their supervisors when they had reached an impasse and needed additional assistance to produce change. The researchers observed that this series of feedback meetings had a very positive influence on initiating and leading change in the organization, but they had been unable to substantiate this observation with data.

In 1950, that changed with a second study conducted in eight accounting departments at Detroit Edison that had participated in the first survey. For this stage of the research, managers reviewed the two sets of survey results with employees (those from the first 1948 survey and those from this second 1950 survey) and again conducted action planning. One difference from the first round, however, was that a natural field experiment was set up. In four of the eight departments, after the initial feedback meeting, no action was taken based on the survey results (two intentionally as "control" departments; two due to personnel changes that made it impossible to continue to include them in the experiment). In the four departments that did take action, managers developed action planning programs that differed significantly from one another. Some programs took as long as 33 weeks, while others took 13; some departments met as frequently as 65 times, while others met as few as 9. Some department action programs involved all employees, while others were limited to the management team. Almost 2 years after the programs were initiated, a third survey was conducted in 1952 to assess the impact of the programs that the managers had developed. Thus, the experiment allowed the researchers to compare the 1950 and 1952 data for groups that had taken significant action and those that had taken no action.

The researchers found that among the groups that had taken action based on the survey results, employees reported a positive change in perceptions about their jobs (such as how important it was and how interested they were in the job), their supervisors (such as the manager's ability to supervise and give praise), and the company work environment (such as opportunities for promotion or the group's productivity) compared to the groups that had taken no action. Moreover, Mann (1957) reported,

> Employees in the experimental departments saw changes in (1) how well the supervisors in their department got along together; (2) how often their supervisors held meetings; (3) how effective these meetings were; (4) how much their supervisor understood the way employees looked at and felt about things. (p. 161)

Mann added that the change was even stronger in groups that involved all levels and employees in the action planning process. The researchers then could conclude that the conference feedback model they had developed was an effective one, in which data were collected and fed back to organizational members who took action to initiate changes based on the data and discussion of it.

Today action research, following a model similar to what was done at Detroit Edison, is the foundation and underlying philosophy of the majority of OD work, particularly survey feedback methodologies. This model forms the basis of the OD process that we will discuss in greater detail in Chapter 5. Employee surveys are now a common strategy in almost all large organizations and action research feedback programs have become one of the most prevalent OD interventions (Church, Burke, & Van Eynde, 1994). We will discuss the use of survey methodologies specifically as a data gathering strategy again in Chapter 7.

Management Practices

Based in part on these findings, several research programs in the 1960s prompted researchers and practitioners to adopt different ways of thinking about management practices. The aim of these research programs was to offer alternative ways of managing in contrast to the dominant methods of the time. Four notable research programs include (1) MacGregor's Theory X and Theory Y, (2) Likert's four systems of management, (3) Blake and Mouton's managerial grid, and (4) Herzberg's studies of worker motivation.

Douglas MacGregor, a scholar at MIT and a colleague of Lewin's during his time there, significantly affected thinking about management practices in 1960 with the publication of his book, *The Human Side of Enterprise.* In it, he suggested that "the theoretical assumptions management holds about controlling its human resources determine the whole character of the enterprise" (p. vii). He believed that managers held implicit and explicit assumptions (or "espoused theories") about people, their behavior, and the character of work, and he noted that it was quite easy to hear how those theories influenced managers. In fact, he gave each of his readers an assignment:

> Next time you attend a management staff meeting at which a policy problem is under discussion or some action is being considered, try a variant on the pastime of doodling. Jot down the assumptions (beliefs, opinions, convictions, generalizations) about human behavior made during the discussion by the participants. Some of these will be explicitly stated ("A manager must himself be technically competent in a given field in order to manage professionals within it"). Most will be implicit, but fairly easily inferred ("We should require the office force to punch time clocks as they do in the factory"). It will not make too much difference whether the problem under discussion is a human problem, a financial or a technical one. Tune your ear to listen for assumptions about human behavior, whether they relate to an individual, a particular group, or people in general. The length and variety of your list will surprise you. (MacGregor, 1960, pp. 6–7)

MacGregor argued that managers often were not conscious of the theories that influenced them (remarking that they would likely disavow their theories if confronted with them), and he noted that in many cases these theories were contradictory. Not only do all actions and behaviors of managers reflect these theories, MacGregor believed, but the then-current literature in management and organizational studies also echoed these assumptions. He categorized the elements of the most commonly espoused assumptions about people and work and labeled them Theory X and Theory Y.

Theory X can be summarized as follows:

1. The average human being has an inherent dislike of work and will avoid it if [possible].

2. Because of this human characteristic of dislike of work, most people must be coerced, controlled, directed, threatened with punishment to get them to put forth adequate effort toward the achievement of organizational objectives.

3. The average human being prefers to be directed, wishes to avoid responsibility, has relatively little ambition, wants security above all (MacGregor, 1960, pp. 33–34).

In contrast to the assumptions about personal motivation inherent in Theory X, Theory Y articulates what many see as a more optimistic view of people and work:

1. The expenditure of physical and mental effort in work is as natural as play or rest.

2. External control and the threat of punishment are not the only means for bringing about effort toward organizational objectives. [People] will exercise self-direction and self-control in the service of objectives to which [they are] committed.

3. Commitment to objectives is a function of the rewards associated with their achievement.

4. The average human being learns, under proper conditions, not only to accept but to seek responsibility.

5. The capacity to exercise a relatively high degree of imagination, ingenuity, and creativity in the solution of organizational problems is widely, not narrowly, distributed in the population.

6. Under the conditions of modern industrial life, the intellectual potentialities of the average human being are only partially utilized (MacGregor, 1960, pp. 47–48).

MacGregor wrote that adopting the beliefs of Theory Y was necessary to bring about innovative advances in products, technologies, and solutions to existing problems, and that managers would need to shed some of their existing assumptions about controlling people in favor of a more expansive and humanistic orientation to human behavior in organizations. His work went on to recommend several ways to put Theory Y assumptions into practice, including documenting job descriptions, restructuring the performance appraisal process, and more effectively managing salary increases and promotions.

At about the same time as MacGregor was arguing for a new set of assumptions about management, Likert (1961, 1967) studied four alternative ways of managing, the foundations of which correlate strongly with MacGregor's work. He agreed with MacGregor's assessment of the current state of management, writing that "most organizations today base their standard operating procedures and practices on classical organizational theories. These theories rely on key assumptions made by well-known practitioners of management and reflect the general principles they expound" (Likert, 1967, p. 1). Likert conducted a study in which he asked managers to think of the most productive and least productive divisions in their organizations and to place them on a continuum reflecting their management practices, which he labeled as Systems 1 through 4:

System 1: Exploitative authoritative. Managers use fear, threats, and intimidation to coerce employees to act. Information flow is downward and is comprised of orders being issued to subordinates. Upward communication is distorted due to fear of punishment. Decisions are made at the top of the organization. No teamwork is present.

System 2: Benevolent authoritative. Managers occasionally use rewards but also punishment. Information flow is mostly downward. Most decisions are made at highest levels but some decision making within a narrow set of guidelines is made at lower levels. Some teamwork is present.

System 3: Consultative. Managers use rewards and occasional punishment. Information flow is both downward and upward. Many decisions are made at the top but are left open for decision making at lower levels. Teamwork is frequently present. Goals are set after discussion of problems and potential solutions.

System 4: Participative group. Managers involve group in setting and measuring goals. Information flow is downward, upward, and horizontal. Decision making is done throughout the organization and is characterized by involvement and participation. Teamwork is substantial. Members take on significant ownership to set rigorous goals and objectives.

Likert found and wrote in two monographs (1961, 1967) that managers reported that the most productive departments were run using a participative group management style, and that the least productive departments were led by managers who modeled an exploitative authoritative style. Despite this finding, Likert reported that most managers adopted the latter, not the former, style. To stress the point more forcefully, Likert (1967) followed up this perception data with quantitative data that showed a rise in productivity after a manager began to increasingly adopt the System 4 behaviors of participative management.

A third research program attempting to demonstrate a new set of management values and practices was that of Blake and Mouton. In *The Managerial Grid,* Blake and Mouton (1964) noticed that management practices could be plotted on a chart where the manager demonstrated a degree of "concern for production" and a "concern for people." Each of these could be mapped on a grid, with a score from 1 (low) to 9 (high). A high concern for production but a low concern for people was referred to as a "9,1 style." A manager adopting this style would demonstrate behaviors such as watching and monitoring employees, correcting mistakes, articulating policies and procedures, specifying deadlines, and devoting little time to motivation or employee development. Blake and Mouton advocate a 9,9 approach to management in which managers demonstrate both a high concern for production and a high concern for people, noting that one value of this style is that there is no inherent conflict between allowing the organization to reach its goals and demonstrating a concern for people at the same time. The 9,9 style, they argue, creates a healthier environment, because "people can work together better in the solutions of problems and reach production goals as a team or as individuals when there is trust and mutual support than when distrust, disrespect, and tensions surround their interactions" (Blake & Mouton, 1964, pp. 158–159). Blake and Mouton's grid OD program, detailed in subsequent volumes (Blake & Mouton, 1968, 1978), defined a five-phase intervention program in which managers are trained on the grid concept and complete team-building activities, work on intergroup coordination, and build and implement the ideal organization.

As a fourth example of research in management practices, in a research program beginning in the late 1950s, Frederick Herzberg began to explore the attitudes that people had about their jobs in order to better understand what motivates people at work. A number of studies had sought to answer the question "What do workers want from their jobs?" throughout the previous decades, with contradictory results. In interpreting the studies, Herzberg suspected that job satisfaction was not the opposite of job dissatisfaction. In other words, he believed that different factors might be at play when workers were satisfied with their jobs than when they reported being dissatisfied with their jobs.

Through a series of in-depth interviews, Herzberg and a team of researchers set out to investigate. They asked people to reflect on important incidents that had occurred to them in their jobs—both positive and negative—and asked participants to explain what it was about that event that made them feel especially good or bad about the job. "The results showed that people are made *dis*satisfied by bad environment, the extrinsics of the job. But they are seldom made satisfied by good environment, what I called the *hygienes*. They are made satisfied by the intrinsics of what they *do*, what I call the *motivators*" (Herzberg, 1993, pp. xiii–xiv). In the initial 1959 publication and through subsequent studies, Herzberg explained the key motivators that contributed to job enrichment, in what has been called his motivation-hygiene theory:

- Achievement and quality performance
- Recognition for achievement and feedback on performance
- Work itself and the client relationship
- Responsibility
- Advancement, growth, and learning

At the same time, Herzberg, Mausner, and Snyderman (1959) point out that hygiene factors will not necessarily contribute to job satisfaction, but can cause job dissatisfaction. "When feelings of unhappiness were reported, they were not associated with the job itself but with conditions that *surround* the doing of the job" (p. 113), such as

- Supervision
- Interpersonal relationships
- Physical working conditions
- Salary
- Company policies and administrative practices
- Benefits
- Job security

Herzberg, Mausner, and Snyderman explain that their research on motivation illustrates why contemporary managers had such a difficult time motivating employees. Then-popular management programs for supervisors and wage incentive programs addressed hygiene factors of supervision and monetary compensation, but did little to address the factors such as achievement and work itself that truly motivated employees.

The work of MacGregor, Likert, Blake and Mouton, and Herzberg is illustrative of an era of research in which scholars and practitioners began to rethink commonly held assumptions about management and human behavior. In many ways it is remarkable how MacGregor's optimistic views of human nature and motivation in Theory Y, in contrast to what he saw as the dominant view of managerial control articulated in Theory X, continue to be as relevant to conversations today as they were more than 40 years ago. At the time, OD had not yet made significant inroads into organizations. Managers strongly held negative assumptions about human behavior characteristic of MacGregor's Theory X or Likert's exploitative authoritative style, and while there was already evidence that alternative styles worked more effectively, executives continued to seek proof of OD's effectiveness (Mirvis, 1988). Consequently, these writers sought to persuade the practitioner community that there was a more optimistic and humanistic alternative to management. Some of the assumptions inherent in these three research programs have become dominant values in OD. The foundational values inherent in the humanistic orientation articulated in Likert's participative management style and Blake and Mouton's 9,9 style strongly influenced the field of OD. These values remain as hallmarks of OD practice today, and they are discussed in greater detail in the next chapter.

Quality and Employee Involvement

A fourth historical tradition in the development of the field of OD evolved as organizations began to increasingly adopt some of the management styles described in the previous section, involving employees more in the management and operations of the organization, beginning particularly in manufacturing and industrial environments. This development appeared to be more strongly embraced in the late 1970s and 1980s as industry firms realized a growing competitive threat to the U.S. manufacturing industry as a result of developments in Japan (Benson & Lawler, 2003). As firms realized that the quality of the product strongly impacted the profitability and competitiveness of the organization, they began to pay attention to management styles that would increase workers' ability and motivation to improve quality. As a result, they began to involve employees in noticing defects and taking action to prevent them or to correct them.

After World War II, Japan began to invest in increasing its manufacturing capabilities and quality programs (Cole, 1999). Japanese manufacturing firms created the *quality circle* in the 1950s and 1960s as a method to involve employees in improving quality in their organizations. Thompson (1982) explains,

> A quality circle is a small group of employees and their supervisor from the same work area, who voluntarily meet on a regular basis to study quality control and productivity improvement techniques, to apply these techniques to identify and solve work-related problems, to present their solutions to management for approval, and to monitor the implementation of these solutions to ensure that they work. (p. 3)

The assumption is that typically employees understand best the work in their immediate area and have the most knowledge about how it can be improved. Quality circles involve employees in improving the work environment and the quality of the output by making suggestions to upper management for areas of improvement. Upper management then is free to accept or decline the suggestions. Employees participate of their own accord but are usually given additional compensation or incentives when they do contribute. Research on the effectiveness of quality circles shows mixed results in terms of productivity and improved output (Cotton, 1993), but it is clear that the use of quality circles in American companies reflected an interest in increasing quality, motivation, and participation through employee involvement (Manchus, 1983).

Also taking a cue from Japan's success, in 1981, after studying and observing Japanese management styles that appeared to result in higher productivity and greater quality, William Ouchi proposed Theory Z (a concept modeled after MacGregor's Theories X and Y) in which he suggested that "involved workers are the key to increased productivity" (Ouchi, 1981, p. 4). Ouchi's book described to Americans how the Japanese style of management worked, with long-term or even lifetime employment for workers, performance reviews and promotions or career movement after only a very lengthy observation period, and shared decision making and responsibility. These values were directly contrary to those held by American managers and made the American values more explicit by comparison. Thus, Ouchi's argument is a follow-up to the management practices arguments made in earlier decades but also took advantage of American business' interest in Japanese management styles and improved competitiveness through employee involvement practices.

Quality circles are part of a family of approaches known as *employee involvement* practices. Employee involvement generally describes any attempt to include workers in order to develop greater commitment, productivity, and quality by granting them decision-making authority, giving them information about the organization (such as goals and finances), and providing incentives (Cotton, 1993).

The quality tradition continued throughout the 1980s and 1990s, manifested in quality programs such as ISO 9000, Total Quality Management, and in the late 1990s and early 2000s, Six Sigma. Quality programs such as these, while not always characterized as OD programs, are important to the OD practitioner as they almost always involve some degree of personal and organizational cultural change and often involve an OD practitioner or change agent to help facilitate this change. Today we see evidence of this trend in OD through the pervasive use of self-managed work teams that are given control and ownership of their work as well as how the team functions and is managed. We will discuss some of these programs in Chapters 11 and 12.

To this point in its history, OD focused on solving internal problems in the organization, centered on change first and foremost at the individual level. Seo, Putnam, and Bartunek (2004) contrast this phase, which they call *first-generation OD,* with *second-generation OD,* which they argue consisted of approaches that gave "explicit attention to the organizational environment and the organization's alignment with it" (p. 85). Beginning in the 1980s, with an increasingly global and more frequently and rapidly changing environment, along with advances in technology, organizations

were forced to more quickly adapt to new market conditions. As a result, OD interventions became more highly focused on systemwide concerns rather than on those
of individuals. Seo et al. write that first-generation OD approaches assumed that
changing the individual (through T-groups, survey feedback mechanisms, changing a manager's assumptions or behaviors, or increasing employee involvement in
teams) would gradually mushroom into change at a system level. They write that
"in the turbulent environments of the 1980s and 1990s, however, individual and
group development became less important to organizational effectiveness unless
the organization as a whole continued to be attuned to its rapidly changing environment" (p. 86).

Even in the 1970s, some writers began to criticize the "soft" T-group model as the
foundation for OD work, and OD became more focused on applications in business
settings to further business objectives (Mirvis, 1988). With the challenges prompted
by a new environment in the 1980s, second-generation OD approaches began to target changes at the level of the entire system. Increasingly, OD practitioners began to
look externally at the organization's connection to its environment and to conduct
transformative change at the structural and system level. OD interventions became
more oriented to strategic change with specific goals for the intervention, in contrast
to earlier, open-ended interventions most evident in the T-groups of the 1940s and
1950s. This trend toward using OD efforts to result in strategic change and increased
productivity became most evident in the popularization in the early 1980s in a tradition of work in organizational or corporate culture.

Organizational Culture

A 1980 *BusinessWeek* article brought the concept of corporate culture into the popular
vocabulary of managers and executives searching for a competitive advantage. It
reviewed such well-known companies as AT&T, IBM, and PepsiCo, highlighting the
corporate values that drove their success and promoting the idea that a company's
strategy and culture must be in alignment for the organization to succeed, directly
linking corporate results with organizational culture. The article concluded that if
strategy and culture were not in alignment, either the strategy or the corporate culture must change ("Corporate Culture," 1980).

The concept of a "culture" predominantly originates from the field of anthro-
pology and conjures images of social scientists observing distant countries and
social groups. Similarly, OD practitioners and those who study corporate or organizational cultures have been called "organizational anthropologists" (Smircich,
1985, p. 65), whose task it is to decipher not only "how things are done around here"
(a common definition of culture) but also the hidden meanings and assumptions
that characterize how organizational members interpret and make sense of what is
happening, or "how people think around here."

Culture has been defined in various ways, but most agree that a shorthand definition of culture is "the shared attitudes, values, beliefs, and customs of members
of a social unit or organization" (Walter, 1985, p. 301). Schein (2004) provides a
more detailed definition:

The concept of organizational learning gained a following in OD because its primary concern, growth and development of individuals and teams, resonated strongly with the founding rationale and values of the field. Organizational learning has now become both an evaluation mechanism of OD effectiveness as well as an intervention in itself. An international academic and practitioner community now comprises the Society for Organizational Learning, which evolved from a center founded in the early 1990s by Senge. Organizational learning plays a major part in both the values of OD and practices that we will discuss in later chapters on values and intervention strategies.

Organizational Effectiveness and Employee Engagement

It may be too soon to characterize organizational effectiveness (OE) and employee engagement as a trend in the development of the field of organization development. Nevertheless, many practitioners are directing their attention toward conceiving of OD as organizational effectiveness, though the academic literature does not appear

Table 2.1 History of Organization Development

Period		Theme	Influence Today
1940s	*First-Generation OD*	Laboratory training and T-groups	Small-group research Leadership styles Team building
1950s		Action research and survey feedback	Employee surveys Organization Development processes
1960s		Management practices	Participative management
1970s		Quality and employee involvement	Quality programs such as Six Sigma, Total Quality Management, and self-managed or employee-directed teams
1980s	*Second-Generation OD*	Organizational culture	Culture work, specifically in mergers and acquisitions
1980s/1990s		Change management, strategic change, and reengineering	Currently practiced, systems theory, large-scale and whole organization interventions
1990s		Organizational learning	Currently practiced, appreciative inquiry
2000s		Organizational effectiveness and employee engagement	Currently practiced

to be making this same shift. In some practitioner circles, *organizational effectiveness* is supplanting *organization development* as a preferred term, perhaps because of the continued perception today that OD is a "soft" practice not connected to the organization's business objectives. It is not entirely clear whether in this new term *organizational effectiveness* differs substantially from OD as practitioners define it, though the former expression stresses the results the organization obtains from an intervention, but at the expense of the emphasis on personal and organizational growth that comes from the term *development*. The term *organizational effectiveness* is not a new one, clearly, as you will recall its inclusion in Beckhard's (1969) well-known definition of organization development. Indeed, academic researchers have been working to define the characteristics, precursors, and determinants of OE for many years (see Cameron & Whetten, 1981). Many early studies of OE concentrated on quantitative and objective measures on outcomes of what constitutes an effective organization. Thus, by adopting this term and referencing this research history, we may be seeing a shift in the practitioner community away from the qualitative (interpersonal, cultural, growth, and learning) aspects of OD toward being able to quantitatively prove the value of an OD intervention.

To contrast with this organizationwide view of effectiveness, *employee engagement* is a second term that is being widely adopted by managers and OD practitioners. The term "refers to the individual's involvement and satisfaction with as well as enthusiasm for work" (Harter, Schmidt, & Hayes, 2002, p. 269). Literature on an individual's job satisfaction, productivity, and motivation is substantial. Some see engagement as a broader concept than these others, however, suggesting that "employees who know what is expected of them, who form strong relationships with co-workers and managers, or who in other ways experience meaning in their work, are engaged" (Luthans & Peterson, 2001, p. 378). The current interest in employee engagement may be reflective of a return to a concern with the health of the individual to complement the emphasis on organizational concerns and outcomes. Thus, the current reference to employee engagement may be a counterresponse to the quantitative movement in organizational effectiveness, resurrecting what is lost by substituting the bottom-line business connotation of OE for OD.

As you can see, threads of OD's history remain with us in contemporary practice. Table 2.1 summarizes the eight strands of OD reviewed in this chapter and shows how OD's history influences the field today.

Summary

Organization development has evolved, adapted, and changed dramatically in the decades since the first T-groups were initiated. Early practitioners and researchers concentrated on individual growth and development through T-groups, action research and survey feedback activities, and emphases on management practices and employee involvement, whereas later approaches beginning in about the 1980s emphasized larger, systemwide concerns such as culture, change management, and organizational learning. Throughout its history, with new experiences and research programs, academics and practitioners have built on previous practices in order to develop the content and process of OD work to continue to change individuals and organizations. We see elements today of each of these trends in the history of OD. Consequently, OD is not a one-size-fits-all approach to organizational change, nor is it a methodical set of rigid practices and procedures, but it consists of multiple methods, perspectives, approaches, and values that influence how it is practiced. Depending on what a client is trying to achieve, the OD consultant may adapt and adopt a number of practices and approaches, traditional and well-tested or cutting-edge and less well-known, in order to develop an appropriate intervention strategy that makes sense for the client organization. Many, perhaps most, of these approaches have their roots in the traditions of OD that we have discussed in this chapter. As we cover the process and content of OD throughout this book, you will see how the field retains traces of its history in contemporary practice.

Note

1. The historical record differs as to how enthusiastic the researchers were about this development. Some have written that the participants were "encouraged" to sit in on the sessions by the researchers (French & Bell, 1999, p. 33), some remark that the request to sit in was simply "assented to" (Hirsch, 1987, p. 18), and others emphasize the "anxiety" (Bradford, 1974, p. 35) and "misgivings" (Lippitt, 1949, p. 114) that the researchers felt by the request.

For Further Reading

Bradford, L. P. (1974). *National Training Laboratories: Its history, 1947–1970*. Bethel, ME: National Training Laboratory.

Bradford, L. P., Gibb, J. R., & Benne, K. D. (Eds.). (1964). *T-group theory and laboratory method*. New York: Wiley.

Kleiner, A. (1996). *The age of heretics: Heroes, outlaws, and the forerunners of corporate change*. New York: Doubleday.

CHAPTER 3

Core Values and Ethics of Organization Development

As we discussed in the previous chapter, organization development (OD) consists of more than just the application of surveys and tools or facilitating meetings, though these are all general activities that can fall within the scope of an OD engagement. As each client application of OD principles and practices is somewhat unique, OD is not the rigid following of a systematic procedure. It involves the kinds of assessments, dialogues, and decisions that we cover in detail throughout this book. Consequently, developing OD skills is less about learning a standard toolkit and more about internalizing the factors that influence an OD practitioner's decisions. Those decisions are guided by a set of values and ethical beliefs about how organizations should be run, how people should be treated, and how organizational change should be managed. OD values and ethics help to direct choices about what client engagements to accept, what data gathering strategy to employ, how feedback to the client should be managed, what interventions to select, and how the intervention should be structured. In this chapter, we will define the core values held by OD practitioners and describe the ethical beliefs that influence their choices and decisions.

The values that have been adopted by OD practitioners have been formed and shaped by its history, so many of the pronouncements of OD values that you will see in this chapter will resonate with what you read in Chapter 2. The work of MacGregor, Likert, and others resulted in a series of statements about the best ways to manage people in organizations, and over time these have been internalized and shaped into a series of explicit values for the field of OD.

Defining Values

A great deal of psychological research and writing has defined and examined the concept of values and how values affect our thinking and behavior.[1] Rokeach (1973) defined a *value* as "an enduring belief that a specific mode of conduct or end-state of existence is personally or socially preferable to an opposite or converse mode of conduct or end-state of existence" (p. 5). Values express what a person believes should happen or ought to happen, and they are relatively stable and enduring from situation to situation, though they can also change and become more complex, particularly as a person gains more experience. Value statements are organized into a person's value system, which is "a learned organization of rules for making choices and for resolving conflicts" (Rokeach, 1968, p. 161). As a system, values help us decide what action to take and how to assess both our actions and the actions of others.

Why Are Values Important to the OD Practitioner?

Values are significant for organization development because they are the underlying beliefs that are enduring and broader than any single consulting engagement or intervention. Values have been a part of the field since its founding, and they have held such an important place in the practice of OD that the field has been somewhat derisively referred to as a "religious movement" (Harvey, 1974). Yet failing to take values into account leaves OD as a list of intervention techniques to be studied without understanding the reasons why those interventions were developed or when the practitioner should apply them. Management scholar Edgar Schein wrote of his frustration in completing a questionnaire about OD intervention techniques that "I did not see OD as a set of techniques at all, but as a philosophy or attitude toward how one can best work with organizations" (Schein, 1990a, p. 13). Margulies and Raia (1990) put the point more bluntly, noting that OD

> *is* value-based and more importantly its core values provide the guiding light for both the OD process and its technology. The very identity of the field is reflected in the existence and application of the values it advocates. Without them, OD represents nothing more than a set of techniques. (p. 39)

Others agree, going so far as to predict that the future of OD rests on the applicability of its core values to practitioners and clients (Wooten & White, 1999).

Values are important to OD practitioners for the following reasons:

1. *They guide choices about how to proceed.* Returning to our values helps to guide us when we are uncertain how to proceed with a client or when we have multiple courses of action that are possible. When a client does not know which solution is best, for example, the OD value of participation and involvement may encourage the practitioner to recommend including organization members in the decision about which solution is most desirable. OD values can give direction and tend to specify guiding principles rather than exact behavior.

2. *They provide a larger vision that extends beyond any individual intervention.* For the OD practitioner, values provide a constancy of purpose that is greater than any single consulting engagement, providing a larger mission for one's career. Many OD practitioners hold values of environmental and social responsibility and social justice, and they see results in those areas as enduring effects of their work. Developing better working conditions in more humanistic and democratic organizations is an overarching value that many practitioners hold, core beliefs that endure regardless of the situation.

3. *They distinguish OD from other methods of consulting and change.* OD and other types of management consulting share important similarities but also important differences. One of these differences relates to the values of OD work. Focusing interventions and the consulting process to ensure growth, development, and learning is a key value that does not show up as a purpose of most other management consulting activities. "It is the humanistic value structure and concern for people that *differentiates* organization development from many of its competing disciplines" (Church, Hurley, & Burke, 1992, p. 14).

4. *They can help to prompt dialogue and clarify positions.* Being explicit about our values and the choices they prompt can help OD practitioners and clients understand one another's behavior. The OD practitioner can explain why he or she believes in a certain course of action by articulating the values underlying this choice, and the manager or client can do the same. We can learn from one another's perspectives and discover underlying similarities and differences (as well as avoid repeating the same conflicts over and over). A client who decides not to implement a mentoring program may still believe in the value of individual growth and shared learning, but may believe that the time is not right for this particular program. The consultant can then work with the client to develop another program that meets the client's needs and also maintains the same objectives and underlying values.

5. *They can help us evaluate how we did.* Values can be a starting point for evaluation of an engagement (as we will discover in Chapter 13) or a point for personal reflection and self-evaluation as a consultant. Whether we acted in accordance with our values and helped to further those values is an important point of learning and evaluation after any engagement.

Core Values of Organization Development

Several humanistic assumptions underlie the core values of the field. By humanistic we mean that individuals deserve respect, are trustworthy, and want to achieve personal growth and satisfaction (Wooten & White, 1999). Humanistic values also include a belief in the equity and equality of people, democratic principles, and a belief in human dignity and worth. "Broadly defined, this humanistic orientation can be summed up as 'improving organizational life for all members'" (Church et al., 1992, p. 11). Adapting from predecessors Likert, MacGregor, and Blake and Mouton, Tannenbaum and Davis (1969) articulated the transition in values taking hold in organizations at the time. Table 3.1 summarizes the alternative values espoused by OD practitioners.

Expanding on the definitions listed on the right side of Table 3.1, Margulies and Raia (1972) were among early proponents of OD's humanistic values, which they described as follows:

1. Providing opportunities for people to function as human beings rather than as resources in the productive process

2. Providing opportunities for each organization member, as well as for the organization itself, to develop to his [or her] full potential.

3. Seeking to increase the effectiveness of the organization in terms of *all* of its goals.

4. Attempting to create an environment in which it is possible to find exciting and challenging work.

5. Providing opportunities for people in organizations to influence the way in which they relate to work, the organization, and the environment.

6. Treating each human being as a person with a complex set of needs, *all* of which are important in his [or her] work and in his [or her] life (p. 3).

Table 3.1　Organization Development Values

Away From . . .	Toward . . .
A view of people as essentially bad	A view of people as essentially good
Avoidance of negative evaluation of individuals	Confirming them as human beings
Seeing individuals as fixed	Seeing them as being in process
Resisting and fearing individual differences	Accepting and utilizing them
Utilizing an individual primarily with reference to his or her job description	Viewing him or her as a whole person
Walling-off the expression of feelings	Making possible both appropriate expression and effective use
Game-playing	Authentic behavior
Use of status for maintaining power and personal prestige	Use of status for organizationally relevant purposes
Distrusting people	Trusting them
Avoiding facing others with relevant data	Making appropriate confrontation
Avoidance of risk taking	Willingness to risk
View of process work as being unproductive effort	Seeing process work as essential to effective task accomplishment
Primary emphasis on competition	Greater emphasis on collaboration

SOURCE: Tannenbaum, R., & Davis, S. A. (1969). Values, Man, and Organizations. *Industrial Management Review, 10*(2), 67–86.

Many who read this list of humanistic values for the first time have an initial feeling that they are worthy values to hold, but they see them as too idealistic to implement in practice, specifically in a competitive organizational environment in which business results are necessary. The OD practitioner sees the possibilities for an improved organizational life in which personal and organizational goals are not at odds. This means, perhaps most fundamentally to OD's values, that personal effectiveness, challenge, learning, fulfillment, and satisfaction can be gained *at the same time* that the organization's effectiveness and objectives are also realized. We will return to this point later in the chapter.

In the next sections we will examine several of OD's current values in more detail.

Participation, Involvement, and Empowerment

Participation is perhaps the most foundational of OD's democratic values. Recall the discussion of Likert's participative management strategy described in Chapter 2. Participative management, and OD activities that support it, offer the ability for employees to contribute to the decision-making process and to have more control and autonomy over their work (Skelley, 1989). This value means that organizational members should be involved and included in decisions and organizational changes that impact them, because "people support what they help create" (Beckhard, 1969, p. 27; Wooten & White, 1999, p. 11). Schein (1990a) writes that the essence of OD is "that change in human systems will not come about without the active involvement of the members of the system who will undergo the change" (p. 16). Change, in this respect, is not imposed on a group or demanded of an individual. Instead, the practitioner's charge is to help the organization develop and manage the change that it seeks to create, giving the opportunity for participation and thereby transitioning ownership to organization members. Creating occasions for participation in decision making means giving employees a choice to contribute (for example, to offer an opinion or to express a perspective) but stops short of mandating it. Providing opportunities for involvement and participation does not necessarily mean that all organizational members will be enthusiastic about the outcome, but it does mean that they will have had an opportunity to express an opinion and potentially to shape it. In this respect, participation is a very important aspect of organizational members' being able to express themselves and achieve personal fulfillment through membership.

Participation is not, however, a silver bullet to eliminate all organizational problems. As Pasmore and Fagans (1992) argue, "One cannot conclude based on any reasonable review of the literature . . . that simply involving people in decision making will produce positive benefits to either those involved or the organization as a whole" (p. 378). Instead, more complex factors are at play. Organizational members may not be prepared or trained to participate. For example, inviting employees to solve complex problems may not be effective if they do not have the skills to do so. Moreover, participation can be a risky prospect in many organizations, where members can feel suspicious of being asked to step outside of long-held hierarchical patterns. This is true particularly since organizations have not created the conditions in which members can participate competently, as Argyris (1957) noted a half-century ago. Characteristics of organizational structure (e.g., a tall organization), relationships (e.g., expectations of who may participate given what status), and societal expectations (e.g., values of not being confrontational or oppositional) all inhibit an individual's choice to participate (Neumann, 1989). Finally, increasing participation can actually be detrimental to members if it is not authentic. Organizational leaders must not choose to involve employees solely for symbolic reasons. Instead, they must develop an environment in which authentic participation is possible and organizational members can have a legitimate impact.

The Importance of Groups and Teams

Beckhard (1969) writes that "the basic building blocks of an organization are groups (teams)" (p. 26). They are central categories in the organizational system and, as a result, the major target for many interventions. Organizational members almost always belong to at least one, if not several, interdependent teams, organized by function (e.g., marketing or human resources) or level (e.g., vice presidents or second-shift managers), for example. French (1969) writes that organization members generally want to participate in at least one group of this type (the immediate department being the most common), to both contribute and to be accepted, and that group effectiveness is at least in some way dependent on the group's taking some of the major task and maintenance responsibilities of the leader. These groups both reflect and affect the larger organization's functioning, since the successful functioning of finance, marketing, or sales affects other departments that depend on them. Therefore, successful team functioning is essential to larger systemwide success. Coghlan (1994) concludes, "As the success of an organization's change endeavors depends on an effective utilization of teams and groups to move the change through an organization, skills at understanding and facilitating groups and teams are essential for the management of change" (p. 22). Because of their prevalence and importance, paying attention to the health of groups and teams is a key value in OD.

In addition to formal groups and teams, individuals are also members of informal groups of colleagues, friends, and associates, often from multiple departments, that exert a powerful impact on an individual's behavior. Formal and informal group norms and cultural beliefs of groups comprise the unwritten code of behavior, and these codes are taught to new members. Understanding these norms and codes, what they tell individuals about how to behave, and what impact this has on the organization is an important part of understanding the group's ability to contribute to organizational change.

Growth, Development, and Learning

Perhaps the value that differentiates organization development from most other management and consulting work is its emphasis on growth, development, and learning. Think about your own beliefs, skills, and attitudes compared to what they were 5 or 10 years ago. In small or perhaps more significant ways, you are likely to be different. You have learned from mistakes or perhaps changed a belief or habit based on experience. In organizational settings, people are no different. They are, and the organization itself is, "in process," meaning that we see people and organizations as constantly evolving and changing. For OD consultants, this value implies that we choose not to give up on a person or group during challenging times, instead finding ways to help them grow and develop. This runs counter to the notion that unsuccessful people should be terminated and unsuccessful departments should be disbanded. Instead, it means first understanding the factors inhibiting success and then providing opportunities for change. This optimistic view of people and groups also implies that engagements and interventions should be constructed as opportunities for learning, so that the organization can learn not only to solve the immediate problem but also to learn how problems or situations like this one can be addressed next time, without fostering dependence on a consultant. Ideally, this learning process will become ingrained into the organization itself so that learning is increasingly a normal part of leadership and management (Schein, 1987).

Valuing the Whole Person

Recognizing and valuing a person as a "whole person" means three things. First, it is often the case that a person who has been in a job or followed an educational path for any length of time can become typecast or pigeonholed by professional category, as an accountant, a marketing person, a receptionist, a manufacturing line employee, and so on. Consequently, work assignments and problems are brought to that person in accordance with people's existing labels for him or her and assumptions about professional knowledge and interests. The accountant will not be brought a customer service problem, the receptionist will not be invited to contribute to a public relations problem, and the manufacturing line employee will not be asked for an opinion on an engineering problem. Presumably, this is because this is how labor is organized, but it is also due to assumptions about what kinds of work people want to do. People also want variety, or perhaps may be interested in a career change, and organizations can structure opportunities to recognize organizational members' multiple interests and skills. Consider what a manufacturing employee knows about the construction and engineering of products or what a receptionist knows about customer service and public relations problems. They can be very knowledgeable about areas outside their immediate job descriptions. It is also true that "most people desire to make, and are capable of making, a much higher level of contribution to the attainment of organization goals than most organizational environments will permit" (French, 1969, p. 24). Unfortunately, many organizations hold their members back from greater contributions. Organizations can provide support for learning, growth, and development that recognizes that people can make contributions beyond those for which they were originally hired.

Second, recognizing organizational members as whole people respects their feelings as people. They may be especially enthusiastic about a recent success and deserve genuine congratulations, or they may desire an opportunity to celebrate the organization's success with colleagues. They may be worried about taking on new responsibilities, concerned about new expectations, or angry at a policy change. OD interventions aim to respect these expressions of emotion and to acknowledge them. The expression of anger and conflict is a natural and normal reaction to organizational change and ought not to be ignored or suppressed.

Finally, respecting the whole person means acknowledging and recognizing diversity and the benefits that individual differences bring to an organization. We come to organizations with multiple identities—gender, age, race, national origin, religion, disability, economic background, and so on. Many organizational practices have historically resulted in ignoring or silencing alternative voices (Prasad, Pringle, & Konrad, 2006). This has been especially true for members whose identities were not identical to those of management. The result has been that ideas and contributions from members with rich backgrounds and experiences have frequently not been heard or included. Recognizing the diverse identities of organizational members implies paying explicit attention to, valuing, and respecting the unique contributions of all members.

Dialogue and Collaboration

As early as 1969, Beckhard noticed that "one of the major problems affecting organizational effectiveness is the amount of dysfunctional energy expended in inappropriate competition and fighting between groups that should be collaborating" (p. 33). Indeed, the same can be said of individuals. A key value in organization development is the creation of healthy environments that promote collaboration rather than competition, with the assumption that a win-win solution is both possible and more desirable than conflict. This does not mean that the suppression of conflict is desired; in fact, the opposite is true. OD interventions seek to bring conflicts to light where they can be addressed in a healthy manner through open dialogue, rather than to allow the suppression of conflict that continues to fester unspoken. Moreover, the goal is for organizational members to learn how to recognize hidden conflict and to deal with it in an appropriate manner.

Authenticity, Openness, and Trust

According to Burke (1977), in a review of organization development trends, authenticity was on its way to overtaking democracy as a primary value in the field. When we create competitive environments, organizations develop as contexts in which it is valued and rewarded to withhold information or mislead to gain status and authority. Collaborative practices cannot succeed in that environment. Instead, they demand that we act in an authentic manner. Being authentic means being straightforward, genuine, honest, and truthful about one's plans, opinions, and motivations. This has implications for how managers communicate with employees, for example, in providing an honest explanation for a project (what the project is intended to accomplish and why) as well as one's own opinions and beliefs about it. Authentic leadership demands consistency in words and actions as followers look to leaders' behavior to assess whether their talk is forthright and can be trusted (Goffee & Jones, 2005). Leaders demonstrate trust by giving employees information; explaining organizational direction, values, principles, and rationales; including them in dialogues and discussions; and allowing them to make decisions. This value applies not only to organizational members but also to OD practitioners, who must be authentic with clients in order to expect the same in return. This means confronting clients where appropriate and being honest with the client in the assessment of the data and one's own feelings.

No intervention or organization holds to all of the values listed in Table 3.2 as static entities. In fact, it is probably not useful to think of values as categories, but instead to think of them as a project or objective. Many practitioners think of OD

Table 3.2 Current Values in Organization Development

- Participation, involvement, and empowerment
- The importance of groups and teams
- Growth, development, and learning
- Valuing the whole person
- Dialogue and collaboration
- Authenticity, openness, and trust

values not as states (e.g., an organization is or is not participative, is team-oriented or individual-oriented), but rather as a continuum or direction. They represent movement away from traditional notions about organizational bureaucracy and human behavior (like Theory X, discussed in Chapter 2) and toward alternative humanistic views about individuals and groups. Any consulting engagement or intervention strategy successfully modeling OD's core values can be seen as moving an organization toward these values rather than turning on one value and turning off another as you would a light switch. This belief demonstrates the value of being "in process," that organizations and individuals are continually growing and changing.

Changes to OD Values Over Time and the Values Debate

The humanistic roots of organization development began with its foundation as a field interested in individual growth and self-awareness. OD has always had theoretical, practical, and humanistic components, with focus varying in one of these three areas at times in its history (Friedlander, 1976). Recently, however, as we discussed in Chapter 2, the movement toward organization effectiveness has taken a greater hold in OD as practitioners are more frequently asked to consult on organizationwide changes. In a survey of OD practitioners in the 1990s, Church, Burke, and Van Eynde (1994) found an increase in practitioners' values toward achieving business effectiveness outcomes (such as increasing productivity, enhancing quality, or developing a competitive advantage) over traditional humanistic values (such as openness, collaboration, and other values described above). (Compared with these first two categories, practitioners ranked lower on the list values related to the external environment, such as caring for the natural environment and enhancing corporate citizenship.) In fact, the major values in both categories (business effectiveness and humanistic concerns) were ranked almost equally in their importance to practitioners. The researchers noted that contemporary practice deals much more frequently with organizationwide, bottom-line results and that experiential activities for individuals and groups are no longer the mainstream of organization development practice.

This business results emphasis in organization development targets bottom-line results that can involve downsizing and job changes for individuals. Many observers have sounded a note of alarm about the business effectiveness addition to OD's humanistic values (see Nicoll, 1998), noting that if OD were to move significantly away from its humanistic roots in favor of organization efficiency and productivity, OD would be "unrecognizable from its origins" (Church et al., 1992, p. 14) and that "a realization of this trend in the extreme . . . would mean the end of OD as a distinct field" (p. 7). However, not all agree that a focus on business effectiveness is harmful to the field of OD. Some have argued that the humanistic values of OD have adapted pragmatically to contemporary organizational challenges (Margulies & Raia, 1990), and that this is just another adaptation to needs. Others note that there may be a generational gap developing between those who have been in the field for a long time, who lament the addition of efficiency and profitability to OD's foundational values (and the concomitant watering down of its humanistic roots), and those who are new to practicing OD, who see OD interventions as a means to help clients achieve the business outcomes they seek (Hultman, 2002). Bradford and Burke (2005) write that there is a downside to OD's insistence on humanistic values, noting that they produce a group of practitioners advocating for their own values and who are perhaps naive about the varying circumstances in which certain values should be emphasized over others.

Implemented appropriately, humanistic concerns and business effectiveness need not be always contradictory objectives, since "we must be concerned with both the people being affected and the way in which they work (the process), as well as what they actually produce (the outcome)" (Church et al., 1994, p. 35). Ultimately, if the job of the OD practitioner is to assist the client in helping them achieve what they desire to achieve, this can be done within the broad context of OD's core values and ethical beliefs. This is not to say that there are no challenges or tensions, however, to holding to these beliefs. For example, what is the consultant's responsibility in helping a client redefine job responsibilities for employees who do not desire to change job tasks? The OD practitioner must hold to the conviction that achieving personal effectiveness and business outcomes are not always by necessity contradictory ends, and the practitioner must therefore learn to navigate the challenges and tensions to holding OD values, being conscious of the choices being made.

What Would You Do?

Consider the statement of ethical guidelines for OD practice at the end of this chapter. What do you think a practitioner should do when confronted with these scenarios? Identify the item(s) in the ethical statement related to each situation.

1. You have learned of a possible project that would allow you to practice your new OD skills with a nonprofit organization. While you have not led a workshop like this before, you are enthusiastic about the opportunity, and this could be a great career move that would also help a deserving organization. You would agree not to charge the group for your services. What ethical considerations exist for your participation? Would it matter if this group would compensate you for your time? Would it matter if this was a private company and you were already employed there?

2. As the manager of corporate quality, you ask members of your staff to interview 15 key stakeholders to determine their support for a new training

initiative. Your staff summarized the data for you and reviewed the summary in a staff meeting. It becomes clear that two of the executives are strongly opposed to the initiative, and two are strongly in favor of it. It occurs to you that you could benefit from knowing who the supporters are so that they could convince the opponents to support your initiative. What ethical considerations exist in this situation? Can you ethically ask your staff to share the names of the supporters? What if your staff offered no promises of anonymity to the interviewees? Would it matter if the subject was a sensitive one?

3. As a favor to a friend who manages a small team of six professionals, you agreed to facilitate a team meeting. Fearing that the meeting would become contentious, your friend asks you to steer the discussion away from several issues that she knows will cause an argument. Knowing that these conflicts are the source of the team's troubles and are necessary discussion points to help the team improve, should you bring up the issues anyway and help the group resolve them, or should you heed your friend's request?

4. You are the director of operations for the emergency department of a local hospital. Recent state regulations now mandate that certain paperwork be completed before and after each patient's visit, and you have redesigned the intake processes to adjust for these requirements. You need the administrative and nursing staff to be on board with these changes, and you know they will be resistant. How might OD values of participation, involvement, empowerment, collaboration, and openness suggest what to do next?

Challenges to Holding Organization Development Values

Schein (1990a) and Church et al. (1992) see tensions and challenges to the practitioner in holding to the values described above:

1. *Financial and economic tensions.* OD practitioners are frequently either external consultants needing to sell clients on an approach or internal practitioners working with managers of the same organization. In either case, it is easier to describe approaches to solving a problem rather than to engage in a philosophical statement about values to a potential client. External consultants making a living in OD may find it easier to talk with clients about OD techniques versus holding nebulous values-based dialogues. They may decide to accept an engagement that does not fit with their values over declining the invitation of a paying client. Church et al. (1992) refer to this as a "tension of being driven by ego gratification, personal success, and financial rewards versus championing traditional humanistic values in the consulting process" (p. 20).

2. *The push to see OD as technology.* OD practitioners find it tempting to quickly and arbitrarily use favorite tools or the latest technique in an attempt to be cutting edge. Businesses and consulting practices have evolved that promote specific OD techniques so that both consultants and clients may be enamored with a popular approach or a sales pitch. In any case, the excitement over a new technique may

overshadow the values on which it is based or the necessity of implementing it in the first place. Margulies and Raia (1990) write,

> Many practitioners have become routine in their applications; they have succumbed to management pressure for the quick fix, the emphasis on the bottom line, and the cure-all mentality. . . . They seem to have lost sight of the core values of the field. (p. 38)

Many students and new practitioners of OD in particular become enamored with books outlining "101 new OD interventions" without full knowledge of when and why they would be applied.

   3. *Management culture and expectations.* Speed and productivity are key values of business culture in the United States. Managers seek rapid solutions to immediate problems and want to be able to quantitatively prove the value of spending money on a consultant. A consultant who spends time with surveys, conducting interviews, giving feedback, or facilitating meetings may appear to be producing very little and taking a long time to do so. This culture of productivity and expectations of speed pushes OD practitioners away from the rigor of values-based diagnostic processes and into rapid discussions of solutions and intervention programs. This creates a "tension between projecting one's own values and normative beliefs onto client organizations versus being only a facilitator for serving management's interests" (Church et al., 1992, p. 20). Managers may see a practitioner who discusses values as out of touch with contemporary organizational challenges.

   4. *Research.* Academic research projects that sought to compare and contrast methods and techniques used in OD work have pushed practitioners to see OD (and the field to evolve) as a set of techniques that resulted in certain outcomes rather than to examine whether those techniques appropriately applied the core values of the field (Schein, 1990a).

Statement of Organization Development Ethics

Ethics follow from values in guiding practitioners in how to implement and enact values. Ethical beliefs outline more and less desirable behaviors, based on a set of underlying values such as those defined above (White & Wooten, 1985). In a survey of organization development and human resources professionals in the early 1980s, practitioners admitted that there was no widespread definition of ethics for the field. Several scholars collaborated on an early draft of a statement, which was further revised. An annotated version was published in a book in 1990 by William Gellerman, Mark Frankel, and Robert Ladenson. The statement of ethical guidelines for OD professionals is reprinted in the Appendix to this chapter. This statement contains many of the categories of OD values discussed earlier in this chapter, including client-centered values.

This clear statement of ethics has many followers and will be a useful guide for you throughout this book. Ethical conflicts do occur for OD professionals, and we will explore some of them in later chapters.

Summary

The values of organization development are a significant part of its identity, and they distinguish OD from other methods of consulting. Its values help practitioners with making choices about how to proceed in an intervention. They clarify our thinking and help to establish a dialogue with clients about what we value and why. They also provide a method for evaluating our work and give practitioners a larger purpose for their work. OD's values include participation, involvement, empowerment, groups and teams, growth, development, learning, thinking of organizational members as whole people, dialogue, collaboration, authenticity, openness, and trust.

Recently, business effectiveness has been added to this list of humanistic concerns to include values such as quality, productivity, and efficiency, which some highlight as a potential conflict with OD's humanistic values tradition. In any case, values conflicts do occur as OD practitioners must cope with economic and cultural forces that push them to see OD as a set of tools or intervention techniques and to neglect the values that underlie these techniques. Finally, a statement of OD ethics has been developed as an explicit statement of desired practitioner behaviors that are based on OD's values.

Note

1. Rokeach (1973) and other psychologists over the past decades have done a great deal of work to distinguish among values, attitudes, beliefs, assumptions, and so on. For our purposes in this chapter, these distinctions are not critical.

For Further Reading

Gellermann, W., Frankel, M. S., & Ladenson, R. F. (1990). *Values and ethics in organization and human systems development: Responding to dilemmas in professional life.* San Francisco: Jossey-Bass.

Margulies, N., & Raia, A. P. (1972). *Organizational development: Values, process, and technology.* New York: McGraw-Hill.

White, L. P., & Wooten, K. C. (1985). *Professional ethics and practice in organizational development.* New York: Praeger.

Appendix

Statement of Ethical Guidelines for Practice for OD-HSD (Organization Development–Human Systems Development)

We commit ourselves to acting in accordance with the following guidelines.

I. Responsibility to Ourselves

  A. Act with integrity; be authentic and true to ourselves.

  B. Strive continually for self-knowledge and personal growth.

  C. Recognize our personal needs and desires and, when they conflict with other responsibilities, seek whole-win resolutions.

  D. Assert our own interests in ways that are fair and equitable to us as well as to our clients and their stakeholders.

II. Responsibility for Professional Development and Competence

  A. Accept responsibility for the consequences of our actions and make reasonable efforts to ensure that our services are properly used; terminate our services if they are not properly used and do what we can to see that any abuses are corrected.

  B. Develop and maintain our individual competence and establish cooperative relationships with other professionals.

    1. Develop the broad range of our own competencies. These include:

      a. Knowledge of theory and practice in

        i. Applied behavioral science generally

        ii. Leadership, management, administration, organizational behavior, system behavior, and organization/system development specifically

        iii. Labor union issues, such as collective bargaining, contracting, and quality of working life (QWL)

        iv. Multicultural issues, including issues of color and gender

        v. Cross-cultural issues, including issues related to our own ethnocentric tendencies and to differences and diversity within and between countries

        vi. Values and ethics in general and how they apply to both the behavior of our client system and our own practice

        vii. Other fields of knowledge and practice relevant to the area(s) within OD-HSD on which we individually concentrate

      b. Ability to

        i. Act effectively with individuals; groups; and large, complex systems.

        ii. Provide consultation using theory and methods of the applied behavioral sciences.

      iii. Cope with the apparent contradiction in applying behavioral science that arises when our "science" is too particular or theoretical to be applicable or when our real approach is intuitive and not clearly grounded in science.

      iv. Articulate theory and direct its application, including creation of learning experiences for individual; small and large groups; and large, complex systems.

  2. Establish collegial and cooperate relations with other OD-HSD professionals. These include:

    a. Using colleagues as consultants to provide ourselves with feedback or suggestions about our own development and to minimize the effects of our blind spots.

    b. Creating partnerships with colleagues to enhance our effectiveness in serving clients whose needs are greater than we can serve alone.

C. Recognize our personal needs and desires and deal with them in the performance of our professional roles and duties.

D. Practice within the limits of our competence, culture, and experience in providing services and using techniques.

  1. Neither seek nor accept assignments outside our limits without clear understanding by clients when exploration at the edge of our competence is reasonable.

  2. Refer clients to other professionals when appropriate.

  3. Consult with people who are knowledgeable about the unique conditions of clients whose activities involve specific areas in which we are inexperienced or not knowledgeable:

    a. In special functional areas (such as marketing, engineering, or R&D)

    b. In certain industries or institutions (such as mining, aerospace, health care, education, or government)

    c. In multicultural settings (such as when we practice in settings in which there is significant diversity in the race, ethnicity, or gender of the people involved)

E. Practice in cultures different from our own only with consultation from people native to or knowledgeable about those specific cultures.

III. Responsibility to Clients and Significant Others

A. Serve the long-term well-being of our client systems and their stakeholders.

  1. Be aware of the beliefs and values relevant to serving our clients, including our own, our profession's, our culture's, and those of the people with whom we work (personal, organizational, and cultural).

  2. Be prepared to make explicit our beliefs, values, and ethics as OD-HSD professionals.

  3. Avoid automatic confirmation of predetermined conclusions about the client's situation or what needs to be done by either the client or ourselves.

4. Explore the possible implications of any OD-HSD intervention for all stakeholders likely to be significantly affected; help all stakeholders while developing and implementing OD-HSD approaches, programs, and the like, if they wish help and we are able to give it.

5. Maintain balance in the timing, pace, and magnitude of planned change so as to support a mutually beneficial relationship between the system and its environment.

B. Conduct any professional activity, program, or relationship in ways that are honest, responsible, and appropriately open.

1. Inform people with whom we work about any activity or procedure in which we ask their participation.

   a. Inform them about sponsorship, purpose and goals, our role and strategy, costs, anticipated outcomes, limitations, and risks.

   b. Inform them in a way that supports their freedom of choice about their participation in activities initiated by us; also acknowledge that it may be appropriate for us to undertake activities initiated by recognized authorities in which participants do not have full freedom of choice.

   c. Alert them to implications and risks when they are from cultures other than our own or when we are at the edge of our competence.

   d. Ask help of the client system in making relevant cultural differences explicit.

2. Seek optimum participation by people with whom we work at every step of the process, including managers, labor unions, and workers' representatives.

3. Encourage and enable people to provide for themselves the services we provide rather than foster continued reliance on us; encourage, foster, and support self-education and self-development by individuals, groups, and all other human systems.

4. Develop, publish, and use assessment techniques that promote the welfare and best interests of clients and participants; guard against the misuse of assessment techniques and results.

5. Provide for our own accountability by evaluating and assessing the effects of our work.

   a. Make all reasonable efforts to determine if our activities have accomplished the agreed-upon goals and have not had any undesirable consequences; seek to undo any undesirable consequences, and do not attempt to cover them up; use such experiences as learning opportunities.

   b. Actively solicit and respond with an open mind to feedback regarding our work and seek to improve our work accordingly.

6. Cease work with a client when it becomes clear that the client is not benefiting or the contract has been completed; do not accept or continue work under a contract if we cannot do so in ways consistent with the values and ethics outlined in this Statement.

C. Establish mutual agreement on a fair contract covering services and remuneration.

1. Ensure mutual understanding and agreement about the service to be performed; do not shift from that agreement without both a clearly defined professional rationale for making the shift and the informed consent of the clients and participants; withdraw from the agreement if circumstances beyond our control prevent proper fulfillment.

2. Ensure mutual understanding and agreement by putting the contract in writing to the extent feasible, yet recognize that:

   a. The spirit of professional responsibility encompasses more than the letter of the contract.

   b. Some contracts are necessarily incomplete because complete information is not available at the outset.

   c. Putting the contract in writing may be neither necessary nor desirable.

3. Safeguard the best interests of the client, the profession, and the public by making sure that financial arrangements are fair and in keeping with appropriate statutes, regulations, and professional standards.

D. Deal with conflicts constructively and minimize conflicts of interest.

1. Fully inform the client of our opinions about serving similar or competing organizations; be clear with ourselves, our clients, and other concerned stakeholders about our loyalties and responsibilities when conflicts of interest arise; keep parties informed of these conflicts; cease work with the client if the conflicts cannot be adequately resolved.

2. Seek to act impartially when involved in conflicts among parties in the client system; help them resolve their conflicts themselves, without taking sides; if it becomes necessary to change our role from that of impartial consultant, do so explicitly; cease work with the client if necessary.

3. Identify and respond to any major differences in professionally relevant values or ethics between ourselves and our clients; be prepared to cease work, with explanation of our reasons, if necessary.

4. Accept differences in the expectations and interests of different stakeholders and realize that those differences cannot always be reconciled; take a whole-win approach to the resolution of differences whenever possible so that the greatest good of the whole is served, but allow for exceptions based on more fundamental principles.

5. Work cooperatively with other internal and external consultants serving the same client systems and resolve conflicts in terms of the balanced best interests of the client system and all its stakeholders; make appropriate arrangements with other internal and external consultants about how to share responsibilities.

6. Seek consultation and feedback from neutral third parties in cases of conflict involving ourselves, our clients, other consultants, or any of the systems' various stakeholders.

E. Define and protect confidentiality in our client relationships.

1. Make limits of confidentiality clear to clients and participants.

2. Reveal information accepted in confidence only to appropriate or agreed-upon recipients or authorities.

3. Use information obtained during professional work in writings, lectures, or other public forums only with prior consent or when disguised so that it is impossible from our presentations alone to identify the individuals or systems with whom we have worked.

4. Make adequate provisions for maintaining confidentiality in the storage and disposal of records; make provisions for responsibly preserving records in the event of our retirement or disability.

F. Make public statements of all kinds accurately, including promotion and advertising, and give service as advertised.

1. Base public statements providing professional opinions or information on scientifically acceptable findings and techniques as much as possible, with full recognition of the limits and uncertainties of such evidence.

2. Seek to help people make informed choices when they refer to statements we make as part of promotion or advertising.

3. Deliver services as advertised and do not shift without a clear professional rationale and the informed consent of the participants or clients.

IV. Responsibility to the OD-HSD Profession

A. Contribute to the continuing professional development of other practitioners and of the profession as a whole.

1. Support the development of other professionals by various means, including:
   a. Mentoring with less experienced professionals.
   b. Consulting with other colleagues
   c. Participating in reviews of others' practices.

2. Contribute to the body of professional knowledge and skill, including:
   a. Sharing ideas, methods, and findings about the effects of our work.
   b. Keeping our use of copyright and trade secrets to an appropriate minimum.

B. Promote the sharing of professional knowledge and skill.

1. Grant use of our copyrighted material as freely as possible, subject to a minimum of conditions, including a reasonable price based on professional as well as commercial values.

2. Give credit for the ideas and products of others.

3. Respect the rights of others in the materials they have created.

C. Work with other OD-HSD professionals in ways that exemplify what the OD-HSD profession stands for.

   1. Establish mutual understanding and agreement about our relationships, including purposes and goals, roles and responsibilities, fees, and income distribution.

   2. Avoid conflicts of interest when possible and resolve conflicts that do arise constructively.

D. Work actively for ethical practice by individuals and organizations engaged in OD-HSD activities and, in case of questionable practice, use appropriate channels for dealing with it.

   1. Discuss directly and constructively when possible.

   2. Use other means when necessary, including:

      a. Joint consultation and feedback (with another professional as a third party)
      b. Enforcement procedures of existing professional organizations
      c. Public confrontation

E. Act in ways that bring credit to the OD-HSD profession and with due regard for colleagues in other professions.

   1. Act with sensitivity to the effects our behavior may have on the ability of colleagues to perform as professionals, individually and collectively.

   2. Act with due regard for the needs, special competencies, and obligations of colleagues in other professions.

   3. Respect the prerogatives and obligations of the institutions or organizations with which these colleagues are associated.

V. Social Responsibility

A. Accept responsibility for and act with sensitivity to the fact that our recommendations and actions may alter the lives and well-being of people within our client systems and within the larger systems of which they are subsystems.

B. Act with awareness of our own cultural filters and with sensitivity to international and multicultural differences and their implications.

   1. Respect the cultural orientations of the individuals, organizations, communities, countries, and other human systems within which we work, including their customers, beliefs, values, morals, and ethics.

   2. Recognize and constructively confront the counterproductive aspects of those cultures whenever feasible, but be alert to the effects our own cultural orientation may have on our judgments.

C. Promote justice and serve the well-being of all life on earth.

1. Act assertively with our clients to promote justice and well-being, including:

    a. Constructively confronting discrimination whenever possible.

    b. Promoting affirmative action in dealing with the effects of past discrimination.

    c. Encouraging fairness in the distribution of the fruits of the system's productivity.

2. Contribute knowledge, skill, and other resources in support of organizations, programs, and activities that seek to improve human welfare.

3. Accept some clients who do not have sufficient resources to pay our full fees and allow them to pay reduced fees or nothing when possible.

4. Engage in self-generated or cooperative endeavors to develop means for helping across cultures.

5. Support the creation and maintenance of cultures that value freedom, responsibility, integrity, self-control, mutual respect, love, trust, openness, authenticity in relationships, empowerment, participation, and respect for fundamental human rights.

D. Withhold service from clients whose purpose(s) we consider immoral, yet recognize that such service may serve a greater good in the longer run and therefore be acceptable.

E. Act consistently with the ethics of the global scientific community of which our OD-HSD community is a part.

Finally, we recognize that accepting this Statement as a guide for our behavior involves holding ourselves to standards that may be more exacting than the laws of any countries in which we practice, the ethics of any professional associations to which we belong, or the expectations of any of our clients.

SOURCE: Gellermann, W., Frankel, M. S., & Ladenson, R. F. (1990). *Values and Ethics in Organization and Human Systems Development: Responding to Dilemmas in Professional Life.* San Francisco: Jossey-Bass. Reprinted with permission.

Case Study 1: Analyzing Opportunities for Organization Development Work at Northern County Legal Services

Read the Northern County Legal Services case and consider the following questions:

1. What is it like to work in this environment? How do you respond to Julie as a leader? Compare Julie as a leader with some of the descriptions of leadership styles provided in Chapter 2.

2. What organizational, team, and individual problems can you identify? What opportunities for organization development work do you see?

3. How do the opportunities you have identified illustrate the values and ethical beliefs of organization development identified in this chapter?

"Good morning. Northern County Legal Services," Christina said. "How can I help you? Yes, I see. Okay, why don't I schedule a time for you to stop by and talk with one of us about your situation and we can see how we can help? I'm free on the 12th at 3:30 p.m. Does that work for you? Excellent. And you know where our office is located? Yes, right across the street. Good. I'll look forward to speaking with you then."

It was already packed in the office of Northern County Legal Services (NCLS), a non-profit organization located just outside the downtown district. In the small waiting room, nearly 20 clients waited for assistance while a team of staff members handled walk-in visitors and made appointments. With no air-conditioning, the room was starting to get hot on the sunny August afternoon as the chairs filled up.

"I'm sorry. Mr. Gaines? I think you're next." Christina looked at the growing crowd.

"Oh, no, no, no, no." A tall woman rose from her chair and stepped forward, raising her voice. "I've been here since 10 a.m. and I was here first. I'm next. He needs to wait his turn." She looked around the room for support, and some heads nodded as those waiting began to look at one another in frustration.

"Yes, I'm sorry that you've waited so long, but Mr. Gaines had made an appointment," Christina said.

"Yeah, for 11:30," Mr. Gaines scoffed.

"It will only be a few more minutes until someone is with you," Christina offered.

"You need to get more organized," the woman said as she rolled her eyes. She returned to her seat, fanning herself with a 2-year-old copy of an entertainment magazine.

Christina looked her watch: 12:20. Her parking meter was already expired. "Have a seat, sir, and I'll be right with you." She grabbed her purse and quickly headed to the front door. "And just where do you think you're going, miss?" a voice came from the waiting room. "She can't take it any more," another voice offered, as laughter rose from the corner.

Christina ran the four blocks to where her car was parked. There was already a yellow envelope with a $25 parking ticket lodged under her windshield wiper.

Northern County Legal Service's mission is to match clients who cannot afford legal counsel with a lawyer willing to offer pro bono services. NCLS specializes in housing and employment law but also matches clients with attorneys who assist with almost any legal need, including domestic violence and family law. The service is free to clients (though some pay for some services on a sliding scale based on their income). The remainder of the funding comes from grants, and the center is staffed almost entirely by a group of 15 volunteers and law school students. Students form the majority of the staff, and they receive internship credit, usually volunteering at the center during their third year of law school. Most students only participate in the center for one semester, and competition among students is tough to receive one of the volunteer slots.

The one full-time employee is a director, Julie, who has been at the center for about 2 years. Aside from running the office, managing volunteers and students, finding attorneys, and conducting training workshops for both students and volunteer attorneys, Julie's main concern is funding, which is a constant issue.

The small office where NCLS is housed consists of a waiting room and four offices. Julie keeps one of the four offices as her own, and the other three are taken by students or volunteers who work for 10 to 20 hours per week, usually in 4- to 6-hour shifts. Each of the four offices has a computer with one printer shared for the center. At any given time, there might be as many as eight volunteers who share the three offices, meeting with clients to perform the "intake" functions.

The intake process begins with a client who arrives on a walk-in or appointment basis, and the initial meeting usually lasts for about an hour. Depending on the client's need, the intake paperwork consists of three to six pages of single-spaced questions that the staff members ask clients in order to be able to provide the most help. Intake forms also contain client demographic data, such as household income and household size, needed for the center to compile monthly, quarterly, and annual statistics that grant funders require in order to measure the center's progress.

It was 7:30 a.m. as Julie walked in to the office. The phone was already ringing, but she let it go to voice mail as she turned on her computer and quickly sorted through the phone messages that had piled up since she left yesterday afternoon. Nothing that couldn't wait until later in the morning, she thought. In the waiting room, the staff began to gather for the monthly staff meeting. This is the time when Julie covers the statistics for the prior month with the staff, gives updates, and answers questions.

"Good morning." Julie looked around the room. About two-thirds of the staff are seated in the uncomfortable assorted chairs, which have been donated or purchased at minimal cost over the past several years. "Today I want to cover a few things. First, the importance of getting the intake paperwork complete; second, scheduling; and third, timely filings." She looked around the room at the bleary-eyed group, many of whom held coffee cups as they avoided eye contact.

"Fine? Good. Melinda? I noticed that many of you are making the same mistake as Melinda in failing to fully complete page 6 of the housing intake form. For example, here's the copy of the one you completed last week. Where the form asks for service date, we really need that to complete the filing motion for the client. If we don't have it, we have to call them to get it. I've noticed a few of these that have been blank in the past week or two. Does everyone understand that?" Heads nodded in agreement.

"Where do we put the intake form for housing after it's done?" Eric asked.

"In the intake in-box on the filing cabinet in Julie's office," Monica offered.

"I thought that was only for urgent motions," Eric said. "I've been putting the nonurgent ones in the in-box in the hallway."

"That's right," Julie said. "Actually I'd prefer it if you handed the urgent ones directly to me and put the nonurgent ones in the hallway box. You can put the urgent ones in my box if I'm not here."

"What's urgent?" Monica asked.

"Urgent means if it's been 4 or 5 days since the client received an eviction notice," Julie said. "The fifth day is the most critical."

"What do we do if you aren't here but it's been 5 days?" Monica asked.

"Then you can either call my cell phone and let me know that it's waiting, or you can call an attorney from the list," Julie said. "Or you can do it yourself but wait to file it until I can verify it after you're done."

"Do we do that for the domestic violence restraining order requests also?" Annette asked.

"No, those should be filed in the top drawer of the cabinet until another staff member can take the intake form and call a volunteer attorney to take the case," Julie said.

"Why can't I just call immediately to get the process started more quickly?" Annette said. "If I've done the intake, why can't I just continue to the next step?"

Julie was beginning to get frustrated. "Look, everyone, we went over this in training. It's important that this all be handled as we discussed it before."

Julie continued as, out of earshot, Annette leaned over and whispered to Monica. "Yeah, training was what, like an hour? I still don't understand why there are so many procedures."

"I know," Monica said, "and I feel so incompetent about housing law. My specialty has been family law. I'd rather learn about that part of the center, but I keep getting these eviction intakes. And the paperwork is incredible. I spent an hour with a client yesterday and only got about two pages' worth of information. I ran over my next appointment trying to get the rest."

"I had the same experience," Annette said. "The clients have such detailed histories, and they need to share their whole story. I talked to a woman whose boyfriend shoved her against a wall and broke her wrist. She started to cry, and I was thinking that I can't very well interrupt her and say, 'Sorry, ma'am, but that's Question 65. We're still on question 14, so can you tell me your combined annual income?' And I had three of those same intakes yesterday. I went home completely drained last night."

Monica nodded. "I've heard stories like that, too. The part I hate is when I have to pick up the paperwork out of the inbox and file the motion when I didn't do the intake. The other day Julie started shouting at me because I missed a note on an intake that

Christina did and I had to refile the motion. I almost missed the deadline but I stayed 2 hours later than usual and got it all done. It was gratifying but emotionally exhausting. It's hard to even come in sometimes. I wonder, are we even making progress here?"

"Now what's she talking about?" Annette looked up at Julie.

"So that's why you need to make sure that Dave has your weekly schedule, so he can keep the appointment schedule accurate with hourly time blocks for intakes," Julie concluded.

Julie returned to her office. There were two messages from the Dylan Foundation president wanting to know about last quarter's statistics. He had threatened to pull funding for next year unless the center began to show more progress in winning cases where disabled clients were about to be evicted. She knew that the staff had done great work recently, but they had only begun to compile the statistics and she could not yet prove it with charts and graphs. He'd be fine after she met with him, she thought. She made a mental note to bring two recent success story case studies to her meeting with him.

Rafael appeared in the doorway. "Julie, what do we do when the service date on the subpoena doesn't match the date on the submission form? Can you show me how we address that in the reply?"

"Yes. Well, actually, ask Kyle because I showed him the same thing last week," Julie said.

"Kyle's not here until 3, and I have to have the motion done for the client to pick up at noon," Rafael said.

"Okay. Just give me a few minutes and I'll be right there," Julie said.

"Thanks," Rafael said.

Jean was right behind him. "Julie, I have an urgent housing motion here that needs to be filed. Do you want this now?"

Julie took the intake form and looked through it. A woman with a $900 monthly income and an infant son and 2-year-old daughter received an eviction notice for being one day late on her $800 rent. A court filing would be due tomorrow.

"I have a meeting this afternoon and can't do it today. Why don't you put it in the hallway box and maybe someone can get to it today, otherwise I'll get to it tomorrow," Julie said.

Jean paused for a moment. "Okay, I'll do that," she said.

CHAPTER 4

Foundations of Organizational Change

In 1996, the *St. Louis Post-Dispatch* hired a new editor, Cole Campbell, to address declining readership and increased competition. Among the changes instituted in the newsroom was a shift away from reporters being assigned to beats and toward journalistic reporting teams. The staff was generally enthusiastic and optimistic that this change would be a positive one that would increase the paper's quality, and they welcomed the team-based governance structure. The vision was that teams comprised of members from the news and business divisions would collaborate on customer-focus and problem-solving initiatives to improve the paper. As the change was instituted, however, morale declined. Several mid-level editor and reporter positions were eliminated or restructured, and both reporters and editors had to reapply for jobs as team members or leaders in the new structure. Many staff members were frustrated that they were not consulted or involved in making the changes successful. Soon reporters began to dislike working in teams and declared that nothing had actually changed in the quality of the paper. Many award-winning and highly respected journalists left the paper voluntarily, citing the changes in the newsroom. In 2000, Campbell resigned. Circulation had declined from 320,000 to less than 295,000 during his four-year tenure (Gade & Perry, 2003).

- What could have been done differently to make this change successful?
- What factors do you think contribute to making a successful change?

As you have no doubt experienced, achieving change is difficult. This story of organizational change at the *St. Louis Post-Dispatch* has likely been replicated at countless organizations. While it may be tempting to blame the leader and to dismiss failed attempts as yet another example of poorly managed change, it is beneficial to understand what happened in situations like this one and what other explanations are possible. They can teach us about where attempts at change go wrong and how organizational change should be managed differently.

As we have discussed in previous chapters, organization development (OD) was primarily concerned early on with incremental changes that organizations could experience through interventions that targeted individual development. In recent years, with an emphasis on organizational effectiveness, OD has directed attention toward larger-scale and strategic change. Organizational change is the context (and purpose) of OD work, and a key competency of OD professionals is understanding the nature of organizational change, including what factors help to make changes succeed and what factors cause them to fail. In this chapter we will explore the nature of organizational change, including how researchers and practitioners think about change. We will explore the levels and characteristics of changes that organizations seek to make, and we will look at the research and writings of scholars and practitioners that develop theoretical models for how changes occur, as well as the fundamental issues that make changes successful.

To do that, we will also delve briefly into organizational theory. We will discuss two ways of looking at organizations: as systems and as they are socially constructed. The organization-as-system model has evolved from general systems theory over the past 50 to 60 years. Organizations-as-socially-constructed is a relatively more recent evolution of organizational theory, becoming prominent in the past 20 to 30 years. While they are contradictory in some respects, containing some fundamentally different assumptions at their core, both of these ways of looking at organizations offer useful and different insights. They both suggest approaches to organizational change that can help practitioners as they interpret how to best help a client achieve change in a particular organization. As you learn about these perspectives and models of organizational change in this chapter, keep in mind the practical challenges faced by those that lead organizational change.

You may be wondering why we need to delve into such theoretical detail just to understand how to manage organizational change at a practical level. The answer is that our approach to change depends on the underlying assumptions and beliefs that we have about how organizations work. In other words, "The way change facilitators think about causes of change determines how they contract, assess, intervene, and evaluate during their interactions with client organizations" (Olson & Eoyang, 2001, p. 7). As we have noted in previous chapters, it is important for OD practitioners to be conscious and intentional about the choices they make and to avoid adopting an intervention or model simply because it is fashionable. By learning more about the assumptions behind the models, you will be a more thoughtful and successful practitioner of organizational change.

Levels and Characteristics
of Organizational Change

When we talk about organizational change, we are referring to many different kinds of changes that occur at many levels. Changes can occur at the individual level when people learn new skills or develop new ways of working through mentoring, coaching, or education and training. Changes can occur at the group or team level as teams develop new ways of working with one another, define their goals and objectives, and learn ways of addressing conflict. Groups can also learn how to work more effectively with other groups (intergroup change) to solve problems or address interdependencies. Changes occur at the organizational level through the development of new strategies and processes, visions for a new desired future, and major system practices that affect all organizational members. Changes can also occur at suprasystem levels, where multiple organizations are implicated. These can involve changes, for example, between multiple organizations (such as mergers and acquisitions), between organizations and government agencies, or between cities, states, or nations.

Practitioners and scholars have noticed that organizational changes differ on a number of dimensions. Changes vary in several ways:

1. *Planning.* Organizational change can be planned or unplanned. Organizational members can be conscious and intentional about the changes that they want to make, often due to environmental factors, strategic or market needs, or other influences. Changes can also be unplanned, perhaps in response to an immediate threat or crisis. Weick (2000) contrasts planned changes with emergent changes, which are the "ongoing accommodations, adaptations, and alterations that produce fundamental change without a priori intentions to do so" (p. 237). Organization development as a field has primarily been concerned with the successful implementation of planned organizational change (Beckhard, 1969) or intentional change programs developed intentionally to improve the organization or address a deficiency.

2. *Magnitude.* OD literature differentiates between first-order and second-order change (Watzlawick, Weakland, & Fisch, 1974). First-order change consists of "incremental modifications that make sense within an established framework or method of operating" (Bartunek & Moch, 1987, p. 484), and second-order change is defined as transformational changes that "are modifications in the frameworks themselves" (Bartunek & Moch, 1987, p. 484). First-order changes tend to be alterations or changes to existing practices rather than a rethinking or reinvention of the practice. Implementation of a computer system that simply automates existing work practices is an example of first-order change, where existing work practices are modified within the existing understanding of how the work is done, maintaining its current purposes, objectives, and processes. First-order change reflects an evolution of existing definitions rather than a revolution or redefinition. Rethinking how the entire organization

used the computer system, including redefining roles, processes, values, and implicit meanings, would be considered second-order change. Because second-order change tends to reflect a more substantial shift, some refer to this type of change as "organizational transformation" (Bartunek & Louis, 1988). Chapman (2002) writes that, historically, most OD models reflect concerns with first-order change rather than second-order change. Others refer to differences in magnitude of organizational change by the labels *transactional* or *transformational* (Burke & Litwin, 1992), *evolutionary* or *revolutionary* (Burke, 2002), and *incremental* or *transformational* (Kindler, 1979).

3. *Continuity.* Weick and Quinn (1999) distinguish between episodic and continuous change. Episodic change is defined as distinct periods of change, usually infrequent and explicitly defined. When seen in this way, episodic change is usually framed as a response to a stable condition in which adverse conditions are present that force a change. Continuous change, on the other hand, reflects the idea that the organization is never truly out of a state of change, and that even in minute ways, change is always occurring.

Models of Organizational Change: Systems Theory and Social Construction Approaches

Scholars and practitioners have developed a number of models to explain how change occurs. Some of these models are based on years of empirical research, whereas others are based in practitioners' experiences of witnessing and implementing change in organizations. These models explain change differently based on different underlying theoretical assumptions about organizations, people, and work. In the first section, we will examine systems theory and models of organizations and organizational change that share systems theory's assumptions; in the second, we will discuss the social construction perspective and models of organizational change consistent with that approach.

Organizations as Systems

The first lens that we will use to look at an organization is as a system. Systems theory can be traced to an Austrian biologist, Ludwig von Bertlanffy, who wrote a series of books and articles beginning in the 1940s (see Bertlanffy, 1968) about the systemic interconnections of the natural world. Living organisms and the physical environment, Bertlanffy noted, displayed interconnectedness among their various parts. Fruit trees under stress due to weather conditions such as drought or extreme heat, for example, produce less fruit in order to conserve energy. General systems theory, according to Bertlanffy, was about understanding the characteristics of these natural systems and the underlying laws that defined their interconnections. Rather than investigate only the subparts of these organisms in isolation from one another, general systems theory tried to understand how the subparts related to one another.

Katz and Kahn (1966) were among the first to adapt this perspective to organizational theory. "All social systems, including organizations," they wrote, "consist of the patterned activities of a number of individuals" (p. 17). They argued that open systems (natural and organizational) displayed common characteristics, such as the importation of energy or inputs, a throughput or transformation process, an output, feedback, homeostasis or equilibrium, and others. Systems theorists refer to these systems as "open" versus "closed" because the system is interconnected with its environment (Kast & Rosenzweig, 1972). Most theorists emphasize, however, that the natural system metaphor for organizations can be taken too far, since "social structures are essentially contrived systems" (Katz & Kahn, 1966, p. 33). See Figure 4.1 for a visual depiction of an organizational system.

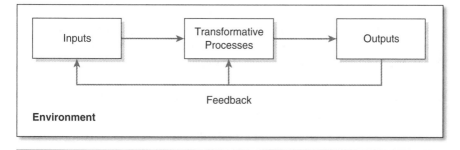

Figure 4.1   An Organization as a System

To better understand these characteristics of a system, consider an automobile factory as an example. Inputs consist of raw materials such as the engine, doors, tires, and so on (or even more fundamental inputs such as sheet metal, plastic, or glass). The factory works with these raw materials through assembly, painting, and other construction processes. The output is a functioning automobile of a certain kind with certain characteristics. The cars are sold for money, which is used to purchase more raw materials, create new car designs, open more factories, and so on. Feedback processes (such as inventory numbers, sales rates, and sales revenue) create information that is fed back into the system to ensure that the system maintains equilibrium and that it can adapt appropriately to environmental conditions.

The system maintains equilibrium through market and consumer demands. For example, if cars are not being sold (e.g., due to competition, economic conditions, or other environmental factors) and too much inventory exists, the factory will slow down production to adapt to these conditions. If demand is high, feedback to the factory will result in higher production rates (again adapting to what is demanded by the environment). When demand declines, without storage or conservation of resources (for example, retaining some money so that the organization can still function even when sales rates are lower than expected), the organization will cease to exist. Systems theorists call this property of systems "negative entropy," meaning the system needs to cope with expended energy without any incoming energy to assist the system in surviving. Moreover, all of these parts and functions are internally interdependent, so that changes in one part of the system will result in changes in other parts of the system (Nadler & Tushman, 1983).

Within these systems, certain functional specialized roles and procedures exist to aid the system in functioning properly. Production workers, for example, work on a specific component of the assembly process. Managers and executives help the system's parts to function effectively and monitor the feedback from the internal and external environment. Procedures help the system to reproduce its processes in standardized ways. The overall organizational system also consists of a variety of interconnected subsystems that depend on one another. For example, the factory depends on human resources to hire and train employees properly. The entire system depends on finance to pay employees, to provide budgets used to purchase raw materials, and to collect money from customers. These departments exist as subsystems within the overall organizational system.

Open systems thinking is the process of considering how people, processes, structures, and policies all exist in an interconnected web of relationships. Systems thinkers see the whole of an organism or organization as larger than the sum of its parts, and as systems that exist within other systems of which they are a part (Burke, 2002). Mayhew (2006) writes that systems thinking is about analyzing the organization on three levels: events, patterns, and structure. Whereas *events* are single occurrences of an episode, *patterns* are the multiple and repetitive "archetypes" (Senge, 1990) that allow events to happen in the same way time after time. These patterns exist in *structures* that support and reinforce them. Systems thinking, as Senge describes it, consists of seeing the interrelationship of structures and components rather than simple and "linear cause-effect chains" (p. 71). Correcting organizational problems requires systems thinking rather than simple linear thinking (A caused B to happen) in order to solve the root of the problem rather than correcting the immediate, surface-level symptoms of the problem (asking questions such as "What caused A? Are there other causes?"). In other words, it requires analyzing structures and patterns rather than isolated events.

Systems theory has been a popular approach in organizational studies because it resonates with how we understand organizations to work at the most general level. Organizations produce something—whether it is a product, such as cars or breakfast cereal, or a service, such as financial consulting or providing Internet access. Changes in the environment, such as legislative or regulatory changes, cause organizations to adapt to new rules. Poor quality inputs lead to problems in transformation processes and result in poor quality outputs. Erroneous information in the feedback process creates unnecessary or problematic changes in the system. Aspects of the system are interdependent on one another, and problems in one part of the system create problems in other parts of the system. These statements about organizational systems provide a commonsense explanation for how organizations and their subsystems seem to us to work.

The Value of Systems Theory for OD Practitioners

For OD practitioners, systems theory offers a number of benefits. First, it can offer useful explanations for human behavior in organizations with attention to roles and structures rather than individual idiosyncrasies. Instead of seeing individual differences, OD practitioners can note where systems may encourage certain behavior patterns, usually subtly and without conscious decision. If a call center regularly measures the number of calls completed per hour, then call-takers may be motivated to quickly complete calls at the expense of careful diagnosis and resolution of customer problems. Service managers may be motivated to dispatch replacement parts for customers via overnight mail (thereby inappropriately increasing expenses) in order to increase customer satisfaction (for which they will receive a bonus). The measurement and rewards system in both cases directs a certain behavior on the part of call-takers and service managers. Narrow job definitions and roles in one division may result in no employee taking responsibility for a certain problem as employees act in accordance with what the system has asked them to do in defining the role they occupy. Structured role definitions can explain how and why certain people interact with each other in patterned ways (for example, the emergency room nurse may take instructions from the attending physician). The systems theory perspective helps us see role-based interactional patterns rather than isolated actions of single individuals.

Second, understanding the system and its dynamics gives OD practitioners a more appropriate place to begin interventions for change, since the object of change is generally the system, not the individual person (Burke, 2002). For example, inadequately maintained or broken equipment can reduce factory output levels. Instead of blaming the production manager's poor management skills for low factory production yields, or placing blame on factory workers for slow work, the systemic issue is a more direct cause. When an organization has unhappy customers due to a quality problem, instead of conducting training for customer service representatives on how to deal with angry customers, the quality problem should be addressed as the source of the problem. Katz and Kahn (1966) wrote that this attention on training was a common error in organizations—and little change results from it:

> It is common practice to pull foremen or officials out of their organizational roles and give them training in human relations. Then they return to their customary positions with the same role expectations from their subordinates, the same pressures from their superiors, and the same functions to perform as before their special training. (p. 390)

An organization that fires an unproductive employee and hires a highly paid, skilled replacement often discovers that the new employee is no more successful because the role exists in a structure (say, low budget, little decision-making authority) where virtually no employee could succeed. As Senge (1990) puts it, "When placed in the same system, people, however different, tend to produce similar results" (p. 42). OD practitioners can delve more deeply into the causes of problems and interconnections among groups, looking at systemic problems rather than at individuals or individual components of the system as the primary sources of error (Harrison & Shirom, 1999). This can lead to more fruitful targets for change.

Third, because changing one part of the system also results in changes to another part of the system, OD practitioners can be more deliberate about changes that are being proposed, and possible negative results can be predicted. If bonuses are given to sales executives who sell a certain product, the factory likely will need to produce more of that product than others. If computer equipment is not replaced in order to reduce expenses, then additional expenses likely will be incurred in repairing equipment. If insurance claim application processing can be completed 2 days more quickly after a work process redesign, then the payment processing department that processes approved claims may have more work to complete more quickly than it can handle. Taking systemic issues into account may mean a more successful organizational change, as undesirable or "downstream" outcomes can be predicted and addressed before they become problems of their own. The organization as a whole can be internally consistent about the changes it wants to make.

Models of Organizational Change Consistent With a Systems Theory Approach

As might be expected given its popularity as a theoretical model for organizations, models of organizational change consistent with a systems theory approach predominate. What they may lack in specificity, they make up in helping the practitioner to see patterns and their relationships in a broader sense. We can thus see patterns in a large volume of data (in fact, we can use these models to analyze data, a point we will return to in a later chapter). They can help us see possible relationships that we may have missed, and they can help us see missing pieces that we might have expected to see but did not. Finally, they can help us see possible areas for change (Burke, 2002). The model may point out the influence of one area on another that may prompt us to note that we devote too much attention to the first topic and not enough to the latter. In short, models are like colored lenses that highlight some aspects of the terrain while they may obscure others, but in any case, they will help us see new things that we may not have seen before.

Four common models of organizational behavior and change consistent with a systems theory perspective are Lewin's three-phase model, the Nadler-Tushman congruence model, the Burke-Litwin model, and the Weisbord Six-Box Model. Each of these offers a different perspective on organizational analysis, highlighting a different approach to organizational change.

Lewin's Three-Phase Model of Change and Force Field Analysis

Kurt Lewin (1951) offered a three-phase model of organizational change in which he described change as a process of (1) unfreezing, (2) moving, and (3) refreezing. Current organizational practices need to be released (or unfrozen) to be changed. Once they are changed, they need to be refrozen as newly adopted regular practices. Lewin pointed out that two forces worked together to maintain equilibrium in an organization: forces promoting a change and forces promoting the status quo. Change can occur only when forces of change are greater than forces maintaining the status quo. This can happen in two ways: if forces promoting change are increased or forces maintaining the status quo are decreased. Examples of factors supporting a change might be customer demand, market need, or the low cost of the change. Factors resisting a change might be the need for extensive training, insufficient employee resources, or lengthy implementation time. (See Figure 4.2.)

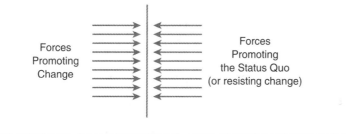

Figure 4.2 Kurt Lewin's Force Field Analysis

Lewin's is an easily grasped description of change that has been widely adopted by managers and practitioners. It explains that to embrace something new, something else must be left behind. The organization must be "freed" from prior practices and must work to sustain the change when it is implemented. The model also reminds us that organizational members must be prepared for a change, and that levels of resistance can mean that the organization remains in a "frozen" state until we work to unfreeze it. Members must be practically or symbolically "released" from previous practices in order to change them, and following a change, conscious attention must be paid to reinforcing the change in order to help it stick. A popular adaptation of Lewin's model refers to an organization's current state, a transition state, and a desired state (Beckhard & Harris, 1977). Despite its popularity among practitioners, many scholars have noted that an "organization-as-ice-cube" model is, however, an oversimplification of a much more complex process, particularly since organizational practices are never exactly frozen (Kanter, Stein, & Jick, 1992).

Lewin's concept of force field analysis has become a useful tool for OD practitioners to use with clients. The tool can help organizational members understand what factors would support a given change effort and what resistance might prevent the change from being adopted. Some practitioners use the model as a formal assessment, asking team members (separately or in groups) to rate the strength of the forces for and against change on a scale from 1 to 5 to prioritize actions where energy should be directed.

The Nadler-Tushman Congruence Model

Noting that systems theory is "too abstract to be used for day-to-day organizational behavior-problem analysis" (Nadler & Tushman, 1983, p. 114), Nadler and Tushman have offered an expanded version of systems theory that contains additional concepts intended to be more useful to practitioners (see Figure 4.3). Nadler (1981) also explains that this model is particularly useful for organizational change. The premise behind the model is this:

The model puts its greatest emphasis on the transformation process and in particular reflects the critical system property of interdependence. It views organizations as made up of components or parts which interact with each other. These components exist in states of relative balance, consistency, or "fit" with each other. The different parts of an organization can fit well together

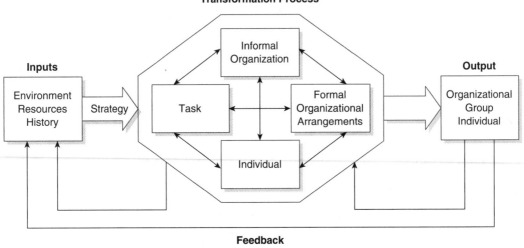

Figure 4.3 The Nadler-Tushman Congruence Model

SOURCE: Nadler, D. A., & Tushman, M. L. (1983). A General Diagnostic Model for Organizational Behavior: Applying a Congruence Perspective. In J. R. Hackman, E. E. Lawler III, & L. W. Porter (Eds.), *Perspectives on Behavior in Organizations* (2nd ed., pp. 112–124). New York: McGraw-Hill. Reprinted with permission.

and thus function effectively, or fit poorly, thus leading to problems, dysfunctions, or performance below potential. Given the central nature of these "fits" among components in the model, we will talk about it as a *congruence model of organizational behavior,* since effectiveness is a function of the congruence among the various components. (Nadler & Tushman, 1983, p. 114)

Like the traditional model of systems theory described earlier, notice that inputs, transformation processes, outputs, and feedback are also included as part of the congruence model. Each of these has been expanded in this model. Inputs include environment, resources, and history, and are merged with organizational strategy to influence transformation processes. Market demands, human resources, technology, capital, information, and prior patterns all comprise the organization's inputs. Strategy is included in the congruence model as it determines what the organization will work on and how the organization must work to achieve its outputs. Outputs are now more specifically defined as not only the "tangible" product of the organization's processes, but outputs also consist of organizational, group, and individual performance. Nadler and Tushman include job satisfaction, stress, and other individual outputs as products of the work environment as well. Transformation processes have been expanded in the congruence model to include four important elements that relate to one another: task, individual, formal organizational arrangements, and informal organization. The task component encompasses the work to be done, but also the skills and knowledge required to do it and the degree of independence or judgment required. The individual component includes employees' knowledge and skills, engagement and motivation, preferences and attitudes, and other influences on individual behavior. Formal organizational arrangements include explicitly defined processes and organizational structures, job definition, metrics, the physical layout and environment, and other officially specified aspects of the work. Informal organization is defined as the less explicitly defined or tacit understandings, processes, methods, and norms that comprise how work is actually done.

Together, these four elements are defined as the primary components of the organization. They interact together in more or less consistent ways as the organization produces its outputs. Nadler (1981) writes about a fundamental notion of the congruence model:

> At the core of this systems-based perspective is the assumption that the interaction among the organizational components is perhaps more critical than the characteristics of the components themselves, and that as systems, organizations fundamentally work better when the pieces fit together. (p. 194)

Nadler and Tushman (1983) refer to this as the "congruence hypothesis," or the idea that the better the congruence between components, the more effective the organization. When an organization has a market demand to produce a new product (new input and new output), that demand requires a specific task to produce the output. If the task's demands require skills and knowledge that individuals do not possess, then there will be a congruence gap (or low "fit") between task and individuals. Organizational effectiveness can only be achieved if the fit is increased.

The model points to areas that affect one another so that changes in other parts of the system can be noted and controlled. Nadler (1981) explains that when parts of a system are changed, they may increase or decrease the "fit" or congruence with other parts of the system. When change happens, other components of the organization may resist the change and encourage regression to the prior state. Thus, Nadler points to the need to motivate change (the individual component), manage transitions, and pay attention to political dynamics of change as well.

The Burke-Litwin Model of Organizational Performance and Change

Burke and Litwin (1992) praised many of the models of organizational change that had been developed up to the early 1990s, but they also saw them as overly simplistic. Many of these models had real-world proven utility and had been developed from practitioners' own experiences. Some prior models could not, however, predict the impact of an organizational change with certainty on other elements of the organization, and other models lacked empirical testing. Burke and Litwin developed their model of organizational performance and change as a causal model that could be empirically tested, that would specify the variables that would be affected by a given change, and that would take into account both first-order (transactional) and second-order (transformational) change (see Figure 4.4).

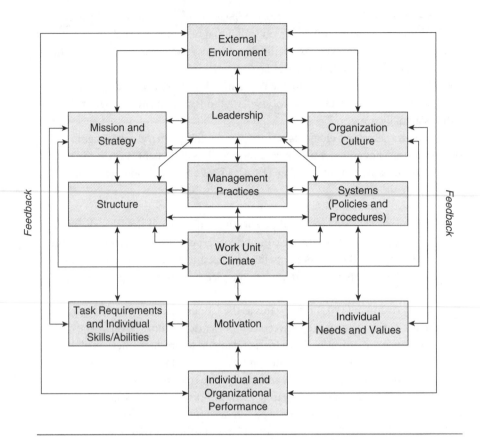

Figure 4.4   The Burke-Litwin Model of Organizational Performance and Change

SOURCE: Burke, W. W. (2002). *Organization Change: Theory and Practice.* Thousand Oaks, CA: Sage. Reprinted with permission.

Theirs is explicitly a model of organizational change based in systems theory that is intended to follow from its basic tenets.

Many observers have remarked on the complexity of this model and express confusion about the number and direction of the arrows. Burke and Litwin acknowledge that the model is complex but state that change is such a complex phenomenon, the model is still likely a simplified version of what actually occurs during change. Similar to systems theory, the external environment at the top of the model represents inputs, the individual and organizational performance box at the bottom of the model represents the output, and all other boxes between these represent the throughput processes. Arrows indicate the greatest directions of influence among the variables, but the downward arrows, they believe, have greater influence on lower boxes than do the upward arrows to the variables above them. Burke and Litwin write that all boxes generally affect all others, but the arrows in the model represent the most important causal links. They define each component as follows:

- *External environment:* Any outside condition or situation that influences the performance of the organization.

- *Mission and strategy:* What employees believe is the central purpose of the organization and how the organization intends to achieve that purpose over an extended time.
- *Leadership:* Executive behavior that provides direction and encourages others to take needed action.
- *Culture:* "The way we do things around here." Culture is the collection of overt and covert rules, values, and principles that guide organizational behavior and that have been strongly influenced by history, custom, and practice.
- *Structure:* The arrangement of functions and people into specific areas and levels of responsibility, decision-making authority, and relationships.
- *Management practices:* What managers do in the normal course of events to use the human and material resources at their disposal to carry out the organization's strategy.
- *Systems:* Standardized policies and mechanisms that are designed to facilitate work.
- *Climate:* The collective current impressions, expectations, and feelings of the members of local work units.
- *Task requirements and individual skills/abilities:* The behavior required for task effectiveness, including specific skills and knowledge required for people to accomplish the work assigned and for which they feel directly responsible.
- *Individual needs and values:* The specific psychological factors that provide desire and worth for individual actions or thoughts.
- *Motivation:* Aroused behavioral tendencies to move toward goals, take needed action, and persist until satisfaction is attained.
- *Individual and organizational performance:* The outcomes or results, with indicators of effort and achievement. Such indicators might include productivity, customer or staff satisfaction, profit, and service quality (Burke, 1993, pp. 130–132).

The authors write that the model attempts to integrate notions of transformational and transactional change. The factors most influential in transformational change are due to environmental causes, so the top four boxes (external environment, mission and strategy, leadership, and culture) have the greatest influence on performance. During transactional change, the other boxes below this level (structure, management practices, and so on) are the major factors of interest. Burke (2002) has described several cases in which applications of the model have been successfully tested.

Weisbord's Six-Box Model

Strictly speaking, Weisbord's Six-Box Model, first elaborated in a 1976 article, was not explicitly articulated as a model of organizational change (see Figure 4.5). In later years, however, Weisbord's model has become a popular diagnostic model to illustrate elements of a system that are out of sync with other parts of the system, in particular to explore how formal and informal systems are often misaligned or contradictory. Consequently, it has become a popular model among practitioners for analyzing and conducting organizational change (Birnbaum, 1984; Ford & Evans, 2001).

Weisbord refers to the model as a "radar screen" (Weisbord, 1976, p. 431) depicting the interrelationships among six of an organization's component parts. Based on his

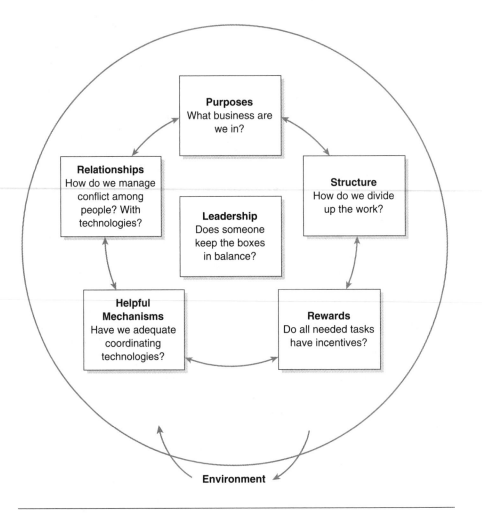

Figure 4.5   Weisbord's Six-Box Model

SOURCE: Weisbord, M. R. (1976). Organizational Diagnosis: Six Places to Look for Trouble With or Without a Theory. *Group & Organization Studies, 1,* 430–447. Reprinted with permission.

experience, the model categorizes six common problem areas in an organization and helps to illustrate how symptoms can be seen in a systemic light. Each of the boxes has both formal (espoused and official) and informal (how things work in practice) components, and a complete diagnosis must attend to both. The model's six boxes include the following:

- *Purposes.* This box includes formal goal clarity (how well are goals explained) and informal goal agreement (how well the goals are truly understood and acted upon).
- *Structure.* How well does the organizational structure match the needed outputs? Is the organizational structure followed or undermined in daily practice?
- *Rewards.* Does a (formal) reward system exist, and does it actually produce results making employees feel as if their contributions are being rewarded (informal)?
- *Relationships.* This concerns the degree to which people can work interdependently and manage conflict successfully.

- *Helpful mechanisms.* What formal mechanisms exist to facilitate work, such as budget processes, meetings, reviews, or other communications? How well do these helpful mechanisms meet their objectives?
- *Leadership.* How do leaders lead? What do they state as their formal expectations? What norms do leaders informally role model or informally communicate?

When formal and informal components of the boxes are not in alignment, the organization may be expending energy maintaining both a formal system and an informal one that may or may not be functioning as needed. It is not the case that one of these systems is better than the other, but understanding how these six boxes function formally and informally can give insight into why an organization may be experiencing problems and where to begin interventions for change (Weisbord, 1976). Additional gaps may exist between the organization and its environment, between individual work and the organization's goals, or between different organizational units. It is this formal and informal gap analysis that Weisbord and others have noted is an especially important aspect of the model. Weisbord's Six-Box Model thus gives great insight into the internal functioning of a system. As some have noted, this advantage of the Six-Box Model may be its drawback as well, as it attends less to elements of the external environment and issues such as scarce resources or demands of external stakeholders (Harrison & Shirom, 1999). It also gives less insight into which gaps may be more serious than others. By placing leadership in the center of the model, it may also overemphasize the role of leadership and understate the role of individual employees in the functioning of the organization.

This model, like the other three models, is consistent with the approach suggested by systems theory, that an organization exists in interaction with its environment, and that managing problems, misalignments, and holes between various components is a key to successful organizational functioning. This has been the dominant approach in OD and organization theory (Shaw, 1997). Assumptions about organizational components and analysis of "fit" remain a key feature of diagnostic recommendations in the practitioner literature (e.g., Harrison & Shirom, 1999). This approach can be enhanced, however, by another perspective, to which we now turn.

Organizations as Socially Constructed

The story goes that three umpires disagreed about the task of calling balls and strikes. The first one said, "I calls them as they is." The second one said, "I calls them as I sees them." The third and cleverest umpire said, "They ain't nothin' till I calls them."

—Simons, 1976 (cited in Weick, 1979, p. 1)

A second view of organizations is a more recent evolution in organizational theory, and it offers a different perspective on change than the models we have just seen. The intellectual history of the idea of social construction in organizational studies is usually traced to Berger and Luckmann's (1967) seminal work *The Social Construction of Reality,* and it has been particularly influential in organizational theory over the past three decades. Consider that in our everyday language, or even in texts such as this one, organizations are frequently personified as actors in their own right. We speak of working "in" an organization, thinking of an organization as a container or physical environment. We speak of organizations "adapting" to their environment, or the production department "deciding" to increase output. Classical organizational theory actually considered organizations to be "living things" with "a concrete social environment, a formal structure, recognized goals, and a variety of needs" (Wolf, 1958, p. 14). Yet organizations are not people, and a number of important ideas are obscured when we personify them.

The social construction view argues that organizations are not exactly things at all, but that the organization is really a concept developed out of our own actions and language. Some scholars suggest that the study of organizations is really the study of the process of organizing, with the verb form emphasizing the active role we take in creating our organizations. If you consider an organization that you know well and try to point to what "it" is, you may point to a building to show where it is located or show an organizational chart as an abstract representation of how that organization is structured, but you will not have pointed to the organization. (The building could still exist without the organization, for example.) Drawing boundaries between the organization and its environment can be an equally challenging exercise. Consider the city in which you live as an organization and try to delineate what is "inside" and what is "outside" it. There is city hall and its employees, but what about the citizens, or those who do business in the city but live in another, or the developers who built the local shopping mall? Are they to be considered part of the organization as well, or do they belong in the environment category? From this perspective, the boundary between the organization and its environment is not a sharp or easily defined one, and can even sometimes be fluid from interaction to interaction. Weick (1995) writes that "*environment* and *organization* conceal the fact that organizing is about flows, change, and process" (p. 187). The terms *organization, boundary,* and *environment* in systems theory become more complex and perhaps less meaningful when we start to delve more deeply into how to define them.

The view of organizations as socially constructed differs sharply from the systems theory perspective in many respects. It challenges the prevailing assumptions of systems theory that organizational environments, inputs, processes, outputs, feedback, and so on are self-evident concepts and categories with predefined singular meanings on which we all agree. Instead, it sees those concepts and categories as created, developed, and infused with meaning by organizational members. The quote above about baseball umpires illustrates the primary difference between systems theory and social construction. In systems theory, the process of pitching to a batter, calling balls and strikes, and tallying outs and so forth would describe a subprocess in a baseball game. While accurate on its surface, it omits the process of constructing meaning (defining what count as balls, strikes, and outs) from an umpire's perspective that actually creates the possibility of the game existing (imagine if all umpires agreed to refuse to interpret a pitch!).

As a second example, let's return to the illustration cited previously about the automobile factory and feedback processes, where information such as sales revenue figures fed back into the factory tells them to build more cars. The revenue figures themselves, as numbers, mean nothing on their own. Instead, they must gain meaning through the process of interpretation. An organizational member (a manager or executive, presumably) must interpret the sales figures and decide (based upon a preexisting agreement, past experience, or even just a hunch) that the numbers mean that enough cars have been sold that additional inventory will be needed. Here, it is the manager's interpretation and judgment that give the data meaning for the organization. Indeed, an incredible amount of information exists in organizational environments that must be given meaning (think, for example, of the competitive landscape, Wall Street expectations, financial performance, past history of the firm, union agreements and employment conditions, customer expectations, and much, much more). To say, as systems theory does, that the environment specifies how the organization must act to achieve equilibrium omits the process of making and creating meaning, and developing and sharing interpretations, that explains how and why organizational members decide to take action. (Notice how few organizational members are mentioned in the descriptions of systems theory.) One could never gather all relevant information before a decision. Instead, information is selectively gathered, made sense of, and shared to create a socially constructed truth that organizational members will use for decisions and action (March, 1994). The category of "environment" is thus invented and invested with meaning by organizational members, and it does not exist outside of their interpretation. Weick (1995) calls this concept *sensemaking,* which he defines as "placement of items into frameworks, comprehending, redressing surprise, constructing meaning, interacting in pursuit of mutual understanding, and patterning" (p. 6).

Interactions and language are important areas of attention in the social construction perspective because it is through regular interaction and dialogue that organizations are developed and through which change can occur. As Benson (1977) wrote, "People are continually constructing the social world. Through their interactions with each other social patterns are gradually built and eventually a set of institutional arrangements is established. Through continued interactions the arrangements previously constructed are gradually modified or replaced" (p. 3). Thus, sensemaking is an ongoing process, not something with a defined beginning or ending (Weick, 1995). (This idea reinforces the value of OD discussed in the previous chapter that organizations and individuals are always in process.)

The social construction perspective has become an attractive one for both researchers and practitioners because it resonates with what we experience in organizations as we make sense of our activities and the actions of others. It also respects the ambiguity and multiple meanings that many organizational members experience and the necessary interpretive processes that characterize much of organizational life. Decisions are considered and rationalized based on complex and contradictory facts. Roles are negotiated and enacted, not predetermined by job descriptions. Press releases and executive communications are scrutinized, debated, and examined for hidden meanings. We leave conversations with colleagues to begin other conversations, sharing information and interpretations in each conversation. Multiple contexts and facts can be brought to bear on any situation to result in ambiguous and inconsistent interpretations. For many students of organizational studies, the social construction perspective fills in the missing elements of systems theory to provide a richer and more dynamic view of how organizations work. It describes how members experience organizations as social environments where interaction is fundamentally how work is accomplished and sensemaking is how it is understood and experienced. Particularly in less mechanistic, manufacturing-oriented environments, in today's knowledge-intensive organizations, the machine view of organizations assumed by systems theory seems less accurate when applied to the globalized and fragmented "postmodern" organization of the 21st century. Many believe that the social construction approach more effectively captures this new reality (Bergquist, 1993).

The Value of the Social Construction Approach for OD Practitioners

The social construction perspective has gained a following among organization development practitioners because it offers several unique benefits. First, like systems theory it offers a useful (but different) explanation for human behavior. It explains why, for example, organizational members would be less willing to take risks after witnessing a layoff in another division in which risk taking was common. Perhaps a logic has been developed in which members believe that taking risks means that losing one's job is likely. As a second example, consider that perhaps an executive decides to terminate a product line that is losing money. Instead of seeing this as a one-dimensional decision based on input from the environment, the social construction perspective helps to articulate the complexities in collecting, interpreting, and sharing the information used to make and communicate the decision. The social construction perspective directs the OD practitioner's attention to the cultural processes of sensemaking that result in action.

Second, the social construction perspective emphasizes the active role that members take in creating the organization. Members may decide to create a new department, change a structure, adopt new titles, or change a process. While an individual member may not have the choice to change a certain policy, the policy is one developed by organizational members and created for the organization's benefit. Relationships among supervisors and employees are not confined to rigid role-based interactions, but are multidimensional and can be friendly, cold, formal, sociable, and so on. Relationships between coworkers or departments are more complex than simply sharing orders or instructions between them and can be cooperative or contentious, relaxed or rigid. The social construction perspective illustrates the active choice that we make in creating these systems and relationships. This implies that OD practitioners should create situations in which people can choose a different organization to create, such as new policies, processes, roles, or relationships. Accepting this adaptability gives practitioners and organizational members the freedom to create changes that they desire to see (within boundaries, frequently, that we also agree to respect). While this does not deny the importance of leadership in change or the financial or environmental realities, it places an equal emphasis on everyday conversations that occur in the organizational network between all participants.

Third, the social construction perspective helps OD practitioners to see the importance of communication in creating change (Ford & Ford, 1995):

> Stories, myths, rituals, and language use are not simply reflections of organizational meanings; they are the ongoing dynamics that constitute organizational life. Meanings, then, do not reside in messages, channels, or perceptual filters. Rather, they evolve from interaction processes and the ways that individuals make sense of their talk. (Putnam, 1983, p. 40)

Words and their context are important, and the interpretive processes that we use to make sense of words often go unexplored. Consider a situation in which an organization, under financial pressure and rumors of layoffs, is required by law to send out an annual benefits notice to all employees. The notice states that following an involuntary termination, employees are eligible for continued medical benefits for a length of time following termination. From the perspective of the human resources benefits department, this is an ordinary compliance activity, but from an employee's perspective, it could be alarming to receive such a notice unexpectedly mailed to one's home considering the context. OD practitioners can become attuned to context, language, and interpretation mechanisms and help organizational members become more explicit about their interpretations. They can understand the context for interpretation of any particular message and make better recommendations about how communication will be received. Ford and Ford (1995) write that communication is not just another part of change, but it is the primary means by which change occurs.

Finally, the social construction perspective stresses that organizational change has as its foundation a change in meaning. Sensemaking logics lie beneath values, beliefs, and attitudes, as well as organizational practices, identities, and processes. Simply changing a practice, a role, a title, or a department name does not always change the underlying interpretive processes that members have adopted. Consequently, the approach assumes that change can best be accomplished when organizational members have the opportunity to work together to define new practices (Weick, 1995).

Models of Organizational Change Consistent With a Social Construction Perspective

Models of organizational change consistent with a social construction perspective look quite different from those explained earlier that are consistent with a systems theory perspective, as they recognize that change is a "messy" and unpredictable phenomenon (Shaw, 1997). Calling them "models," in the sense that we have just seen, is also misleading, because they question the very structures that systems theory assumes. Instead of locating organizational change in categories such as leadership, strategy, or rewards, the social construction perspective explains change as a change in interpretive mechanisms, conversations, communication, meaning, and cognitive schema. In fact, the very idea of organizational change is rethought in this perspective. Weick (2000) argues that "the breathless rhetoric of planned transformational change, complete with talk of revolution, discontinuity, and upheaval, presents a distorted view of how successful change works" (p. 223).

He argues that most models contrast change with inertia, whereas if we recognize that organizations are never really in inert states at all, we become more interested in the ongoing "ebb and flow" (p. 230) of organizational life.

As Ford (1999) points out, what constitutes a change is ambiguous and can mean different things to different people. Most change models tend to presume that a change is a single, easily identifiable phenomenon that members could point to and identify as "the change." Most practitioners and organizational members, however, recognize that change has multiple parts, some of which may or may not be successful, and that these have multiple meanings for various audiences. A widespread organizational change affects different employee groups in different ways, so a single definition of the change may not be possible. Instead, as we have learned, the social construction approach is interested in what the change means to people, recognizing that this meaning may shift and adapt at various points in time. Consequently, social construction approaches to change tend to emphasize continuous change rather than episodic change, privileging the role of language and discourse in change (Weick & Quinn, 1999).

Ford (1999), for example, argued for a definition of organizational change as "shifting conversations," in which people use different language to understand and accomplish change. When change occurs, it does so "when one way of talking replaces another way of talking" (Barrett, Thomas, & Hocevar, 1995, p. 370). Ford and Ford (1995) describe four different kinds of conversations that occur during organizational change: conversations that initiate change, conversations that seek to understand change, conversations for performance, and conversations for closure. No one mix of conversational types is right for every change, they note.

> The successful implementation of change is a function of conversations that reflect the evolving context and progress of the change, including the results produced and breakdowns to be resolved. Identifying an appropriate conversational pattern, therefore, is a pragmatic issue of determining which type of conversation is most likely to work in the current situation, trying it, seeing what happens, and making adjustments in and to subsequent conversations. What this means is that change managers may find a conversational mix that is effective in one change but ineffective in another. (Ford & Ford, 2008, p. 448)

This model can explain how, when change does not proceed as expected, certain conversations may not have taken place at all, or may have taken place unsuccessfully.

This model of change-as-communication calls into question the categories discussed in earlier models (e.g., structure, systems, leadership, culture), because those factors are only relevant to the extent that organizational members draw upon them in conversation. Understanding how a change is proceeding depends on careful study and attentive listening to how language has changed (Anderson, 2005b). Echoing MacGregor's recommendation to listen carefully to managers' implicit theories, Ford and Ford (1995) write, "Managers' assumptions about how ideas are related can be discovered through a study of their conversations about change, particularly during conversations for understanding" (p. 563). Thus, this approach sees change not as an abstract set of influences among boxes, but as a series of conversations where change can be discussed and debated, and new ideas can emerge.

Also proposing a social construction model for change in their popular work *How the Way We Talk Can Change the Way We Work,* Kegan and Lahey (2001) have written about seven new language shifts that leaders can encourage to support change:

1. From the language of complaint to the language of commitment

2. From the language of blame to the language of personal responsibility

3. From the language of "New Year's Resolutions" to the language of competing commitments

4. From the language of big assumptions that hold us to the language of assumptions that we hold

5. From the language of prizes and praising to the language of ongoing regard

6. From the language of rules and policies to the language of public agreement

7. From the language of constructive criticism to the language of deconstructive criticism (pp. 8–9)

They argue that these seven languages play a role in conversations that we have at individual, team, and organizational levels, and that they often inhibit us from making the changes we seek to make. New conversations can encourage greater learning and achieve change.

The role of the change agent implied by social construction models of change is to facilitate an appropriate environment for these conversations. Managing change in this vein is more like coaching an improvisational jazz band than turning a series of levers and dials on a machine. Creating change does not mean following a well-defined process, but being inventive and creative with how it is achieved, negotiating among different stakeholders to produce the dialogues that need to happen for change to succeed. "The job of a change agent . . . is to initiate, maintain, and complete conversations so as to bring into existence a new conversational reality in which new opportunities for action are created and effective action takes place" (Ford, 1999, p. 492). How effective change is depends on how well new conversations are initiated and adopted.

Ford and Ford (2008) have developed a practical tool called the conversational profile for change managers to use in analyzing and interpreting the four kinds of change conversations described earlier. They invite managers to log their conversations during a period of two weeks or so. Managers write, as in a journal, who participated in the conversation and what was said, as close to a verbatim record of the conversation as they can recollect. Managers then identify which types of change conversations they have engaged in most frequently, and they can then alter their approach if the results of those conversations have not resulted in the outcome they expected or desired. "After seeing analysis of their conversations and results, managers come to their own conclusions about what might be missing or not working;

that is, develop a hypothesis, which they can then test by altering either the type of conversations they use or the content of those conversations," Ford and Ford explain (2008, p. 455). Managers might realize, for example, that they engage in conversations for understanding, assuming that action will follow, but that they have not been explicitly engaging in conversations for performance in which actions are discussed.

In addition, related to the social construction approach to change, a new paradigm is emerging in organization development, one influenced by the study of self-organizing systems in biology and other disciplines. The complex adaptive systems perspective, like the social construction approach reviewed above, rejects the notion of the organization as a machinelike set of interconnected and systematized parts that form a predictable whole. Instead, this view sees the organization as ever-changing based on emerging patterns of self-organization created by the interactions of those agents acting as part of it (Olson & Eoyang, 2001). This approach questions the belief inherent in systems theory that systems are generally alike and general principles can be applied to predict how they will react and respond. Instead, complex adaptive systems thinking believes that individuals and organizations respond differently depending on the circumstances, so behavior cannot be predicted and controlled so systematically. This implies that managing change does not work from a top-down perspective, as in systems theory, but instead, "the role of the change agent is to use an understanding of the evolving patterns to . . . affect the self-organizing path, to observe how the system responds, and to design the next intervention" (Olson & Eoyang, 2001, p. 16). For many observers, this approach resonates because it highlights how changes can adapt and spread throughout a system to illustrate how even small changes made to a single project team can have expansive effects across the organization.

At this point you may be wondering which of these explanations of organizational change is the most appropriate one to use. Each offers benefits and contains drawbacks, making some elements of the organization visible while it obscures others. From a philosophical perspective, there are some fundamentally incongruous assumptions between the two schools of thought, so buying into both would seem impossible (e.g., the nature of organizational structure as representing an empirical reality versus being socially constructed). Indeed, some authors argue that OD is fundamentally different from a social construction perspective, contrasting the classic diagnostic approach to OD with an alternative dialogic approach (Bushe & Marshak, 2009).

From a practitioner's pragmatic view, however, each of these models offers unique insight into a client's environment. What matters is not so much which model is right, but instead which model helps to facilitate additional understanding and is most consistent with both a practitioner's approach and the client's need. For example, in a highly structured hierarchical environment, clients may be more drawn to systems theory approaches. Alternately, practitioners may find it enlightening to examine a team's language during meetings to better understand team conflict or motivation. Using multiple models may also help to illuminate new aspects of a situation, since being overly wedded to one particular model may blind the practitioner to important information (Burke, 1993). What is important is to be conscious of the assumptions of the approach being taken and the consequences of those assumptions.

Practices in Leading Change

No matter the model of change that guides it, many scholars and practitioners believe that there are several practical steps and ideal leadership practices that will facilitate change. Kotter (1996) has outlined eight steps that leaders should follow in instituting a major change in their organizations:

1. *Establishing a sense of urgency.* Fight complacency about current performance by examining current performance and measuring it against competitors or other benchmarks.

2. *Creating the guiding coalition.* Build a team of energetic, capable leaders who have expertise and credibility to lead the change.

3. *Developing a vision and strategy.* Create an engaging description of the future and the path that will be taken to get there.

4. *Communicating the change vision.* Communicate regularly, using multiple media, in jargon-free language what the change will mean and why organizational members should be enthusiastic.

5. *Empowering broad-based action.* Remove organizational, systemic, skill, and policy barriers to making the change successful.

6. *Generating short-term wins.* Implement a number of immediate and visible changes to prove the success of the change effort and provide motivation.

7. *Consolidating gains and producing more change.* Overcome the tendency to become complacent and continue to promote even greater changes.

8. *Anchoring new approaches in the culture.* Ensure that new employees and new leaders represent the desired culture (p. 21).

Summary

Organizational change is the explicit purpose of most organization development work. Practitioners intervene in organizations at the individual level, at the level of group or team, with multiple groups or teams, at the whole organization level, and between organizations, states, or nations. Change can be planned or unplanned, one-time or continuous. It can also be first-order change, or minor modifications within existing patterns, or it can be second-order change, which are creations of new frameworks and patterns.

Scholars and practitioners have developed models and approaches to explain how change occurs, and each model has benefits and drawbacks. Some of these models are based in systems theory, seeing an organization as a set of input, throughput, output, and feedback processes. Lewin's three-phase approach to change as unfreezing, moving, and refreezing, as well as the Nadler-Tushman congruence model, the Burke-Litwin model of change, and Weisbord's Six-Box Model all are consistent with the basic tenets of systems theory. These models explain how change can be successful when the basic components of the organization fit together effectively, and that changes to one area often result in necessary and perhaps unintended changes to another area. A different approach to change has a social construction perspective at its core, which sees organizations as they emerge and unfold in communication patterns. This approach sees change as a continuous process rather than a specific project.

With a good understanding of organizational change, the OD practitioner can be more conscious of the most appropriate interventions that will help produce change. In the next chapter we will focus more specifically on the practitioner's role, how an OD practitioner works with a client, and the process that the OD practitioner follows during change.

For Further Reading

Burke, W. W. (2002). *Organization change: Theory and practice.* Thousand Oaks, CA: Sage.

Holbeche, L. (2006). *Understanding change: Theory, implementation and success.* Amsterdam: Elsevier.

Hosking, D. M., & McNamee, S. (Eds.). (2006). *The social construction of organization.* Herndon, VA: Copenhagen Business School Press.

Katz, D., & Kahn, R. L. (1966). *The social psychology of organizations.* New York: Wiley.

CHAPTER 5

The Organization Development Practitioner and the Consulting Process

Once upon a time, I did a wild and crazy thing. I accepted an offer from one of my clients to become their senior vice president for organization development. Because most of my career has been as an outside consultant and I had never even been a junior vice president of anything, this was quite a leap. But, because I had worked for almost a year with the management team of which I would be a part, and I respected, liked, and trusted the other members of the team, particularly the COO and the soon-to-be-my-boss CEO, I decided to take the leap.... Every day is a new game, and well, marriage changes everything (O'Connell, 2001, p. 274).

- What do you think are the greatest differences between being an internal and external organization development practitioner?

To this point, we have discussed the history and foundations of the field of organization development (OD). We have also explored the values and ethics of OD practitioners and described how the process of organizational change is the general context for most OD work. In this chapter, we will explore the practitioner's role in the OD process more deeply and begin to introduce some of the common issues in practitioner-client relationships that we will explore throughout the book. We will differentiate OD consulting from other types of consulting that you may be familiar with, we will explore internal and external consulting relationships, and we will identify the profile of an OD consultant, including the educational background, experience, skills, and competencies needed to be a successful consultant. We will conclude this chapter by discussing the OD consulting process in detail, following an action research model that will become the outline for subsequent chapters in the book.

The Consulting Relationship and Types of Consulting

As we have already discussed, OD practitioners include a much larger group than those who hold the title of consultant. They include executives, managers, project managers, and others who devise and implement organizational change, no matter the role. Hanson and Lubin (1995) believe that OD work is highly consistent with a manager's work, from a manager's role as an administrator and supervisor, to a manager's work in promoting learning, development, problem solving, teamwork, and more. "Fundamental to their work are their skills and competencies as social change agents" (p. 87). OD can provide concepts, tools, theories, and techniques that help managers, executives, and other organizational members in implementing change.

In addition to these groups, many organizations employ OD consultants to assist with change. Consultants work closely with managers and executives as change agent partners to help the organization accomplish its objectives. This consulting relationship can be defined as follows:

> A voluntary relationship between a professional helper (consultant) and a help-needing system (client), in which the consultant is attempting to give help to the client in the solving of some current or potential problem and the relationship is perceived as temporary by both parties. (Lippitt, 1959, p. 5)

The consultant's role generally exists as an outsider to the client's system. Less formally, in popular terminology a consultant is someone who gives advice, opinions, counsel, or mentoring, typically in an area of specialized expertise. This definition is both applicable and misleading when applied to the role of the OD consultant.

An OD consultant has a particular kind of role and responsibility in a consulting engagement. Schein (1969, 1999) has described common consulting models or approaches, those of the expert and doctor-patient, that are familiar to many readers (to this I add the mechanic model). By *models*, we mean that these are common perspectives or assumptions that clients have about consulting and consultants. Each of these models of consulting differs in important ways from the role of the OD consultant. As a result, it is important for OD practitioners to understand what expectations and assumptions the client may be bringing to the consulting relationship.

Expert Model

Schein (1999) refers to the expert consultant as the "purchase of expertise" or "selling and telling" (p. 7) model of consulting. This is a common consulting role among information technology consultants, financial consultants, strategists, supply chain consultants, and others who are hired by a client specifically for knowledge and expertise in a narrow subject area. An expert consultant is often hired when an organization does not possess resources internally to complete a project. Expert consultants are usually hired to solve a specific problem or implement a solution that the client has chosen. Consequently, expert consultants often enter situations in which clients have already identified a problem and perhaps may have even chosen a solution to be implemented by the expert. A client who hires a technology consultant, for example, has already decided that technology is the problem. Not surprisingly, technology solutions will be the only ones offered by the consultant. The client hiring an expert consultant has often already framed the problem as a gap in knowledge that the expert can fulfill. This approach presents several difficulties. Since the consultant's specialized knowledge is usually greater than the client's, supervising the consultant's work is especially challenging (Freedman & Zackrison, 2001). As a result, "The client gives away power" and "is vulnerable to being misled" (Schein, 1999, p. 8). For this model to work effectively, Schein notes that the client must have already conducted an accurate assessment and clearly defined the problem for the consultant.

Doctor-Patient Model

Most of us have experienced what happens when we visit a physician for an unknown medical problem. Typically, the doctor asks a number of questions that the patient answers, with the patient unaware of the implications of the question or the response. "Where does it hurt?" "When did you first notice it?" "How often have you felt this way?" "Is the pain isolated to this one area or does it spread?" Following this diagnostic series of questions asked for the doctor's benefit, the doctor announces the result and the solution: "I think you have sprained your ankle. Take one of these twice a day, elevate your ankle, and place ice on it for 20 minutes at a time until healed." The patient leaves satisfied that the problem has been solved, and the doctor is satisfied to leave the patient once the solution has been identified.

Though it is a very popular and easily assumed model of consulting, it presents several problems. When clients adopt the doctor-patient consulting model, they are looking for someone who will analyze their situation and prescribe a solution to the problem. The responsibility for gathering data, processing information, making a diagnosis, and choosing solutions rests on the consultant. The primary responsibility for implementing the solution relies on the patient/client. While the doctor-patient model is a less time-consuming model (Cash & Minter, 1979), success in this model relies on the ability of the consultant to accurately gather information about the client's situation, diagnose the underlying problem, and prescribe an appropriate intervention. Rarely can the consultant alone do this accurately, however. Members of the organization may not know how or may not want to give accurate information to the consultant. In addition, the doctor-patient model frequently results in low success following implementation. Often no one other than the consultant has seen the data or believes that the diagnosis is the correct one. As a result, interventions that are completed tend to be for the consultant's benefit, not the client's, so long-term change is unlikely. Even when the problem is successfully solved, clients likely will not know how to solve the problem themselves (Schein, 1987). The next time a problem occurs, the client is forced to call the consultant again.

Mechanic Model

Related to the doctor-patient model is a third popular model for consultants, called the mechanic model (Kahnweiler, 2002). Many who visit an auto mechanic, for example, have little interest in the technical details involved in the inner workings of their cars. When we have a problem, we often tell the mechanic something like "It's making a grinding noise when I turn left," and we want to pick up our car a few hours later, pay the bill, and leave. The mechanic is responsible for figuring out what is wrong and fixing it. If the repair does not successfully solve the problem, the responsibility is the mechanic's, not ours. We do not want to see complicated diagrams or explanations of how the mechanic discovered the source of the problem, removed the broken part, replaced it, and verified that the solution worked. Most of all, we do not want to get our hands dirty under the hood, inspecting parts and learning more about the car's functions. It is good enough for us when the problem has been fixed.

The mechanic model underlies interaction with clients who have little patience or time to deal with problems. It is rarely a successful consultant role. It is occasionally the result of a client's actively chosen ignorance of the details of a problem or a solution. Clients preferring a mechanic-consultant would prefer to place a phone call to a consultant, describe a problem ("Jim and Ted can't get along"; "Our team never gets anything done"), and wait for the consultant to return to report that the problem has been fixed. The mechanic model gives the consultant responsibility over virtually every aspect of the problem and the solution, and it permits the client to relinquish both accountability and responsibility for the problem. Unsuccessful solutions or problems that recur can be blamed on a poor consultant. Clients avoid the messy and sometimes uncomfortable processes "under the hood" and are not forced to confront their own role in the problem being experienced. It goes without saying that in this consulting model the client rarely gains any insight into the process of assessing problems and implementing solutions.

The Organization Development Consulting Model

Organization development consulting differs in significant ways from each of the three models just described, even though clients frequently approach an OD consultant with one of these alternative models in mind. Consequently it is the consultant's responsibility to invite the client to share expectations about roles and working expectations early on so that misunderstandings can be corrected and implicit expectations can be made explicit. We will discuss in greater detail in the next chapter how consultants do this when we discuss the process of contracting. Table 5.1 compares organization development consulting with the three models discussed here.

In contrast to the expert model of consulting, OD consultants are hired as experts in process consulting and human systems rather than in specific content areas, though content expertise in areas such as operations, finance, marketing, or strategy can help a consultant more quickly identify with the client. Schein (1969, 1999) calls OD consulting "process consulting" to set it apart from consulting in which the practitioner offers content expertise. In general, however, OD consultants view clients as the experts, because they are the most knowledgeable about the

Table 5.1   How Organization Development Consulting Differs From Other Approaches

	Expert	Doctor-Patient	Mechanic	Organization Development
Responsibility for data gathering	Primarily client	Consultant	Consultant	Shared
Responsibility for diagnosis	Client, with consultant recommendations	Consultant	Consultant	Shared
Responsibility for selecting interventions	Primarily consultant	Consultant	Consultant	Shared
Responsibility for implementing change	Client, with consultant recommendations	Client	Consultant	Shared

organization, people, culture, processes, problems, and history of the organization. They are generally more knowledgeable than the practitioner about what interventions may or may not work best, what order the activities should be conducted, who should be interviewed or surveyed, where the most fruitful data may be gathered, and how data should be interpreted for subtle and underlying cues. Seeing the client as the expert puts the consultant in a more humble position in which he or she can ask the client relevant questions to unleash the client's hidden knowledge and then offer useful insights from an outsider's perspective (Schein, 1999).

In contrast to the doctor-patient model, OD consultants often prefer to conduct data gathering and decide on a diagnosis jointly with a client. OD consultants prefer an equal relationship in which the client has primary responsibility for the problem and the solution as opposed to the consultant taking ownership of the problem and solution. As a result, the consultant's role is to assist the client in the diagnostic process in a partnership. As Schein (1987) notes, joint diagnosis is important for the following reason:

> The consultant can seldom learn enough about any given organization to really know what a better course of action would be or even what information would really help. . . . However, the consultant can help the client to become a sufficiently good diagnostician. (p. 9)

Moreover, the success of an intervention tends to be greater when clients and consultants jointly agree upon a diagnosis and intervention strategy. This is being addressed more frequently in real doctor-patient interactions as well, as research has indicated that when physicians and patients agree on a medical diagnosis, patients are more satisfied with the interaction and are more likely to adopt the physician's treatment recommendations (Bass et al., 1986; Stewart et al., 2000).

In contrast to the mechanic model, in OD engagements the client has a significant role to play in understanding and making sense of the problem and in implementing the solution. The client's active participation is necessary to ensure that once the consultant leaves the engagement, the intervention can be a sustained change. Without a client's active participation, the results are likely to be short lived.

In contrast to both the doctor-patient and mechanic models, a primary objective of any consulting engagement is for the client to learn the OD process so that problem-solving skills (including gathering data, diagnosis, and interventions) are transferred to the client. In fact, Schein (1999) writes, "Unless clients learn to see problems for themselves and think through their own remedies, they will be less likely to implement the solution and less likely to learn how to fix such problems should they recur" (p. 18). Some beginning consultants see perpetuation of a client's ignorance as advantageous. After all, they think, if I teach clients how to solve these problems themselves, won't my own services be obsolete and I will be out of a job? There are several problems with this view. It goes against one of OD's core values to contribute to growth, learning, and development. When a consultant holds this belief and acts upon it, it contributes to a power imbalance in which the client is encouraged to be helpless, needy, and reactive, while the consultant maintains power and control. In many organizations this relationship imbalance is typical among organizational members and it often contributes to some of the conflicts and organizational problems that the consultant has been brought in to help solve. It is therefore hypocritical for the consultant to advocate a new kind of relationship among organizational members when the client-consultant relationship is not a role model for it. Last, the OD process is not a set of secrets that are closely guarded and revealed only to paying clients. Clients who do not see progress are less likely to call a consultant back to solve the same problem, but clients who have learned how to address problems on their own are more likely to call a consultant again to solve a different problem and to recommend a consultant to colleagues and friends.

In summary, the OD consultant is a different kind of consultant, one that maintains multiple and unique roles and deals with a diverse set of circumstances and problems. For many practitioners this is why it is an interesting and rewarding profession. The OD consultant, according to Marshak (2006), must be a professional practitioner that is also a skilled diagnostician, social scientist researcher, interventionist, educator or trainer, facilitator, and coach. Learning to successfully perform these roles in a consulting engagement requires content knowledge, process knowledge, and interpersonal skills. In the next section we will explore the profile of the OD practitioner in greater depth.

OD Practitioners: Who Are They and Where Do They Work?

As we noted in Chapter 1, change agents who do OD work are a diverse community, consisting of managers, HR professionals, IT project managers, and more. Some organizations employ internal consultants that hold the titles of organization development consultant, organizational effectiveness consultant, or human resources specialist. These are generally roles in which the practitioner is hired as a full-time employee to provide internal consulting to managers, executives, and teams that are experiencing problems or implementing change. OD consultants that work as internal practitioners in an employee capacity generally work in the human resources department, but larger organizations may also have OD consultants reporting to a business area instead, particularly in business areas in which implementing change is a frequent project, such as in information technology.

Some observers have noted that where an organization has an internal OD function, it is often "buried within HR," where internal consultants lack access to executive clients and "it is difficult for OD practitioners to experience positive regard, much less have organizational influence" (Burke & Bradford, 2005, p. 9). Burke (2004) has described the advantages and disadvantages of five possible scenarios in which the OD function is (1) a division of HR, (2) a freestanding unit in the organization, (3) a decentralized function where OD practitioners report to business units, (4) an integrated part of every HR function (such as compensation, benefits, etc.), and (5) a part of the strategic planning function. He concludes that while the latter two are not common structures for an OD function, there may be benefits to strengthening the organization and the field by integrating OD with both human resources and strategic planning for systemwide change.

Organizations also employ external OD consultants who work independently or as part of a larger consulting practice. Often the external consultant is contacted directly by an executive or manager, generally establishing a contract with the external consultant on a per-project basis, even if the consultant has a long-term relationship with the client organization. These consultants may have several client engagements at any given time, sometimes travelling between sites, depending on the magnitude and time commitment required of the engagement.

Internal Versus External Consulting: Advantages and Disadvantages

In the chapter's opening vignette, one consultant made a career transition from being an external to an internal consultant. Whether one chooses a career path as (or to hire) an internal or external consultant, there are many advantages and disadvantages of either role. Table 5.2 explores some of the pros and cons of holding these two roles.

Clearly these advantages and disadvantages will vary among consultants and among organizations. Some organizational members, for example, place a high degree of trust in an outsider's perspective and may discount the recommendations of those inside the organization, assuming that consultants must be more skilled if they maintain client relationships and earn a salary as an independent consultant. In other organizations the opposite is true: Internal perspectives are more valued than external ones, and those solutions "not invented here" are suspect. In some organizations, internal consultants may be trusted with confidential information more easily, and external consultants may find it hard to draw out information from organizational members. In other organizations, internal consultants may be perceived as already taking on management's side, and external consultants may be seen as more neutral and a positive symbol of "change to come" (Kaarst-Brown, 1999). Internal consultants may face increased pressure to avoid being honest with clients for fear that they will retaliate. These consultants do themselves and their clients a disservice when they "collude" with clients by refusing to confront difficult issues (Scott, 2000). External consultants may do the same to avoid angering a client who may be important to future business. Indeed, some challenges are common to both roles.

Table 5.2   Advantages and Disadvantages of Internal and External Consulting

	Internal Consulting	*External Consulting*
Advantages	More knowledge of organizational culture, history, and practices.	More experience with a variety of clients.
	Already has relationships with organizational members.	Does not enter organization with bias from past experience with organizational members.
	Perceived as having a longer-term view and potentially greater stake in success of outcome.	Less political involvement; can be truthful with less consequence.
	Earns a regular salary.	May have greater "star power."
	Less need to market services.	Organizational members may feel more comfortable sharing confidential information without fear of leaks.
Disadvantages	May be blind to seeing some issues because of history with culture.	May have trouble seeing the hidden meanings or subtle issues.
	Less variety in clients, industries, and issues.	Must build relationships and trust with organizational members.
	May be presented with ethical challenges where it is hard to refuse.	May be perceived as short term.
	May be confronted with confidentiality concerns, particularly with an internal manager.	Must seek out clients to earn paycheck.
	Organizational members may be reluctant to share sensitive information for fear that it may leak internally to colleagues.	May have recommendations perceived as selling or extending work unnecessarily.
	May be seen as an agent for management.	May not be able to follow through beyond interventions to see long-term results.

Because there is no perfect scenario, organizations can sometimes reap advantages by having both an internal and external consultant work together throughout a project, from data gathering through interventions. An internal consultant can provide background information to the external consultant throughout the project, and the external consultant can point out issues that the internal consultant may have missed.

Ethical Issues for Internal and External Consultants

Ethical issues differ for internal and external consultants. For example, internal consultants may face increased pressure from peers or coworkers to violate a client's confidentiality by disclosing the existence or purpose of an engagement, what participants said during an interview or in a focus group, or even simply to disclose what problem the consultant was contacted to discuss. An internal client may not want information shared widely about the existence of an executive team-building engagement, a reorganization, or a merger/acquisition, and the consultant has the ethical responsibility to maintain this confidentiality. While it may be awkward to respond to a colleague that those areas are confidential, it can be especially challenging for an internal consultant to deal with when the consultant's manager or the vice president of human resources is asking. The most effective way to deal with this challenge is to predict it and to develop working agreements between consultants and managers about what information will be or cannot be shared. Block (2000) calls this "contracting with your boss" to clarify expectations and assumptions and to anticipate the issue before it becomes a problem.

> If you were a manager hiring an organization development consultant, for what kinds of projects would you prefer an internal consultant? An external consultant? What skills would you look for?

The Organization Development Consulting Profession

A number of professional associations have been formed for OD practitioners. The National Training Laboratories, the American Society for Training and Development (which has an OD practice subarea), the Organization Development Network, and the OD Institute are targeted toward the practitioner community. Among academic associations, the most popular are the Organization Development and Change division of the Academy of Management, and the Society for Industrial and Organizational Psychology. Academic journals such as *The Journal of Applied Behavioral Science* and *Leadership and Organization Development Journal* frequently publish articles of interest to both practitioners and academic readers.

A sample of about 400 members in these groups was studied by Church, Burke, and Van Eynde (1994), who found that practitioners were about equally split between being internal and external consultants. The majority held master's or doctoral degrees, had been practicing in the field of OD for just over 11 years, represented a wide variety of industries (including real estate, health care, education, military, and automotive), and had diverse educational backgrounds. Many (over half of those surveyed) maintained active relationships with the academic world through teaching, administration, or participation on advisory boards.

Becoming an OD Consultant

While there are an increasing number of academic and professional programs that teach OD concepts and practices, not much has changed since Burke (1993) wrote that "there simply is no clear and systematic career path for becoming an OD consultant" (p. 185). There is not yet a single, universally accepted certification or degree that would qualify one to be an OD consultant. In fact, skills and levels of experience differ greatly among OD practitioners, who may specialize in certain intervention types such as coaching, strategic planning, or process design. Bunker, Alban, and Lewicki (2005) note that "knowing that someone is an 'OD practitioner' does not tell you much about the person's training, preparation, background or expertise and skill base" (p. 165). Like our clients, OD practitioners are a diverse community.

Most observers agree that a background in the social and behavioral sciences is a good starting point to expose beginners to introductory OD concepts. Burke (1993) recommends academic training in areas such as organizational psychology, group dynamics, research methods, adult learning, career development, counseling, OD, and organizational theory. Head, Armstrong, and Preston (1996) and McLean (2006) also recommend courses in business, since most OD work is done in that context, a point echoed by Burke and Bradford (2005), who concur that the OD consultant needs to "understand the language and how profit is made and costs contained according to various business models" (p. 8). Supplementary study in areas such as organizational communication, sociology, public administration, and political science can also provide useful concepts that can add to a practitioner's theoretical and practical knowledge. Participation in groups such as professional associations, conferences, and training courses offered by those associations can be good ways to increase one's knowledge of OD concepts and to expand a professional network. Practical experience, however, is a prerequisite to successful consulting, so shadow consulting with a skilled mentor is among the best ways to gain experience. Those wanting to break into the field might volunteer to help an internal consultant with a project at work. Assisting an internal consultant with data gathering, data analysis, taking notes during interviews, or simply sitting in on a workshop or facilitated meeting can be excellent ways to watch OD work in action. In addition, a popular way to gain experience is to seek pro bono opportunities to work with a nonprofit group. One caveat: Because it is important to present oneself ethically and not to overstate one's level of knowledge, working with an experienced consultant is usually necessary until the beginning consultant gains enough experience to be able to take on the engagement alone.

Individual development and growth is a personal exercise. Different individuals will need and want to develop in different areas of competency and skill. As Varney (1980) put it, "Professional development comes through a variety of different kinds of experiences" (p. 34) that are customized to the individual. Participating in a program or activity because it is popular or because it is available may not be the best choice. Reading journals, attending conferences, observing other consultants, and obtaining an advanced degree are all possible options depending on the practitioner. In summary, while there are multiple paths to a career in OD, there are also many opportunities for those eager and motivated to develop the necessary knowledge, skills, and experience.

Skills and Competencies for OD Consultants

There have been many attempts to define the set of skills and competencies that a practitioner needs to be considered a fully competent organization development professional.[1] Some of these efforts have been conducted by individual researchers, some have been sponsored by professional associations, and some have been associated with a college or university OD program. Each has offered a different set of skills and competencies, and a single approach has not yet been adopted (Eubanks, Marshall, & O'Driscoll, 1990). Moreover, these skill and competency definitions differ in whether they describe interpersonal skills, behavioral skills, or knowledge of content areas needed to be successful (O'Driscoll & Eubanks, 1993). Varney (1980), for example, describes three areas in which OD practitioners need to be skilled: (1) self and impact awareness; (2) conceptual, analytical, and research skills; and (3) organizational change and influence skills. Focusing on behaviors that contribute to successful results, Eubanks et al. (1990) list six competency categories: using interpersonal skills, managing group process, using data, contracting, implementing the intervention, and maintaining the client relationship. Sullivan and Sullivan (1995) present no fewer than 187 essential competencies for internal and external OD consultants in a list that has been revised more than a dozen times since the late 1970s.

Table 5.2 presents a subset of core and advanced skills contained in many of these surveys of OD competencies. The list is indeed daunting, but rest assured that it is unlikely that any single practitioner will be highly skilled in all of these areas. Some practitioners choose deep expertise in a number of these areas instead of breadth in all of them (McLean, 2006). Nonetheless, most of the interpersonal skills on this list are needed whether one specializes in large-group interventions or one-on-one coaching. Many of the intervention areas described in this chart are covered later in this book.

The OD Consulting Process and Action Research

Recall from Chapter 2 that *action research* was the name that Kurt Lewin gave to the process of using social scientific research practices to gather data about groups, intervene in their processes, and to evaluate the results of the intervention. Action research is described as follows:

> A participatory democratic process concerned with developing practical knowing in the pursuit of worthwhile human purposes. . . . It seeks to bring together action and reflection, theory and practice, in participation with others, in the pursuit of practical solutions to issues of pressing concern to people, and more generally the flourishing of individual personas and their communities. (Reason & Bradbury, 2001, p. 1)

Lewin envisioned that research findings would not only improve practices in the immediate organization but would also be shared widely to improve theory, which would be used by other practitioners in their own organizations. Thus, action

Table 5.3 Example Competencies for Success as an Organization Development Consultant

Interpersonal Skills and Personal Characteristics	Organizational Behavior	Data Collection and Analysis	Training and Development	Business and Management Knowledge Areas	General Professional Skills	Consulting Skills	Interventions
Self-awareness and self-management	Organizational theory	Research design	Adult learning	Finance and accounting	Public speaking	Entry and contracting	Strategic planning
Objectivity/ neutrality	Strategy	Interviewing skills	Instructional design	Human resources management	Written communication	Design of data gathering program	Vision/mission development
Imagination	Open systems	Survey preparation	Training delivery skills	Sales and marketing	Translate theory into practice	Diagnosis	Goal setting
Flexibility, dealing with ambiguity	Motivation and rewards	Data analysis (quantitative and qualitative)	Assessment of learning	Information systems and technology	Project management	Designing interventions	Process analysis and redesign
Honesty/ integrity	Change theory	Statistical analysis	Performance management	Operations and production	Ethical issues for OD consultants	Giving and receiving feedback	Role development and clarification
Consistency	Organization design	Participant-observation	Technology and learning	Legal issues	Cross-cultural knowledge	Evaluating results of interventions	Restructuring
Building trust and rapport	Power	Interpreting and reporting results					Coaching and mentoring
Open-mindedness	Leadership	Measurement and testing					Team building
	Conflict						Future search conferences
	Organizational culture						
	Mergers and acquisitions						

Interpersonal Skills and Personal Characteristics	Organizational Behavior	Data Collection and Analysis	Training and Development	Business and Management Knowledge Areas	General Professional Skills	Consulting Skills	Interventions
Listening	Group development						Appreciative inquiry
Sense of humor	Change management						Quality approaches (Six Sigma, Total Quality Management)
Risk taking	Change resistance and stakeholder engagement						Conflict resolution
Political awareness	Communication (metaphors, stories, etc.)						Facilitation skills
Persuasiveness							
Collaboration							
Tact and diplomacy							
Role modeling							
Rational-emotional balance							
Negotiation							
Managing stress							

research projects owe a debt not only to the organization and its sponsor but also to other practitioners and to the research community at large (Clark, 1972; Greenwood & Levin, 1998). The term *action research* encompasses a number of activities, such as defining the problem, planning a research process, understanding and evaluating theory, and more. In its ideal form, action research is a scientific process (Cunningham, 1993) in which the researcher is actively engaged *with* those experiencing the problem versus conducting research *on* them (Heron & Reason, 2001). Thus, participation by organizational members in diagnosing the issues and solving the problem is a key feature of action research. Action research projects generally proceed in the manner described in Figure 5.1, where an initial problem prompts diagnosis, planning action, taking action, and evaluating results. Once results are evaluated, the cycle begins again.

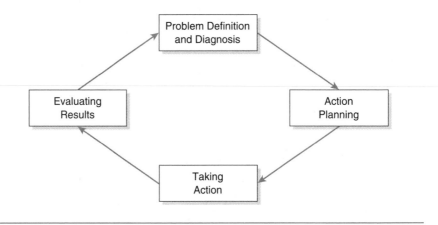

Figure 5.1 A General Action Research Cycle

Traditional action research programs strive to contribute to both theory and practice, bridging the divide between them, and this has been a central objective of OD throughout its history. The purpose is not just to create new theory but to create new possibilities for action where theory and action are closely intertwined (Coghlan & Brannick, 2001): The two components of action (practice) and research (theory) are combined in practice as they are in the name.

Over time, however, many believe that the gap between theory and practice has widened as practitioners have devoted less attention to contributing to theoretical knowledge (Bunker et al., 2005). Regardless, action research and OD consulting share similar objectives in developing a participative and inclusive process where practitioners and organizational members jointly explore problems, initiate action, and evaluate outcomes, and where the overall purpose is social or organizational change.

Though practitioners today may not necessarily see contributions to theoretical knowledge to be a central objective of every OD project, practitioners have adopted an OD consulting process that generally follows an action research model, borrowing the major tenets of action research. While different practitioners may label the phases differently, the consulting process in Figure 5.2 is generally consistent with what most OD practitioners do. The consulting model looks like a linear process, but most consulting engagements rarely proceed in such a step-by-step manner.

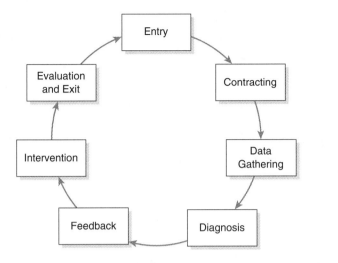

Figure 5.2   Stages of the Consulting Process

What is also similar in both OD consulting and action research is the disciplined reexamination and analysis of actions and data to evaluate results (Freedman, 2006). Consultants and action researchers both return to different stages throughout the engagement, gathering additional data where needed, or validating the process with the client and recontracting as new issues emerge. The process is more iterative than linear.

Let's look at each of these stages in turn:

Entry. The first stage of the consulting process is entry, which begins with an initial contact between a consultant and a client.

Contracting. Next, the consultant and client come to agreement on what work will be accomplished. The client makes the request by describing the problem or OD consulting opportunity, and the client and consultant discuss the engagement and how to create a successful consulting relationship. The consultant responds with a formal or informal proposal about what he or she will do.

Data gathering. Third, data are gathered about the situation, the client, the organization, and other relevant aspects of the problem. This can involve one or more methods or sources of information.

Diagnosis and feedback. Next, the client and consultant jointly analyze and interpret the data. The consultant presents the client with feedback from the data gathering stage. The problem may be reevaluated, additional data may be gathered, or an intervention strategy may be proposed.

Intervention. The consultant and client agree on what intervention(s) would best address the problem, and the intervention strategy is carried out.

Evaluation and exit. The consultant and client evaluate the outcomes of the intervention(s) and whether the intervention(s) have resulted in the desired change.

Additional data are gathered at this point and the client and consultant may agree to terminate the engagement or to begin the cycle again (reentry, recontracting, etc.).

The remainder of the book follows these stages of the OD consulting process. In the next chapter we will cover the first two stages of the consulting model in depth: entry and contracting. In Chapter 7, we will focus on data gathering, and in Chapter 8 we will discuss diagnosis and feedback, followed by an introduction to interventions in Chapter 9. Chapters 10 to 12 describe intervention types, and in Chapter 13 we describe how consultants evaluate the success of interventions and consulting engagements.

Summary

The function of the organization development consultant is varied as the consultant plays multiple roles throughout the consulting engagement, from facilitator to coach, teacher to researcher. The OD consultant is a specific type of consultant that approaches organizational problems differently than would a consultant taking on an expert, doctor-patient, or mechanic role. Expert consultants are hired for specialized content knowledge in a particular field. Doctor-patient consultants are hired when consultants possess content knowledge and clients want to be told what the solution is. Mechanic consultants are hired when the client wants the consultant to deal with virtually all elements of the problem and to propose and implement a solution. By contrast, the OD consultant works jointly with the client throughout the consulting engagement and also strives to share problem-solving knowledge with the client to increase the client's ability to solve the problem alone next time. The OD consultant can be an internal or external role, each of which hold advantages and disadvantages for the consultant and the client.

The varied roles of an OD consultant have implications for the knowledge and skills required to be a successful practitioner. While no practitioner is likely to be an expert in the competencies listed in Table 5.2, the list can become instructive for those who wish to enter the field and to increase their personal development.

OD practitioners follow a consulting process modeled on that developed in action research programs. Key practices adopted from action research include involving organizational members in the process, conducting data gathering, joint evaluation and interpretation of data, joint diagnosis of an intervention strategy, and joint evaluation of the outcomes.

Note

1. For examples, see Carey & Varney (1983); Esper (1990); Eubanks et al. (1990); Eubanks, O'Driscoll, Hayward, Daniels, & Connor (1990); Freedman & Zackrison (2001); Head et al. (1996); McLean (2006); McLean & Sullivan (2000); O'Driscoll & Eubanks (1992); Scott (2000); Sullivan & Sullivan (1995); Varney (1980); Warrick & Donovan (1979); Worley & Feyerherm (2003); Worley & Varney (1998).

For Further Reading

Coghlan, D., & Brannick, T. (2001). *Doing action research in your own organization.* London: Sage.

Freedman, A. M., & Zackrison, R. E. (2001). *Finding your way in the consulting jungle: A guidebook for organization development practitioners.* San Francisco: Jossey-Bass/Pfeiffer.

McLean, G. N., & Sullivan, R. L. (2000). Essential competencies for internal and external OD consultants. In R. T. Golembiewski (Ed.), *Handbook of organizational consultation* (2nd ed., pp. 749–753). New York: Marcel Dekker.

Schein, E. H. (1999). *Process consultation revisited.* Reading, MA: Addison-Wesley.

Scott, B. (2000). *Consulting on the inside: An internal consultant's guide to living and working inside organizations.* Alexandria, VA: American Society for Training & Development (ASTD).

Sullivan, R., & Sullivan, K. (1995). Essential competencies for internal and external OD consultants. In W. Rothwell, R. Sullivan, & G. N. McLean (Eds.), *Practicing organization development: A guide for consultants* (pp. 535–549). San Diego: Pfeiffer.

CHAPTER 6

Entry and Contracting

The client was a petrochemical plant with 1,000 employees in a North American corporation.... At the plant, we were greeted with statements of goals ranging from hard-nosed interest in increasing productivity to enlightened aspirations for improving human relations in the organization. But whether the outcomes desired of OD were utilitarian or humanitarian, the nature of OD was, for virtually all members of the organization, shrouded in mystery. As is generally true, prospective clients in this organization had a difficult time understanding what they were getting themselves into. At a meeting to discuss the possibility of working with cross-functional task forces, for example, the consultants sketched in typical fashion the outlines of a team-building scenario. They stressed the importance of the group's willingness to help themselves, held out the possibility of increased self-awareness, and emphasized the absence of any guarantees of improved effectiveness. In response, one member of the task force remarked, "This is the strangest sales pitch I've ever heard" (Kaplan, 1978, pp. 45–47; Kaplan notes that the initial stages of the consulting process took 2 years).

- How would you describe the organization development (OD) process to a potential client?
- How would you clarify the OD practitioner role in an initial client meeting?

I n any consulting engagement, well before the team-building session is planned or the strategic planning meeting is designed, a great deal of time is invested in setting up the intervention for success. This is done in the first three stages of the consulting process: entry, contracting, and data gathering. In Chapters 6 and 7 we will describe the purpose and structure of these phases for both the client and the OD practitioner. By the end of these two chapters, and the case study that follows them, you will more clearly understand the importance of these three stages, and you will be able to apply what you have learned about contracting and data gathering by developing a data gathering strategy that will seek to reveal the underlying issues behind a problem presented by a client.

In this chapter we will first discuss the entry process, in which the client and consultant make contact for the first time. In this stage, the client presents an initial description of the problem or request, and the OD practitioner must consider whether and how to continue the relationship. In the contracting process, the practitioner and client explore both the formal and psychological contractual elements of their relationship, such as further exploring the problem, the request for consulting support, each others' needs and roles, and how the engagement will progress. The consultant must determine who the client is, a trickier proposition than it may seem. With a successful foundational relationship established, the consulting engagement has a much greater likelihood of success.

It is difficult to understate the consequence of these phases, since many (perhaps most) problems that occur later on can be attributed to shortcuts or omissions in contracting. Investing time early on can save considerable time later. Cunningham (1993) describes this fact persuasively:

> The planned change process requires more time in the formative sequences of the process. Participants or organizational members are involved in the definition of the need, and have the opportunity to use their creativity in developing the idea and its proposal. As a result, less time may be needed during the implementation stage for making adaptations or dealing with resistances. The investment of time in assessing and focusing can significantly reduce the amount of time required to implement and institutionalize the change. It should also reduce the possibility of having to scrap an unworkable idea and start over again. (p. 68)

While consultants and clients find it tempting to jump to solutions, assuming they have a good understanding of the problem, skipping the early phases of the consulting process can have serious consequences later on.

Entry

Entry is the first step in the consulting process and consists of the first contact with a client before the formal contracting process has begun. It can occur in the form of an unsolicited phone call from an acquaintance, or may it occur as the result of informal networking or even a discussion on a plane or train with a stranger. Gaining entry occurs generally as the result of a number of intentional and accidental factors. For external consultants, gaining entry is often as the result of marketing and selling one's expertise or success to a potential client. External consultants are more likely to use strategies such as networking, phone calls, direct mail, websites, or presentations at conferences to build awareness among potential clients (Freedman & Zackrison, 2001). Even for internal consultants, marketing one's services is a part of the job.

Geirland and Maniker-Leiter (1995) recommend that internal OD practitioners give presentations, lead lunchtime "brown bag" discussions, create marketing materials, and "take all opportunities to speak before any audience in the company" (p. 45). These marketing events can give examples to internal audiences of how an OD engagement can add value and provide results.

While most think of entry in these pragmatic terms, comprising a process of marketing, taking the first phone call, agreeing to take on the assignment, and scheduling a meeting to develop a contract, the entry phase has greater symbolic significance and complexity. Beyond these events, the entry process is the first stage in the consultant's becoming connected to the social environment of the organization, including building relationships with organizational members who understand first and foremost that the consultant will only be a temporary member (Glidewell, 1959). Thus, the entry phase should also be seen as the first stage in a relationship and trust-building process, and the consultant's actions during this stage will be perceived as at least symbolic of the working relationship to come. A good entry process will thus entail the consultant listening carefully to the client, showing good faith in expressing care and concern for the client's request. Glidewell (1959) argues that during this stage, the client wants reassurance that the consultant not only understands but shares the client's goals and values. It is the first impression that a potential client has of a consulting relationship.

Ethical Issues During the Entry Stage

It is during the entry stage that the consultant has the first hints about the type of project being requested. Just as clients often approach consultants with assumptions of a different model of consulting in their minds (as discussed in Chapter 5), clients often request projects that consultants are unable to (or should not) fulfill for one or more reasons. This occurs most often when a client asks for a consultant to perform an activity that is inappropriate for the OD practitioner role. Examples of inappropriate consulting activities include advice and counsel to a client on the qualifications or behaviors of specific individuals or job applicants, or confidential advice to a client on the performance or structure of a team. Borderline activities include those activities that fall into the "expert" consulting role, when the consultant is asked to offer content advice (French & Bell, 1999). In some cases, the entry conversation between practitioner and client can reveal the influence of organizational politics on the decision to bring in an OD practitioner. The consultant may be selected to function as a scapegoat to eventually be blamed for the problem, or the project may be designed to fail so the client can remind organizational members how difficult the manager's job is.

When a client wants to hire a consultant to sit in on a team meeting and tell her or him "what's really going on in those meetings" or "what you think of the leader or team members," these activities put the consultant in an uncomfortable and unethical position. Ethical challenges can be even greater when the client prefers to keep the consultation hidden from or misrepresented to organizational members. When the consultant role, which must be founded on trust of and by organizational members, begins with a misrepresentation, the consultant and organizational members may no longer be working toward the same objectives. It is at this point, when a client begins to suggest what the consultant considers an inappropriate role, that the consultant should be quick to point out the limits of the consulting activity before misunderstanding occurs. Schein (1969) writes of making these limits explicit early, "so that they don't function as traps or sources of disappointment later on if and when I refuse to go along with something the client expects of me" (p. 83).

Ethical problems can occur when consultants misrepresent or overstate their background or experience (educational background, experience with similar problems, organizations, or industries) (White & Wooten, 1983). In their zeal to be hired for an assignment, consultants may also overpromise results, offer an "armchair" diagnosis without background data, or agree to implement an intervention strategy without additional analysis. Even statements to the client such as "We'll have it taken care of" and "This is easy," or "I've fixed this before," while reassuring to the client, offer promises that the consultant may be unable to meet.

Who Is the Client?

A central question to be answered during entry and the initial phases of the engagement is "Who is the client?" On the surface this appears a simple question, especially for internal consultants who may already know the voice on the other end of the phone. Even for internal consultants, however, defining the client is not a simple matter (Geirland & Maniker-Leiter, 1995). Cummings and Worley (2001) write that "it is not unusual for an OD project to fail because the relevant client was inappropriately defined" (p. 46). Schein (1997) has developed an instructive typology of six "client types" that complicate how the client can be defined, noting that "one can find oneself not knowing for whom one is working, or working with several clients whose goals are in conflict with each other" (p. 202):

1. *Contact clients.* Contact clients are the initial points of communication in the client organization.

2. *Intermediate clients.* Intermediate clients are those that are included in meetings or from whom data are gathered during the course of the engagement.

3. *Primary clients.* Primary clients have responsibility for the problem the consultant is working to address. Primary clients generally are the ones paying for the consultant's services.

4. *Unwitting clients.* Unwitting clients will be affected by the engagement or intervention but may not know of the engagement activity or that it will concern them.

5. *Indirect clients.* Indirect clients are not known to the consultant but are conscious that they are stakeholders in the outcome.

6. *Ultimate clients.* Ultimate clients consist of the larger system or organization, "or any other group that the consultant cares about and whose welfare must be considered" (Schein, 1997, p. 203).

The consultant often meets a number of people during the entry phase, and sorting out who is a primary client and who may be an intermediate client can be a challenging endeavor. A contact client may indeed be the primary client or may be a peer, assistant, or subordinate of the primary client contacting the consultant on his or her behalf, and who will later introduce the consultant to the primary client. A contact client eventually may also become an intermediate client, participating on the project at a later time. The primary client may make a request that conflicts with the goals and objectives of the ultimate client. Differentiating between client types is instructive to the consultant who "is always dealing with more than one part of the client system, and some parts may not have the same needs or expectations as do others" (Schein, 1997, p. 203). Being clear about these needs can sensitize the consultant to the potentially conflicting needs that may exist and that may be necessary to be accounted for later.

Many practitioners approach the client question differently. Some argue that the entire organization or system should always be thought of as the client. Burke (1994) argues that the client is not always a single individual or the larger system, but the client should be thought of as the *relationships* between individuals, groups, and the larger organization. This means that all of the consultant's actions and decisions are directed toward improving these relationships rather than satisfying the demands of a single individual or small group. Schein (1997) describes how the client can change depending on the target of the intervention. When interpersonal issues are involved, then the relationship can be seen as the client. When one group or multiple groups are involved, then the group process can be seen as the client. When multiple systems are involved, society at large can be seen as the client. It may appear to be an insignificant decision, but defining the client can be instructive to the consultant and can help frame how the problem is defined, how and what data are gathered, and what interventions are selected. Reminding oneself who the client is, especially when a difficult decision presents itself, can help to clarify allegiances and desired outcomes, and to guide the consultant's next steps.

The entry phase usually concludes with a scheduled face-to-face or telephone meeting at a later time, delay of a potential contract until a later date, or termination if either consultant or client is unwilling to continue.

Contracting

Contracting is the process of developing an agreement with a client on the work to be performed. It is a particularly important time, when communicating about the client-consultant relationship is of interest to both the client and the change agent/consultant. It is also the most natural time when both parties are interested in discussing mutual expectations, clarifying roles, and setting expectations about the work to be done by both parties. It also can correct (or cause) misunderstandings as the following personal example illustrates.

As an eager young consultant, I took on an assignment for a senior executive, enthusiastic about the opportunity to work on an important project. The client was frustrated that many projects in the division were missing their goals, either missing deadlines or over budget. He wanted to understand how the division could get back on track with projects. Willing to jump in and be of assistance, and flattered by the opportunity, I asked very few questions in our initial interview. Knowing the importance of data gathering, I agreed to come back to him in 3 weeks with additional data from employee interviews.

The interviews seemed to go well. Employees freely shared their opinions about the problems they found in working on projects for the executive. They vocally complained about the time it took him to make decisions, the seemingly impossible budget constraints they were placed under, and the lack of communication from the management team about linkages between major programs that required them to conduct last-minute rework. I summarized the feedback and brought it to the executive at a feedback meeting. So that we could jointly develop solutions to the problems that had been posed, I left a page titled "Next Steps" blank in the presentation.

At the feedback meeting, the executive listened intently without saying a word. I summarized the top areas of feedback that the employees had shared with me, including the issues related to his own style. He did not speak during the presentation, until at one point he began flipping through the pages, scanning the feedback and looking for something. He reached the blank page and interrupted, holding the page at arm's length. "This is it?" he asked. "Well," I stammered, "we're going to develop those together." His frown clearly told me that I had missed his expectations. He wondered where my recommendations were for fixing his problem. Only at that point did I share my expectations about my role, his role, and the process for us to work together. With mismatched expectations about the role of the consultant (his more closely approximating the "mechanic" model described in the previous chapter), we were unable to agree on what to do next. He filed the presentation and chose to take no action.

Had I asked more (and better) questions during our initial interview, I could have clarified his expectations much earlier. What did he want to see from me? Could he provide an example of the problems he saw, and how had he tried to solve this problem before? How long had this been going on? What role in the project did he want to take? What action did he anticipate taking? I missed the opportunity to negotiate role expectations, to clarify my own actions, and to delve into the client's description of the problem in ways that could have opened up an opportunity for joint problem solving and exploration of deeper issues.

What Is Contracting?

The contracting conversation is a time to explore some of the initial issues that have prompted the client to call, but also to clarify how the consulting process will work, from negotiating expectations to discussing roles and outcomes. While contracting usually begins with a face-to-face meeting before a project begins, it is not confined to that single meeting. Contracting is a continual process, and consultants return to validate agreements and negotiate expectations at many points throughout the engagement. Weisbord (1973/1994) writes that "I'm never finished contracting. Each client meeting requires that I reexamine the contract" (p. 409).

The word *contracting* can conjure frightening images of lengthy documents and unwieldy legal forms, and as a result many internal consultants believe that this does not apply to them. However, a contract can come in many forms, from a simple phone call or e-mail to a formal written legal agreement. Whereas external consultants and their clients generally expect to develop a written agreement on the services to be performed that cover minimally the work to be performed, the time frame of the engagement, and the financial compensation to be paid, many internal consultants bristle at the notion of a contract of any kind. They think that clients will be frustrated by their attempt to nail down expectations and timeframes, sometimes under the mistaken impression that they do not have the right as internal consultants to share their own needs and requirements. Moreover, they are sometimes placed in situations in which they cannot refuse a client's request, and they assume that they cannot make requests of the client as a result. However, all consultants should be reminded that generally the client has invited the consultant's assistance and (usually) wants the engagement to be successful. Most clients appreciate an explanation of the consultant's process and a statement of what must be done to make the engagement a success. While developing written documents allows both parties to clarify their understanding, for internal consultants this does not need to be an overly formal document, drawn up by attorneys or notarized (Gallant & Rios, 2006). A follow-up e-mail may be sufficient to allow the client to clarify anything that the consultant may have missed or misunderstood.

When consultants fail to contract, they do not realize that even not contracting is actually contracting. By not setting expectations in advance, the consultant gives the impression of compliance with the client's framing of the issues, definition of the process, and tacit assumptions about roles. It becomes not only more difficult to negotiate changes after this time, but it can frustrate both client and consultant and strain the relationship.

Thus, contracting, according to Schein (1969), has both formal and psychological components. The formal contract consists of topics that one might initially think of when developing an official professional agreement, such as the agreed-upon time span of the relationship, steps in the consulting process, and payment to be made to the consultant. The second part of the contract is psychological and may not even be documented. The psychological contract for the consulting relationship is just as important as the formal contract. It is an explicit agreement about the consulting relationship, such as how the client and consultant will communicate with each other, building a relationship ideally on authenticity and openness. "The psychological contract consists of a preliminary definition of the organization's problems (from the CEO's point of view) and an agreement concerning what each party may expect of the other" (Boss, 2000, p. 122). Table 6.1 lists some of the initial questions that might be part of the psychological contract. Not all of these questions will be answered in the first client meeting, but the answers to initial questions may point to areas that can be addressed in later meetings with the client or other members of the organization.

Table 6.1   Some Questions to Have Answered During the Entry and Contracting Phases

---

About the Presenting Problem

(The client may be unable to describe the problem in such detail. In these cases, exploratory diagnostic activities may be appropriate to help the client develop an initial statement of the problem.)

What problem is being experienced? How does it appear? When is the client most aware of the problem? Can the client give an example of a recent time when it was witnessed?

What are the consequences of the problem to the organization, its customers, or its employees? What could the client do better if the problem were solved?

What does the client think caused the problem?

How long has the problem occurred?

Who is involved in the problem? What is the client's role in the problem?

Has the organization experienced this problem before? What has the organization done about this problem in the past? With what results?

Is there energy/resistance for fixing this problem? Why now? Where is there energy and where is there resistance? Who is hurt most by the problem? Does anyone benefit from this problem's existence?

What is the client asking the consultant to do?

About the Consulting Relationship

How will the client be involved in the engagement?

What expectations does the client have in terms of how to work together? (Consider number and frequency of meetings, communication preferences such as voice mail, e-mail, telephone, in-person meetings. Also state the practitioner's preferences in each of these areas.)

How should the client and consultant communicate? Approach one another with disagreements or requests? How will they each react when this occurs?

What kind of confidentiality is required?

How will the consultant role and project be described and framed to organizational members?

How will progress be evaluated along the way and at the end?

How will the client and consultant know when the engagement should end?

About the Consulting Engagement

What time pressures are there? When should the engagement (or its stages) be completed? Can time extensions be negotiated if progress is being made?

Who else will be involved? Other consultants or employees?

How will the consultant provide feedback to the client? Are there limits to what feedback is being requested?

Who will get a copy of the final report, if there is one?

About the Organization

(Only if the answers cannot be obtained before the meeting through research)

What are the organization's products and services?

Who are the key executives? How is the organization structured?

How large is the organization or group involved? What is its experience with change recently? Has it experienced other changes like this one?

What is the organization's culture like? What norms or values are espoused formally or followed informally? What is the general attitude or level of engagement of organizational members?

The Purpose of Contracting

Contracting has a number of purposes:

1. *To further explore the problem.* Clients sometimes call a consultant with a vague idea of what the problem is and what needs to be done, but these initial statements of the problem can be little more descriptive than "We have a communication problem" or "We're not meeting our goals." Thus, the consultant's objective during the contracting phase is to understand the root of the problem and its components: how the problem is experienced, when it was first noticed, who is involved, how the organization has tried to solve it and with what results, and what barriers have prevented the problem from being solved to this point. The consultant can more clearly understand the problem's impact on the organization and how solving (or failing to solve) the problem will affect the business. While this is contracting, it is also an early stage of data gathering and diagnosis. Some clients may not have a good understanding of the problem, and thus the practitioner may wish to conduct an initial set of diagnostic activities (discussed in the next chapter) as a starting point.

2. *To clarify the client's goals and objectives for the request.* The contracting meeting is the appropriate time to elucidate what the client expects to see when the engagement is finished. The discussion of goals and objectives for the project will also determine how the engagement will be evaluated, and failing to specify this in advance will lead to wandering scope of the project and an evaluation phase in which it is virtually impossible to show success. Weisbord (1973/1994) recommends that goals and objectives be stated as concretely as possible. Instead of "improved communication" or "better meetings," goals are more clearly stated and more likely to be met when they can be as specific as possible, such as "I want our meetings to start and end on time, covering each of the topics on the agenda," or "I want team members to approach each other with conflicts rather than coming to me." Without these goals specified, the engagement is on a "flight to nowhere"

with the potential to "end up in a worse place than you started" (Freeman, 1995, p. 26). The client and consultant should discuss how the engagement will be terminated by agreeing on how they know the goals have been met. In addition, the consultant can assess whether the client has motivation to investigate the problem or whether the request is at heart a desire on the client's part to have a change agent implement a solution already chosen.

3. *To allow the client to get to know the consultant, the consultant to get to know the client and the organization, and for both parties to validate that the project is one that the consultant has the knowledge and skills to accept.* The consultant should do as much early research as possible on the organization's customers, products and services, and history. During the contracting meeting, both consultant and client can get to know one another if they do not already. Importantly, the consultant can explain the role and purpose of OD to clarify any misconceptions for a client who may never have approached an OD practitioner before. The change agent can ask additional questions about the organization's norms and culture. The client can assess the practitioner's content and interpersonal skills and assess whether a good relationship can be established and whether the consulting process meets the client's needs. By exploring the problem, the practitioner has a better idea of the range of potential approaches and can be assured that this engagement matches the consultant's skill level. The practitioner can validate that it is a project that he or she is willing and able to accept. The contracting meeting is not the opportunity for "grandstanding" by reciting one's resume, past client list, successful engagements, or educational background (Stroh & Johnson, 2006, p. 20). Instead, the practitioner should plan to do more listening than talking.

4. *To understand the organization's commitment to change.* By asking questions about the problem and the client's suggested approach, the consultant can validate the likelihood of being able to carry out an intervention. One OD practitioner shared a story about contracting with a client who had an urgent request to help implement a technology system that was being piloted in just a few weeks. Organizational members were already resisting the pilot and angry about the changes. The practitioner asked what the client would do if she recommended that the pilot be postponed. The client replied that she would go forward anyway because the system was already late. Without much opportunity to change, the engagement would have been frustrating for both consultant and client and both agreed that a consulting engagement probably was unnecessary.

5. *To create an environment in which consultation can succeed by agreeing on mutual roles and needs.* This includes both the client's role in the engagement and what the consultant will do. The contracting meeting is the time for both client and consultant to share their expectations about their involvement and mutual support for one another during the project. The consultant must explain his or her needs for support. Different consultants develop their own lists of needs over time based on experience, but generally include such items as time needed from the client, public commitment, required meetings, communication preferences, involvement from other staff members, and other organizational resources needed (e.g., office

space or computer equipment). The client may need the practitioner to schedule meetings formally rather than drop in, to let the client determine the timing of meetings with certain stakeholders, or to limit requests for organizational members' time to a certain number of hours per week.

The practitioner should also explore the client's role in the project, from participating in data gathering and diagnosis to planning and carrying out the desired interventions. Recall that the consulting relationship is an equal partnership and that the client "owns the problem and the solution" (Schein, 1999, p. 20). The contracting meeting is the time to discuss the implications of this value and what it will require in terms of the client's own time and actions. Schein (1969) writes that as a consultant it is important that he not be seen as the one "selling" ideas across the organization or pushing for change, but instead helping the client to clarify this process and to implement solutions.

6. *To clarify time pressures and expectations.* The client and consultant should explore time expectations for not only the overall engagement but also the stages along the way, from data gathering and feedback to implementing interventions and measuring outcomes. Time pressures can intervene if either the consultant or client has commitments during the course of the engagement that would cause them to be absent or to put parts of the project on hold.

7. *To clarify how the client and consultant will interact.* This involves not only practicalities such as the number and schedule of meetings but expectations for an equal relationship in which authenticity and honesty are a necessity. Many consultants, especially internal ones, see themselves in a "one-down" position due to role or status in the organization, working "for" the client rather than "with" the client. As a result, they often fear direct statements and view them as confrontational. They avoid confronting a client with questions such as "Why don't you want to collaborate with your colleague on this project?" or "What is your own role in this problem?" By not approaching the relationship equally, the consultant fails to act authentically, ignoring difficult issues and leaving the tough problems unexplored. As Weisbord (1973/1994) states with his clients, "Part of my job is to raise sticky issues and push you on them. You have a right to say no to anything you don't want to deal with. If you feel free to say no, I'll feel free to push" (p. 408). Setting up the relationship in this way and getting the client's reaction to these expectations can help to begin the relationship with an equal partnership.

8. *To clarify confidentiality needs.* As Block (2000) puts it, confidentiality is a concern "since you are almost always dealing with a political situation as well as a technical one" (p. 65). OD practitioners frequently handle sensitive personal concerns, from executive coaching sessions to career development to team-building activities. In some organizations, using a consultant can be a mark of defeat, signaling a failure to solve a problem alone. The change agent needs to be sensitive to a client's fears and anxieties about hiring a consultant and should use the contracting meeting to clarify these concerns. The practitioner should explore who is entitled to know about the existence of the consultation, how the consulting project will be positioned with others, and who will have access to data or receive copies of reports or other documents. If a possible result of the consulting engagement is a layoff, reorganization,

work redesign, or process changes, how should the practitioner respond when questions arise from organizational members about the possible consequences of the engagement? Internal consultants need to speak with clients about whether or how the consultant's manager will know of the purpose and outcomes of the consultation. The most important point about client confidentiality is that it is the client's decision, not the practitioner's, and the client's wishes must be respected. If at any time the consultant has a doubt about the nature or extent of the confidentiality agreement, this must be clarified immediately with the client.

9. *To plan next steps.* By the conclusion of the contracting process, both consultant and client should have an understanding of what each person will do next. This may involve, for example, submission of a formal proposal or contract, an agreement that the consultant will validate what was heard in an e-mail or memo, or that data gathering can take place. Contracts can be written as a formal letter, a document or memo accompanied by a letter, or as simple as an e-mail. Regardless of the form it takes, most contracts should include the following elements described in Table 6.2.

Table 6.2   Elements of a Contract

1. Statement of the problem as explained by the client
2. Implications of the problem on the business or organization

3. Methodology or approach to the engagement
   a. Data gathering proposal, including what data are to be gathered and from whom
   b. Specific requests that the client has for the project

4. Timetable for the overall engagement, with milestones listed for intermediate stages

5. Agreed-upon needs and roles
   a. The client's needs and role
   b. The consultant's needs and role

6. Confidentiality
7. Fees
8. Qualifications to take the engagement

Success in the Contracting Meeting

A successful contracting meeting has occurred if the consultant and client have come to agreement on the process for moving forward with the engagement, have appropriately negotiated needs and roles, and are each satisfied with the relationship. Holding a contracting meeting can be a challenge with several pitfalls, however, and consultants should do three things as they conduct the contracting meeting:

1. *Listen.* Many practitioners are tempted to interrupt a client's description of the situation or problem by explaining their experience addressing similar problems with other clients. Other practitioners, desiring to demonstrate knowledge and expertise, present a laundry list of educational credentials and high-status clients. However, rarely does a client, in the middle of an explanation of a high-anxiety, perhaps personal problem, want a consultant to interrupt and talk about the consultant's self. Putting the client and the client's situation first means careful and active listening, as well as waiting until the right moment to speak. Let clients have the opportunity to express themselves first, doing most of the talking initially.

2. *Ask questions carefully and sensitively.* Practitioners need to ask questions (see Table 6.1) to learn more about the situation and the potential for a successful engagement. Schein (1969) recommends two types of questions:

> I usually ask questions which are designed to (1) sharpen and highlight aspects of the presented problem, and (2) test how open and frank the contact client is willing to be. If I feel that there is hedging, unwillingness to be critical . . . and/or confusion about my potential role as consultant, I will be cautious. (p. 83)

A practitioner's questions can sometimes come across as an attack on a client or the organization ("Why hasn't something been done earlier about this problem?"). At other times the practitioner can ask so many questions that the client may feel as though the discussion is wandering away from the immediate problem or become overwhelmed by the barrage of questions. A practitioner can narrow an exhaustive list of questions to ones that the client can address immediately and ones that can be discussed at another time or through another mechanism, such as e-mail, a follow-up telephone call, or through interviews with other organizational members.

3. *Do not accept a role, activity, or framing that does not meet your needs for a successful engagement without being explicit about it.* Practitioners must be clear about what they absolutely must have in order to work with a client. These "must haves" can include compensation, time, support, or other resources from the client, and they can include relationship issues such as honesty and accountability. When clients and practitioners cannot agree on these issues, they must make a decision about whether and how to proceed. Block (2000) describes the process of getting "stuck" in contracting and how practitioners should address it. They may choose to forego one of their must-have issues (perhaps settling for lower fees, fewer client meetings, or a shortened cycle time) or they may renegotiate the offer (agreeing to a shorter cycle time if the scope of the engagement is narrowed). Regardless of what the practitioner chooses, this should be a conscious choice. Listening to the uncomfortable gut feeling a practitioner may have about the low likelihood of an engagement's success is instructive. The practitioner can put this reluctance into words and more clearly set up the engagement for success by negotiating these wants and even turning down an engagement if it is unlikely to succeed.

Recontracting

Recall Weisbord's (1973/1994) statement that a consultant is never finished with contracting. Each meeting with a client is an opportunity to evaluate progress, retain previously discussed roles and processes, or change them based on past experience or anticipated future needs. Recontracting in this sense is an implicit evaluation and renegotiation that occurs at each stage. In addition, recontracting can be done explicitly. For example, this is necessary when any of the following occur:

- New information gathered during the data gathering stage expands or narrows the scope of the agreed-upon engagement.
- The consultant feels that additional data gathering is necessary.
- Either the consultant or the client no longer sees progress being made.
- The project experiences barriers such as lack of a client's time or reduced availability of organizational members to participate.
- Organizational circumstances imply modifications of the original agreement (changing goals or budget).
- Personnel changes result in a new client.
- The consultant finds obstacles to completing the original agreement.

Recontracting follows a process similar to the original contracting session. The consultant and client should schedule a formal meeting to discuss the engagement, review the original agreement, discuss the new situation, and agree on how the new situation presents any changes to the contract.

Ethics in Contracting

There are at least three ethical dilemmas that a consultant must navigate during the entry and contracting stages (White & Wooten, 1983, 1985):

1. *Misrepresentation and collusion.* We have already discussed the potential for a consultant to purposefully or inadvertently (by omission) overstate one's qualifications for an engagement. Consultants may lead the client to believe that they have experience with similar problems, industries, or organizations, and they may also overstate their certifications or other specialized skills. They may also misrepresent the potential for change or success by promising results. Collusion can occur when the consultant and client agree to "exclude outside parties for personal gain or protection" (White & Wooten, 1985, p. 149). This can occur when the consultant agrees to omit focusing on a difficult problem, agrees to a short-term change that may have long-term negative consequences, or agrees to serve a narrow interest benefiting a particular group to the detriment of other groups or the organization as a whole. Collusion can also occur when the consultant implicitly or explicitly agrees to accept the client's framing of the issues without additional confirmation, agreeing to implement a solution solely because the client wants it. Because consultants generally want

to help the client and are eager to accept an engagement, the potential for an ethical conflict that misrepresents the consultant or colludes with the client is very high during the entry and contracting stages. Misrepresentation and collusion have such potential for negative consequences for the consultant and the OD consulting profession that skipping or minimizing contracting discussions can be seen as not only a poor process but also a violation of professional ethics.

2. *Value and goal conflict.* Value and goal conflict can occur when the objective for the consulting engagement violates one or more value principles of OD consulting, such as when clients seek to use the consultant as a "spy" or hidden observer, or when clients want to hide the purpose of the engagement. Value conflict can also occur when a consultant agrees to conduct an engagement with an unwilling client or one that has been coerced into participation. Other ethical problems can occur when consultants who work for multiple clients fail to be explicit about any potential conflicts of interest that may result from serving multiple clients who may have conflicting goals.

3. *Technical ineptness.* Technical ineptness refers not to information technology, but to the technical ability of a consultant to appropriately follow the OD consulting process. In the entry and contracting stages, consultants may not know how to articulate their needs or may omit a discussion of their needs, or they may seek harmony with clients by agreeing to take engagements that do not contain the seeds for success.

Contracting as Data Gathering

When both parties agree upon a contract, the next step of the consulting process begins: data gathering. While the consultant may be thinking of formally proposing interviews or surveys or some other data gathering method, he or she already has a lot of data, in fact. The problem has been described from one perspective (the client's), and the client may even have formally presented some data to the consultant, perhaps in the form of numbers or written feedback from surveys. In addition, the contracting process itself can be seen as data gathering. Did the client appear nervous, brusque, excitable, anxious, distant, or aloof? Was the problem described as annoying, impossible to solve, typical, or devastating? Did the client feel like a willing partner in trying to solve the problem, or did the consultant have to "sell" the client on equal participation in the engagement? Such responses, as well as the consultant's gut feelings about the project, can be illustrative or symbolic of how others in the organization may be feeling and can be instructive as the consultant approaches the data gathering process.

In addition, the consultant has learned a great deal about the organization's culture from the contracting process. Gallant and Rios (2006) explain, "Attention to words, tone, metaphors, and other linguistic differences that are peculiar to the client and the industry is essential" (p. 190). The consultant can become aware of communication patterns during these initial meetings that give insight into the organization's norms and values. The consultant likely has observed the physical environment and met some organizational members. In short, these first meetings with a client are the first steps in gathering data about the organization, and the consultant's own experiences with the client are an important source of information not to be discounted.

Summary

The foundation of a successful engagement is laid when the consulting relationship begins in the entry and contracting stages of the organization development process. The entry process begins with the initial contact between consultant and potential client. Clients can be of different types, from the initial contact client to other clients that may be marginally affected by the project, to the whole organization.

Contracting is a critical skill for a consultant to learn. Many problems that consultants experience later in the engagement, such as a lack of commitment to taking action, disagreements about the consultant's role, lack of contact with a client, or confusion about the objectives of the engagement, can be attributed to ineffective contracting. Contracting has formal components, such as the fees to be paid, the amount of time to dedicate, and the actions the consultant will commit to taking. It also has psychological components, such as when the consultant and client must contract with one another about how they will interact together, and the sharing of mutual needs. While the contracting stage may appear to conclude when the project is agreed or the documents are signed, it never really does. Consultants return to contracting discussions each time they meet: to validate progress so far, correct any misunderstandings or missteps to that point, and agree on what to do next. In that sense, each engagement is a never-ending process of contracting.

For Further Reading

Block, P. (2000). *Flawless consulting: A guide to getting your expertise used* (2nd ed.). New York: Jossey-Bass.

Boss, R. W. (2000). The psychological contract. In R. T. Golembiewski (Ed.), *Handbook of organizational consultation* (2nd ed., pp. 119–128). New York: Marcel Dekker.

Schein, E. H. (1997). The concept of "client" from a process consulting perspective: A guide for change agents. *Journal of Organizational Change Management, 10,* 202–216.

Weisbord, M. R. (1994). The organization development contract. In W. L. French, C. H. Bell Jr., & R. A. Zawacki (Eds.), *Organization development and transformation: Managing effective change* (4th ed., pp. 406–412). Burr Ridge, IL: Irwin. (Reprinted from *OD Practitioner,* 5(2), 1973, 1–4)

CHAPTER 7

Data Gathering

Promotion, Inc., is a privately held company in the Midwest that serves the direct mail industry with printing and mailing services. A junior organization development consultant agreed to conduct an employee survey, specifically with the Mail Division, to determine why turnover rates were much higher than in other divisions within the company. An internal committee developed 16 possible causes of the turnover based on interviews with 20 employees. The 102-item questionnaire (which included a separate page of demographic data as well) was organized into 11 categories, and the survey was pilot tested with a small group of employees and revised based on their feedback. In the end, all 480 employees in the division were sent a survey in order to ensure that no employee was omitted and that employees could remain anonymous. The results of the survey held negative feedback for management about roles between departments, work policies, and employee compensation. Results of the survey were presented to management in five separate sessions, beginning with top management and continuing with the internal committee and Mail Division managers. Results took many by surprise, and some managers walked out of the feedback sessions. Managers were unwilling to take action based on the feedback and decided to shelve the reports. In the end, employees were provided only a brief and highly edited version of the feedback report almost 2 months after the survey was administered (Swanson & Zuber, 1996).

- What do you think was done well in the administration of the survey in this case? What do you think should have been done differently?
- Was a survey a good choice for a data gathering method in this case? Why or why not?

With a formal and psychological contract successfully established, a data gathering strategy is developed to further explore the causes and consequences of the problem described by the client. Using methods such as interviews, focus groups, surveys, observations, and unobtrusive measures, the consultant can develop a nuanced and detailed understanding of the situation so that interventions developed can be both applicable and more effective. In this chapter we discuss the methods of data gathering used by organization development (OD) consultants and describe how consultants choose among them to formulate a data gathering strategy.

To both consultants and clients alike, spending time gathering additional data can seem like a trivial and costly exercise. After all, the client has at this point already seen many instances of the problem being discussed and likely has been able to describe it in detail. This can be a troublesome view to maintain, however. Clients see one angle of a problem from one perspective, and additional perspectives can add useful insights that cannot be seen without additional data. Gathering data and presenting the information back to the client can present a more complete picture of the organization and expand both the client's and practitioner's knowledge. It is an intervention in itself, and in many cases it is the most powerful intervention that a consultant can execute.

The Importance of Data Gathering

Comprehensive data gathering takes time, however, and "many managers and consultants show a bias for quick intervention and shortchange diagnosis" (Harrison & Shirom, 1999, p. 8). In an attempt to quickly solve the problem that may have existed for quite some time, both managers and consultants are tempted to take a shortcut through the data gathering process, assuming that the information available is sufficient. However, "managers and other decision makers run serious risks if they eschew diagnostic inquiry and systematic decision making altogether when uncertainty and pressure for quick action intensify" (p. 9). Despite these warnings, speed frequently trumps accurate data and careful diagnosis.

Nadler (1977) writes that there are three reasons that consultants should take data gathering seriously. First, good data collection generates "information about organizational functioning, effectiveness, and health" (p. 105). Argyris (1970) explains,

> Without valid information it would be difficult for the client to learn and for the interventionist to help. . . . Valid information is that which describes the factors, plus their interrelationships, that create the problem for the client system. (p. 17)

Good data collection should expand the practitioner's and client's knowledge of the problem.

Second, data collection can be a force that can spark interest in change. It can bring organizational members together on a common definition of the situation that they can then agree to change. Nadler (1977) writes that in this respect, "Collection can be used for consciousness raising—getting people thinking about issues concerning them and the organization" (p. 105).

Finally, practitioners who do data collection well can "continue the process of relationship-building between the change agent, his or her internal partners, and the organization" (p. 106). The change agent has the opportunity to meet organizational members, demonstrate empathy and credibility by focusing on individuals and their perspectives, and develop cooperative and trusting relationships so that the practitioner can help the organization to change.

Presenting Problems and Underlying Problems

In initial meetings with practitioners, clients describe *presenting problems*. Presenting problems are those initial explanations of the situation that highlight symptoms of which the client is most painfully aware. Beneath presenting problems lie *underlying problems*. Underlying problems can be described as the root cause or core, fundamental issues that are producing the symptoms. Interventions designed to address presenting problems but that do not address underlying problems are likely to produce only a short-term, negligible impact. These interventions are commonly the "simple fix" that clients may actually prefer. After all, they usually match the client's framing of the issues, they are frequently easier to address, and they often involve process issues or other task-oriented changes that avoid personal change or interpersonal conflict. Unfortunately, they rarely solve the underlying problem contributing to the surface-level symptoms that are easier to see.

For example, Block (2001) describes several common presenting problems framed by clients that consultants may erroneously try to fix. If a client wants more cooperation from a team, the change agent may try to get all relevant parties in a room, discuss their objectives, discuss working relationships, and agree upon communication patterns. Reframing the problem as one of territory between groups changes the problem from the lack of cooperation to a negotiation of boundaries and group identity, where each individual or group may need to give up something for the good of the larger organization. Another common example concerns training: A client sees low results and wants more training or education for organizational members. The client may not see that there are process and motivational barriers inhibiting organizational members from acting. If a consultant acts on a request for training without understanding why organizational members act in the way they do, the consultant will take up time and resources developing a training program that may have very little to do with why results are not being achieved.

The point is that without greater detail as to the nature and extent of the problem from different perspectives, the chosen interventions may target the wrong areas, and they may even deepen conflict and frustrate organizational members. Presenting problems are an initial place to start, but the practitioner's real concern must be with the underlying problems. These can be best explored through data gathering.

Data Gathering Process

Noolan (2006) recommends a five-step process for data gathering:

1. *Determine approach to be used.* Each method of data gathering has advantages and disadvantages. Based on the client's description of the problem, the consultant should determine what data should be collected and why.

2. *Announce project.* The client or another representative should explain to organizational members what data are being gathered, by whom, using what methods, and for what purposes.

3. *Prepare for data collection.* Surveys or interview guides should be prepared, along with a list of potential interviewees. Interviewees should be contacted and a time and place scheduled.

4. *Collect data.* Use appropriate protocols, depending on the data gathering approach selected.

5. *Do data analysis and presentation.* Practitioners may choose to use one or more diagnostic models to analyze the data and give feedback to the client. (This part of the process is discussed in the next chapter on diagnosis and feedback.)

This approach can vary somewhat, with different considerations for successful data gathering, depending on the data gathering method used. Each approach requires a different length of time for gathering information and analyzing it, a different level of expense, and a different investment on the part of organizational members, clients, and consultants. Some approaches, such as interviewing, can have a psychological effect on the organization, whereas unobtrusive measures generally occur behind the scenes without much fanfare or publicity. In this chapter we expand on the specific details for each step of the data gathering process for each method.

Data Gathering Methods

Organization development practitioners use five common methods of data gathering to explore presenting problems. In the following sections, we explore these methods, including why practitioners use that approach, what advantages or disadvantages each approach presents, and what pitfalls or potential problems practitioners can experience in using each approach. We also explore tips for successful data gathering using each approach:

1. Interviews

2. Focus groups

3. Surveys/questionnaires

4. Observations

5. Unobtrusive measures

Interviews

Interviews are generally one-on-one meetings during which practitioners speak directly with individual organizational members. The practitioner is interested in the individual stories and perspectives of organizational members and in a personal setting can explore their history, experiences, beliefs, and attitudes in depth. Seidman (2006) writes that "at the root of in-depth interviewing is an interest in understanding the lived experience of other people and the meaning they make of that experience" (p. 9). The primary advantages of interviewing as a method for data gathering include the ability to understand a person's experience and to follow up on areas of interest. Interviews can yield surprises that a practitioner may not know enough in advance to ask about. In many cases interviews can be the only choice in getting at specific issues, such as employee experiences with a manager of a small group or a conflict between two managers. In these cases, employees may be unlikely to respond to a written questionnaire with adequate detail to truly understand the problem, and it may not be possible to witness the situation personally through observations. Even if a practitioner could see the situation personally, interviews can allow the practitioner to better understand how organizational members interpret a situation or what attitudes and beliefs they have about it.

Data gathering through interviews relies heavily on cooperation from organizational members who will only open up to discuss serious issues if they trust the interviewer (Seidman, 2006). Interviews can be threatening, as members may feel defensive if they are personally involved in a problem and they may be motivated to stretch the truth to present themselves in a positive light. Consequently, among the five data gathering methods, interviewing requires the greatest interpersonal skill of OD practitioners. Interviewers should be adept at placing people at ease in a one-on-one situation, excellent listeners, and skilled conversationalists. Interviews can generate a tremendous amount of data, with organizational members sharing stories, examples, and personal beliefs, including issues relevant to the issue the practitioner is investigating and those tangential to it. These data can be difficult and time-consuming for the practitioner to sort through after the interviews, and they may suffer from the practitioner's or client's biases or interest in seeing certain facts that may not be as apparent as the practitioner wants to believe.

To conduct data gathering successfully using interviews, an interviewer should follow these guidelines:

1. *Prepare an interview guide.* Interviews can be formal and structured, with each interviewee asked the exact same set of questions without straying from the list of questions, or they can be semistructured, with an interview guide containing a general list of open-ended questions addressing the major topics of the interview. With semistructured interviews, the interviewer adds probes, or follow-up questions, where appropriate, and can explore other areas that were not predicted in the interview guide. Follow-up probes can include questions such as "Why do you think that is true?" or "Can you give an example?" Most OD interviews are semistructured.

2. *Select participants.* When only a small team is involved, interviewing every team member is a reasonable approach. However, because interviewing can be time-intensive and resource-consuming for both the organization and the interviewer, it may not be possible to interview every relevant organizational member. For example, to gather data from employees on a manufacturing floor, the practitioner may have to sample a certain number of employees from the day shift and night shift, or to select employees from line A and line B. How many interviews to conduct likely will depend on the time available, the problem to be investigated, and the population from which participants are selected. A practitioner can be more confident that enough people have been chosen when interviews begin to get repetitive and substantiate the same common issues. The selection process can be random (using an established randomization protocol such as a random numbers table or computerized selection method) or stratified (taking every third person on an ordered list by employee number, for example). The selection of interviewees also can be intentionally based on the participants' knowledge or involvement in the topic being discussed. (With their greater knowledge of the organization, clients should help in selecting interviewees.) Still another approach is to conduct what social science researchers term "snowball" sampling, in which a researcher begins with one or more participants and concludes each interview by asking the interviewee who else he or she would recommend interviewing. Thus, the network is tapped for its own knowledge and access to another interviewee is potentially smoother. In any case, the practitioner should be prepared to justify these choices, since organizational members in sensitive situations may attribute meaning to interviewee selection, even if it was random.

3. *Contact participants and schedule interviews.* When contacting each potential interviewee, the interviewer should explain the purpose of the interview and how long it is expected to take. It can be helpful to have the client or sponsor contact interviewees first to invite their participation, promising contact from the OD practitioner to schedule the interview. This approach can have the advantage of easing access and encouraging responsiveness, particularly for an external consultant, but it can have the disadvantage of associating the consultant with a client's goals and objectives. The change agent can be more explicitly seen as an "agent" of management, and interviewees may be suspicious or withhold important information if they do not trust the sponsor. In any case, interview participation should be framed as a free choice with no consequences for refusing to participate, and potential interviewees should be given the option to participate free from any coercion. In

sensitive situations, practitioners may advise that the client suggest a list of possible interviewees from which a certain number will be chosen.

Contact methods for scheduling interviews commonly include telephone calls and e-mails. The more sensitive the topic of the interview, the more the OD practitioner should consider the most personal method of contact. Simply scheduling interviews to get feedback on noncontroversial matters such as employee satisfaction with general working conditions or whether a new process is working correctly may be easily done by e-mail. Interviews discussing interpersonally sensitive topics such as conflict with a manager or coworker are best done in person or by telephone.

Descriptions of the purpose of the interview should be consistent between the client's description and the practitioner's, as well as between interviews. Participants are likely to speak with other colleagues or their managers about the interviews, sharing the topics and questions among each other. If these descriptions are not consistent, participants may rightfully be apprehensive about the stated purpose or intent of the interviews.

Finally, a location for the interview should be selected that allows for the best interaction possible. This means a private location free from distractions such as phone calls and personal interruptions. The interview should be conducted in an environment in which conversation can take place without disturbing or being overheard by others.

4. *Begin the interview and establish rapport.* The interviewer should begin with a personal introduction, again explaining the purpose of both the engagement and the interview, including what topics will be discussed. The interviewer should also take the time to explain what he or she will do with the data from the interview and who will see it (if anyone). The interviewee may want to know how interviewees have been selected and who else is being interviewed, which the practitioner may be able to share in a broad categorical sense such as "all managers," "about half of the second engineering shift," or "five people at random from each of the company's four sites." The practitioner can also state what notes will be taken and what will be done with the notes, in order to explain why the interviewer may be writing during the interview. Waclawski and Rogelberg (2002) recommend that seating be arranged so that interviewees can read the interviewer's notes to further put the interviewee at ease regarding what is written, and that interviewers alter their notes if there is anything written that makes the interviewee uncomfortable.

To put the interviewee at ease, it is a good practice to begin the interview with a relatively safe set of questions about the interviewee's background, length of time with the company, and current and previous roles. It can also be useful for an interview to begin with a "grand tour" question (Spradley, 1979) in which the interviewer opens up the interview with a broad, general subject, such as "Tell me about a typical day for you at work" or "Tell me about your involvement with this group since you joined the company." While such questions tend to produce somewhat longer and wandering responses, they can be instructive as an overview without asking too many questions or introducing bias.

Many practitioners make a useful distinction between confidentiality and anonymity in interviews. Information is *confidential* if no one other than the consultant will know what was said in the interview—in other words, what is said stays with the consultant. Information is *anonymous* if it can be shared outside the interview but separated from the source (i.e., the interviewee's name). Generally interviewers can promise that information from interviews will remain anonymous but not confidential. That is, to be able to use the data and act upon them, the practitioner must be able to share the data outside of the interview, but the practitioner should not share who said what without a participant's explicit permission (Freedman & Zackrison, 2001).

5. *Conduct the interview by following the interview guide, straying from it when appropriate.* Interviews are primarily a conversation, albeit one with a specific purpose. Interviewers need to listen carefully to the current response, think about any follow-up questions, remember the other areas that are listed in the interview guide, and be conscious that time is limited. The best interviewers can maintain the character of the interview as a conversation without being distracted by other tasks.

6. *Close the interview.* Close the interview by inviting the participant to pose any questions that he or she may have. Conclude by thanking the interviewee and reiterating the timeline for what will happen next and when the participant will hear results, if at all. Most people are naturally curious about what will happen next, and it is important that the conclusion of the interview sets the appropriate expectation. The interviewer can also choose to provide a business card or other contact information in case additional questions arise or the interviewee wishes to clarify something after the interview.

Tips for Successful Interviews

1. Listening is a critical skill in interviewing. It is important to avoid interrupting an interviewee with another question in earnestness to move on to another area. Listening for emotion as well as content can suggest areas for follow-up questions. Noticing hesitancy in the interviewee's voice, the practitioner can ask, "You seem reluctant to talk about the budgeting process. Can you say more about your thoughts?"

2. Avoid indicating agreement or disagreement with the interviewee, or suggesting that the interviewee's responses are similar to or different from other interviews. Even head nodding, nonverbal feedback such as "yes" or "uh huh," used to encourage the interviewee to continue, can be seen instead as a sign of agreement that may change the interview. Likewise, Seidman (2006) recommends only rarely sharing your own experiences that are similar to an interviewee's, since the interviewer can become the focus and can potentially alter the direction of the interview. The best advice is to emphasize interest in the interviewee's experience, not in one particular answer.

3. Take notes sparingly during the interview, and write more immediately after it ends. It is rarely possible to take verbatim notes and participate fully in the conversation. Taking very brief notes with key words, followed by a more

complete record after the interview, can allow the consultant to pay closer attention to what is being said. When verbatim quotes are desired, the consultant can ask the interviewee to repeat what was just said, noting that "what you just said is so important I want to write it down word for word." To allow extra time to take notes after interviews, avoid scheduling them back-to-back.

Some consultants choose to audiotape or videotape interviews, thinking that it will save time taking notes. This practice can actually take more time, however, since it requires spending time equal to the length of the interview listening to or watching a tape. Given concerns about where the tapes may end up, potential technical problems with equipment, and an interviewee's likely discomfort, this approach usually presents more disadvantages than advantages. If additional note-taking is desired to capture a great deal of data, and the consultant cannot do this alone, another consulting partner could attend the interview only for the purpose of taking notes. This can be very appropriate in some circumstances but may make some interviewees uncomfortable.

In summary, interviews are probably the most common method of data collection in OD. Good interviewing requires a consultant to have good interpersonal skills in establishing rapport, maintaining a conversation, steering the conversation to relevant areas of interest, and listening actively. While they can be time-intensive, they can be well worth the additional effort expended to gain knowledge and background detail into the organization. Because gaining the time to conduct one-on-one interviews can be difficult, many consultants turn to the group interview, or focus group.

Focus Groups

Focus groups are groups of usually a small number of organizational members facilitated by a consultant who poses questions and then allows for group discussion. Focus groups have been used by social scientists as a research tool for many years, and in recent years they have also been used frequently for public relations and market research activities (Smithson, 2000). Like interviews, focus groups allow the consultant to explore experiences and situations in depth and to follow up on specific areas of interest. They are not observations of group behavior in the group's ordinary work activities, but a special conversation instigated by a consultant's questions and consultant-facilitated and directed. Unlike one-on-one interviews, focus groups are rarely appropriate for very sensitive issues (Waclawski & Rogelberg, 2002). Issues of a general nature, such as how employees feel about the company's benefit plan or what they feel should be done to improve executive communications, can be good candidates for focus groups. In focus groups participants can build on one another's ideas. They can brainstorm, discuss, and debate. Because they can allow for a wide range of participation and orient members toward group or team involvement, two key values of OD, many practitioners like to use focus groups as a method of data gathering. As a disadvantage, focus groups can generate a tremendous amount of data that can be difficult and time-consuming to analyze.

To conduct a focus group, consultants should follow a process similar to interviewing. The considerations are somewhat different, however, since the subject matter and structure of a focus group are different from individual interviews:

1. *Prepare an interview guide.* Interview guides for focus groups are likely to be shorter than those used in one-on-one interviews, since the participation level will be much greater for a similar amount of time. Consequently, it is likely that fewer subjects will be covered. In addition to the interview guide, the consultant should prepare some opening and closing remarks that explain the purpose of the interview, what will be done with the data, and how the data will be recorded.

2. *Select participants.* Participants can be selected randomly, as in interviews, or they can be selected based on some other criteria. Groups can be homogeneous, that is, selected based on some criteria they share. Examples include intact teams, managers, all employees in the New York office, salespeople, college interns, employees with 10 or more years with the company, or customer service personnel. Groups can also be heterogeneous, or a mixed group, where the group's composition is more diverse. The advantage of homogeneous groups is that these employees may share a similar background because they have something in common, and they may be able to provide depth and detail into a problem from that perspective. Customer service personnel, for example, may be able to build on one another's contributions to create a more complete picture of quality problems with the company's products. By having different backgrounds or roles in the organization, mixed groups can offer the consultant the advantage of seeing patterns common to all organizational members regardless of role or demographic characteristic. The question of whether to use homogeneous or heterogeneous groups thus depends on the focus group's purpose. Waclawski and Rogelberg (2002) find an advantage in having each group be homogeneous, but recommend conducting enough focus groups so that a heterogeneous population participates in the overall data collection.

As with interviews, a location should be selected that is free from distractions and interruptions for the length of the discussion. It is best for the location to contain a large oval table or for chairs to be arranged in such a way that all participants can see one another (Waclawski & Rogelberg, 2002). The number of participants per group depends on the subject's complexity but should be somewhere from 5 to 15 people. Successful focus groups can be conducted with more participants, but since time is likely limited, participants may struggle to contribute if the group numbers more than 20. Again like interviews, invitations to participants should explain the purpose and structure of the focus group, and participants should be reminded that attendance is voluntary and there should be no consequences for nonparticipation. There should be no peer pressure to participate (or not) and it is best that consultants minimize the potential for organizational members to know who did and who did not participate. For this reason, it is wise to issue invitations not to a large group at once but directly to each individual invited to participate. Thus, those who decline will remain known only to the consultant.

3. *Hold the focus group.* The consultant or focus group facilitator should begin by welcoming participants, and reiterating the purpose and explaining the structure of the focus group. Participants should introduce themselves if they do not know one

another already, in order to understand one another's organizational roles and backgrounds. The facilitator should explain what and how notes will be taken, as well as what will happen with the results of the focus group(s). The facilitator should next propose several ground rules for participation, including the following:

- What is said during the course of the meeting should remain known only to the participants and should not be repeated to others.
- Roughly equal participation is the goal, so the facilitator is likely to intervene from time to time to ensure that all voices are heard.
- The facilitator may intervene to keep the group on track or focus conversation back to the question under discussion.
- The purpose is to explore issues; personal comments or attacks are not appropriate.
- The group may wish to agree on other ground rules as well, and the distinction between confidentiality and anonymity should be made at this point.

The facilitator can begin with an open-ended, safe question to encourage participation if the group seems hesitant to begin. So that each person's voice can be heard and any initial hesitation to contribute can be lessened, the facilitator may wish to begin with a directive question such as "What one word comes to mind when you think of the physical environment of the building?" or "In one sentence, what's the best thing about your job?" It is not necessary to go around the circle in order (a conversation is the objective), but that is an option for groups that are especially quiet.

As the facilitator follows the interview guide, it may be necessary to quiet any monopolizing participants and to encourage those that are shy or have a difficult time jumping into the flow of conversation. Making eye contact with those who look as though they are waiting to participate is a very subtle way of encouraging participation, but more directive comments may be necessary, such as "Ray has been trying to say something," or "Just a minute, Rick, I think Shanthi has something to add." Frequent contributions from one member can bias the facilitator's perception and give the impression that the entire group shares a single view. It may be important to test this with the group from time to time if the group does not comment. This can be done by saying simply, "Sheila has offered her suggestion for what should be done about the procurement process. Does everyone agree with that?" or "Who can offer another idea?"

Because the focus group often results in individuals sharing a group experience, some participants may be reluctant to offer a different view, especially if members have a close relationship outside of the focus group. Such *groupthink* should be tested by the facilitator as well. When participants know one another outside of the focus group, the facilitator should be reminded that the members have a previous history and other organizational roles that will change the course of the conversation. Members may work together frequently, they may have had a contentious relationship in the past, or they may have unequal status. Current or past conflicts, tight coworker relationships, or strong team identification likely will be manifested in the focus group setting. (Recall the OD value of the "whole person." People are greater than their organizational roles in the focus group.) To the extent possible, the facilitator should try to be aware of these dynamics to better understand what is being said and why.

The facilitator must also balance the need to get through the interview guide and to explore topics of interest. Since the goal is an in-depth exploration of issues, the facilitator will need to listen carefully to the various contributions and offer additional probing questions, such as "I've heard a theme from many people saying that they don't seem to trust the management team. Tell me what they could do to change that."

Like interviews, focus groups are conversations among several participants. Careful listening and skilled conversational and facilitation practices are central to the success of the focus group.

4. *Conclude the meeting.* When time has ended or the conversational subjects have been exhausted, the participants should be invited to pose any questions they may have of the facilitator. The consultant should repeat the objective of the engagement and the focus groups and what will be done next with the data.

Tips for Successful Management of Focus Groups

1. Listening is just as important with focus groups as it is with interviews. Focus groups can be somewhat more complex at times because the facilitator is listening to the speaker, thinking of the next question, and watching group dynamics.

2. Also as with interviewing, it is important to maintain objectivity to the extent possible and to avoid indicating agreement or disagreement with the group's contributions. This can be especially important in group settings, when participants may convene alone later to discuss the group. Any impression of agreement that the facilitator gives can lead the group to think that the facilitator was taking sides ("She seemed to agree with us that the management around here is terrible").

3. In some environments where organizational members may be particularly disgruntled about a situation, a mob mentality can develop in focus groups, where negative emotions can escalate and spread rapidly. This can promote a self-defeating tone to the group where participants may leave feeling more discouraged than when they arrived. The facilitator should be attuned to this possibility and may want to develop strategies to combat a downward negative spiral, perhaps by calling attention to it.

4. As in interviews, having two facilitators is an option where one can participate in the conversation and another can take notes. This can free the facilitator to listen and participate. When exact wording is necessary and budget is available, some consultants have hired court reporters to transcribe focus group dialogue, though this requires that participants only speak one at a time, which can occasionally stifle dialogue.

In summary, focus groups can be an excellent method for gathering data. They can elicit contributions from many people in a shorter time than can be done with one-on-one interviews. Group members can also build on one another's ideas, which can result in better solutions and explorations of a situation. If a facilitator is skilled at managing the conversation and addressing the challenges of a focus group, the data gathered from this approach can be very useful to diagnosis and planning interventions.

Surveys/Questionnaires

In the history of organization development, the survey or questionnaire has been one of the most commonly used methods of data gathering. Since Mann's (1957) study of Detroit Edison, the survey has developed as a means by which consultants can solicit input from a large number of organizational members at once. Surveys or questionnaires are typically paper- or Internet-based methods to allow for a large number of participants. Today, a number of free or inexpensive online survey tools make it very easy to survey a large number of organizational members very quickly. Social media sites (though not anonymous) can also allow a wide number of organizational members to be contacted and surveyed.

Generally surveys address a broad number of subjects and explore a wide range of issues, as opposed to a deep investigation of one or two issues. Used alone, surveys are best used as exploratory mechanisms, and they are typically inappropriate for sensitive subjects. Some practitioners use surveys following interviews or focus groups to understand how prevalent the issues are that have been brought up in interviews. In combination with other methods, surveys can provide breadth where others provide depth.

Falletta and Combs (2002) write that surveys used in OD engagements are primarily action-driven. In this respect, "Surveys are more than instruments for gathering information" (Kuhnert, 1993, p. 459), but they are instruments for prompting change. The change agent does not conduct a survey solely to report the results to management and to conclude the project, but instead works closely with the client on interpreting the data and planning actions to address the results. Surveys can be quick and easy to administer. Each consumes time from organizational members, so it is important to be clear about the purpose of the survey and to gain at least some initial commitment for action. Without a commitment to take the results seriously and act on them, an organizational survey that appears to promise change will only deepen any existing cynicism among members when nothing is done with the results.

Having at least a moderate background in survey design and both qualitative and statistical analysis is necessary in most circumstances. Whether practitioners conduct the analysis themselves or get assistance with the statistical procedures, most will need to at least be able to read and interpret the results for their clients. A graduate-level course in qualitative and quantitative research methods can be extremely useful to the practitioner who plans to conduct surveys. In addition, there are a number of helpful guides to conducting organizational surveys (see, for example, Fink, 2002, 2005; Smith, 2003).

The following process can help a practitioner to successfully conduct an organizational survey:

1. *Determine the reason for the survey.* Surveys can be used to assess management interaction, organizational communication, work processes, training needs, and

employee engagement. Each has a different implication for the structure of the survey. Annual satisfaction or engagement surveys are common in many large organizations, when every organizational member has the opportunity to participate. Such surveys have become "institutionalized," often separated from the daily functions of the organization (Smith, 2003). Because these surveys are often done out of habit rather than need, the reason for the survey is often unclear and commitment to take action is unknown.

2. *Determine who will take the survey.* Organizationwide survey topics typically imply that all members will be given the opportunity to participate in the survey. In some situations, a smaller sample of members may be more appropriate, less expensive, and less time-consuming. Such samples, however, can increase the statistical error rate, depending on the population to whom the results are being generalized. If a census is chosen, then it is important that all necessary measures be taken for each member to receive a survey. Security employees who work the night shift, employees who travel from site to site, those who work from home, and manufacturing employees who may not have access to computers for Internet-based surveys can often be inadvertently left out of the survey process. If a sample is chosen, it may be a good idea to publicize the survey to the wider population to indicate that a random sampling technique is being used and that not all members will be receiving a survey invitation.

3. *Design the survey.* A practitioner may choose to use an existing survey instrument rather than design one. Many private companies have developed surveys that can be used to assess topics such as employee engagement, and academic researchers have developed highly tested surveys of organizational commitment, identification, and job satisfaction, among others. More frequently, practitioners use surveys to address specific issues, and in these situations, they often customize the questions to suit the organization. Falletta and Combs (2002) write that such surveys are frequently model-driven; that is, consultants sometimes use organizational models such as the Burke-Litwin model or the Weisbord Six-Box Model to develop questions. These models can be limiting, however, as they each frame the organization and its structure in its own way. This can lead to the model predetermining the outcome, and the consultant may feel that the model forces questions or issues into certain categories that may not match those being used by organizational members.

The length of the survey is a common concern. If the survey is too long, participants may become fatigued or busy with other work and may not complete it. If it is too short, it may not provide enough information or detail to act upon (Smith, 2003). Most surveys use a combination of fixed-response questions (for example, the Likert scale tends to use a 5-point scale with choices from *strongly agree, agree, neutral, disagree,* and *strongly disagree*) and open-ended or short-answer questions. Participants may not take the time to respond to a large number of open-ended questions, and analysis can be complex. However, if used judiciously, such questions can be well worth the additional analysis time.

4. *Administer the survey.* Survey instructions should be clear about how long the survey is likely to take and how participants should return it (for paper-and-pencil surveys) or submit it (for electronic surveys). The deadline should be clearly communicated, and a reminder issued shortly before the survey will close.

Tips for Successful Administration of Surveys

The most common errors in the use of surveys involve the questions or survey items themselves. The following list does not delve into all of the possible errors with question design, but these are a few important issues for OD practitioners to consider:

1. Avoid questions that indicate bias toward or against a particular group of people. Questions should use language that is neutral toward any racial group, gender, religion, or any level, role, or category of organizational members.

2. Avoid questions that could be answered accurately in multiple ways. For example, a survey question that reads "I am satisfied with my pay and benefits" could be answered both "strongly agree" and "strongly disagree" if the respondent is very satisfied with the benefit plan but is dissatisfied with monetary compensation.

3. Keep in mind the need to translate or localize questions. In a global environment, many organizational surveys need to be accessible in various languages. Survey items will need to be translated as well as localized. That is, translation is a matter of linguistic change, whereas localization is a matter of cultural accuracy for the context. Items should avoid idioms or slang unique to American English, as well as U.S. work practices that may not be applicable to employees in other countries.

4. Clarify important terms. Even phrases that might appear to be self-evident such as "senior management" or "your work team" may need to be defined at the beginning of the survey. Employees in a regional office, for example, may wonder whether "senior management" refers to the highest ranking local management or whether it refers to the executive team at headquarters.

5. Survey items should be tested with a small sample of organizational members who can later be interviewed to determine whether questions were clear and whether the respondent understood the survey items in the manner in which they were intended.

Technological advancements have made issuing and responding to surveys easier than ever before. It is now possible for a consultant to develop and issue a survey to a targeted population and receive responses within a matter of days. Consequently, surveys remain one of the most popular ways that consultants gather data in OD engagements. The disadvantage of this ease of use is that some organizational members can become oversurveyed, but when used occasionally and conscientiously, surveys can be an excellent addition to the consultant's data gathering approach.

Observations

A fourth method of data gathering is direct observation. Compared to the first three methods we have discussed, observations allow the consultant to collect data on actual behavior rather than reports of people's behavior (Nadler, 1977). Self-report data can be erroneous because the information relies on the memory of the person being asked. For several reasons people may report their behavior in error, may not be accurate in their perceptions of the behavior of others, or may represent behavior to give the interviewer a positive impression. Interviewees may not be conscious, for example, of whether telephone interruptions during a task cause them to make more errors, whether they handle customer complaints on a certain product differently from their coworkers, or whether they compliment certain employees more often than others. They may report only what they remember (perhaps only the last few days, or an event that was extraordinary and thus stands out) or they may report what they want to make known (avoiding a complaint about a coworker, but sharing frustrations about this year's salary increases). Questionnaires may also be unlikely to elicit accurate data on these points. Observations allow the practitioner to get closer to seeing how these issues play out during the course of an ordinary day and to avoid errors in self-reporting. Moreover, self-report data are always a reflection of past events, whereas observation collects data on what is happening in the present (Nadler, 1977).

The OD practitioner can use observations to gain a better understanding of the actual work that people are doing. Instead of only interviewing members to understand how patient registration or building inspections are handled, or reading the formally documented process, the practitioner can learn much more about the process by sitting with an intake nurse for a day or following a building inspector as she completes her rounds. By doing so, the practitioner will have a greater understanding of the process, will build credibility and relationships with organizational members, and will have a richer understanding of how any changes to the job will impact those who perform it.

Data gathered through observations, however, are prone to being filtered through the eyes of the observer. The observer who has heard complaints that employees in the billing department are unproductive because they socialize frequently may be more likely to observe that. Observing a staff meeting to watch for conflict may mean that the consultant interprets certain behavior as conflict that organizational members may not see in that light. Thus, bias is not omitted in this method of data gathering, but it is a different kind of bias than that which occurs during interviews, focus groups, or surveys.

In addition, observations are likely to alter the circumstances and potentially change the behavior of those being observed. This fact about observations has come to be known as the Hawthorne Effect, named after a now-famous experimental study of working conditions in a manufacturing plant described by Roethlisberger and Dickson (1939). Listening to a customer service agent handle customer complaints likely will expose the consultant to the kinds of calls that agents receive, but it may not be the best choice to learn how agents truly deal with complaints. Anyone being observed in that circumstance is likely to want to make a good impression and to complete the work in the most diligent way. Staff meetings conducted with an observer watching from a corner may be more cordial and agreeable than one without an observer. Unless the observer is trusted and builds rapport, observation may not work well to see conflict, to learn how informal systems subvert the formal ones, or to understand how employees work around official processes.

While observations can give a general sense of how things happen, a consultant is not likely to see the entire range of situations. One or two team meetings' worth of observation, or a few hours watching patients in a hospital waiting room, can be very instructive but does not substitute for the knowledge and expertise of those who work there and have seen many more examples. The observer should not overgeneralize from only a small sample of observations and assume knowledge equal to that of organizational members.

Finally, observation would not be a good choice in situations where the phenomenon being observed is rare or infrequent. A practitioner may observe for many hours without witnessing what happens when a machine breaks down if it only happens every 3 months. Observations are less useful for studying unusual problems or infrequent interactions.

Tips for Successfully Conducting Observations for Data Gathering

1. Observers should show an interest in learning what usually happens, demonstrating interest in the activity observed. Observers can be intimidating. Making it clear that the point of the observation is not to act as a police officer for an official process usually puts people at ease. In addition, no matter how quiet the observer is, observation is still usually an intrusive activity that interferes in some way with the ordinary course of organizational life.

2. Consider observing with explicit permission rather than hiding the purpose of the observation. It can be useful to observe interactions in the lunchroom or the lobby, and such observations rarely need widespread publicity or long explanations. When observing people doing their daily jobs, most consultants find it more ethical and comfortable to make their purpose known. However, the consideration to share one's purpose is situation-dependent. The more those observed know about the purpose of the observation, the more the behavior may change. Telling a team that the purpose of the observation is to see "whether staff meetings remain on topic or whether they wander off onto tangents" (or even a more general "to watch the flow of the meeting") probably will mean that team members pay much more attention to the content and process of the discussion, and the observation will be of an atypical meeting. This can be unavoidable, however, so the more general explanation probably would suffice.

3. Observations can be unstructured or formally structured. Unstructured observations can be as simple as moving from location to location, watching and listening to what people are doing. The observer can simply make notes about what is being seen. Formally structured observations can be used as well, sampling different times and locations to get representative observations. Other structured observations can be useful for group interaction, using forms that have been designed for that purpose (with check boxes that represent the number of questions asked, for example).

4. Note-taking can heighten participants' anxiety about being observed and can give away the purpose of the observation if it has not been disclosed in detail.

It may be best for the observer to take short notes and frequent personal breaks where additional detailed notes can be taken.

5. Because observation can be prone to observer bias, it may be appropriate to use multiple observers, whether internal or external to the organization, to observe multiple times and locations. The observers can share their notes and interpretations with one another to test bias and determine whether they may share multiple interpretations of the same event.

Though they can be time-consuming, observations can be a good choice when the practitioner would like to witness a situation personally. They usually bring the practitioner closer to the situation or problem being experienced than do interviews or focus groups. It can be enlightening and humbling to witness the complexities and challenges of organizational life in action, and it can make a consultant more aware of the organizational culture so that interventions can be appropriately directed at the right sources of the problem.

Unobtrusive Measures

A fifth type of data that can be gathered consist of unobtrusive measures (Webb, Campbell, Schwartz, & Sechrest, 1966; Webb & Weick, 1979). As the name suggests, these data are generally readily available because they are produced during the ordinary course of organizational activity. They can usually be gathered in an inconspicuous manner without changing the data themselves. As discussed earlier, observations can be intrusive, and the very nature of observation can change what is being observed. With unobtrusive measures, the data usually already exist, and gathering the data does not usually change what is being studied. Like the Sherlock Holmes mystery in which the absence of a barking dog led Holmes to conclude that the dog knew the intruder, unobtrusive measures can be a source of data that can give the consultant insight into the organization without making a direct inquiry or conducting observations. Because these data exist separate from the consulting engagement itself, the data are likely to be less influenced by the presence of the observer or practitioner. As a result, unobtrusive measures can be highly valid sources of data. They can contradict or substantiate data gathered elsewhere (through interviews or observations, for example).

There are a variety of types of unobtrusive measures that can be useful to consultants:

1. *Historical data.* Historical data and archives consist of both public and non-public records. A consultant who wants to learn the history of a union strike or a company's bankruptcy can certainly rely on interviews with organizational members, but may also look up articles in a local newspaper to learn this history as well. These articles are less likely to be influenced by changing perceptions and interpretations of the event over time. The organization may maintain its own library of historical artifacts that can be examined as well, such as employee newsletters or correspondence with customers.

2. *Official documents.* These consist of a wide variety of documents that are often used for financial, legal, or human resources purposes, such as job

descriptions, goals and objectives, personnel files, or meeting minutes. Obviously these data only represent the formal and official record, which may differ substantially from what organizational members experience. Meeting minutes, for example, may not document everything that was said during the meeting, but do tend to define what organizational members considered to be worthy of documentation (Anderson, 2004). Presentations, e-mails, and other documents can also be helpful background information, as can internal websites.

3. *Databases.* Most organizations maintain databases of customer, financial, and employee records. These can be useful sources of data to determine, for example, how many people were hired last year compared to the year before or where most customers live.

4. *Online environment.* Social media sites, wikis, online bulletin boards, and review websites can illustrate past, current, and prospective employee and customer attitudes about the organization. Prospective employees might share their experiences about the interview process, and current employees might share what it is like to work at a certain site, for example. Current customers might share frustrations with aspects of customer service.

5. *Physical environment.* An organization's physical environment can say a great deal about its culture. In organizations where status and hierarchy are important elements of the culture, executives maintain large offices with expansive windows on the surrounding landscape. Middle managers may have smaller offices and windows, and employees may sit in cubicles. In other organizations, all employees regardless of role may have an office or may have a cubicle. Other objects of the formal physical environment to observe include the following:

- Architecture and signage (e.g., layout, building construction materials, lobby furnishings)
- Design of work areas, formal gathering locations, and meeting rooms
- Lunchroom, break room, and cafeteria
- Posters, photographs, or art
- "Costumes, company uniforms, standard attire" (Jones, 1996, p. 6)

The personal physical environment, or how organizational members design their own work environments, can also be a source of data to illuminate the organizational culture. Examples include the following:

- Employee bulletin boards (newspaper articles, comic strips, papers posted by employees to be read by other employees)
- Desk or office decorations, such as personal photographs, diplomas, and certificates

Environments designed or customized by employees can give a consultant insight into employee satisfaction and morale. The number and content of currently popular Dilbert cartoon strips can provide a source of data about employee frustrations, for example.

6. *Language use, including stories and metaphors.* As Burke (1992) puts it, "Metaphors used by executives and other members of an organization are windows into the soul, if not collective unconscious, of the social system" (p. 255). Members describing the organization as "one big family" or "a sinking ship" (Brink, 1993, p. 369) give great insight into how they think about the culture. Common organizational metaphors concern sports (often used when people describe working in teams for a common goal) or the military (used to highlight urgent or competitive activities, such as beating the competition). They are more than shortcuts for longer explanations or mere poetic devices, but are ways of calling on and even creating a set of values that organizational members ought to share (Jacobs & Heracleous, 2006; Tietze, Cohen, & Musson, 2003).

Similarly, stories serve a teaching function. Values and lessons historically have been passed down from generation to generation through storytelling, and the same can be said for organizational stories. Members may recall "the lesson of the product failures of the 1980s" or tell a story about the vice president who was fired after making a major decision. These stories can be illuminating for a consultant who wants to understand the organizational culture and context.

Language such as stories and metaphors occurs naturally in organizational discourses but can be elicited during interviews or focus groups as well. An interviewee may be asked to tell a story that would give a newcomer an insight into the organization or to pick a physical object that describes how the office functions.

Tips for Gathering Unobtrusive Measures

1. Despite the impression that may be given by the name, some unobtrusive measure data gathering is still resource-intensive. Unless the consultant has access to the database, for example, an organizational member who knows how to use it must do the work, so exploratory or "just to see" data gathering may not be appropriate.

2. Unobtrusive data gathering is not always hidden from organizational members. Nadler (1977) adds that searching through filing cabinets or employee records can cause a great deal of unease among organizational members, reminding us that such methods are not emotionally neutral. It may still be necessary to explain to organizational members what the goal is of the data collection.

3. Not all data may be unambiguously interpreted. For example, simply because all organizational members have the same office size does not mean that the organization is free from hierarchy or status. Nadler (1977) writes, "It's not always clear, for example, what constitutes an incident of absenteeism or lateness. The data can be interpreted in several different ways" (p. 139). It may be helpful to check an interpretation with someone with experience in the organization's culture to validate whether it is accurate.

4. Be careful not to overgeneralize from observations or examples that represent only one occurrence of a phenomena. Online comments, for example, might represent only one particularly good or bad example, posted with the benefit of anonymity by a motivated writer, and not representative of the experiences of others.

Used in combination with another method, unobtrusive measures can be a useful source of additional data to help the consultant interpret the problem the client describes and the organizational culture. They can validate or contradict information gained from other sources. It can also be a rapid way of collecting data with less intrusion than other methods.

Creating a Data Gathering Strategy and Proposing an Approach

Choosing a method of data gathering involves several considerations. Each of the methods described in this chapter presents various advantages and disadvantages, so the consultant and client must choose between them with the knowledge that none is perfect. As Schein (1969, p. 99) puts it, "No data gathering method is right or wrong in the abstract." Table 7.1 compares the pros and cons of the five approaches.

Consultants must balance several criteria when choosing a data gathering strategy:

1. *Investment required.* Each method has a cost to the organization and the consultant in terms of time and monetary expense for both data gathering and data analysis. Methods such as interviews take time to gather the data, whereas methods such as surveys can produce volumes of quantitative and qualitative data that can be time-consuming to analyze. While one-on-one interviews may be ideal to explore a certain problem, the client may not be willing to devote the time needed to execute such a strategy. In addition, the organization may not have the resources available to devote to substantial data mining from databases or files.

2. *Access.* The client may not allow the consultant to have access to data or it may not be practical. It may not be possible to interview each organizational member due to work schedules, travel, or vacation. The organization's policies may prohibit use of personnel files or may not allow external consultants to have access to financial or technical files.

3. *Relevance to the problem.* Some methods of data gathering are better suited to particular types of problems. Unobtrusive measures are less likely to yield useful data about how a team feels about a management change, and observations are unlikely to give significant insights into whether employees are satisfied with the training programs provided. Thus, each method of data gathering selected must be relevant to the problem described by the client. Each method selected should be chosen because it is likely to yield useful valid information about the presenting problem and its underlying problems. If clients do not believe that a proposed data gathering strategy is relevant to the problem described, they will question the consultant's choices, since it may appear that the consultant is wasting time or following an unfruitful path.

4. *Accuracy.* Some methods are more prone to respondent and consultant bias than others. The consultant may be less likely to gain highly valid data from respondents in some situations, or the consultant's own biases may color what is seen in

Table 7.1 Advantages and Disadvantages of Five Data Gathering Methods

Method	Advantages	Disadvantages
Interviews	May prompt interviewees to be more forthright in a personal environment. Interviewer can follow up on important issues and explore situations in depth. More personal than surveys or focus groups. Consultants can capture examples and quotes effectively. Interviews may reveal new issues.	Time- and data-intensive if many interviews are to be conducted. Potentially expensive. Rapport must be established; interviewees must trust interviewer. Gives only the interviewee's perspective. Interviewers may unwittingly encourage certain response bias. Analysis can be time-consuming.
Focus groups	May save time compared to individual interviews. Access to many people at once, thus can be more efficient at getting information than interviews. Group can build on one another's thoughts, stimulating thinking.	Potential for groupthink or for people to "go along" with one point of view to avoid conflict. Confidential issues may not be discussed with peers. A few members may dominate the group.
Surveys/ Questionnaires	Data from many people can be gathered at once. Can take a short time. Allows a broad range of topics to be addressed. Data can be quantified and compared across groups. Can repeat survey to show differences over time.	Data analysis can be intensive. May require statistical knowledge beyond the capabilities of the consultant. Difficult to follow up in depth on a single issue. Response rates may be low or may bias the results. Respondents may give socially desirable answers.
Observations	Allows data collection "in the moment" when an	Can be time-intensive. Can be expensive.

Method	Advantages	Disadvantages
Observations (continued)	event occurs rather than after the event. Allows behavior to be seen rather than self-reported. Can be initiated with little preparation. Can build relationships with organizational members.	Observer may be biased to see an event based on how others have explained it. May be difficult to observe multiple instances of a behavior that occurs sporadically. Observer may intimidate or affect the group or individual being observed.
Unobtrusive measures	Data exist separate from individual interpretation or motivation. High validity. Can substantiate or contradict data gathered elsewhere (triangulation). Can be less intrusive.	Can be time-intensive. Can be more subtle to interpret. Can be more difficult to access. Potentially poor quality.

observations. Thus, the ability to obtain valid information from a certain approach will differ based on the situation and the consultant's relationship with the client and organizational members.

5. *Flexibility.* Some methods allow the consultant to have greater flexibility in terms of following up on particular questions of interest or items that come up during the course of data gathering. A survey can be inflexible, for example, because once it has been designed and administered, it is not possible to add subsequent follow-up questions. Interviews tend to be more flexible since consultants can alter the questions during the course of the conversation.

How should a consultant balance these criteria and choose among the five approaches? Each client situation presents a unique negotiation between the problem described and the factors listed above. In other words, consultants may have to settle for what is possible as opposed to what is ideal. To compensate for the disadvantages of one approach, it may be a good idea to balance it with another, combining different methods to yield the most detailed data. Surveys, for example, can be followed by interviews or focus groups where organizational members can help to interpret the results. Alternately, interviews done before surveys can give the consultant insight into what survey questions should be asked. The point is that

> by using several methods to gather and analyze their data, practitioners can compensate for many of the drawbacks associated with relying on a single method. They will also need to choose methods that fit the diagnostic problems and contribute to cooperative, productive consulting relationships. (Harrison, 1987, p. 21)

Mixing methods and triangulating the same issue from different perspectives can solidify an interpretation as well and make it more persuasive in the client's eyes. As Swanson (2007) concludes, "In almost all instances, using more than one data collection method is necessary to ensure valid conclusions about the trends, factors, and causes of organizational, process, team, and individual performances" (p. 122).

To select an approach, it may be useful to create a chart such as the one shown in Table 7.2. Based on the client's description of the presenting problem, the consultant can list other possible interpretations or underlying problems that might be contributing to the situation that the client is describing. Then a data gathering approach can be selected that would generate the greatest amount of useful information on that issue. Because this approach is likely to spawn an exhaustive list of possible data gathering methods, the consultant should choose only those that seem most relevant to the client's problem and that fit the five criteria described above. In Table 7.2, for example, a client may have shared a problem with the cycle time of insurance claims processing, perhaps even noting that new employees seem to take longer than tenured employees. There could be a number of reasons for this. One might be that they did not learn the process accurately when they joined the organization. Interviews would be well suited to determining how they learned the claims process. A chart such as this one can focus the data gathering effort by forcing the consultant to retain a disciplined concentration on the client's problem, as well as to be explicit about the rationale for the data gathering approach.

Table 7.2   Selecting a Data Gathering Approach

Facts From Client's Description of Problem	Possible Interpretation or Reason	Data Needed	Best-Suited Method
New employees do not process insurance claims as quickly as experienced employees.	Employees do not learn the process accurately.	Ask new employees about their orientation experience and training.	Interviews
Sales figures in Midwest are significantly lower than East or West regions.	Salespeople in Midwest make fewer sales than in other regions.	Gather revenue per employee data in each region for past 3 quarters.	Unobtrusive measure

Ethical Issues With Data Gathering

Data gathering is itself a response to ethical concerns. It is an ethical consulting practice in that its purpose is to avoid colluding with the client's initial statements of the problem, and in doing so, the consultant seeks to expand on the client's view in order to solve the right problem for the long term. By gathering data, the consultant can avoid some of the ethical issues described in the previous chapter.

However, data gathering also presents consultants with a number of opportunities to face further ethical challenges, some of which have already been hinted at earlier in this chapter. The primary opportunity for an ethical dilemma concerns "misuse of data" that "occurs when the voluntary consent or confidentiality of the client system is violated or abridged" (White & Wooten, 1985, p. 150). This ethical principle is violated most flagrantly when a practitioner discloses who made a particular comment during an interview or focus group session even after pledging to the respondent that comments would remain anonymous. For a change agent, quotes from interviews, paper-and-pencil surveys, and facts gathered through unobtrusive measures are a typical and sometimes mundane part of the job. What the practitioner considers sensitive or risky matters less than what organizational members consider sensitive. It is no stretch to say that inappropriately leaked data could have serious life consequences for organizational members, including career limitations or termination from a job.

In addition, before gathering data, practitioners owe organizational members an explanation about what will be done with data gathered from them, giving them an opportunity to participate with free and informed consent or to decline to participate without consequences. In academic research, researchers are usually required to present research subjects with an informed consent form that lists the researcher's purpose, contact information, and any benefits or risks to the subject for participating. OD practitioners should consider their own research practices no less seriously.

These ethical principles require that practitioners be vigilant in protecting data. Notes from interviews and handwritten surveys should be kept with the consultant or in a secure location under lock and key. Practitioners should consider taking notes by using pseudonyms instead of actual names, or by using a personal shorthand method. Any audiotapes or videotapes must be only heard or watched by the consultant (or those with permission) and should be destroyed immediately after they have been transcribed. It is also easy to inadvertently "leak" information between interviews by stating "I heard the same thing from the last person I interviewed" (Farquhar, 2005, p. 227).

Finally, data gathering is conducted to benefit the client, not the practitioner. The practitioner should aim to gather data relevant to the problem described or that would illuminate related areas of the problem, all with the client's consent. The practitioner should avoid collecting data simply because it is interesting or useful for another engagement.

Summary

The most effective way that a consultant can learn about the client's problem and propose an effective intervention is through data gathering. Consultants use data gathering methods to delve into a client's description of a presenting problem to determine what underlying problems may be contributing to what the client is seeing. By gathering valid information about the organization, the client and consultant have a better understanding of the problem. Five data gathering methods that consultants use most frequently include interviews, focus groups, surveys/questionnaires, observation, and unobtrusive measures. Each has its advantages and disadvantages, so a mixed method approach may be the ideal solution. Consultants must balance the pros and cons of each method with what clients may accept, based on the investment needed in the approach, access, relevance, accuracy, and flexibility. Thus, proposing a data gathering strategy to a client is to propose another kind of contract, one in which the consultant is pledging to help the client understand the underlying problem in exchange for the organization dedicating energy to analyzing it in order to work toward an appropriate solution.

In the case study that follows this chapter, you will have the ability to practice analyzing a client's initial presenting problem and to propose a data gathering strategy that will explore other elements of the situation and any underlying problems.

For Further Reading

Fink, A. (2002). *The survey kit* (2nd ed.). Thousand Oaks, CA: Sage.

Seidman, I. (2006). *Interviewing as qualitative research* (3rd ed.). New York: Teachers College.

Waclawski, J., & Rogelberg, S. G. (2002). Interviews and focus groups: Quintessential organization development techniques. In J. Waclawski & A. H. Church (Eds.), *Organization development: A data-driven approach to organizational change* (pp. 103–126). San Francisco: Jossey-Bass.

Webb, E. J., Campbell, D. T., Schwartz, R. D., & Sechrest, L. (1966). *Unobtrusive measures: Nonreactive research in the social sciences.* Chicago: Rand McNally.

Case Study 2: Proposing a Data Gathering Strategy at AeroTech, Inc.

Read the AeroTech case and consider the following questions:

1. What is the client requesting? *— team / manager intervention*

2. What are the presenting problems? What do you think may be any underlying problems? Which of these underlying problems is most likely, in your view?

3. What data would illustrate whether these underlying problems are occurring? Which method of data gathering would you use and why? (Consider using the method of analysis shown in Table 7.2.)

4. What are the advantages and disadvantages of that method? Include a proposed timeline for your approach and any details about the data gathering method itself, including possible interview or survey questions, documents to gather, or observations you would conduct.

"I want to thank you for meeting with me," said Patrick Delacroix. "We have an *issue: $ + time* important issue that I'm hoping you can address. It's costing the company a lot of *project= help solve* time and money, and I think that the project that we're going to plan out will really *—proposed to* help solve a major problem in our group." *execute Up*

Patrick Delacroix, executive vice president of engineering for AeroTech, an aerospace technology research and products firm, was sitting behind a large walnut desk *enviromnt* at AeroTech headquarters. Cassandra Wilson, an organization development consultant in the AeroTech human resources department, had been assigned to consult with the engineering organization and was anxious to hear more about the problem that Patrick had called her to discuss.

AeroTech headquarters is located in the suburbs of a large metropolitan area. It is *environmnt* housed in an older concrete building that was built in the 1970s without many windows *—old fashnd* or the showy glass and steel architecture characteristic of many of the other companies in the area. In fact, these days it would be easy to drive by the headquarters and not know *enviromnt shows* that this major, multimillion-dollar company was even located there. AeroTech has a long *lack of improve* and distinguished history, having been a major supplier to the top government contractors contributing to U.S. space and defense programs in the 1980s. In the past 20 years, however, it has fallen out of favor among government contractors as quality problems *— funr decreast* plagued the company's products. The company briefly considered bankruptcy but averted *new CEO,* a Chapter 11 filing when its new CEO was named 4 years ago. The CEO helped the com- *chngd —> reivsid* pany to partially recover by revising its strategy, and as a result, AeroTech has now begun *strateg yb* to diversify into other areas in which there is higher demand. Some of these new business segments have become very successful enterprises, but it is clear that the pressure is high to succeed in the new lines of business. An article in the local newspaper predicted the *—lyoff needed* demise of AeroTech if annual losses continue at the present rate, and it suggested that *due to* based on financial analysts' projections, layoffs this year are almost certain to repeat last *annual losses* year's 16% reduction of AeroTech staff. "With financial performance mirroring last year's," the article concluded, "we may be witnessing the slow death of one of the metro area's original companies. Unless it merges or is acquired, we would be surprised if we are still reporting on AeroTech news a few years from now."

Patrick began at AeroTech nearly 25 years ago as an associate engineer, a few years after he finished his doctorate in engineering from a local university. He has witnessed the extensive changes in research and development of engineering products in his various roles as engineering manager for metals fabrication, director of the new component division, and now as vice president of the entire engineering operation. He lived through the decline in personnel and morale after quality problems forced the closure of the fabrication operation, but he also oversaw the rise in revenues following the successful component products released in the past 6 years. Most recently he presided over the largest loss of engineering talent that the company had seen through voluntary and involuntary termination programs. Much of the new strategic direction is riding on his shoulders.

"I'll get right to the point. As you can imagine, I'm under a great deal of pressure to get the new laser systems released to the market," he began.

"I can understand," Cassandra said. "I've heard that everything is on track with product development at least, is that right?"

"I wish it were that simple," Patrick said. "Developing advanced laser systems is a complex operation. We're relying on our best and brightest engineers to create some of the most innovative applications of advanced laser technology on the market today. If we pull it off as planned, it will be an incredible success for the company. Unfortunately, we can't always predict how long it will take to develop a product. How long it takes to be creative is a volatile challenge that's always present in our division. We also have to balance cycle time with our financial investments in research and development. We put a lot of pressure on our engineers, and we count on them to deliver."

Cassandra nodded. "I do hear that many of them are working nights and weekends. So what brings you to requesting our meeting today?"

"First let me give you a bit of background. As you know, we have five engineering teams in this division: laser systems, component systems (which are separated into two teams, new components and enhancements to existing components), satellite technology, and custom design. The laser and satellite teams are relatively new, having only been organized in that way since last year, and you'll recognize that they're the two critical areas in the new direction of the company. The other teams have the same charter that they've had for the past few years."

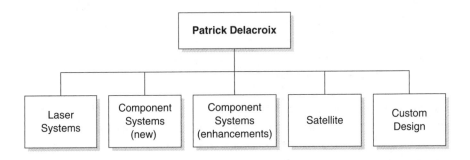

Patrick continued. "Productivity is my main issue. We have very limited budgets and very short delivery windows in which we're expected to produce results for the business. If we don't produce, a competitor will get to the market faster and we'll essentially have lost the battle. Right now we're not doing a very good job of that."

"Tell me more about what you mean by productivity," Cassandra said.

"I mean that in general we're not meeting our commitments to getting our products out. As a result, we're losing market share each time we're late to reaching the point at which our products are generally available. That impacts our sales force, marketing efforts, and the credibility of the engineering team."

"What do you think is causing low productivity?" she asked.

"Well, I think that there are many factors, but the most basic seems to be time management. Obviously how our engineers spend their time is critical. We need them to be skilled at prioritizing their time to spend it on the most value-adding activities so that the development activities can be completed on time." Patrick paused. "We need them to be self-managing and productive. That's why I called. I'd like to ask for your help in designing a time management and prioritization seminar to address some of the issues that I see among the engineers. You might throw in a little project management as well."

"We can certainly consider that," Cassandra said. "Let me ask you a couple of questions to better understand what's happening with your group. What's led you to the conclusion that they can't manage their time well?"

"Well, I'm obviously nervous about the laser systems team," Patrick said, "so I walk downstairs pretty frequently to get an update and to see how things are going. Almost every time I'm down there I see people working, but the results just don't seem to be there."

"What have you done so far?" she asked.

"I prefer to let my managers do the managing. I don't like to bypass them. And they know that the entire company is waiting for the product to be ready. But I have to be fair here. It's not everyone, it's mostly Todd's group."

"Who is Todd?" Cassandra asked.

"Todd Lyman is the manager of the laser systems engineering group. He joined the company last year at this time, right after we reorganized the engineering group after the layoffs," Patrick said. "We brought him in from the outside to lead the development of the new laser systems. We were lucky to recruit him, since he has extensive background in laser engineering management at one of our competitors. He's incredibly intelligent, well liked, and came with great credentials."

"I think I may have heard his name. So the problem with productivity is really in Todd's group?" Cassandra asked.

"Yes. Since he arrived his team has led three new product releases. Two were product upgrades and one was a new product. Two of the three were delayed beyond their original expected release date," Patrick said.

"How did the laser products group perform before the reorganization and before Todd joined?"

"Just fine," Patrick said. "That's what's so frustrating about these product delays. There's no apparent reason for them. Before, the group was like a machine. They would get a product design request, and they would do it. Many times they operated under budget. Now they're over budget and missing deadlines. It's really getting embarrassing to me personally, actually. Since Todd's arrival the group's performance has declined considerably. That leads me to my second request. I'd like to ask for you to engage Todd in some management coaching to build his management skills."

"Before we talk about Todd, let me ask you a few more questions about the group and its history. Who led the group before?" Cassandra asked. "How was that person perceived by the engineers in the group?"

"Ed Herman was a very popular manager. We were sorry to lose him. He was really a good company guy who knew how things were done around here, but he is now on a golf course in Florida having a great time in retirement. I envy the guy." Patrick smiled.

"So when Ed left, what happened to the group? How would you describe the team's reaction?" Cassandra inquired.

"Ed left right before the reorganization. In fact, it was Ed's departure that led me to rethink how we would organize things differently. In order to get some cross-pollination of Ed's excellent and productive team, I moved a few of them into satellite technology, and a few of them into custom design. I figured that would enhance the skills of both of those teams, since satellite is a new team, and custom design is a high-margin business. Ed's team was really close-knit. After that move was announced, a couple of the remaining engineers that were left behind asked to be moved with their colleagues into the other two groups. I guess they missed their old colleagues, but I couldn't afford to have the entire team disbanded like that, so they stayed behind."

"After you hired Todd, how did the team respond?" Cassandra asked.

"The team was small at the time, but they participated in the interview process, interviewing each of the candidates and providing feedback to me, and I agreed with their recommendation to hire Todd. I think that was a good process to get their buy-in for their new manager. Once Todd arrived, he had the responsibility of hiring about six new engineers to replace some of the staff that were reassigned during the organizational structure change," Patrick offered.

"The team is a mix of new and tenured engineers, then," Cassandra said. "What else can you tell me about the composition of Todd's team?"

"Let's see. There are probably a dozen engineers, ranging in age from late twenties to mid-sixties. Most are in their late forties to early fifties. The new ones joined only within the past year, obviously, and among those that were already a part of the team, the average tenure is probably 15 years or so. They have extensive educational backgrounds and are among the most highly skilled engineers I've met."

"What's been the morale among those engineers that were transferred and those that stayed behind in the laser group?" Cassandra asked.

Patrick shrugged. "Fine, I assume. I haven't heard any specific complaints."

"Other than Todd's group, how are the other engineering teams doing, in your assessment?" Cassandra asked.

"Very successful," Patrick said. "I haven't been more pleased with the performance of the satellite and custom design teams. They've really come through during a difficult time, especially with budget cutbacks that have affected each of our teams a great deal. That's what makes it so strange that Todd's team, with the existing tenured employees that he has on his staff, just can't seem to contribute in the same way that the other teams have."

"It sounds like Todd came with an excellent background with a wealth of experience as a manager and engineer, and that the team was fully behind his hiring," Cassandra summarized. "With those qualifications, under the circumstances what leads you to think that he needs management coaching?"

"Well, there's management experience and there's management at AeroTech. We have our own unique ways of doing things here. I think that Todd just needs to understand the Aero way specifically," Patrick said.

"Tell me more about what you mean by the 'Aero way.' You've said that Todd's group is missing deadlines and is over budget?"

"Right," he said. "We ask each of our engineering managers to develop a quarterly plan that we use as commitments across the business. I take the product development timeline that they send to me, and I share it with marketing and sales so they know when to begin the major sales push. I send it to operations so they know what components and parts to order in advance of volume manufacturing. I use the financial commitments to share with our chief financial officer so that she can make revenue projections and calculate financial projections. My credibility rides on those commitments. Todd's projections are consistently inaccurate, which has caused problems, obviously, for the marketing, sales, and finance teams."

"What do you think is causing the inaccurate forecast for budgets and delivery times?" Cassandra asked.

"There could be many things, but I have to say that when I was a manager of an engineering group, I could always come up with a realistic forecast," Patrick reminisced. "Maybe I didn't always get it right, but even when I got a commitment from an engineer that it would take him 2 months to deliver, I always added 10 to 20% to the budget and cycle time, just to be safe. My group may not have been the fastest, but we were always within projections." Patrick smiled.

"Is that a standard practice in most engineering environments?" she asked.

"Yes, it's pretty typical in my experience," Patrick said.

Cassandra looked through her notes. "OK. So let me summarize. There is a new manager with a team composed of new employees and tenured employees. That's the newest team in the division and also the team with lowest productivity compared to other similar teams in the division. Specifically, Todd's team is not producing products within his own projections of cycle time and budget. You're asking me to conduct two interventions. One would be a training program for the engineers on Todd's team that would teach time management, prioritization, and project management. A second intervention would be management coaching for Todd to help him better work through the management issues with his team, including cycle time and budget projections. Do I have that right?"

"That's it exactly." The phone rang on Patrick's desk. "I'm afraid I have another meeting scheduled now. Is there any other information I can provide to help you get started?"

"Perhaps. At this point, however, I'm not sure that the training and management coaching programs that you wanted me to work on are the right solutions to your problem. I'm not exactly certain what the true problem is, but I have some ideas. I think I'd like to gather some additional data before I make a recommendation. How does that sound?" Cassandra asked.

"What kind of additional data do you want to gather? How long will that take?" he asked.

"I'll tell you what. Why don't I write up a short proposal that specifies the additional data I would like to gather, and I can explain what I think the data would tell us. I'll include some of my thoughts about our roles in this project, including what I would need from you and what you can expect from me. I can send that to you within the next week."

"That sounds fine, but keep in mind the time pressure we're under here. I'll look forward to hearing back from you," Patrick concluded.

CHAPTER 8

Diagnosis and Feedback

The Board of Cooperative Educational Services (BOCES) in New York had hired a new school superintendent. Early in his new role, the superintendent decided that he needed to focus on several important constituencies, among them the BOCES administrative staff. To better understand and address the concerns of the internal group, he hired consultants to conduct interviews and observations of staff members. The staff concerns centered on issues of communicating common goals, understanding the vision and direction of the organization, participation in decision making, and teamwork. As a result of the diagnosis, the consultant, client, and staff all agreed that a series of workshops and action planning sessions would be useful to improve teamwork, clarify goals, and increase trust and engagement. The workshops were held as agreed and were rated as very effective by attendees. The group seemed to be making progress.

Just as the engagement was to conclude, a hidden conflict became apparent through a confrontation between the supervisor and the staff. Seven administrators sent a formal letter to the superintendent expressing significant concerns about many issues that had not yet been discussed or addressed, reporting barriers that inhibited them from being successful in their jobs. The initial diagnosis was now questionable, and additional data were gathered. A second round of staff member interviews now revealed deep conflicts about the superintendent's agenda, and the staff reported that they lacked confidence in the supervisor and his direction. The superintendent considered resigning. A second workshop was conducted to clarify roles, improve conflict resolution skills, and develop trust between team members and the superintendent so that open communication could occur. The consultants recognized in retrospect that while the data hinted at the hidden conflict, the initial diagnosis only showed part of the picture (Milstein & Smith, 1979).

- Why do you think the conflict was not discovered in the data gathering phase?
- What, if anything, could the consultants have done differently to make the conflict apparent earlier?

To many organization development (OD) practitioners, there is nothing quite as overwhelming as the volume of data that is generated from conducting interviews, focus groups, surveys, observations, and collecting unobtrusive measures. Depending on the length of the engagement, the size of the organization and data gathering effort, or the magnitude of the problem, such data can easily amount to hundreds or even thousands of pages of notes and reports. These notes may contain individual stories and interpretations, vivid observations, and statistical data from surveys, each of which may be consistent or contradictory with each other or the client's or practitioner's initial interpretations. At this point, the practitioner is faced with the challenge of sorting through it all to answer a deceptively simple question and discuss it with the client: "What is going on here?" This is the objective of the diagnostic and feedback phases of the OD process.

In this chapter, we explore the purposes of the diagnostic and feedback phases and we will discuss how consultants sort, analyze, and interpret data to arrive at conclusions that can be fed back to the client. We will address what kinds of conclusions consultants reach during the diagnostic phase, as well as how the feedback meeting should be conducted in order to present and discuss the data most effectively. We will address client reactions to feedback, including client resistance and the consultant's response to resistance. Finally, we will address ethical issues in the phases of diagnosis and feedback.

As you may have already noticed, while data gathering, diagnosis, and feedback are separated here as distinct phases of the consulting process, they bleed and blend together in most consulting engagements. This can happen when, for example, during data gathering, preliminary conclusions (diagnoses) prompt the consultant to follow new data gathering paths. Also, client feedback can offer a new interpretation on the data, which can add depth and nuance to the diagnosis. Taken together, these analytic stages represent the process of addressing a client's presenting problem with a complete picture of the underlying problem or situation so that the right intervention can be chosen and structured in the most effective way possible.

Diagnosis: Discovery, Assessment, Analysis, and Interpretation

While *diagnosis* is a common term among practitioners, it is unfortunate that it holds the connotation of the doctor-patient consulting model described in Chapter 5. For this reason, some writers prefer terms such as *discovery and dialogue* (Block, 2000), *assessment* (Franklin, 1995; Lawler, Nadler, & Cammann, 1980; Noolan, 2006), or *analysis and interpretation*. Regardless of the label, practitioners agree that the purpose of diagnosis is to "help an organization understand its behavior and its present situation—what's going on, how it's going on—so that something can be done about it" (Manzini, 1988, p. 148). Diagnosis is not only an informational activity, it is aimed at generating action.

It is during the diagnosis and feedback phases that the consultant presents the client with a more thorough and balanced view of the problem, a view that has been incomplete to the client to this point. This is because, as Argyris (1970) writes,

Organizations are composed of human beings whose behavior and attitudes are influenced by the positions they occupy, the roles they play, the groups and intergroups to which they belong, and their own personality factors. Thus, each individual may see a problem differently. (pp. 156–157)

Different interpretations of problems exist depending on job roles, organizational locations, individual experiences, and more. An executive will have one view of the problem and its causes, and there will be yet another view by a middle manager, and still another by a frontline employee. Showing the client how the problem can be viewed from these multiple angles can mean that "consultants and clients understand and attack causes of problems, rather than symptoms" (Harrison, 1994, p. 16). Indeed, Block (2000) reports that managers turn to consultants because they have typically tried unsuccessfully to solve a problem based on their own limited view of it, and that "the consultant's primary task is to present the picture—this is 70 percent of the contribution you have to make. Trust it" (p. 217). Done well, the diagnostic and feedback processes can act as interventions on their own and can motivate the client to take action to solve the underlying problem.

Practitioners often make two common mistakes in the diagnosis phase. First, they take diagnosis as an event rather than as a process. As the opening example illustrates, diagnosis is not a one-time occurrence—organizations, situations, groups, and people change. Additional data will surface and the picture will continue to build. Diagnosis is not a conclusion to come to in one day, but a set of preliminary beliefs about what is generally happening to be adapted as the organization changes. As the organization evolves, so must the diagnosis.

Second, practitioners often make the mistake of single-handedly shouldering the burden of diagnosis. Instead, diagnosis ideally would not be a process conducted by the change agent alone. In fact, many OD practitioners prefer to involve clients or even client teams in the diagnostic process. Bartee and Cheyunski (1977) state that diagnosis is most successful when the practitioner can create a process for the client to participate in developing an accurate set of conclusions. In this process, they write, "The client system becomes the authority in determining what information is important to share," and "The clients immediately tend to own and take responsibility for the data generated" (p. 56). Some advocate conducting workshops in which data can be presented and interpreted by organizational members rather than by the practitioner alone (Bartee & Cheyunski, 1977; Moates, Armenakis, Gregory, Albritton, & Field, 2005). Following a low response rate on an employee survey, for example, Moates and colleagues initiated a set of action groups that were presented the findings from the survey and interviews. The groups were asked to interpret the data, rate the importance of various themes, and to develop ideas for addressing the problems described. In doing so, the diagnostic and feedback process was facilitated by the consultants, but the interpretation and choice of actions to take belonged to the client organization. This may not be appropriate for some organizational cultures or diagnostic subjects, but for many situations it is likely that such an approach would increase the client's trust in the outcome (Harrison & Shirom, 1999).

The diagnostic phase consists of a number of interrelated activities, listed below. Each is described in greater detail in the following sections:

1. *Analyze the data, including sorting them into key themes.* Obviously, handing a stack of interview notes or completed survey forms to a client with no analysis is not useful. Instead, the consultant must summarize and abstract key points from the data. The consultant will look for common themes in the data and organize them in a way that helps the client understand the problem.

2. *Interpret the data.* Interpreting means drawing conclusions that are supported by the data. The consultant's role is to present the facts, as well as to facilitate understanding and implications of the interpretations, beliefs, attitudes, opinions, and inferences offered by organizational members.

3. *Select and prioritize the right issues that will "energize" the client.* Almost all data gathering activities will produce a long list of issues, concerns, and contributing problems, and some will be only minimally related to the current problem. Selecting those that are most energizing will help the client to be motivated to focus on a narrow set of issues to be addressed, implying a shorter list of actions. The issues will not all have equal relevance or contribution to the problem, so the consultant can help the client to see which issues may have higher impact or priority than others.

Finding Patterns by Analyzing Data

The objective of the analytic exercise for the organization development practitioner is to reduce a large amount of data to a set of "manageable patterns which will help to organize the problem into a useful conceptual map" (Argyris, 1970, p. 157). Data analysis, as some social scientists have observed, can be a "mysterious" activity (Marshall & Rossman, 1989) and an "open-ended and creative" act (Lofland & Lofland, 1995). It can be perplexing to decide where to begin and how to tackle such an endeavor. Fortunately, social scientific researchers who have coped with this problem for many years have developed useful solutions, whether the data are quantitative (such as in surveys) or qualitative (such as in interview notes). Though academic research projects and OD data gathering programs have different objectives and audiences (Block, 2000), OD practitioners can learn from and apply a great deal of social science research practices in the data analysis stage.

Many practitioners struggle to get the data analysis "right," as if there was (to use a metaphor) a needle of a true answer buried in the data haystack. This results from a misguided assumption that there is only one true interpretation. As some OD practitioners put somewhat philosophically, "The question of what is 'truth' remains tentative and subject to revision" (Massarik & Pei-Carpenter, 2002, p. 105). Data can be organized in any number of ways, and the interpretation and analysis of the data is often inseparable from the experience of the person doing the interpreting and sorting. This, in fact, is what distinguishes academic research from OD practice—the practitioner's judgment and experience have a great deal to add to the creative and intuitive process of analyzing the data (Block, 2000). Levinson (1994) agrees, adding that the "practitioner is his or her most important instrument" (p. 27). In addition, despite the practitioner's best efforts, it is probably a healthier attitude to take and less stressful process to follow when the OD practitioner admits to never being able to know as much about the organization as the clients themselves (Schein, 1999). A more realistic outcome would be for the practitioner to develop a set of data-based and data-supported preliminary conclusions that lead to a useful conversation with a client who can ideally learn from the practitioner's conclusions and participate in developing appropriate actions.

Procedures for analyzing data are generally derived from two logical methods for reasoning from data (Babbie, 1992). The first is a *deductive process,* in which the analyst applies general principles or a theory to a particular circumstance or (set of) observation(s). The second is an *inductive process,* in which the analyst reasons from the observations or the data to elicit general principles or a theory. These methods can be applied to data analysis for OD practitioners as well. A deductive process of data analysis consists of using models or theories about organizations, organizational change, and human behavior to help sort and interpret the data. An inductive process consists of reading and sorting through the raw data to develop the key themes from them. Both are common approaches, as is statistical analysis of surveys and questionnaires.

Deductive Analysis: Using Models for Diagnosis

One popular method of analyzing data is to use a diagnostic model. Particularly if a model has been used to develop the data gathering approach, such as a survey or interviews, using a model to analyze the data is a natural next step. Using a model has several benefits (Burke, 1994):

1. *It makes coding data easier.* Models present a finite number of categories into which data can be sorted. With preestablished categories, the practitioner can more easily sort interview comments into various groups.

2. *It can help with data interpretation.* The practitioner can notice which categories contain more or fewer comments, or can notice which aspects of the model are over- or underemphasized. Models also show relationships among categories that can be used for action planning.

3. *It can help to communicate with clients.* Unlike lengthy theories or complicated academic language, models are often graphic depictions that may be more easily understood and that can more clearly direct a client's attention to particular areas of interest.

We have already explored a number of popular diagnostic models in this book. Weisbord's Six-Box Model, the Nadler-Tushman congruence model, and the Burke-Litwin model of organizational performance and change (each of which is described in Chapter 4) have all been used successfully in numerous OD engagements to diagnose problems and suggest areas for attention. Each model differs in its choice of language and relationships, and thus each offers something a little different for the practitioner to consider (Nadler, 1980). One drawback is that these three are all models of whole organization functioning. Using one of these models to analyze data generated from interviews on a team's satisfaction with how projects are assigned would not be very useful. Specific models such as those developed for leadership or management (such as Likert's four systems or Blake and Mouton's managerial grid discussed in Chapter 2), employee engagement, or team functioning might be more useful in some circumstances.

Burke (1994) gives an example of how this categorization process worked in one situation in which he used Weisbord's Six-Box Model to analyze data from interviews with eight managers in a financial services company. He sorted the interviewees' comments into strengths and weaknesses by each of Weisbord's six components, also labeling each comment as part of the "formal" or "informal" system. When the data were categorized in this way, he noticed that the informal system appeared to be stronger than the formal system, particularly in the area of leadership, and that the category of purposes was particularly weak compared to the others. An off-site meeting agenda was designed to focus on goals, objectives, and strategies, as well as to build the formal leadership team through relationships that had already been informally established.

In addition to these widely known models, many practitioners use their own models that have been developed from their own experience. Burke (1994) points out that most of these are not published, and that 100 different practitioners would produce "100 different diagnostic models" (pp. 53–54). Thus, there is not always agreement about which model is best for which situation, and the diversity of models can be both an asset and a drawback, because of the assumptions contained in models. As we discussed in Chapter 7 when we addressed the use of models in survey design, models can be constraining. Systems theory is a popular diagnostic model, for example, yet it also focuses our attention on formally structured organizational processes and neglects interpretive acts of organizational members, which can be important in understanding many organizational problems. The very benefit of models in helping us narrow and focus the data can also be a drawback. Models can highlight attention to certain areas but allow us to overlook others, often oversimplifying complex processes (Golembiewski, 2000c).

Another danger is that we may become overly dependent on the model so that we cannot see connections or patterns ourselves without the model. A final note of caution about using the deductive approach with a model is that while it lends itself to categorizing and counting issues and comments, these do not necessarily represent the issues about which there is the most energy or emotion. In other words, a few participants may feel very strongly about one theme, which may also be very important to the current problem, and others may feel less strongly about a more frequently mentioned theme. Simply stating that five comments related to "leadership" may also not be instructive enough to take action.

Inductive Analysis: Pulling Out Key Themes

Unlike deductive analysis, inductive analysis is done without a predetermined set of categories. That is, the data analyst determines what the categories will be. One benefit of an inductive approach is that the label for the categories can more closely align with the language of organizational members. The categories can also be customized to the project so that more or fewer categories can be used depending on how the consultant wants to present the data. This approach can even lend itself to creating a model specifically tailored to the client's situation, showing interrelationships between categories, topics, and organizational groups or members. Here is a short example of how this approach can be used.

Imagine that a client has engaged a consultant to determine why a team's past three major projects have missed their schedules, and that the following 10 comments are derived from individual interviews with team members:

"Our project manager did not complete an accurate budget."

"Management took too long to decide which proposal to accept."

"We do not have the necessary systems in place for project managers to use."

"Vacation schedules disrupted the work when team members were not available."

"Management took members from the team for another critical project."

"The schedule was inaccurate to begin with."

"We do not pay enough to hire the most qualified people."

"Project managers do not get paid for overtime."

"Management changed the project scope halfway through the project."

"No conference call capability to include remote team members."

These data could be categorized into these four areas:

Project planning (budget, scheduling)

Compensation/rewards (overtime, salaries)

Management (scope, resources, decision making)

Tools (systems, conference calls)

A second categorization system could be based on the focal person identified in the comment (omitting two that do not fit this scheme):

Project managers (budgets, overtime, systems)

Managers (decision making, scope, moving resources)

Team members (vacation schedules, remote members)

Still a third method:

Financial systems (budgets, overtime, compensation)

Technology systems (conference calling, systems)

Human resource processes (vacation schedules)

Management processes (decision making, project scope, resource planning)

Any of these is an accurate categorization of the comments. In fact, a number of other categories could be used as well, so determining how these comments get sorted would depend on the consultant's experience, the client's preferences, and the organizational culture. Ask yourself what the client will learn when you present the data each way. What do you see in the three ways that this same list above is organized? Do you learn more through one presentation than another? Does it accurately reflect the data or does it make it look like one concern is more or less important than it deserves to be?

Learning data analysis of this type is best done through practice, and practitioners each have their own preferred methods of coding data. Generally, most practitioners perform inductive coding following these seven steps:

1. First, read through a good portion of the data again without taking notes. The purpose of this is to become very familiar with the general data rather than to take any action at this point.

2. Then, setting aside the data, write down several key ideas or themes that stand out in what you have just read. This can be a challenge, and you may draw a blank, but persevere. "Don't be surprised if, after doing this, you are no better off than before. You may have difficulty detecting particular trends. . . . Don't be alarmed" (Manzini, 1988, pp. 77–78).

3. Next, go back through the data again and ask yourself what this comment is trying to say or what idea or concept it is an instance of. Give the comment the appropriate label(s). In the example above, the comment "The schedule was inaccurate to begin with" could be labeled as "project planning."

4. Proceed through the list of comments, with each comment being placed into a category (or more than one) already in place or becoming an instance of a new category if it is unlike any that have been created so far.

5. When all comments are analyzed, sort them by category and validate that each comment has been accurately placed. Look for categories where there are very few comments and those where there is an abundance.

6. Determine whether the "saturated" categories could or should be broken down further and whether the "single-instance" comments are truly unique or whether they could be combined with another category.

7. Write a description of what each category means and which categories may be related to others.

As you may conclude from the explanation and example above, an inductive analytic approach can be time-consuming and even frustrating when data are plentiful. It requires reading through the data numerous times to become very familiar with the issues, and it demands flexibility and an open attitude from the practitioner. Because the categories do not exist until the practitioner creates them, the inductive approach may require more knowledge of the organization, the data, or organizational theory in general than the deductive approach.

A final note of caution is that because the analyst is generating the categories, there is a danger of particular comments resonating with the practitioner's own opinions or beliefs (this may be particularly true for internal consultants) so that certain comments or categories gain more weight than they should. A practitioner who has had a bad experience with senior management on another project may be inadvertently looking for comments about management to support his or her own view. On the other hand, the practitioner's own intuition is a powerful source of data, and listening to this inner voice can be instructive in determining how to analyze the data. We will discuss ways to address this dilemma below.

Statistical Analysis

For surveys (especially those with Likert-type items) or sophisticated analyses of themes generated through inductive or deductive categorization processes, statistical analysis can be a powerful tool for data analysis. Statistical analysis is very common with organizationwide employee satisfaction or engagement surveys, for example. Methods for conducting statistical tests are much too complex to present here, and compared to qualitative analysis, such quantitative procedures are probably necessary in fewer circumstances. Most OD practitioners should be familiar enough with basic statistical charts (e.g., frequency distribution tables, histograms, x- and y-axes, bar and line charts) and descriptive statistics (e.g., mean, median, mode) to interpret their meaning and to explain them to a client.

For the statistical research–oriented practitioner, powerful statistical tests can be very persuasive ways of diagnosing an organization. Often, however, clients without the research background of the analyst find these tests less persuasive. "Frequently, one sees consultants or researchers piling volume upon volume of computer output onto an overwhelmed, confused, but supposedly grateful client," Nadler (1977, p. 149) writes. The time and effort the practitioner may need to invest to explain the conclusions drawn from an independent samples *t*-test or ANOVA may result in distracting the client from the genuine issue that ought to be addressed. Too much statistical detail can also lead the client to ask a number of purportedly "interesting questions" ("Are there statistically significant differences in mean responses on Question 15 between sales and marketing?") that lead to additional statistical tests and thus permit the client to delay an action phase, a potential form of resistance that is described later. The best approach may be to be judicious with the use of statistics to include just enough to build a persuasive case without overwhelming the client with too much data. Nadler (1977) recommends including a small set of relevant data, simple enough for a nonexpert to interpret, with visual displays to help condense the important facts.

Interpreting Data

When the data are sorted into categories and reduced from the volume of raw comments into the most prominent themes, the task remains to develop interpretations or inferences from the data to determine what conclusions can be drawn. The practitioner can now ask a number of questions about the data, such as those discussed when contracting with the client: What are the strengths and weaknesses being described? What is the nature of the problem according to the data? What are the contributing sources of the problem in the data, and how do these differ from the client's view? What is being done about the problem today? Are there differences in the data according to any demographic variables of interest?

In this process, it is easy to subconsciously slip from facts and data to inferences, including some inferences that may not be supported by the data. Levinson (1994) offers an instructive recommendation: "The practitioner should be able to cite the facts from which the inferences were made, specify the alternative inferences that were possible, and explain the reason for choosing one over another" (pp. 43–44). A conclusion that "employees do not trust senior management" can be drawn from various facts reported in interviews: employees feel punished for taking risks, they choose not to report bad information, and they offer examples of managers' promises left unfulfilled. Having the facts available to support the inference helps to bolster the likelihood that it is a reasonable interpretation, and it gives both clients and change agents more confidence in the conclusion.

One reason that it is easy to make a dangerous slip to inferences not supported by the data is that practitioners may draw conclusions based on their own experience, potentially looking through data to back up a view they already hold. Kahn (2004), for example, describes a powerful consulting experience he had in a social services agency in which, because of his own personal family background, he began to side with organizational members as they blamed the agency director for the organization's problems. Assumptions about leadership, power dynamics, follower behavior and responsibility, and his personal sympathy with certain organizational roles all combined to push Kahn toward a particular interpretation about who held responsibility for problems and away from addressing sensitive issues including racial and gender dynamics.

There are many ways that practitioners can avoid this problem and develop more sound conclusions. One way is to conduct the analysis multiple times in different ways. Re-sorting the data into new categories or using multiple models can validate the analysis or offer alternative conclusions. Try both inductive and deductive analysis to see what results. A second method is to invite a colleague who is not familiar with the data (if confidentiality agreements with the client allow it) to either conduct a "second opinion" analysis of the data or to listen while the analyst describes the conclusions that have been drawn. The second practitioner can test inferences to ensure that they are supported by the data. A third method, perhaps the most obvious, is to work through the interpretive process with the client. If multiple interpretations are possible, holding a dialogue with the client can clarify which of these is most reasonable. Again, the consultant's role is less about bringing the right, true answer to the client and more about facilitating a learning process that allows the client to explore an alternative picture and to have access to an angle that has been missing to this point. Figure 8.1 summarizes these three options.

Re-sort	1. Try sorting the data again, using a different approach (inductive or deductive). Try using a different model, if one was used the first time.
Get help	2. If confidentiality agreements allow it, invite a peer to assist with data collection or analysis.
Ask the client	3. Invite the client to analyze the raw data to see if he or she reaches the same conclusions.

Figure 8.1   Avoiding Bias in Interpreting Data

Selecting and Prioritizing Themes

With themes developed and preliminary conclusions drawn, the practitioner must consider what issues should be brought up to the client. Not all of them will be germane to the current engagement and not all can be addressed. Thus, a careful prioritization process is necessary to "avoid presenting management with a huge laundry list of problems, which may appear overwhelming in its totality. Isolate the truly significant problems and issues, and prepare summaries that describes their nature and extent" (Manzini, 1988, p. 143). How does a consultant decide, however, that employee complaints about workload should be shared, but that complaints about the cafeteria food should be lower on the list? What about the complaints of a small but emotional minority who bring up a highly charged issue? Choosing what themes to select is a function of the problem, the data, the engagement, the contract, and the consultant's own experience and intuition. Golembiewski (2000a) offers a useful set of "features of energizing data," or those criteria that, when met, are likely to energize the client toward action rather than deepening cynicism or frustration that the issues seem unresolvable. Among them are the following:

1. *Relevant.* Issues shared with the client should be relevant to the problem for which the consultant and client have contracted. The client is not likely to be interested in issues that are remote or not among the most influential causes of the problem. Cafeteria food may not be relevant to the team's challenges in agreeing on a work schedule that meets each team member's needs.

2. *Influenceable or manageable.* It will build energy when the consultant presents issues that the client can change. Sharing data about problems that the client cannot control ("Two of your problems are that the price of oil is too high for your

budget, and you are in an industry that is declining at the rate of 11% per year") pushes responsibility for the current problem further away and drains the client of energy to take action. Not only should the issue be manageable, but Block (2000) recommends choosing themes that people *want* to work on.

3. *Descriptive.* The most useful data will describe current facts, rather than using themes to judge, evaluate, pinpoint blame, or isolate individual contributions to problems. Data that are evaluative and that punish are likely to be resisted. This does not mean that emotion should be ignored. Feelings and opinions of organizational members fall into the category of facts that can be described. "I heard these three themes from my interviews" is an appropriate descriptive statement that outlines the issues with a minimum of evaluation.

4. *Selective.* Not all of the themes in the data can or should be discussed. It is tempting to present too much in order to expand the client's picture of the situation, but such efforts are likely to overwhelm the client, who may then have trouble deciding what to do next. Choosing the top few issues to present will focus attention on those that are the most important, leaving out those issues mentioned less frequently.

5. *Sufficient and specific.* The tradeoff of selectivity, Golembiewski (2000a) writes, is that too little information may be presented, which may not be enough to fully understand the situation. Enough detail should be provided so that the client can consider specific actions to take. Using the example earlier, stating that "management issues" are a key reason why projects are behind schedule may be accurate but, without additional explanation, it is also too vague to decide what action would remedy the problem. Also, issues selected should be described in relatively equal conceptual categories, to avoid very specific feedback such as "Employees would prefer that you answer voice mail within 4 hours" mixing with more general descriptions such as "Employees feel that you do not manage change well."

Figure 8.2 summarizes these five guiding principles for selecting and prioritizing themes to share with a client.

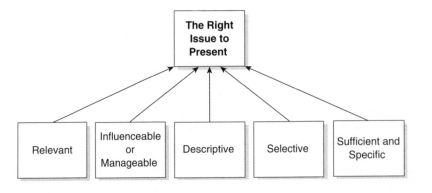

Figure 8.2 Selecting and Prioritizing Themes

Feedback

After the data are analyzed, sorted, and selected for the degree to which they will energize action, the practitioner shares these findings with the client. This can take the form of a written feedback report, a feedback meeting, or most likely both. How and when the feedback is presented is best discussed as a part of the contracting process (Noolan, 2006). As a practical matter, creating a report and sending it to a client is not a very difficult process. As Argyris (1970) writes,

> If the basic objective of feedback is simply to offer a clear presentation of results, the interventionist need only develop a well-written, well-bound, easily understood report . . . and select a capable lecturer who will tend to prevent difficulties from developing. (p. 322)

The feedback meeting has a more important purpose, however, in engaging the client in taking action. To do that, the change agent's presentation of the data can put even the most willing client at a crossroads of what may be a difficult and even personally painful process.

Feedback to a client, even if the client has invited it, can be a sensitive process with high anxiety for both the consultant and the client. The client has exposed the organization to the consultant, and as a part of the system, the client is implicated in its problems. Even if the data are not about the client but about the organization in general, the client may see the feedback meeting as a personal and professional evaluation of competence. Because the objective of data gathering is often to develop a description of the problem that enhances what is understood by the client, the tacit implication in a feedback session may be that the client did not adequately understand the problem, and such a situation can produce a "sense of inadequacy [that] can arouse anxieties and guilt feelings" (Argyris, 1970, p. 323). The client may become defensive and resist the data in ways we will describe later. To maximize the likelihood that the client will receive and understand the feedback and be motivated to take action, the feedback meeting must be set up for success by creating an environment in which exploration of issues, learning, and action planning are possible.

Feedback has both motivating and directing functions (Nadler, 1977). Feedback *motivates* action when it is inconsistent with what is already believed, so that it produces a level of discomfort and the recipient is prompted to take different actions to reach different results. Feedback also *directs* attention to the *right set* of actions that will produce better results. Not all feedback will motivate or direct change, however. The data will not produce energy if they violate the characteristics described earlier. If the information is not seen as relevant, specific, or sufficient, for example, the client will resist it.

Structuring the Feedback Meeting

Organization development practitioners should consider how feedback meetings can be set up for success even before they begin. The practitioner should think carefully about the environment in which the meeting will be held and whether it is conducive to learning, exploration, and dialogue in a confidential setting. If the client's office is a desk in an open room in which other organizational members frequently walk in and out, the client will not be focused enough to hear the feedback and confidentiality may be violated. Other common interruptions in a client's office such as a ringing telephone, frequent visitors, and the immediacy of incoming e-mails all can be distracting. For this reason, it may be useful to choose a different locale. Also, enough time should be dedicated to the meeting so that the consultant can review the contract, the data, details behind the data, and discuss actions or interventions. Too little time will not allow the issues to be explored fully in a single meeting. Even seating matters, as well. Sitting across from the client can create an adversarial environment where client and consultant seem to be working against one another. Sitting at a round table or side by side looking at notes or a presentation may create a more collaborative environment.

Experienced practitioners have developed their own preferences for how to structure the feedback process. Levinson (1994), for example, recommends that the consultant and client agree to set aside the last 2 hours of one workday and the first 2 hours of the next morning for review and discussion. In the first session, he reads the report to the client aloud, and only then gives the client a copy of the report for review in the evening. The following morning, the client, after having read the report alone and considered it, works with the practitioner to clarify the issues and to develop action plans. Block (2000) takes a different approach, quickly reviewing the original contract and presenting findings, with the bulk of the meeting dedicated to exploring client reactions, discussing recommendations, and deciding what actions to take next. He argues that most practitioners spend too much time on the data and themes so that little time remains to explore how the client feels about the data and what should be done with the feedback. To take yet a third approach, Argyris (1970) refuses to develop recommendations on the grounds that the clients must own the feedback as well as the recommendations. He argues that providing recommendations robs the client of the opportunity to explore and internalize the issues first.

Giving an early copy of the feedback to the client can be a double-edged sword. On the one hand, the client has the opportunity to review it before a personal meeting and may be better prepared to accept particularly difficult feedback after a few days of absorbing its meaning and implications. On the other hand, action-oriented clients may be tempted to act hastily on the feedback before discussing the data with the practitioner and may act on a misunderstanding or emotional reaction. The practitioner alone can make this determination based on personal preference, experience, and knowledge of the client.

Presenting Data in the Feedback Meeting

The discussion in the feedback meeting presents several opportunities to increase or to decrease client acceptance of the data. Here are a number of recommendations for managing the feedback session and presenting the data:

- Even though the client may see it as ritualistic, begin with positive data. Encourage the client to accept and appreciate the organization's strengths. This is a fine approach as long as the feedback is genuine and authentic. To some clients, this can feel like being set up before being hit with the bad news. Understanding strengths can be especially helpful when the client can use them to compensate for or to address weaknesses.

- Ensure that the themes described in the feedback report provide enough detail to be accurately defined and useful. Some consultants pick one or two representative quotes from interviews as an explanation of a particular theme. One caution in using this approach is that quotes can contain identifying information that may violate an interviewee's anonymity. Beyond the simple category label "improve team meetings," the practitioner should be able to define what interviewees wanted improved.

- Quantitative data can illustrate trends and how widespread agreement is across the organization, but they can also provide too much detail for clients. A healthy sprinkling of statistics may be all that is necessary to illuminate the trends.

- Language choices are important in presenting the data. Using nonevaluative descriptive language such as "employees mentioned that decision making on the executive team seemed slow" will be feedback that is more likely to be accepted and acted upon than "you are a slow decision maker." Also report "the specific impact on self or other's behavior, attitude, or value" (Golembiewski, 1979a, p. 65) so that it is not just the behavior that is understood, but the implications of it as well.

- A common problem is that the practitioner will project his or her own feelings on the client (Block, 2000; Scott, 2000). The practitioner may assume that the client will be angry, hurt, or embarrassed, because that is how the consultant might feel in the same situation. Consequently the practitioner makes assumptions about the client's feelings instead of focusing on the facts.

- "Be willing to confront the tough issues" (Scott, 2000, p. 149). However painful it may be for the consultant to say or for the client to hear, it is necessary to share. Avoid minimizing the feedback in order to create a harmonious relationship or to avoid upsetting the client (for example, by saying "I've seen many managers have this same problem," or "I do the same thing myself"). Such statements water down the significance of the message and encourage the client not to take it seriously.

Recognizing Resistance

The diagnostic process and the feedback meeting can surface negative feelings about change that the client may be unable or unwilling to address, including feelings of loss of control, that are common when one's ideas and beliefs are confronted by new data. A client's resistance to the data and to taking action is a natural part of the process and is commonly expressed in feedback settings. Resistance can also be frustrating for the change agent, who may harbor a fantasy that "if our thinking is clear and logical, our wording is eloquent, and our convictions are solid, the strength of our arguments will carry the day" (Block, 2000, p. 21), but just as organizational problems are often both technical (e.g., the strategy is unclear) and personal (e.g., employees lack motivation), a client's reaction to feedback is often both rational and emotional. No matter how good the data collection and thematic analysis, an emotional response is likely. Resistance is a reaction to the emotions being brought up by uncertainty and fear. Resistance is not always negative, however. It may also be a healthy coping and protective mechanism, as change can threaten the status quo and the ability for the organization to achieve its objectives (Gallagher, Joseph, & Park, 2002). Recognizing resistance is an important skill, and the ability to work with it is an even more advanced skill.

People resist change for a variety of reasons. O'Toole (1995) provides a list of 33 reasons that lie at the heart of resistance to change, including fear of the unknown, fatigue over too much change, cynicism that change is possible, and a desire to keep the status quo and one's comfortable habits. A comprehensive description of client resistance is found in Block (2000), who describes the following 14 ways that it may be expressed by clients:

1. *Give me more detail.* The client continually asks for more data, more descriptions, and more information. Even when presented with the extra facts, it is not enough and even more is desired.

2. *Flood you with detail.* The client spends most of the meeting talking, providing history, background, and commentary on not only the immediate situation but tangential issues, too.

3. *Time.* Resistance is expressed as a complaint about not having enough time to complete the project, to gather data, to meet to discuss the diagnosis and feedback, or to plan the intervention.

4. *Impracticality.* The client complains that the solutions are not practical or feasible in this group, this division, this company, this industry, and so on. This may be expressed as a complaint about what works in "theory" versus what will work "here."

5. *I'm not surprised.* The client accepts the feedback and diagnosis with agreement, nodding that it makes perfect sense. "Of course that is what is happening; it is what I knew all along," the client seems to be saying, avoiding the discomfort that can arise by being confronted with new information.

6. *Attack.* Direct attack is a clear form of resistance, when the client expresses anger, frustration, and irritation through a raised voice and angry words. It is among the easiest to recognize because it is the most explicit.

7. *Confusion.* Much like a desire for more information, the client wants another explanation, expressed in a different way. Then this explanation seems unclear and another is requested.

8. *Silence.* The client remains silent during the entire presentation, and the consultant may be tempted to keep pressing forward until the client speaks up. If confronted, the client may say that the presentation is "fine" or "good," or that "nothing occurs to me to say at the moment, but keep going."

9. *Intellectualizing.* The client asks about underlying theory, perhaps desiring models or articles that apply to this situation. Instead of planning or discussing action, the client prefers to philosophize about the organization and its theoretical patterns.

10. *Moralizing.* The client wants to blame others, often as a group, stating what they should be doing or what they do not understand. Moralizing shifts the focus away from the client's own actions and sets up a hierarchical and non-cooperative situation.

11. *Compliance.* Compliance with the consultant's proposal may be the most challenging for a consultant to see. After all, it is validating to work with a willing client who apparently sees the value in the change agent's proposed solutions. Underneath the agreement, however, lies doubts and reservations. When the time comes to take action, the client finds a reason to delay. If no doubts are expressed and everything seems perfect, the client may be compliant on the surface, but simmering underneath.

12. *Methodology.* As Block (2000) puts it, "questions about method represent legitimate needs for information for the first ten minutes" (p. 146). Beyond that, a barrage of methods questions may represent an attempt to invalidate the feedback and avoid taking action.

13. *Flight into health.* When the time comes to accept the feedback and take action as a result of it, the issue that the client noted in the first meeting has mysteriously vanished. It becomes easier to ignore the problem or change one's opinion of it than it is to take a risk in trying to address it.

14. *Pressing for solutions.* The client expresses frustration at any additional explanation about the problem, where it came from, who is involved, what problems underlie the presenting problem, and so on, pressing the practitioner to get to the point where solutions are described. As we have already learned, however, clients who do not understand the problem are less likely to solve it effectively.

Each of these expressions of resistance may at its heart be a desire to avoid, downplay, redirect, invalidate, or delay internalization of the feedback and taking action. If it were expressed directly, it could be understood and discussed, but when it is indirect and covert, it looks like a different conversation. The change agent who addresses the surface conversation (perhaps responding as requested with additional data or solutions) but who does not address the underlying concerns will be surprised later at the client's subtle delays to taking action.

Many change agents approach a feedback meeting bracing themselves for resistance, but secretly hoping that it is never expressed, desiring to meet with a client who enthusiastically embraces the feedback and looks forward to the opportunity to take action. When that does not happen, they leave despondent and look at their own presentation or action for clues about what they did wrong. They lose hope themselves that change is possible and begin to wonder whether this was a project they should have taken.

A more effective route is to realize that resistance is a natural and expected part of the OD process and to learn how to find words that aid the client in describing what they are resisting. The best prepared consultants will learn how to recognize the forms of resistance that Block describes and to learn what questions or statements will best help the client to express the resistance more authentically. Asking the compliant client "What reservations or concerns do you have about these results?" can make it acceptable to express those concerns if the client did not feel comfortable stating them earlier. To the client who expresses numerous concerns about methodology: "You seem to have a number of concerns about the methods by which I found these themes. Is there something in the data that is making you uncomfortable?" It can be challenging for many change agents to ask such a direct question, but it can also help to diffuse tension by allowing it to be expressed and addressed honestly. Consider looking back at each of Block's 14 kinds of resistance and deciding what you would do if confronted with a client who demonstrated it.

The client may not be resisting when he or she refuses to continue with the project. A direct and honest statement of reluctance to continue with a project is an acceptable conclusion to a feedback meeting, however unfortunate it may feel for the change agent. The client may genuinely understand the data but choose to take no action. Perhaps the next step is not clear or the organization's political environment makes it personally risky for the client to take action. That is not an indictment of the practitioner's process, but it is a conscious choice on the client's part, and it is not a form of resistance (Block, 2000). The practitioner can be confident that the right data were presented and fed back, and the client exercised the right to conclude the engagement.

Ethical Issues With Diagnosis and Giving Feedback

The diagnosis and feedback phases of the organization development process provide a number of potential ethical dilemmas for the change agent. First among them is the possibility of using data in the feedback meeting in a manner that violates the anonymity of the participants. A client may desire to know which quote came from which interviewee, or more subtly, whether it was from the morning shift or the evening shift, or whether it was from a long-tenured employee or a new one. The client may want to read all comments verbatim rather than a subset or a summary of them. Each of these requests presents an ethical dilemma for the consultant who would like to make the data known in order for the client to appropriately interpret and act upon the information but who also owes anonymity to the participants.

In the data analysis phase, the practitioner faces the dilemma of interpreting data in a way that genuinely reflects the data, not the practitioner's own choices of issues or concerns. The consultant may be tempted to highlight, omit, or distort particular points in the data. This can be especially true for internal consultants who may have a personal stake in what data the client sees and chooses to address (White & Wooten, 1983).

In the feedback meeting, the greatest ethical dilemma occurs when the consultant chooses to collude with the client by avoiding or minimizing difficult feedback. This kind of dilemma means that "objectivity is lost. This can occur through assimilation of the change agent into the organizational culture of the client system" (White & Wooten, 1985, p. 149). Most consultants do not desire to intentionally cause personal hurt or to inflict emotional distress on their clients. When they discover through the data gathering process that organizational members find their manager incompetent or aloof, the consultant may be reluctant to address it for fear of the manager's emotional response. It is true that the change agent can face some challenging conversations, but as Block (2000) writes, "The client has the right to all the information that you have collected" (p. 219).

Summary

The diagnosis and feedback phases translate the volume of data gathered into meaningful insights that expand the client's understanding of the presenting problem and feed it back in ways that help the client to take action. In the diagnosis phase, the change agent uses deductive, inductive, and/or statistical techniques to sort and interpret data. Deductive techniques commonly involve models that help the consultant to organize the data using predetermined category labels. Inductive analysis techniques use the data itself to create categories not previously defined. Both are common techniques and have different advantages and disadvantages. Armed with a set of key themes from the data, the change agent selects among them which to share with the client. Some data will be more useful and energizing to the client than others. The most energizing data will be relevant, issues that the client can influence, descriptive, selective, sufficient, and specific. In a carefully thought-out feedback meeting, these themes are shared with the client. The feedback meeting is an opportunity to return to the client's initial presenting problem and to share what the data say about any underlying issues or problems that may expand the client's views. This can be a difficult conversation in which the client may express resistance to the data or to acting on the information, and the best response to an expression of resistance is for the change agent to understand what is being expressed at a deeper level and to learn how to bring out the client's genuine underlying concerns. Consultants act ethically in the diagnosis and feedback stages when they use the data ethically, bring up the issues from the data, distortion-free, avoiding collusion or omissions of difficult problems.

In the case study that follows, you will have the opportunity to analyze data, to choose key themes, and to structure a client feedback meeting in which you would present it.

For Further Reading

Block, P. (2000). *Flawless consulting: A guide to getting your expertise used* (2nd ed.). New York: Jossey-Bass.

Burke, W. W. (1994). Diagnostic models for organization development. In A. Howard & associates (Eds.), *Diagnosis for organizational change: Methods and models* (pp. 53–84). New York: Guilford.

Harrison, M. I., & Shirom, A. (1999). *Organizational diagnosis and assessment: Bridging theory and practice.* Thousand Oaks, CA: Sage.

Nadler, D. (1977). *Feedback and organization development: Using data-based methods.* Reading, MA: Addison-Wesley.

Case Study 3: Sorting Through the Data From Logan Elementary School

The following data are quotes taken from interviews of parents, faculty, and staff of an elementary school by request of the school's principal, Nancy:

1. Organize these data to present to Nancy. Notice demographic details such as grade level, interviewee role, and tenure.

2. Try organizing the data a different way. Did you notice anything different from the first time you analyzed the data? Which method do you think was more effective?

3. How would you structure the feedback meeting with Nancy? Which themes would you present and why?

Logan Elementary School is a suburban, Grades 1–6 elementary school in a middle-class district in the southwestern United States. It is a large school campus with five wings, each with six to eight classrooms. Grades 1–3 (lower grades) are located in wings A and B, while Grades 4–6 (upper grades) are located in wings C, D, and E. The school was built in the late 1980s, though it was recently painted in bright colors, showcasing three elaborate murals, with funds raised from the Parents Association.

You have been called in as the organization development practitioner to help the principal better develop relationships among the school's faculty and staff. There are 38 faculty members, eight staff members, and a part-time librarian at the school. The principal, Nancy Mestas, 2 years into her role at this school, wants to improve relationships among faculty and staff, build consistency in approach among teachers at each grade level, and improve the relationship between the school and the community. She has made several dramatic changes over the past year.

You agreed to conduct interviews of staff members, faculty members, and parents over the course of one week to better understand the issues facing the school. With interviewees, you agreed that all interviews would be documented anonymously and data would be shared primarily in summary form, with quotes shared only when a single individual could not be identified. You are scheduled to meet with Nancy next week to present the data and to hold a feedback meeting.

Monday

"Nancy's been just great with the kids. A couple of times she's joined our recess or physical education outdoor activities to cheer them on as they play kickball. They call her 'Miss Nancy.' I've never seen the kids act that way with a principal before." (Teacher, Grade 5)

"I know Nancy wants us all to have a consistent set of books and materials, but that's just not the way I've always worked at this school. I've been here for 9 years and I've always been able to choose my own books. Nancy needs to understand that that's part of the freedom we have in the classroom." (Teacher, Grade 3)

"Faculty meetings are generally productive. It is a good opportunity to meet with other teachers and release the stress of the day." (Teacher, Grade 5)

"Nancy could do a better job of equalizing participation in the faculty meetings." (Teacher, Grade 4)

"The first open house for parents last year was a nice idea. Same thing for the monthly bulletin." (Parent, Grade-6 child)

"Nancy's style has been very easy to work with. She's very accommodating and approachable." (Staff member, 3 years' tenure)

"When she asked Jaime to pick the Grade 3 reading book, the rest of us weren't consulted. I really felt that was unfair, and Nancy seemed to ignore our complaints. I know she wants consistency, but there's a better way to handle that." (Teacher, Grade 3)

"Nancy gives us a lot of support. She has been at every one of our grade-level meetings and has given us a lot of resources from her days as a fifth-grade teacher. I think she understands the challenges we're faced with." (Teacher, Grade 5)

"Nancy has been very supportive of the staff." (Staff member, 2 years' tenure)

Tuesday

"The district's new grade standards have been very frustrating. We were notified just a few weeks before the school year began—didn't Nancy know about this?—and we had to scramble to meet the new expectations. I basically had 2 weeks to redo my entire plan for September and October. Nancy didn't seem to have much sympathy. She just said, 'We all have to be flexible.'" (Teacher, Grade 2)

"Faculty meetings never seem to get around to any of the topics that I'm concerned about. They're run in a rigid and inflexible manner and we can never bring up any new topics unless we've reserved time on the agenda 2 days in advance. Sometimes things just come up and you need to have them addressed." (Teacher, grade unknown)

"I've been impressed by some of the changes that I've seen over the past year. I really like the new monthly bulletin for parents. It helps me know what Sarah is doing at school." (Parent, Grade-5 child)

"The addition of voice mail has been a helpful communication mechanism to be able to contact the teachers whenever I have a question about my son's homework." (Parent, Grade-2 child)

"I don't feel that Nancy has been accessible to me. I have tried several times to reach her to share my concerns regarding our textbook selection and she has been too busy to meet with me." (Teacher, Grade 3)

"Working with Nancy in the office has been excellent. It's been a huge improvement over the previous principal." (Staff member, 5 years' tenure)

"The upper grade teachers seem to get most of the attention. We hardly ever see Nancy in our wing of the school." (Teacher, Grade 1)

"One thing is clear—Nancy has her favorites." (Teacher, Grade 3)

Wednesday

"It's much easier to know what's going on at the school than it used to be. Things like the parents bulletin each month have been a great resource." (Parent, Grade-4 child)

"The kids love it when Nancy comes to read to them in my classroom. She has been very accessible to me and to our class." (Teacher, Grade 5)

"My working relationship with Nancy is good. I have a lot of experience at this school and I think she respects that. My only concern is that sometimes she tends to forget to notify us of some changes (like the lunch schedule last week) and it causes some problems." (Staff member, 8 years' tenure)

"I think that Nancy should have been open with us regarding the reading textbook issue." (Teacher, Grade 3)

"I'm not sure how frequently Nancy interacts with the superintendent or anyone at the district office, but I think it would help if she would build that relationship. We used to have a lot of credibility with the district because our students have been very successful and it would help us in the past when it came to budget time." (Teacher, Grade 4)

"I wish the district had given us some additional funding to deal with the new math standards for our school." (Teacher, Grade 2)

"There are times I think, 'Nancy who?' Except for faculty meetings and memos, I don't think she knows that I even teach here." (Teacher, Grade 2)

Thursday

"As the librarian, I'm only here a few days per week, but I've really appreciated Nancy's efforts to include me in the faculty meetings and treat me like a full-time member of the staff." (Staff member, 4 years' tenure)

"Our faculty meetings are tense and awkward. Only about half of the group participates. I don't generally get a lot out of them." (Teacher, Grade 3)

"I think Nancy is generally doing a good job, though I think she could have fought the district more on the new standards and getting us some additional funds." (Teacher, grade unknown)

"Nancy redirected our arts funds to the Grade 6 teachers this year, so I'm not able to do my spring painting activity like I have done for the past 6 years. I don't think that was right." (Teacher, Grade 2)

"Nancy's really approachable and sympathetic to our concerns. It's nice to have her support." (Teacher, Grade 6)

"I feel that the way that Nancy assigned teachers this year was unfair. I indicated my preference and that was not taken into account. I have never taught a combination class before and it has been a lot of additional work with very little support." (Teacher, Grade 2/3 combination)

"I had the opportunity to meet with the principal and my son's teacher during the first open house. I haven't used the voice mail feature but I do tend to read the monthly bulletins." (Parent, Grade-1 child)

Friday

"Faculty meetings are well run and structured. I don't think everyone participates equally, unfortunately. Nancy sends around an agenda a few days before the meeting, which works well, and I know what to expect and prepare for." (Teacher, Grade 6)

"If there's one complaint I have, it's the budget. We can't even afford construction paper! Everything we're doing is to support the new curriculum standards, and it's wiped out any additional funding for field trips or other projects." (Teacher, Grade 5)

"I have to sympathize with Nancy. The budget was cut at the same time as we had entirely new requirements to meet from the district, and it's been impossible. I wish she were more aggressive in pushing the district." (Teacher, Grade 1)

"I have had a few opportunities to meet one-on-one with the principal because of my daughter and I have found her very approachable." (Parent, Grade-2 child)

"I left a voice mail for Kelly's teacher a few days ago, but I haven't heard back. I'm not sure how useful that is." (Parent, Grade-3 child)

"We have occasionally seen the quarterly parents bulletin that the teacher sends home. It could be more frequent." (Parent, Grade-3 child)

"Nancy has high standards and is demanding, which makes the staff perform at a very high level. At times I think she could include us in some of the communications that are going to all of the teachers so we know what's going on, too." (Staff member, 3 years' tenure)

CHAPTER 9

An Introduction to Interventions

The UK-based client was one of three leading companies in a specialized global market. The past several years had seen a great deal of change in the company's structure and culture that had led to greater market share and faster cycle times to market. External organization development consultants were called in to help the senior management team through a strategic planning workshop, which had not been done for the past 2 years, and which was increasingly becoming necessary given the company's expectations about future growth. A workshop was planned to discuss the company strategy, to assess implications for internal corporate culture, and to develop the skills and capabilities of the senior team. The consultants first conducted individual interviews with the senior team and believed that the team was entirely committed to the workshop's goals and objectives. While they had discussed these objectives with each individual, however, they had never discussed them with the team together.

At the workshop, the consultants noticed a sudden, marked decline in the participants' levels of enthusiasm and energy for the organizational culture and team issues they had agreed to address. Two dominant members refused to address the previously agreed topics of team-building and culture issues. A coalition of the managing director and production director had become evident, and the consultants realized that team members were reluctant to engage in conflict or confront these two forceful teammates. Not only was the strategic planning work the only remaining acceptable topic to the participants, but the company's senior leader now monopolized the discussion, dictating the outcomes. A month after the workshop, the consultants again stressed the need to work on culture and team dynamics in addition to strategy, but the team resisted. The consultants, surprised by the political environment experienced during the intervention that presented a major obstacle to change, realized that the long-term objectives of the engagement had not been achieved (Beeby & Simpson, 1998).

- Was this team ready for change? Why or why not?
- Why did this intervention fail? What factors do you think lead to a successful intervention?

The impatient manager or change agent will have turned to this chapter after reading the table of contents and will want to quickly skim a list of diagnoses and intervention types and choose one to get on with implementing a solution. After all, the intervention stage is explicitly action and solution oriented. Unfortunately, this quick-to-act mentality is too often the case and often results in unsuccessful change. Most organization development (OD) practitioners rightly consider the intervention to be the heart of the consulting engagement and the point at which change usually becomes the overt objective. At the same time, as we have discussed, it is only after the data are collected, discussed, interpreted, and internalized that the client and change agent can be confident that they are choosing the right intervention for the circumstances. It is only when the diagnosis is agreed upon that the natural next step is to answer the question "What should we do about it?" Deciding what to do can be enough of a challenge, but figuring out how to do it well can be even more difficult, as a number of environmental, organizational, and interpersonal factors can present obstacles to an effective intervention.

Yet as we have hinted, intervening has already occurred well before an intervention strategy has been discussed, planned, or implemented. That is, for the change agent, "Everything you do is an intervention" (Schein, 1999, p. 17). In fact, an intervention can be as little as a single question. One internal consultant tells a story of working with a project team that had the responsibility of redefining procurement processes. As the team presented its work to a larger group, the consultant asked a clarifying question. After the employee presenting the process answered the question, another employee spoke out to contradict the presenter, saying that the group had agreed on something different. A lively conversation ensued, and everyone realized that clearly the group had not yet come to agreement. The change agent can also intervene during the data gathering process by asking questions in an interview or focus group, encouraging people to talk explicitly about situations they may not have been consciously aware of. The feedback meeting intervenes by providing information that may be new or may confirm the client's current knowledge. Even the change agent's entry into the system communicates to organizational members that the problem is deserving of an intervention. But it is the intervention stage itself that is arguably the most formal and structured opportunity for organizational change.

In this chapter and the next three, we will discuss many of the most prevalent interventions in use by OD practitioners. In this chapter, we will address why interventions succeed and fail, and examine the consequences of managing an intervention that does not succeed. We will also discuss what factors practitioners consider as they select the right intervention strategy, matched to the data and diagnosis, and how they can structure the intervention activity to maximize the likelihood that it will be successful. Formal studies are not plentiful on the subject, but there are several lessons that practitioners have learned and shared from their experiences about how to select, plan, and structure interventions for success, regardless of the target of the intervention.

In the chapters following this introduction to interventions, we will discuss different kinds of interventions. Interventions can be focused on individuals, teams, multiple groups and teams, the whole organization, and multiple organizations, and they include a wide variety of activities that range from organization design to team building, mentoring, and coaching.

Interventions Defined

Argyris (1970) writes that "to intervene is to enter into an ongoing system of relationships, to come between or among persons, groups, or objects for the purpose of helping them" (p. 15). There are three important points to stress about this definition.

First, the system is ongoing; that is, an intervention enters into the ordinary and continuous stream of organizational life, and as such, it is influenced by all of the complexities inherent in organizations, such as politics, organizational goals and workload, environmental constraints, interpersonal relationships, past history, and more. Because the intervention does not occur in a vacuum, the change agent must be conscious of the relationship between the intervention and the organizational context.

Second, interventions "come between" or deliberately interrupt existing processes, thinking, people, groups, and relationships. Because they often try to unsettle current practices, interventions can be uncomfortable enough that people may not be ready to change and will resist the intervention. Understanding readiness to change is an important part of intervention planning, which we will discuss later in this chapter.

Third, the objective of interventions is to help or to improve the effectiveness of organizations, groups, teams, and individuals. Solving problems, improving relationships, clarifying roles or goals, and building skills are all worthy and common objectives of interventions. Improperly selected and poorly defined and managed interventions do not help, and they can actually hurt.

Interventions consist of two interrelated activities: first, action planning, or devising an appropriate intervention strategy to address the organization's problem(s), and second, implementing the chosen intervention(s) by structuring them to be the most appropriate for the given individual, team, or organization. An intervention can be as small as a single meeting, event, or workshop, or it can be a series of events that help a group or organization change in progressive steps. We refer to the latter as an *intervention strategy* and the former as *intervention activities* or *events*.

An intervention strategy may consist of a number of different events, as may occur in the example that opened this chapter, where consultants proposed strategic planning, executive team building, and cultural change interventions. A process redesign intervention may also include individual skill building and management coaching. For example, Figure 9.1 lists an intervention for a new finance team, with the overall objective being the rapid start-up of a healthy, well-functioning team. The intervention strategy consists of three activities to follow each other in sequence with a 3- to 4-week gap between them. The first activity would be to conduct a team start-up workshop and to discuss the group's strategic plan. The second, to occur a few weeks later, would have the group discuss goals, clarify roles, and continue to build team relationships. In the third activity, again to occur a few weeks later, when the group has worked together for 2 months, the group would

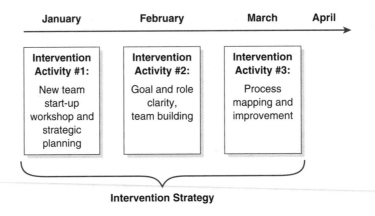

Figure 9.1 An Example of an Intervention Strategy With Three Intervention Activities

map its processes and discuss ways to improve them. While each of the individual events is an intervention (with goals for each individual workshop), they are combined and sequenced into a deliberate and coherent strategy with its own overall objective.

As clients and organizations are different, so too are the interventions that are applied in each case. While there are some standard approaches and ways of conducting interventions, no two applications of an intervention are exactly alike. Each may be adapted or changed somewhat depending on the client or circumstances. Interventions may function differently in different organizations, so flexibility in the application of any intervention is a necessary skill for the change agent. Depending on the organizational structure, processes, age, technology, and cultural factors such as organizational members' tolerance for ambiguity or flexibility, what has worked for one group may not work for another (Meglino & Mobley, 1977).

Why Interventions Fail

Organizational change interventions of the type proposed by many organization development practitioners are implemented in a challenging environment today in which many members may be cynical about change. Many companies choose to implement "fad" programs they have read about in the popular press or heard about from colleagues in other organizations. They start up initiatives such as Total Quality Management, empowerment, or reengineering programs, only to see them result in little or no change, and then they give up on the program (Beer & Eisenstat, 1996; Hedge & Pulakos, 2002a). Such programs are begun and abandoned with relative frequency, so that most people likely have more practice and experience with unsuccessful interventions than successful ones.

This environment raises the bar for most OD interventions today, and puts additional pressure on the practitioner to implement successful programs. Jackson and Manning (1992) write,

Table 9.1 Why Interventions Fail

1. Wrong problem
2. Wrong intervention
3. Unclear or overambitious goals
4. Implementing an event rather than a program
5. Not enough time devoted
6. Poorly designed intervention
7. Unskilled change agent
8. Ownership not transferred to client
9. Resistance to change
10. Lack of readiness for change

No matter how well consultants sell their services, and no matter how pure their motives and insightful their diagnoses, unless interventions are well-conceived, skillfully facilitated, and carried out with client commitment, the intended changes in the client system will not be likely to occur. (p. 5)

Indeed, interventions fail to achieve their desired objectives and result in lasting organizational change for a number of reasons (see Table 9.1), including the following:

1. *The intervention tried to solve the wrong problem.* Stories abound of organizations that sent all managers to training only to realize too late that the real problem was an ineffective performance management process. Or, change agents may be called in to conduct team-building interventions when the real problem was the manager's ineffective leadership. Solving the wrong problem is often a result of a poor (or nonexistent) data gathering and diagnostic process. Consultants who consent to a client's definition of the problem may conduct an intervention resulting in little or no change because the client had a limited view of the problem and the consultant failed to investigate further. As Weisbord (1976) puts it in relation to the Six-Box Model, interventions solve the wrong problem when "the intervention deals with the wrong (less salient) blip on the radar screen" (p. 445). Many managers choose to terminate an underperforming employee, thinking that the problem belongs to a single individual, only to find that the next person in the job is equally unsuccessful. They blame the person rather than examine the systemic problems that contribute to poor performance. Often when we leap to conclusions without proper data, we solve the wrong problem.

2. *The wrong intervention was selected.* In other words, multiple interventions were possible, and the problem was the right one to address, but the primary activity selected did not have the most relevance for the circumstances. Perhaps team

building may have been an appropriate intervention, but a poorly designed process had more influence on customer satisfaction and should have been the initial target for an intervention. Perhaps the intervention began at the senior management level, when training of the frontline salespeople would have had a greater impact. Often change agents and clients are concerned with implementing an intervention effectively and do not necessarily stop to examine whether the right intervention was chosen in the first place.

3. *Goals were ambiguous, unclear, or too lofty.* The outcomes of the intervention were not clearly articulated or were not possible to achieve through a certain intervention event. The client may have unrealistic expectations that sales would double, customer complaints would be cut in half, or employee turnover would stop entirely.

4. *The intervention was undertaken as an event rather than as a program of activities with multiple targets for change.* Many organizational problems require working at multiple times and levels. For example, to increase the pace of a software development process, there may need to be discussions about providing new tools, software engineers may need to learn how to work differently to solve problems, and managers may need new ways of managing performance and measuring success. A single workshop on only one of these topics is unlikely to produce a long-term change. In addition, if the intervention is considered to be an event rather than a long-term effort, often little follow-up activity occurs and organizational members quickly return to former habits and practices. Finally, interventions undertaken as events may not take the larger organizational context into consideration, so that politics, other team members, the needs of other important and relevant stakeholders, and more will force people back into old routines (Massarik & Pei-Carpenter, 2002).

5. *Not enough time was devoted to change.* Closely related to the previous example, clients or change agents may not devote enough time to making the intervention successful. They may give up too quickly or expect too much too soon.

6. *The intervention was poorly designed to reach the specified goals.* There are a number of important design criteria for successful interventions, including everything from the invitation, the agenda, and the participants to the room setup. Perhaps the attendees did not include the right participants who had the most knowledge or responsibility for making the change occur.

7. *The change agent was not skilled at implementing the intervention.* Perhaps the practitioner had never led a certain intervention before or was a poor facilitator. Dyer (1981) finds that "there seems to be good evidence that one factor in change failure is the effect of change agents trying actions they are not prepared to handle" (p. 65).

8. *Responsibility for change was not transferred to the client.* Organizational members may place responsibility for the change on the change agent and not own the change themselves. When the change agent fails to transfer ownership of the

change to the participants, the change does not last beyond the current engagement. When the change agent leaves, organizational members return to their previous ways.

9. *Organizational members resisted or were not committed to the intervention.* There may not have been agreement about the nature of the problem, or organizational members perceive too much loss, risk, or personal consequences to the intervention. They may have been cynical about the likelihood for change or not motivated to participate.

10. *The organization was not ready for change.* Perhaps the organization faced a chaotic time in which organizational members could not focus on or devote attention to change. Organizational members may not be ready to engage in the emotional cost of confronting an authoritarian manager, or they may consider it too risky. In addition, Nadler and Pecorella (1975) write of organizations that are overloaded: "In its enthusiasm to bring to bear as many resources as possible, an organization may contribute to a lack of coordination and integration of change efforts by having a confusing number of activities going on at the same time" (p. 365).

Last, it is important to be reminded that what counts as a "failed" intervention is a matter of perspective. A client, such as the one in the example that opens this chapter, may be pleased with an intervention that allows a team to avoid uncomfortable conflict or surface past anger and consider it a success to have escaped without discomfort. The change agent may be disappointed that these issues were not addressed, realizing that the underlying problem may never be solved as long as members refuse to engage in these important discussions. The opposite can occur as well—a client may consider an intervention to be a failure because it was difficult to achieve or because it surfaced conflict and negativity, while the practitioner may consider it a success to have exposed underlying conflict that is vital to the team's long-term welfare.

Implications of Failed Interventions

If the only cost of a failed intervention was the time wasted in implementing it, that might be frustrating enough, but the costs of a failed intervention are much higher. The consequences to the change agent include not only losing the current client engagement but developing a poor professional reputation and losing other potential clients (since previous clients will share their experience with others). Argyris (1970) states that consultants who experience failed interventions will become less likely to trust their own instincts and interpretations, and suffer more self-doubt. Organizational members who experience a failed attempt at change, for any of the above reasons, can also face the same self-doubt (e.g., *Is it possible for us to change even if we want to?*) and be less likely to trust their own interpretations (e.g., *Do we really understand our problem?*). Consider some of Argyris's (1970) other effects of a failed intervention on the change agent and how organizational members may experience them as well, as follows:

- *Increase in defensive behavior.* Change attempts may be delayed until every possible factor is taken into consideration to defend against all possible points of failure.
- *Decrease in the use of appropriate coping mechanisms.* There may be an increase in unhealthy expressions of conflict or aggressiveness.
- *Increase in psychological tiredness.* Few members have the energy to devote to another change project.
- *Decrease in tolerance for stress and ambiguity.* Participants experience an increase in frustration and cynicism, or they may become rigid, controlling, or demanding.
- *Increase in unrealistic level of aspiration.* It may be that aspirations become too high for change, or they may be aiming at an inappropriately low standard to avoid risk or failure.

Some of these effects may be visible in an organization, even before a well-meaning change agent approaches organizational members for the first time, as residual effects of previous change attempts. For organizational members in this situation, failure becomes a cycle, a self-fulfilling prophecy that members can feel doomed to hopelessly repeat. Even when surrounded by it, the change agent cannot fall into this same thinking. Change agents need to maintain "confidence in [their] intervention philosophy, [an] accurate perception of stressful reality, [and] trust in [their] own experience of reality" (Argyris, 1970, p. 141). Recall the underlying values of OD—a foundational optimism that change is possible and that people, groups, and organizations are in process, not doomed in a failure cycle. A positive outcome is also an option and, fortunately, success can also become a cycle. As the pattern is broken, organizational members relearn what success feels and looks like, and they are increasingly able to make it happen again. The point is that the significance of selecting the right intervention strategy and managing it well cannot be understated.

Considerations in Selecting the Right Intervention Strategy

How is a change agent to select the right intervention strategy and customize it to the current client when there are so many relevant factors to consider? Early in an engagement, many change agents fear that they will be unable to suggest an appropriate intervention. A more common problem is that the practitioner and client together can generate too many options and may be uncertain which of these to select. No matter how solid the diagnosis, it is not always evident which intervention is best (Dyer, 1981) as various situational elements come into consideration. In fact, selecting the right approach is more than a matter of finding the best OD technique to solve the client's problem. Johns (1993) finds that the best choices of an intervention are not always the ones to be adopted, as political interests, alliances, and other contextual factors present obstacles to the selection of an intervention. A given intervention strategy will be more effective if it takes the following points into consideration:

1. *Matching the intervention to the data and diagnosis.* Perhaps the most important criterion in the selection of any intervention is what Bowers, Franklin, and Pecorella (1975) called the *principle of congruence*: "Change activities must be matched appropriately with the nature of the problems and their cases and with the nature of the organizational units under consideration" (p. 406). As discussed above, one of the biggest dangers to an effective intervention occurs when the intervention is not matched to the diagnosis and either the wrong problem is solved or the intervention is not designed to solve the agreed-upon problem. (Recall Argyris's point about the necessity of "valid information" in making a diagnosis.) This can sometimes occur when change agents determine what intervention should be implemented "without careful consideration as to whether that type of method is indeed suited for the organization's particular problems" (Kilmann & Mitroff, 1979, p. 26). This danger is echoed by Massarik and Pei-Carpenter (2002), who write that many OD practitioners "do a particular thing and that's that. They may try to apply an intervention simply because it is their specialty, without clear-cut focus in context of what is required, as long as the client buys it" (p. 109). The best lesson is that taught by Hanson and Lubin (1995), who remind us of the following:

> Regardless of how attractive some of these techniques are, consultants must always ask themselves, "Is this exercise appropriate or relevant to the learning goals of this client or to the situation being addressed, or is it just one of my favorite interventions?" Remember, it is the client's needs that should be met, not the consultant's. (pp. 114–115)

Practitioners can also use one another's expertise and counsel, by discussing the situation with colleagues or other outsiders to test whether a chosen intervention is indeed the most appropriate for the circumstances. One test is that a given intervention is likely to be well-matched to the diagnosis if it results in a high "probability that the problem will be solved with the least probable recurrence" (Argyris, 1970, p. 170).

2. *Considering client readiness for change.* Readiness refers to the involvement, willingness, energy, time, capability, and motivation of the organization to change (Armenakis, Harris, & Mossholder, 1993; McLachlin, 1999). If the client is not ready or willing to change, then the consulting engagement's goals tend to belong to the change agent, not the client, and any intervention is unlikely to be successful. If a client is willing to change in a certain direction and not another, or has a preference of one intervention over another (both choices being equal otherwise), many consultants suggest starting where the client has energy (Block, 2000; Dyer, 1981; Harrison, 1970; Schein, 1999). Harrison (1970) writes that many consultants overemphasize "the overcoming of resistance to change and have underemphasized the importance of enlisting in the service of change the energies and resources which the client can consciously direct and willingly devote to problem solving" (p. 199).

When readiness is a problem of motivation or willingness to change, Armenakis et al. (1993) write that change agents can increase the organization's readiness for change through three influence strategies:

a. Persuasive communications, both orally and in writing, in which leaders can emphasize the urgency and need for change

b. Participation in meetings or events related to the change, where organizational members can discover the reason for the change themselves, such as examining customer complaint reports or market share data

c. Sharing external information to back up the internal communication with other credible sources, such as news media, reports from consulting firms, or academic research

Readiness can also concern the organization's capability and competence to change. For example, a team may not be capable of changing if a manager does not have the budget authority to purchase new tools for organizational members that are necessary. Organizational members may not have the necessary skills or competence to implement a change effectively. For example, before implementing a new supply chain design that requires employees to aggressively negotiate price breaks with suppliers, appropriate negotiation training may need to be provided.

Scholars have developed a number of instruments to help practitioners assess change readiness. Beckhard and Harris (1987) offer a rough but instructive rating system in which various targets of interventions (e.g., individuals, teams) can be ranked as having high, medium, or low readiness, and high, medium, or low capability for change. Before any intervention begins, low readiness and low capability for change situations can be addressed. More recently, Holt, Armenakis, Feild, and Harris (2007) have tested a "readiness for change" scale that assesses (1) whether organizational members see the organization as engaging in an appropriate change program, (2) whether they believe management support exists for the change, (3) whether they believe the organization is capable to be successful at the change, and (4) whether they believe the change would be advantageous to them personally.

In conclusion, the right intervention has been selected if the client, change agent, and organizational members are confident that the organization is ready and capable of implementing it to achieve change.

3. *Deciding where to intervene first.* Where to begin can be one of the most challenging questions to face:

- Should the problem be addressed first at the frontline, or with senior management?
- Should we tackle the task issues first, or should we begin with the relationship issues?
- Should we begin with a pilot project in one group, or implement organizationwide from the start?
- Organizational structure or process?
- Easiest change to implement or most difficult?

Unfortunately, there is no step-by-step recipe that will address these questions, but experts advise that "if one asks questions systematically, one is likely to come up with better judgments and better choices than otherwise" (Beckhard & Harris, 1987, p. 73). Asking questions about the client's goals, the organizational culture, motivation, and the other considerations identified in this chapter likely will help to narrow choices and select an appropriate starting point. In addition, Beckhard and Harris (1987) note that changing an established system using its established processes can be quite difficult, since it can be challenging for organizational members to step outside of current practices in order to change them. They recommend the establishment of "temporary systems" such as pilot programs.

Many consultants recommend starting with task interventions over personal or relationship interventions. Harrison (1970) notes that in his experience, intervening first at the level of the interpersonal relationship often makes organizational members uncomfortable, and he finds that they react with a high level of negativity. When he shifts his strategy to focus on the group's tasks and processes, such as communication patterns, roles, decision making, meetings, and so on, the group rarely resists him and complaints about the intervention stop. "Members who exhibit hostility, passivity, and dependence when I initiate intervention at the interpersonal level may become dramatically more active, collaborative, and involved when I shift the focus to the instrumental level" (Harrison, 1970, p. 200). After working at the task level, the change agent may build enough trust and credibility with a client that deeper personal issues can be discussed. Schein (1999) agrees, writing that the primary task is the most direct contribution that the change agent has been asked to make. He argues that interpersonal issues should be observed and only targeted for intervention if the client specifically wants to do so. Beer (1980) argues that it is more efficient to begin with process interventions and to follow them with individual interventions, as individuals can be given an opportunity to experience a new process, which will then surface data about individual needs, such as training. Golembiewski (1979b) notes that some organizations such as the military may not be "culturally prepared" (p. 332) for the interpersonal depth of some interventions and might be better served by starting with structure, task, and policy activities.

Beer and Eisenstat (1996) offer a somewhat different perspective. They agree that task-related interventions are more easily "sold" to organizations because they are seen as more germane by organizational members, yet they also note that "interventions that focus on harder elements of structure and systems typically do not develop the softer elements of skill, values, and leadership" (p. 599) and recommend an integrated approach. In some organizations, the task intervention may only be able to accomplish so much without intervening in the accompanying interpersonal dynamics.

Finally, the complexity of many changes may dictate starting smaller at first. While a number of interventions may be appropriate, "There are limits, it seems, to the number of interventions that an organization can sustain and benefit from" (Mohrman, Mohrman, & Ledford, 1989, p. 150). It may be that either a smaller scope or a pilot team can build a client's confidence that larger changes can be successful, and organizational learning from the initial activity can provide valuable insights that can help with later implementation.

4. *Considering depth of intervention.* Reddy (1994) argues that there are five levels of depth to groups:

a. The work content

b. Overt group issues such as communication and conflict

c. Hidden group issues such as coalitions and power

d. Values and beliefs

e. The unconscious (p. 93)

The first two are at a surface level and are most easily observed, whereas the final three often lie beneath the surface. While interventions can be targeted at any of these levels, Harrison (1970) argues that a change agent should intervene no deeper than necessary to achieve the client's objective. For example, clarifying roles or building new skills are relatively surface-level interventions. An example of going deeper might be an intervention to address job satisfaction or discussions of communication patterns, expectations, or styles, or a manager's ability to delegate. Still deeper might be interventions targeting a group's level of openness and trust, or team members' accountability or commitment to the success of the team. Harrison writes that the deeper the intervention,

- The less information is available, since individual emotions become involved
- The individual as the target of the intervention becomes more likely, as compared with changes in organizational processes or structures
- The more personal risk and uncertainty is involved
- The more dependent individuals become on the skills of the change agent
- The less likely the results of the intervention are to become transferred to others

The more the purpose of the intervention deals with surface issues (such as role clarity or process design), the less deep the intervention needs to go to address them. Deeper interventions may also be less appropriate for groups that are relatively new, meet infrequently, have a short life span, or work on technical rather than interactive tasks (Reddy, 1994).

5. *Considering sequence of activities.* When an intervention strategy consists of a number of separate activities, change agents should think about how those events are sequenced for maximum benefit. Beer (1980, p. 217) lists six considerations for how different intervention activities should be sequenced in an overall intervention strategy:

- *Maximize diagnostic data.* Interventions that provide more data about the organization should be conducted first to allow better customization for those that follow.
- *Maximize effectiveness.* Initial interventions should build enthusiasm for a change or confidence in success so that later interventions can be more effective.

- *Maximize efficiency.* Interventions should conserve time, energy, and money to the extent possible.
- *Maximize speed.* Interventions should be structured so that they do not interrupt the client's desire for the pace of change.
- *Maximize relevance.* Interventions should be chosen so that the primary problem is addressed first.
- *Minimize psychological and organizational strain.* Early interventions should be safer and produce low anxiety.

Table 9.2 summarizes these five considerations for choosing the right intervention strategy. They are guidelines; they may even contradict each other in certain situations. The best practice is to work closely with the client to determine what engagement is most appropriate for the problem and the client organization.

Table 9.2 Selecting the Right Intervention

1. Match the intervention to the data and diagnosis.
2. Consider client readiness for change.
3. Decide where to intervene first.
4. Consider depth of intervention.
5. Consider sequence of intervention activities.

An additional approach to selecting the right intervention is to create a table such as the one shown in Table 9.3, listing the key theme from the data or the problem being experienced by the client, along with the consequences or effects of the problem, its possible cause, and a possible intervention to address that issue. Listing out the possible interventions and analyzing them together with the considerations listed here may help the change agent and client logically sort through which are most or least appropriate for the situation, and which may be appropriately combined into an overall intervention strategy. It may be helpful to construct a chart like this one to help a client see the possible interventions and to prioritize those that the client finds most relevant and useful for the circumstances.

Structuring and Planning Interventions for Success

Regardless of which intervention is chosen, it is important to be conscious of why and how the intervention strategy is intended to work, since "effective change is brought about by planned, integrated interventions which work consistently on a number of different behavioral and organizational targets" (Nadler & Pecorella, 1975, p. 363). Effective and long-term change is also most likely when

Table 9.3 Choosing an Intervention

Problem, Issue, or Theme From Data	Consequences or Implication of Problem	Possible Cause	Possible Intervention
Conflict between marketing and sales with regard to customer discount levels.	Loss of revenue as sales gives significant discounts.	Approval process for discounting is inconsistent and unclear.	Intergroup intervention and process design
Sales is missing deadlines on proposals to customers.	Low customer satisfaction with proposal content, missed revenue opportunities.	Unclear who is responsible for getting proposal content completed.	Role analysis

the intervention is well structured for success. The structure of intervention activities, and how organization development practitioners plan and facilitate them, relies heavily on the foundational values on which OD is based.

Chin and Benne (1976) write of three approaches to change: The first is an *empirical-rational* approach, in which change is accomplished by persuading people that a change is necessary, providing data to support the argument, and justifying the need for change. A second approach they term *normative-reeducative,* which is based on the notion that change will occur when people change their attitudes, values, skills, and relationships, and when group norms encourage new behaviors rather than old ones. A third strategy they define as a *power-coercive* approach, based on policy, law, economic incentives or punishment, guilt, and embarrassment. OD interventions are primarily normative-reeducative approaches to change, and as such are constructed so that as participants accomplish the content work of the intervention, individuals and groups can also develop new attitudes, skills, beliefs, and values.

Three important principles on which OD interventions are structured include creating opportunities for learning, giving free choice to participate, and presenting clear and explicit outcomes.

Creating Opportunities for Learning. As we have said, the objective of OD is to improve organizational effectiveness, and learning and growth is a central value. For interventions, this implies that they should be developed as opportunities for learning. Argyris (1970) writes that "one of the most important sets of criteria . . . is to generate choices that enhance system competence" (p. 170). In other words, the intervention not only solves the immediate problem, but it also provides organizational members the opportunity to examine how the problem-solving process occurs so that the activity enhances their ability to solve problems like this in the future. This can occur through a number of means, such as experiential exercises and opportunities for reflective discussion on both the content and the process of the intervention. OD practitioners can also develop opportunities for low-risk experimentation and exploration so that organizational members can try out new ideas and analyze the outcomes. By participating in such experiential and reflective activities, organizational members become more conscious of their choices and patterns.

Giving Free Choice. Free choice implies both choice to participate in the activity and legitimate choices in directing its outcomes. "Intervention activity, no matter what its substantive interests and objectives, should be so designed and executed that the client system maintains its discreteness and autonomy" (Argyris, 1970, p. 17). The intervention should not be structured to accomplish what the change agent wants the group to do, but what the client thinks should be accomplished in consultation with the change agent. To the extent possible, participants should be given the opportunity to attend or not to attend, free from shame or coercion. OD practitioners should avoid situations in which an unwilling client is being forced or coerced to participate in coaching sessions. Team members should not be pressured into revealing more of their personal background, history, values, or beliefs than they so desire. Leaders should not be "set up" so that they feel as though they have little choice but to accept a task force's recommendations or risk further alienation from the team, or to be "ambushed" with a team confrontation.

Yet free choice does not necessarily mean that every part of the intervention is open for a collaborative decision. For example, organizational members participating in a process design may not have the ability to choose new technology or hire additional staff. They may need to be informed about what approvals may be necessary after they design the process. Free choice in this context implies that if the intervention is designed to develop a new process, and participants are told what the boundary conditions are for the process, the leader will not bring a predesigned process after a group has developed its own and dictate its implementation. Clients occasionally prefer to structure intervention activities so that their preferred outcome is the only seemingly reasonable solution, providing the illusion of choice. Such manipulation often results in little or no commitment to the final solution by organizational members.

Providing Clear and Explicit Outcomes. Change agents should be forthright about what the intervention activities are designed to accomplish. Effective client relationships are founded on authenticity and trust of both client and change agent. If the meeting is designed to help a manager to better understand how her leadership style affects the group, then the change agent must not trick or manipulate the manager into attending by hiding or glossing over the meeting's purpose. If the meeting will be a confrontation between two groups that do not work well together, then attendees should be informed about that as the target of the intervention. The risks of participation should be known to participants and, to the extent they can be predicted, should be shared in advance of an intervention.

Practicalities in Intervention Design

Everything about an intervention should be consistently directed toward its outcomes. Unfortunately, the objectives of the intervention and its design are often in conflict. The most flagrant violation of this practice occurs when, for example, a group wanting to engage in more effective collaboration is forced to sit through a 1-hour lecture from a leader on how to engage in collaboration (not modeling a very collaborative event). Instead, if collaboration is the goal, participants should be given the opportunity to practice it from the start. They can be given a small task to accomplish in groups of three, for example. This contrasts with a common start to many meetings in which the change agent and client define the agenda, give a motivational speech, and ask participants to introduce themselves by sharing their favorite vacation spots.

The room and room setup matter as well to the achievement of a successful intervention. Putting people in close proximity in a circle with moveable chairs is more likely to result in participation and an actively engaged group than holding a design session in an auditorium with fixed chairs (Block, 2000). Tueke (2005) observes that "most meeting rooms block participation rather than beckon it by the arrangement of the furnishings" (p. 75) by putting people in lecture-style or theater seating that does not allow participants to make eye contact easily with one another. Tueke has developed an instructive guide for facilitators that outlines how room size and layout, physical arrangement of chairs, and lighting and sound can be organized to encourage participation.

The point is that the design of the session should role model what is expected out of it. If change is the goal, then each meeting has the opportunity to reinforce it through the structure of the meeting agenda and space.

The Change Agent's Role in the Intervention

The intervention stage presents the change agent and client with another opportunity to negotiate roles. Will the change agent "be an active participant in the project or more of an outside expert/adviser?" (Stroh & Johnson, 2006, p. 139). Stroh and Johnson (2006) write that some consultants take on highly involving roles where they essentially become "surrogate managers" (p. 139), whereas others may choose to substantially decrease involvement after their recommendations are made. While too much ownership of the change is probably inappropriate, so is too little involvement in the intervention phase, and the right level usually depends on the engagement. The client may prefer that the change agent facilitate a group strategic planning meeting so that the client can participate, or the client may prefer to take ownership of the issues and facilitate alone. In any case, being explicit about roles will help to "avoid duplication or gaps in the execution of the intervention" (Hanson & Lubin, 1995, p. 65). Among the roles that change agents take on in an intervention are the following (see Golembiewski, 1979b, 2000b), each of which can vary in the change agent's involvement:

1. *Facilitative:* Helping a client or group attain its desired outcomes by clarifying alternatives, processes, and decisions

2. *Gatekeeping:* Acting as a boundary-spanner between groups or between a supervisor and a team, negotiating between them and giving objective feedback

3. *Diagnostic:* Pointing out what has been seen, heard, or learned to enhance group or individual awareness

4. *Architectural:* Designing situations, events, and conversations so that awareness, learning, and change can occur

5. *Mobilizing:* Advocating for a particular approach or perspective

While the change agent is likely to be active during the intervention stage, eventually it may be most appropriate for the change agent's involvement to become more limited over time as the responsibility for sustaining the change will need to be transferred to the client.

Ethical Issues With Interventions

The action planning and intervention stages of an organization development engagement represent arguably the highest susceptibility for ethical conflict (White & Wooten, 1983, 1985). "During this stage collusion of parties, technical ineptness, and value and goal conflict can create dilemmas resulting in inappropriate choice of change goals, targets, depth, and method due to a lack of skill, objectivity, or differing needs and orientations" (White & Wooten, 1985, p. 141). We have already discussed the importance of and considerations in selecting the right intervention. It is important to note that for many OD practitioners, selecting the right intervention rises to the status of an ethical issue. Other ethical challenges include the following possibilities.

Misrepresentation of the Intervention. Change agents may be tempted to misrepresent the time, cost, or difficulty of an intervention to please a client, or to overpromise that a given intervention will achieve certain outcomes. The change agent may also be challenged to limit the cost of an intervention to what the client can afford. The following is recommended in these situations:

> The change agent would be well advised to tell the client honestly that it would be better not to start a program at all than to do something that would not be appropriate or would be too limited in scope or impact. (Dyer, 1981, p. 65)

Misrepresentation of the Consultant's Skill Level. As we discussed earlier in this chapter, change agents may also be tempted, consciously or unconsciously, to propose and carry out interventions that are familiar and comfortable to them instead of proposing an intervention that is appropriately matched to the data. The opposite can also occur, when the most appropriate intervention is one with which the change agent has no experience. In these cases, rather than use the client as a test case, the change agent's responsibility is to admit not having conducted such an intervention, perhaps recommending a colleague who can provide assistance.

Collusion With the Client. A common example of collusion occurs when change agents may agree to implement an intervention despite having data to support its use. Collusion can also occur when the consultant becomes a "native" part of the culture and desires to see it succeed, and this identification with the client affects the structure of a particular intervention so that it is misrepresented to organizational members or is structured to exclude certain organizational members.

Coercion and Manipulation of the Client or Organizational Members. Participants in an intervention may not be told about its purpose, or the intervention may not be structured for genuine choice to participate.

Overview of Intervention Techniques

Intervention techniques differ along many dimensions. The following chapters differentiate interventions by their target audience and consider them to exist in three broad categories: those that apply to (1) individuals, (2) stand-alone groups and teams, or multiple groups and teams, and (3) whole organizations and multiple organizations (see Figure 9.2 for a graphic description of how these intervention types relate to one another).

Figure 9.2 presents a generic organizational chart showing a leader, multiple managers, and individual team members and shows how the three intervention categories we discuss apply to that structure. Note that there are a number of ways that the intervention types could be applied to this chart. Individual interventions apply to any of the individuals on the chart, and the circle around the single team could also be drawn horizontally around the leadership team, for example. This point will become clearer as we explore these intervention types in subsequent chapters.

No book could possibly list or review the variety and possible adaptations of the universe of organization development interventions that have been created in the past seven decades, so while we will not cover all known interventions, we will discuss those that are most commonly used. In addition, some of these interventions can be adapted to more than one target area (such as those used both for teams and organizations, for example), so where that occurs we will concentrate on the most common application of the intervention.

Summary

Interventions are explicitly designed to accomplish individual and organizational change. They often consist of an intervention strategy, or overall plan, which may

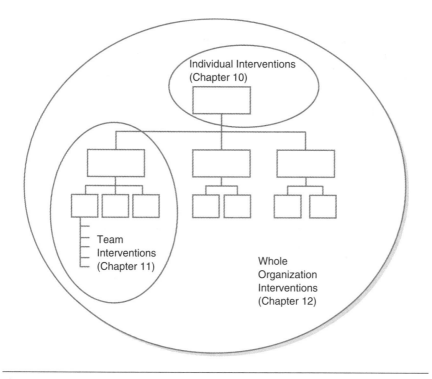

Figure 9.2   Organization Development Intervention Types

be composed of individual intervention activities or events. Many organizational members today have become cynical about organizational change, in part due to the number of unsuccessful interventions they may have experienced. There are a number of common reasons for this, including using an intervention to solve the wrong problem, selecting an inappropriate intervention, having unclear goals and objectives, working with an unskilled change agent, and implementing change in an organization that was not ready for change. As a result, failed interventions have significant costs in time, money, and motivation of organizational members.

Choosing the right intervention involves several considerations. The intervention should be matched to the data and diagnosis. The change agent should consider the organization's readiness for change and where to intervene first. The intervention should also be at the appropriate depth, matched to the problem being solved, and the intervention strategy as a whole should consist of activities that are effectively sequenced for maximum benefit. No matter the intervention, it should be structured as an opportunity for learning, giving organizational members the opportunity to participate with choice and with clear and explicit outcomes. The intervention should be consistently structured so that everything from the invitation to the agenda to the client's initial presentation works steadily toward the established purpose of the intervention. The change agent and client should also discuss roles in advance so that the client's involvement and ownership in the intervention are established and that the change agent can take on an appropriate role in helping the client achieve the objectives of the intervention.

Finally, interventions present a new set of ethical challenges to the change agent, including the possibility of misrepresenting the intervention or one's skills, collusion with the client in choosing an inappropriate intervention, and potential misrepresentation of the intervention to organizational members.

For Further Reading

Argyris, C. (1970). *Intervention theory and method: A behavioral science view.* Reading, MA: Addison-Wesley.

Harrison, R. (1970). Choosing the depth of organizational intervention. *Journal of Applied Behavioral Science, 6,* 181–202.

Hedge, J. W., & Pulakos, E. D. (Eds.). (2002). *Implementing organizational interventions: Steps, processes, and best practices.* San Francisco: Jossey-Bass.

CHAPTER 10

Individual Interventions

Ann had been promoted to oversee the complex operations of a major publishing operation. In addition to a direct staff, she had managerial responsibilities for the management board of two journals and another set of staff members who worked at a different office location. After a year of working in this role, Ann's manager felt that she lacked certain management and interpersonal skills and thought that she would benefit from one-on-one sessions with a coach.

In the first session, the coach and Ann contracted for six coaching sessions, one per month. The coach and Ann determined that the objectives of the coaching engagement would be to increase Ann's skills in working with her team and to gain positive feedback about her performance from her team and her manager. In each 2- to 3-hour session, the coach used several methods to help Ann. Ann completed instruments to help her see her work preferences and how those preferences played themselves out in working with her team. Ann and her coach discussed how Ann related to and managed individual members of her team, how she made strategic decisions, and how she managed team meetings. In addition, they discussed interpersonal skills such as how Ann managed conflict, received and delivered feedback, and communicated with colleagues. The coach's role in these dialogues was to ask questions to help Ann clarify her thinking and see multiple options and possibilities, listening and reflecting what Ann had said rather than instructing her how to act or giving directive advice.

After the six sessions were completed, Ann and her coach agreed to continue coaching as needed on a distance basis (telephone and e-mail) for another 6 months. When she looked back at her progress, Ann noticed how she had improved her working relationships with her manager, specifically with regard to how they could work more collaboratively and how Ann could provide more effective business updates. Ann's manager gave her positive feedback about improvements in Ann's management skills. Team members expressed support for Ann's management abilities, and she noticed that they now worked together in a more unified and consistent manner. Perhaps most important to Ann, the journals grew market share, turnover declined, productivity increased, and staff morale had improved (Wade, 2004).

- What is the purpose of a coach? What do you think makes an effective coach?

Ａs you recall from our discussion of the history of organization development (OD) in Chapter 2, in the early years of OD the T-group and individual change were considered to be the foundation of organizational change—organizations would not change until the individuals that comprised them changed. After all, organizations are not people but are comprised of individuals, so at its heart, organizational change must arise first and foremost out of personal change. While that view has expanded somewhat to include team and organization-level interventions as specific areas for change, individual change through personal interventions remains an integral aspect of achieving organizational change. In this chapter, we will consider several of the ways that change agents and OD practitioners work with individuals to encourage their personal growth and development. These include administering individual assessments and instruments, coaching, mentoring, 360 feedback, and career planning and development.

Individual interventions can be extraordinarily influential to encourage personal growth, development, and change. Ultimately, however, two cautions should be noted about them. First, as Peter Block (2008) puts it, "we have already learned that the transformation of large numbers of individuals does not result in the transformation of communities" (p. 5). Individual change can be an insufficient method for achieving organizational change because, as we have discussed, organizations are comprised of many processes and systems, as well as people with strong cultural values and beliefs. These systems, processes, and beliefs can contradict and work against any individual's attempt to change. For example, an organization may administer a training program to teach employees how to be better at customer service, but such an effort will be wasted if employees lack management support or the appropriate tools to do the job. Put differently, organizations develop regular and usual practices that become institutionalized, and these can be potent forces to retain the status quo and resist any single individual's attempt to change (George & Jones, 2001). Changing individuals may be an important part of the change that an organization needs, but it is not likely to be the only change needed, since individuals work in interconnected systems. Individual interventions may need to be supplemented with team-based or organization-level interventions as part of a comprehensive intervention strategy (see Chapter 9). Second, as most of us have experienced personally, individual change is rarely successful or long-lasting if it is forced or mandated. Whether it is weight loss, quitting smoking, or changing one's communication style with coworkers, personal growth is most effective when the individual is motivated to change. An understanding of the psychology of the individual change process is useful to understand how people respond to and achieve personal change, in order to select interventions most appropriate for the given individual(s).

Individual Change and Reactions to Change

An important part of how people think at work is through *schemas*. Schemas are the familiar cognitive concepts and beliefs that govern how we approach our lives and work environments (George & Jones, 2001). Schemas help us develop familiar patterns that aid us in interpreting what is happening to make sense of our work. We develop schemas so that that we know how to make sense of and act on a new product order received via the Internet, or how to interpret the role a new employee will take on the team. Schemas help organizational members organize not only the work itself but also how that work relates to other schemas they have developed about the organization, coworkers, the physical environment, and more. Change threatens these existing schemas and requires the development of new ones, forcing us to question what was once familiar, known, and comfortable. Whether it is a personal change that we seek (e.g., to become more effective at making and communicating difficult decisions) or change that happens to us (e.g., the company has been acquired and jobs are changing), change disrupts what is familiar. It is the discrepancy and inconsistency between existing, known schemas and new, unfamiliar ones that first prompts individual change (George & Jones, 2001). This is also the time when individuals may resist change as they first recognize the need to shed old schemas and adopt new ones.

It is a truism that people respond to change in different ways. Some are energized by learning new skills or experiencing a different environment, perhaps motivated by the possibilities of a brighter future. Others may be frustrated or anxious when faced with the unknown, perhaps uncertain how to adapt to change, or sad that an enjoyable current state is about to end. Many have mixed emotions. Whatever the emotions, personal change is very often an affective process as individuals go through stages of transitions that Bridges (1980) calls *endings, the neutral zone,* and *new beginnings.*

Endings. All transitions begin with endings, or the recognition and liberation of the past. Endings can prompt confusion and fear. Change can require letting go of past processes, beliefs, and ways of working, but change can also mean letting go of relationships and familiar places. It can also mean changes to one's personal identity, which may happen when career transitions prompt people to rethink who they have been and the meaning that their work has for them personally. The comfortable identity I have developed of myself as a good administrator, police officer, teacher, marketing representative, or book editor is now threatened, and an important piece of my identity may feel lost. Endings are experiences of loss, and people naturally "grieve" during this process, experiencing emotions of shock and denial when confronted with change.

The Neutral Zone. The neutral zone is a time when "neither the old nor the new ways work properly" (Holbeche, 2006, p. 74). It can be frustrating and confusing to recognize that a change is taking place, without the comfort of established routines and practices. People can feel bombarded and overwhelmed by new information and may not know how to evaluate or interpret all of it. It can feel uncomfortable and risky to try new things without the knowledge of what may happen next. It may feel as if the transition is taking forever without a clear sense of when the confusion will end.

New Beginnings. Beginnings may occur with stops and starts as people transition to new ways, perhaps experiencing personal setbacks, frustration, or failure as they attempt to change but find it difficult. Disappointment may set in if the new beginning is not all that it was anticipated to be. "It is unrealistic," Bridges (1980) writes, "to expect someone to make a beginning like a sprinter coming out of the starting blocks" (p. 148). Gradually the new beginning may itself become as familiar and comfortable as the old way.

Individual interventions are designed to help organizational members through various stages of the change process, including recognizing the need to change, motivating acceptance of change, respecting the benefits and drawbacks of the past, learning new skills, and more. They work under the assumption that "if people are to positively embrace the change, it is important to create safe opportunities for people to come to terms with the change and adjust" (Holbeche, 2006, p. 71). Many managers or change agents trying to promote individual change in organizations, however, take the perspective that employees need to "get on with it," "get over it," or "just deal with it." This belief overlooks the role of the manager in helping employees through the challenges of interpreting and adapting to a change (Isabella, 1992). As Bridges (1980) puts it, "Treating ourselves like appliances that can be unplugged and plugged in again" (p. 130) is an ineffective method for personal change, and we need methods for "making sense out of the lostness and the confusion that we encounter when we have gone through disengagement or disenchantment or disidentification" (p. 130). Individual interventions can be one step in that direction. They can prompt endings, encourage reflection during the neutral zone, and facilitate transitions to new beginnings.

Individual Instruments and Assessments

Diagnostic instruments and assessments provide individual feedback to participants in any number of areas such as conflict style, leadership style, work preferences, learning style, work aptitudes, and more. They are often referred to colloquially as "tests," though this is usually a misnomer because diagnostic instruments of the type used in organization development interventions have no right or wrong answers. Individual instruments might ask participants to assess their level of agreement with the statements, "In a group setting, I like to take charge," "I prefer to work alone most of the time," or "Statistical data is necessary for me to make an informed decision." Instruments are usually theory-based and are almost always rigorously tested for validity and reliability by psychologists or other research experts before being published. They are usually either pencil-and-paper or computer-based, completed individually, and can take anywhere from several minutes to several hours to complete, depending on the instrument. Once completed and scored, they can give valuable feedback to the participant to encourage self-awareness, recognition of personal strengths, and identification of any areas the individual may want to change. While they are usually focused on the individual, instruments can often be useful in team settings as well. In these cases, the instruments are completed individually and results are discussed among team members in a facilitated meeting (sharing one's work style preferences, for example, can help team members know how each member approaches the team's objectives).

Individual instruments have a number of advantages (Pfeiffer & Ballew, 1987). Because they are completed individually and feedback is given directly to the participant (usually in writing), instruments can be a relatively low-threat way for an individual to gain self-awareness and personal feedback. Often the process of completing the instrument can engage even a reticent participant and develop some curiosity about the results, which can encourage him or her to consider the feedback. The instrument itself gives participants a language and theoretical constructs to understand their behavior, style, preferences, as well as those of people around them, and this can encourage them to become more aware of how their styles play out in daily interaction. Some instruments allow comparison to other people, which can be liberating when people feel alone or isolated. Instruments can also be administered on multiple occasions (for example, each year) to identify changes that may occur over time.

Using instruments as interventions also can have a number of disadvantages as well. Some people resent or fear being psychologically exposed, figured out, or otherwise discovered, seeing the instrument as pinning them down or labeling them. Despite a facilitator's insistence to the contrary, participants may seek what they consider to be a socially desirable answer, thinking that there is a right and wrong answer. They may be disappointed to find that what they thought was the "best" leadership style does not match their own, according to the instrument, and this may induce feelings of denial or disappointment. The facilitator may try to respond to this by encouraging acknowledgment of the results, whatever they may be, and by stressing that there are no right answers. For some participants, because there are no correct answers, this can encourage relativism and blind acceptance ("My style is fine, and so is yours") instead of building awareness that one may have flaws or behaviors that may not be effective (for example, strong angry reactions that may inhibit employees from being honest with a leader). Some may have emotional reactions or become overwhelmed by the amount of feedback produced by some instruments, and some may become dependent on the facilitator for feedback, interpretation of results, or personal coaching. In group settings especially, instruments can encourage labeling or stereotyping of others (e.g., "He has no emotional reactions because he's an ESTP," "She's a Stage 2 manager") or participants can feel pressured to reveal results they were not prepared to share. Table 10.1 summarizes the advantages and disadvantages of using instruments.

Pfeiffer and Ballew (1987) outline a process for using instruments effectively. First, they recommend establishing a safe and nonjudgmental atmosphere prior to administering the instrument. Participants should understand the reasons they are completing the instrument, how it will be used, and who will see the instrument responses and overall results. The facilitator may want to stress that the instrument is only as accurate as the participants' answers, so honest and forthright responses are important. Next, after participants have completed the instrument, it may be helpful for the facilitator to provide some background about the instrument itself, explaining its theoretical base and any theoretical concepts or ideas that may help

Table 10.1 Advantages and Disadvantages of Using Individual Instruments

Advantages	Disadvantages
• Gives people language and constructs to understand themselves • Relatively low threat; individualized • Allows comparison to others • Promotes involvement in self-discovery • Can administer at multiple times to compare changes • Can allow person to explore areas previously unknown to self	• People may seek the right answer or right style • May encourage labeling or stereotyping • May encourage relativism instead of confrontation • Fear of exposure, being "discovered" psychologically or "figured out" • Can foster dependency on the facilitator • Can be too much information to confront at once; can be overwhelming

participants to understand the instrument. Third, participants can try to predict their outcome on the test before the next step, receiving the results.

As participants receive results, the facilitator may wish to allow several uninterrupted quiet moments for participants to read through, absorb, and consider the feedback. They may wish to compare their predicted results with the results provided by the instrument and to read through any written comments or scoring guides. If the instrument is easy to interpret, the facilitator may wish to simply give scoring or interpretation handouts with the results. In some cases, however, instruments and scoring results can be complex to interpret, and a one-on-one session with someone trained to interpret the results will be necessary. In group settings, with the agreement of everyone present, group members may wish to share their results (anonymously, if desired) for the entire group to see.

Interpretation and processing of results is the most important stage of the process. After all, the goal is self-awareness and knowledge, not clinical diagnoses. The instrument itself is simply a means by which participants can learn and grow. For individuals, facilitators can ask questions such as the following to encourage processing of the results:

- Did the results match or differ from your prediction? How so? Why do you think that is?
- What strengths do you see? What are you satisfied to see?
- What opportunities for change or growth do you see? Is there anything you are surprised or disappointed to see? Is there anything you find dissatisfying?
- How do these patterns play out for you in everyday life and work?
- Is there anything that you would like to do differently based on these results? What actions would you like to take next?

Throughout the process, the facilitator must remain nonjudgmental, open, and respectful, being sensitive to the fact that some individuals may have strong emotional reactions. Even examples that are used may give the impression of some results having a better or worse connotation, so facilitators must be highly attuned to how they are describing the theory and interpretation of results.

There are a number of ethical considerations in the use of instruments. Facilitators should be trained in the administration and interpretation of the instrument, and they should have completed the instrument themselves in order to understand possible participant reactions. Judgments or diagnoses should be carefully considered if they are made based solely on the results, and participants should not be pressured to reveal scores or adopt the facilitator's interpretation of any individual result. Obviously, facilitators should obtain instruments through ethical means and use them as agreed (respecting intellectual property and copyright laws in the purchase and duplication of instruments).

The Myers-Briggs Type Indicator

Perhaps the most common instrument in use in organization development engagements is the Myers-Briggs Type Indicator (MBTI). According to Hoffman (2002), in fact, more than 2.5 million people annually complete the MBTI. The MBTI was developed in the 1920s based on the psychological theories of Carl Jung who believed that "people are different in fundamental ways even though they all have the same multitude of instincts (archetypes) to drive them from within" (Keirsey & Bates, 1984, p. 3). The Myers-Briggs classifies personality into 16 types, based on four preference categories:

- *Extroversion (E) or Introversion (I).* The E-I preference reflects how people gain energy. Extraverts are energized by time spent with other people, whereas introverts gain energy from time spent alone. At a large party or social gathering, the extravert will find more energy as the night goes on, and the introvert will generally feel less.
- *Sensing (S) or Intuition (N).* The second preference pair refers to how people collect information. A person preferring sensation trusts facts, data, and personal experience, and values realistic and practical ideas. A preference for intuition indicates that the person trusts hunches, "gut feelings," and speculative imagination, and values ideas that reflect possibilities and visions.
- *Thinking (T) or Feeling (F).* The T-F preference reflects how individuals make decisions. Thinking types tend to make decisions based on logic, general principles or criteria, policy, and analysis, whereas feeling types tend to make decisions based on subjective and interpersonal considerations, values, harmony, and effects on people.
- *Judging (J) or Perceiving (P).* The final pair indicates a preference for whether people like things closed, settled, and completed (J) or prefer to keep options open and flexible (P). J types plan ahead to get work done well in advance of deadlines, whereas P types prefer the flexibility of emergent ideas.

The MBTI results in a four-letter score, one from each category, so examples of MBTI types are ENFP, ISTJ, INTP, and so on. It scores each of these preference pairs on a scale, so that one might demonstrate a strong preference for introversion but have a weak preference for judging. The strength of these preferences might change over time, but several studies have shown that the four-letter preference tends to remain relatively stable. The test has been found to have good reliability in repeated administrations over time for the same individual (test-retest reliability), but some experts continue to question other aspects of the test's validity due to a lack of evidence (Carlson, 1985, 1989; Pittenger, 2005).

Consultants have found the MBTI to be useful in a number of areas, including team building, training, career development coaching, and conflict resolution (Clinebell & Stecher, 2003; Coe, 1992; Hoffman, 2002; McCaulley, 2000). The MBTI can provide an explanation and point of discussion for individuals who are experiencing a conflict, for example, by showing that two different attitudes toward deadlines are rooted in different preferences on the J-P dimension. In a team, a majority of thinkers may approach a decision logically, and thus be considered hard-hearted by the feelers in the group. A team made up entirely of strong N types may neglect hard facts and data that perhaps ought to be taken into account. In these cases, the MBTI can be especially helpful in reminding us that there are alternative ways to think and work, and that these sources of difference can be beneficial. Individuals can learn to see that their preferences have strengths but also weaknesses, and moreover, these strengths and weaknesses exist in colleagues as well.

Like most instruments, perhaps, the disadvantages of the MBTI tend to lie in dysfunctional uses of the instrument rather than in the instrument itself. First, the MBTI is often used because it is interesting, fun, nonthreatening, well-known, someone else did it, or the consultant is trained in it, rather than being used because the situation calls for it. The change agent should have a relevant reason for using the MBTI and a goal for the session. Second, despite the subtleties that exist in the MBTI rating scales, most uses of the MBTI tend to stress the four-letter preference category, which tends to typecast individuals and ignore the reality that most of us exhibit some aspect of both pairs at some points. Third, individuals may place too much emphasis on the MBTI and make assumptions or explanations for all behavior based on it (Pittenger, 2005). In some organizations, the MBTI has become so popular that individuals who simply experience the instrument themselves begin to train others in typewatching, with inaccurate explanations that neglect the subtleties and power of the instrument (McCaulley, 2000).

Coaching

Coaching is a one-on-one intervention in which an individual works to improve a specific personal, interpersonal, or skill area, or to take actions to reach a desired future goal, working with a facilitator on the process of personal change. In the past, seeking out the assistance of a coach might have been seen as weak or a symptom of incompetence. That view has changed so that the vast majority of U.S. companies now offer some kind of coaching to top executives (Stone, 2007), and executive coaching is perhaps the most common type of coaching practiced today. As a result, the practice of coaching grew dramatically in the 1990s to the point that leadership coach, life coach, executive coach, and career coach are often seen as specialized career roles unique from that of the OD consultant (Schein, 2006a). Many observers now recommend coaching roles for managers as well, noting that there are significant benefits to employees and organizational performance when managers take an active role in helping employees to grow and develop (Hunt & Weintraub, 2002). Despite the growth of the manager-as-coach role, this section will primarily address the internal or external coach who does not have a management-employee relationship with the person being coached.

Coaching is done for different purposes and coaches develop different roles and techniques depending on the client. In the example that opened this chapter, Ann worked with a coach in several areas to improve her effectiveness at work, a common goal of coaching. "Coaching is the process whereby one individual helps another: to unlock their natural ability; . . . to increase their sense of self-responsibility and ownership of their performance; to self-coach; to identify and remove internal barriers to achievement" (MacLennan, 1995, p. 4). In other words, a coach may be a sounding board, asking questions and directing conversations through a process whereby the individual can learn to self-assess and work through thought processes and obstacles. Goals of executive coaching include helping the client to improve "the client's capacity to manage an organization—planning, organizing, staffing, leading," "the client's ability to manage self and others," "the client's ability to manage his or her career," and the ability to "improve the effectiveness of the organization or team" (Kilburg, 1996, p. 140). The coach may help the client to develop a personal vision for the future, define gaps between where the client is today and where he or she would prefer to be, analyze internal and external obstacles and barriers to achieving that vision, and to set short- and long-term goals. Witherspoon and White (1996) write that there are a number of coaching roles depending on the goals of the client:

- Coaching for skills (learning focused on a specific task)
- Coaching for performance (to improve the job functions of the client more broadly)
- Coaching for development (to develop the client for a future role)
- Coaching for the executive's agenda (the coach acts as a third-party observer to assist the executive with business decisions)

Many wonder about the difference between coaching and therapy. After all, in relationships where one person is there as an outside party to help the other, a therapeutic or counseling relationship can easily evolve. Yet coaches and therapists differ significantly in the process they use to work with a client. "Coaches see themselves as partners, ready to work in tandem with a client to solve an interesting challenge. The issues that coach and client address are rarely life-and-death, so the coach uses a less diagnostic, analytical approach" (Grodzki & Allen, 2005, p. 28).

Goals of coaching are also different from those of therapy. In general, coaching tends to focus more on clients' skills and abilities at work and how they can reach their future goals more effectively (Stone, 2007), and much less on their psychological states or analyzing troubles of the past. As Gooding (2003) puts it, "A coach is hired to assist in designing a person's future rather than reliving their past" (p. 36). The coach may help the client to recognize "untapped potential," helping him or her to become more "self-generative and productive," versus therapy that focuses more on "retrospective" issues and "uncovering unconscious material" (Grodzki & Allen, 2005, pp. 28–29). Levinson (1996) writes that "executive coaching does not allow time for developing a therapeutic alliance" (p. 115) and that Levinson's style is to concentrate on current circumstances while addressing patterns in the executive's behavior that are contributing to present problems.

Executive coaching in particular offers unique challenges to the coach. The coaching relationship, while generally an interpersonal relationship, exists within the larger landscape of the organization, including its goals, strategies, culture, and politics. Thus, the coach must be adept at understanding and navigating political waters and cultural dynamics while helping the client achieve the desired outcome. Often the coach is not just a coach but also a consultant:

> Today's executive coach is a hybrid of these prototypes and whole playground is the management of an entire socio-technical business system. As such, he or she must be adept in engaging the mesh of political-behavioral and strategic-philosophical components of the organization. (Lyons, 2006, p. 15)

As in the field of OD generally, there are no special degree requirements or certifications needed to become a coach. Professional publications and associations include *Choice,* a magazine for professional coaches, which started in 2003, the International Coach Federation (ICF), which offers certification for coaches, and CoachVille, a global network of coaching professionals. Good coaching is a highly interpersonal activity. The best coaches:

- Have good communication skills
- Offer encouragement and support
- Take time to listen
- Build a positive environment
- Listen actively
- Let people figure things out for themselves (Thorne, 2004, pp. 64–65)

Ennis and colleagues (2007) have developed a comprehensive list of competencies for executive coaches in particular, which includes such skills as the ability to ask good questions, knowledge of leadership styles, theories, and principles, assertiveness, self-confidence, and interpersonal sensitivity. For executive coaches, business acumen is an important skill because, as Orenstein (2002) puts it, executive coaching is not offered solely for the benefit of the individual, but that "every individual intervention [is] a simultaneous organizational intervention" (p. 372).

The coaching process usually follows the OD process we have addressed in this book. First, coach and client meet to develop a contract to ensure that the relationship will meet the needs of both parties. The coaching intervention may not be appropriate, for example, if the client is unwilling to be coached or is being forced or pressured into coaching (Gauthier & Giber, 2006). The contract outlines the goals and timeframe for the coaching relationship and makes explicit other concerns such as the function of the coach's role, whether and how the coach may challenge the client, confidentiality, and how they will evaluate progress (Megginson & Clutterbuck, 2005). Coaches may use a number of the intervention techniques described in this and subsequent chapters, including conducting an assessment using individual instruments, gathering 360 feedback, facilitating the client through simulations and role playing, and more. No matter the intervention used, the coach will almost always begin with a coaching conversation to explore the client's motivations to change and desired future. Hudson (1999) notes that coaches should ask questions that stimulate the client's thinking, helping to facilitate the conversation and reflecting back what the client says, but that the coach should avoid taking over the conversation or imposing too much structure. During the coaching conversation, the coach can help to encourage goal setting and action planning. Some coaches offer "homework" for the clients to consider between sessions, and in each subsequent session the client may wish to report back on results from taking action or to reflect on any changes or new insights gained since the previous coaching session. When coaching engagements are concluded, many coaches conduct an evaluation session to improve their own coaching practice, inviting feedback about the coach's style and process.

Mentoring

Mentoring programs are growing in popularity in organizations (often where there are a significant number of older workers who are retiring and taking with them their institutional knowledge and experience). A mentor is a counselor, adviser, and teacher who usually works in a one-on-one relationship with a protégé. MacLennan (1995) defines a mentor as "someone available for the performer to learn from" (p. 5) as a teacher, role model, or expert. In some apprenticelike models of mentoring, the mentor may demonstrate how a task is accomplished or provide an example, watch the performer complete the task (or assess completed work), and then provide feedback or an assessment on how it was done. In others, role modeling the skill may be less important. In both cases, mentoring usually involves an expert-protégé relationship with a skilled and knowledgeable teacher who can provide guidance, and is less often a relationship with a "hired" change agent or external consultant. Today, a protégé is likely to have a number of mentoring relationships with mentors inside and outside the organization as a network of advisers who can serve multiple roles and provide diverse perspectives (Whiting & de Janasz, 2004).

Mentoring programs "can shorten learning tracks, speed up managerial advancement, and build the next generation of leaders" (Stone, 2004, p. ix).

Definitions differ among practitioners, and the roles can overlap considerably, but coaching and mentoring differ primarily in the degree of expertise on the facilitator's part and content knowledge to be shared with the performer. Mentoring tends to involve a stronger focus on the skill development of the learner than does coaching. Unlike a coach, the mentor may provide explicit advice or direction rather than wait for the mentee to find the answer through self-discovery (Stone, 2004).

360 Feedback

Multisource, or 360, feedback systems are methods by which individuals can receive feedback from a wide range of people with whom they work. It can be powerful source for personal reflection and change, and it became increasingly popular in the 1990s, prompted in part by trends toward gathering more customer feedback as well as a *Fortune* magazine article that proclaimed that "360 feedback can change your life" (O'Reilly & Furth, 1994). Feedback data are generally collected via written (computer or pencil-and-paper) questionnaires, though one-on-one interviews are also a common method for soliciting feedback. Most 360 feedback systems are anonymous. Generally 360 feedback is used for individual development, most often for managers and leaders of an organization, but some organizations use 360 feedback during the annual performance appraisal process or for team interventions (Lepsinger & Lucia, 1997).

The topic for the feedback itself can vary widely among different methods and can range from feedback solicited about personal attributes, interpersonal skills, and job performance. Many organizations customize feedback questionnaires to reflect the organization's values or desired attributes of leaders. Regardless, what the approaches all have in common is the aggregation of multiple sources of data. This method, as opposed to a small set of feedback ratings or interviews with one or two people, offers several advantages. The idea of 360 feedback is that "observations obtained from multiple sources will yield more valid and reliable (and therefore more meaningful and useful) results for the individual" (Church & Bracken, 1997, p. 150). When peers, subordinates, supervisors, customers, and others all offer feedback on a single individual, the individual can observe common themes and consistent ratings that can transcend any individual situation or relationship. Moreover, it can be instructive to sort out ratings by respondent type to learn whether feedback from peers differs from that of supervisors or subordinates. In addition, some groups may have more opportunities to observe a given trait than others. For example, subordinates may have more data about a manager's leadership abilities, and peers may have more opportunities to observe a manager's ability to work across organizational boundaries collaboratively (Brutus, Fleenor, & London, 1998). Individuals can get a well-rounded assessment about their professional effectiveness from a wide variety of colleagues.

The assumption is that the 360 feedback process will augment the recipient's self-awareness. The feedback provides insights into how others perceive one's own behaviors and skills, and it allows them to compare their self-concepts with how others see them. This can give insight into areas in which recipients may wish to grow and develop. Thus, 360 feedback tends to work best when both raters and ratees see it as developmental. Individuals tend to vary with regard to how much developmental feedback they will accept. If individuals seek out the feedback, are willing to consider it, see it as important to their personal and professional success, and see it as important to understand how they are viewed by others, they are more likely to take the feedback seriously and take action based on it. Also, how the feedback is used and presented has a large impact on how much individuals will accept it. Using 360 feedback during the performance appraisal process, Silverman, Pogson, and Cober (2005) note, likely will encourage participants to reject, resist, or dispute any negative feedback, because there may be more serious consequences to the performance appraisal. At the same time, if there are no consequences to the individual, it will be easy to ignore feedback and to avoid taking action (London, Smither, & Adsit, 1997).

Antonioni (1996) writes that there can be five positive outcomes of a successful 360 feedback process:

1. *An increased awareness of appraisers' expectations.* The 360 feedback process can help to make explicit the unexplored or tacit assumptions and expectations that we have of one another.

2. *Improvements in work behaviors and performance.* Antonioni (1996) writes that research shows greater improvement when feedback data are reviewed with a trained coach who can help participants analyze the feedback and create action plans.

3. *Reduction of "undiscussables."* Since raters usually have an anonymous way to provide feedback about things they ordinarily may not have discussed openly, the 360 feedback process provides an avenue to open up these topics for discussion, which may be done in person following the feedback process. London et al. (1997) suggest that personal change and improvement will be greater when raters and ratees openly discuss the feedback.

4. *Increase in periodic informal 360-degree performance reviews.* The 360 feedback process has the potential to break down walls in organizations that prevent colleagues from honestly sharing feedback with one another. If done well, organizational members may learn how to give and receive feedback more frequently and informally.

5. *Increase in management learning.* Managers as a whole may see patterns in responses to see how the organization as a system may need to be changed in addition to personal change for any single individual.

As an individual intervention, a change agent or OD professional may be asked to participate in gathering the feedback data and presenting the information to the individual. Interview practices described in Chapter 7 can be applicable in these circumstances, and in presenting the feedback to the individual, some of the recommendations from Chapter 8 on gathering feedback and presenting it remain applicable as well. Setting up the feedback meeting, encouraging reflection on common themes, acknowledging strengths, recognizing resistance, and confronting tough issues are all relevant concerns for individual feedback meetings using a 360 process.

Career Planning and Development

In the current environment of organizational restructuring, mergers and acquisitions, outsourcing, and downsizing, the concept of a career has changed. What were formerly clear and stable upward career paths have given way to a flattened organizational structure, changes in the scope of responsibility, increasing job mobility, lateral moves, team-based working, and more. The concept of a career identity has changed from what was once an expectation of moving up to a management level, to individuals wanting to balance work and family or resist frequent relocation for work (London & Stumpf, 1986). More midcareer and late career employees who have had a lengthy career with the same organization now find themselves confronting new assumptions and expectations about work and careers, and as a result the transition can be particularly stressful.

Many organizations have developed career development systems internally to retain and motivate employees, to develop employees internally and promote from within the organization, and to provide opportunities for upward mobility (Gutteridge, Leibowitz, & Shore, 1993). Some even hire career counselors (Niles, 2005). The concept of an organizational career development system originated from organizations' interests in balancing what employees want for career growth and personal development and what the organization needs given its strategic objectives. Yet most organizations still believe that the primary responsibility for career growth and development remains with the individual. Given the frequent downsizing and restructuring in the contemporary organizational environment, changes to the notion of careers, and changes in the employment "contract," it makes more sense than ever for individuals to be conscious of their own career plans and development. Career development programs and one-on-one career interventions can help employees through a forced transition such as a merger, restructuring, or downsizing. They can also help employees proactively choose to take action in anticipation of a transition in the future (seeking out new skills to plan for a new job).

Stages of the Career

Early research and writing on career development emphasized a linear progression of career shifts throughout an employee's life, though recent research indicates that this concept has now been outgrown. Consider Schein's (1978) book *Career Dynamics,* in which he outlined nine stages of a career life cycle:

1. *Growth, fantasy, exploration.* During this stage, individuals explore career options and make educational choices based on careers they find desirable.

2. *Entry into world of work.* Individuals search out, interview for, and experience the first job. They experience the transition to becoming an employee, working for an employer, and navigating the challenges of completing initial job tasks.

3. *Basic training.* The individual begins to develop job skills, becoming an effective contributor. The individual is in a learning mode as a novice organizational member, learning not only job skills but also interpersonal skills in relating to and working with colleagues. He or she may be highly concerned with developing competence and meeting performance expectations of a supervisor or colleagues.

4. *Full membership in early career.* Individuals experience first major job assignments not in a training or apprentice role. They learn how to accept work assignment and the complexities of working with coworkers for extended periods. They evaluate whether this work represents what they would like to be doing in the future or whether a different job or organization would better suit them.

5. *Full membership, midcareer.* Individuals develop self-assurance and trust in decisions and job skills. They may have increasing responsibility and a professional reputation. They consider how to remain current in their areas of expertise and how to continue to grow and develop.

6. *Midcareer crisis.* Individuals begin to reassess their career choices and options. They may evaluate their strengths and weaknesses and think through their goals for their lives and how their careers fit or do not fit with that vision.

7. *Late career.* Individuals will customize a path based on the previous stage to determine the next steps. Those who take a leadership role will learn how to manage the work and performance of subordinates and make broad-ranging decisions, while those who do not choose a leadership path may develop breadth or depth in their areas of expertise.

8. *Decline and disengagement.* Individuals begin to change job roles and perhaps take less responsibility. They may develop increasing interests outside of work.

9. *Retirement.* Individuals transition from a day dominated by full-time work to nonwork concerns. They may reevaluate their personal identities in noncareer terms and may decide how to use work skills in a different capacity.

Schein (1978) writes, "People in different occupations move at different rates through the stages, and personal factors strongly influence the rate of movement as well" (p. 48). Some individuals may remain in one stage for an extended time, and some may find themselves rapidly progressing through stages.

While this once may have been a relevant description of most employees' career development experiences, many observers now suggest that these stage theories no longer fit for the majority of employees. In the changing work environment in which individuals may change careers or jobs or choose to be away from the workforce for any period (e.g., to raise children, take a sabbatical, travel, obtain an advanced degree), some research suggests that people may not progress through the stages in sequence, but cycle through them quickly and return to previous stages (Sullivan, 1999). Rather than presuming that individuals follow a single, well-defined career path through stages, some have proposed the concept of the "boundaryless career" (Arthur & Rousseau, 1996), which transcends any individual job, occupational function, profession, and organization. Career progression in a boundaryless career is defined more by learning milestones and skill capabilities rather than age and job titles. With the rise of flexible contract work, part-time, and temporary project work, employees may choose to work independently, taking advantage of their multiple and diverse skills to work for several employers. Thus, in a boundaryless career, employment may be with many firms rather than a single company, and job security exists not because of tenure and long-term loyalty to the organization but because of the individual's ability to successfully perform the work and contribute to organizational goals (Sullivan, 1999).

Individuals experience different challenges and needs at different points in their careers, and many need support as they tackle these challenges on their own. As Arnold (2001) writes, "From an individual's point of view career management means deciding or finding out for oneself what it is best to do" (p. 120). The OD practitioner and career development practitioner can often provide support for individuals through individual career interventions. The next sections describe examples of career-related interventions that can be appropriate for individuals with different career needs, such as (1) choosing a career direction and identifying work interests, (2) setting career goals, and (3) developing career transitions and new employment relationships.

Choosing a Career Direction and Identifying Work Interests

It may be even more important in the contemporary work environment for individuals to be conscious of their career interests and abilities. A number of individual assessments have been created and tested to help individuals with career choices, such as the Vocational Preference Inventory and Self-Directed Search (see Holland, 1985, 1997) to name just two. The VPI is based on Holland's RIASEC typology, which argues that personality types correspond with vocational interests and satisfaction. The six RIASEC dimensions of vocational preference are as follows (Holland, 1996):

- *Realistic:* A preference for manipulating machines, tools, and things
- *Investigative:* A preference for exploring and understanding natural and social phenomena
- *Artistic:* A preference for music, artistic, and literary activities

- *Social:* A preference for helping, teaching, or counseling
- *Enterprising:* A preference for persuading and managing others
- *Conventional:* A preference for routinized tasks and orderly activities

Researchers who have examined career progression and the RIASEC typology have found that individuals may tend to change jobs or careers, but do so most frequently within the same career typology category. Early research also suggested that individuals were more satisfied with their careers when their careers were consistent with their personality type (Holland, 1996). Such occupational interest inventories, combined with individualized coaching, may help individuals anticipate which career choices may be most satisfying for them.

Setting Career Goals

Some individuals may not yet have a fully developed sense of their own strengths, weaknesses, or even work preferences, so career options may be broad and overwhelming to contemplate. Without conscious attention to their career progression, many people in this stage end up wandering from job to job without goals that help them choose among diverse options. For these individuals, an exercise such as the 5-year resume (Laker & Laker, 2007) may be a useful activity. In this exercise, the individual imagines that it is 5 years from today and writes a resume that he or she would like to describe him or her. The resume includes everything that would be included on a typical resume such as advanced degrees, educational credentials or certificates, and professional experiences. Participants complete short- and long-term action plans and identify the resources that are required for them to meet these objectives. The 5-year resume activity encourages individuals to proactively manage their own career changes.

Other individuals may be concerned with whether they are successfully advancing in their career as much as they would like, either developing and using new skills in a different job, or moving to increasing levels of responsibility. Different individuals judge success differently, so these will be unique concerns. They may notice others around them being promoted and wonder whether their career has stalled. There is often a need to develop a new routine, as the old ways may no longer work effectively. Hall (1986) writes, "The task in early career is to reduce exploratory behavior and establish a career routine, while in midcareer there is a need to disrupt habitual behavior and trigger exploration" (p. 133). At any point in a career, however, individuals can feel stuck. For these individuals, formal training (through university programs or professional seminars) or informal training (through job rotations or new assignments at work) may provide an occasion to reawaken interest in the job and to enhance one's contributions at work.

Developing Career Transitions and New Employment Relationships

Often later in their careers, individuals may benefit from the opportunity to share their career and life experiences with others. Mentoring or consulting may be appropriate and rewarding roles for these individuals, and many organizations have developed human resources systems for late career employees to reduce their time at work (4-day work weeks, retirement but with extended consulting arrangements on an as-needed basis, etc.), which allows experienced employees to begin a phased retirement but allows the organization to continue to benefit from the employees' wealth of knowledge and experience.

Summary

Individual interventions have historically been the foundation of organizational change, though this has broadened throughout the history of organization development to include team and organizationwide interventions. Individual interventions are intended to promote personal growth, development, and change. People's responses to change vary, however, and they often follow a pattern of working through the transition stages of endings, the neutral zone, and new beginnings. Individual interventions can help people manage through these transitions. Instruments, assessments, and 360 feedback can all provide information to an individual about his or her own style and behaviors, as well as others' perceptions about the individual. This can prompt reflection on one's strengths and effectiveness, and can encourage people to think through how they may wish to change. Coaching can be a resource to prompt creation of a new desired future and action plans to reach short- and long-term goals, encouraging clients to move out of the neutral zone stage and establish a new beginning. Similarly, mentoring can help individuals learn new skills and reflect on their actions with the help of a counselor and adviser. Career development interventions reflect the challenges that individuals face at various points in their career life cycle and can help individuals as they struggle through the unique concerns depending on their career stage and interests.

Individual interventions are often but one piece of a larger intervention strategy, particularly when larger organizational concerns are at stake, such as team effectiveness or organizational design. In the next chapters we will consider these team and organizational interventions.

For Further Reading

Bridges, W. (1980). *Transitions*. Reading, MA: Addison-Wesley.

Goldsmith, M., & Lyons, L. (Eds.). (2006). *Coaching for leadership* (2nd ed.). San Francisco: Pfeiffer.

Lepsinger, R., & Lucia, A. D. (1997). *The art and science of 360 feedback*. San Francisco: Pfeiffer.

Schein, E. H. (1978). *Career dynamics: Managing individual and organizational needs*. Reading, MA: Addison-Wesley.

Case Study 4: Individual Type Styles at the Parks Department

Read the parks department case study and consider the following questions:

1. What was the purpose of this individual assessment for this team? What should be the purpose of an individual instrument?

2. How did Lori explain the instrument and its meaning? What do you think she did well and what could have been improved in her explanation of the instrument?

3. What activities did Lori do to use the results of the instrument? Do you think these were effective? Why or why not? What would you have done differently, if anything?

4. How would you respond to Tai's question at the end?

5. What were the results of this intervention for this team? What did the team learn from this activity? Were the client's goals met?

The Franklin Meadows City Parks and Recreation Department is responsible for more than 200 city-managed public parks, golf courses, and recreation facilities. It manages the city trail system, open space, summer camps for children and teenagers, and adult softball leagues. Ken is the city director of parks and recreation, and the staff consists of six managers of the major divisions of the department:

- Cindy, manager, public parks
- Tai, manager, golf courses
- Aron, manager, recreation centers
- Tasha, manager, trails and open space
- Felix, manager, leagues and activities
- Rachel, manager, parks rentals and special events

At the department's quarterly management retreat, Ken decided to conduct a team-building activity. He contacted Lori from the city's human resources department for ideas.

"I want to do something different from what we usually do, which is an operations and goal review, and then we all go to dinner," Ken explained when he and Lori met. "While this team has worked together for about 18 months, and we know each other pretty well, I think it would be enjoyable to mix it up a bit."

"What's going on with this team that you think could be improved?" she asked.

"I think interpersonally the team is quite solid," he said. "I think there's an opportunity for them to open up to each other, however, which I think always helps to smooth the team interaction."

"I have just the instrument to help this team. I have recently become certified in the Team Type Alphabet assessment," Lori said. "It's a way for team members to learn more about one another's individual work styles. Once they take the instrument, I will score it and print reports for each of them."

"That sounds interesting," Ken said. "Why don't you send each member of the team an e-mail and let them know that we've spoken and you will be helping with the retreat."

"I look forward to helping out," she said.

The next day, Lori sent the following e-mail to the team.

Dear Parks Department Managers,

Ken has asked me to assist with next month's offsite meeting, during which we will spend some time on team building. The Team Type Alphabet assessment we're going to discuss will tell you what your individual preference is on a team. Please spend 15–20 minutes taking the test on the website listed below. I will provide you with your individual results at our offsite meeting.

Lori

At the Retreat

Lori joined the team late in the afternoon of the third day of the offsite meeting to review the instrument with the team. She quickly noticed that the team was a little drained from such a long meeting, but hopefully they would enjoy the change of pace she could bring with the activity. The team was seated around several tables forming a U-shape pattern. Ken motioned for Lori to begin.

"You all remember a few weeks ago when you completed the Team Type Alphabet instrument? Today we're going to go through the results of that instrument for each of you.

"The Team Type Alphabet tells you what your preferred style is on a team. This does not mean that you always display this type style in every interaction, but it does tell you what your preferred style is when you are part of a team, whether it's a baseball team or a work team. According to the theory, there are six basic team type styles." Lori wrote the following on the whiteboard in the conference room:

Type E: Energy. Desires harmony and cooperation on the team.

Type C: Controlling. Likes to lead and be the focus of attention.

Type Q: Quiet. Observant, sometimes hesitant to get involved in group discussion.

Type A: Assertive. Forceful, ensures that his or her perspective is heard by members of the team.

Type W: Wondering. Asks questions, enchanted by theory and new ideas.

Type D: Detailed. Enjoys examining data and focusing on specific details.

"I'd like to buy a vowel," Aron joked.

"These are just basic descriptions," Lori continued, "but there's much more to each of them. There are longer descriptions of each style in your handout. Your report will contain your dominant style as well as your secondary style. I'll hand these out and give you a moment to think about it."

The group sat for a minute flipping pages in the lengthy report, quietly reflecting on their individual styles, until Cindy broke the silence.

"Controlling? Somehow that doesn't seem right. I don't feel like I always want to be the center of attention. And why is that called Controlling?" Cindy frowned and stared at the team.

"This is all backed up by years of theory showing that these are people's style preferences," Lori said. "The research shows that you tend to not change very much throughout your life, though your secondary preference might change slightly."

"It's just that Controlling sounds like a very negative description to me," Cindy added, her voice cracking slightly. "I don't think I always have a negative impact on this team. Look at item 35: 'I will follow the team's decision even if I don't agree with it.' I marked 'strongly agree.' That doesn't fit someone who is controlling."

"What's important is not how you responded on any individual item, but how it fits within an entire pattern of responses on the instrument," Lori said.

Cindy looked down at the table and closed her booklet. She looked out the window as a landscape worker shaped the hedges outside the conference room.

Lori continued. "Let's get everyone with a Q style to stand up and go to the right side of the room." Felix walked to the right side of the room and stood alone facing the team.

"Just one? Okay, now let's get all of the A types to stand on the left side of the room." Rachel and Aron went to the other side of the room and faced Felix.

"Okay. Now As, tell me what you think of the Q when you see him."

"Well, I think Felix is a great manager," Aron said. "His department has been very effective lately, with a nearly 20% increase in league signups this season. And—"

"I mean what do you think about his Q style on this team? Felix, why don't you tell us how you feel about the As. Do they dominate the discussion?"

"Well, I guess sometimes that's true." He looked very uncomfortable.

"I always think this is so fascinating," Lori said. "The Team Type Alphabet describes exactly how these styles play out for us in everyday life. So as a team, what can you do about the fact that you have a quiet member and some dominating members?"

Tasha said, "This is so interesting, because I think this explains perfectly why we sometimes go around and around in our discussions. I mean the As tends to always speak first, and the discussion tends to steer in that direction, but it's an hour later when our Q gets to speak that we learn so much more and get to a better suggestion because of what his ideas bring."

"Spoken like an E," Aron said. The group laughed.

"I'm not an E; I'm a W," Tasha said, a little defensively.

"Is there anyone who would like to share his or her primary and secondary style type?" Lori asked, trying to refocus the discussion.

"I guess Felix probably won't go first, since he's a Q," Rachel said. "I'll go."

"But we shouldn't let her, as one of the As, dominate the discussion, right?" Tai asked Lori. "Should we make someone else go first?"

"So because I'm an A, I can never speak until others speak?" Rachel asked. "Is that really the point?" Another uncomfortable moment of silence passed.

"My secondary style is a D, which made a lot of sense to me," Aron said. "It's really accurate. I do tend to focus on the data, results, and numbers. I actually think that seems like more of my primary style. You guys know that I'm always the one trying to make charts and graphs." He smiled at the others. "Maybe I need to focus less on the number crunching."

"Well, everyone's style is different, and everyone's style should be appreciated for what it is," Lori said. "But you should be aware of what effect your different styles have on the productivity of the team."

"But you're the expert in this instrument. Based on what you know about our styles and this team, what do you think we should be paying attention to?" Tai asked.

The team looked up at Lori in unison, waiting for her response.

NOTE: The instrument described in this case study is fictional.

CHAPTER 11

Team Interventions

The faculty of Highland Park Junior High School in Beaverton, Oregon, experienced the challenges that most other elementary and secondary schools experience today—to continually adapt to the needs of students, parents, and the community. To do so, they would have to learn flexible organizational problem solving to be aware of their current approaches and results, to understand the internal and external environment, to assess the gaps between their current and desired outcomes, and to cohesively develop action plans that they could agree to implement. The faculty and staff worked with organization development consultants over a series of workshops to improve communication and participation in faculty meetings, develop better problem-solving practices, take more initiative as a team to recognize and solve problems, and to develop better interpersonal relationships with increased openness and skills in giving one another feedback. The consultants designed sessions to maximize face-to-face interaction, first through simulation activities and then facilitating sessions where the team solved real organizational problems. The team identified and diagnosed their own problems, developed action plans, and tried out new ways of interacting as a team. As a result of the intervention events, cohesiveness and the quality of team relationships increased substantially. Turnover decreased to one fourth to one fifth of that of comparative local schools. Faculty began to take the initiative to call and run their own faculty meetings without the principal's involvement, and they designed and facilitated the next intervention workshop on their own, without the use of consultants. Soon, other schools in the district began to adopt the approaches of the faculty (Schmuck, Runkel, & Langmeyer, 1969).

- Do you think this team's problems are common to many teams? What other common problems do teams experience?
- How do you define a successful team?

E ngagements where the target population is a team are among the most common applications of organization development (OD) interventions. The use of teams in organizations is not a new phenomenon, but use of and attention to work teams and their functioning has increased over the past several decades. Organizations have implemented new forms of teams, such as self-directed work teams, virtual teams, and cross-functional teams. These new types of teams, combined with the complexity of work today that frequently requires increased collaboration and problem solving in a global environment, mean that organizations rely heavily on teams for their success and must devote attention to the effectiveness of their teams (Buzaglo & Wheelan, 1999). Put another way, "The effective functioning of groups and teams is central to the effective functioning of organizations" (Woodman & Pasmore, 2002, p. 164). In addition, teams not only play a central role in an organization's effectiveness, but they also play a central role in the accomplishment and implementation of organizational change, such as shifts in strategy (Coghlan, 1994).

Unfortunately, leaders often fail to pay much attention to team effectiveness, not knowing how to develop the team or assuming that the team will work things out on its own (Dyer, Dyer, & Dyer, 2007). When they do tackle team effectiveness, many leaders and change agents fall into the traps discussed in Chapter 9, directing interventions at the wrong issues, implementing the intervention at the wrong time, or failing to address substantive issues of concern to the team.

In this chapter, we will define what we mean by a team, identify different kinds of teams used in contemporary organizations, and consider the elements of effective teams as well as common points where teams struggle. We will then examine some of the more commonly practiced team interventions directed at improving team effectiveness on work tasks and team relationships, such as role analysis, work redesign, and Workout. Teams also frequently come into contact (and conflict) with other teams, so this chapter also describes intergroup interventions applicable when more than one team is involved.

Defining Teams

Many practitioners and scholars find it instructive to distinguish between a group and a team. Katzenbach and Smith (1993) define a *team* as "a small number of people with complementary skills who are committed to a common purpose, performance goals, and approach for which they hold themselves mutually accountable" (p. 45). Others stress the importance of member interdependence on a team, noting that team members must rely on each other and feel accountable to one another in the accomplishment of their goals to be considered a team (Dyer et al., 2007; Levi, 2001). To account for this fact, Larson and LaFasto (1989) believe that "a team has two or more people; it has a specific performance objective or recognizable goal to be attained; and coordination of activity among the members of the team is required for the attainment of the team goal or objective" (p. 19). In other words, a group might consist of a large number of individuals, all of whom perform the same general job task but do not count on other members in the accomplishment of individual tasks, so they are not a team by these definitions. Students in a class held in a large lecture hall are likely to be considered a group, but if they divide into smaller units to accomplish a task such as a class project (becoming interdependent and accountable to one another in the achievement of a common goal), they are forming teams.

Other commonly held characteristics of teams include the following:

- Members participate in decision making and setting goals.
- Members communicate frequently with one another in the accomplishment of team tasks.
- The team has a defined and recognized identity by others in the organization, outside the team.
- Members have defined roles and they recognize how these roles interrelate.

Barner (2006) writes that contemporary teams are very different from those of the past. Most people hold a model in their heads of a team as an intact collective of members who reported to a single manager, with egalitarian membership, located physically at a single work site, and made up of members from similar cultural backgrounds. Today, rather, teams are much more likely to be ad hoc, called together for a single purpose and a short period, perhaps self-directed without a single manager. Instead of being egalitarian, power relationships now intrude when members increasingly represent multiple functions and hierarchical levels. Teams may be geographically distributed, and thus may be comprised of members from different countries and diverse cultural backgrounds. Contemporary teams may demand that members perform multiple roles on multiple teams rather than specialized roles on a single team (Katzenbach & Smith, 1993). All of these factors challenge our traditional assumptions about what constitutes a team, they introduce new complexities into the inner workings of a team, and they complicate our implementation of interventions to improve team effectiveness.

What Makes a Successful Team?

Much work has been done by researchers to identify the characteristics that distinguish high-performing, effective teams. In an extensive survey of different types of teams in different types of organizational environments and circumstances, Larson and LaFasto (1989) conducted detailed interviews of members of high-performing executive teams, project teams, sports teams, government, and military teams. They concluded that eight characteristics set the successful teams apart:

1. *A clear, elevating goal.* That is, the goal is understood and seen as challenging to team members.

2. *A results-driven structure.* Team members must have clear roles, effective communication processes, and an ability to use available data to evaluate progress and take corrective action when necessary. Members must also understand how their roles interrelate.

3. *Competent members.* The team must be comprised of members with the right technical knowledge and interpersonal skills to contribute to the team's goal.

4. *Unified commitment.* Team members must be willing to dedicate effort and energy to the team.

5. *A collaborative climate.* The team must develop a climate of trust in one another in order to collaborate.

6. *Standards of excellence.* High-performing teams have high standards for individual performance and members feel pressure to achieve.

7. *External support and recognition.* Teams need external rewards but also support in the form of resources necessary for the team to accomplish its work.

8. *Principled leadership.* Leaders provide the necessary motivation and alignment to complete the team's work.

All too often, teams fail in one of these categories. Low-performing teams consistently demonstrate some of the characteristics listed in Table 11.1, missing one or more of these elements of high-performing teams. These can often be clues that a team would benefit from an intervention.

Special Types of Teams

In addition to a new model of team being used today, many organizations employ special kinds of teams to accomplish tasks. Three of these worth noting in detail are

Table 11.1   Common Problems in Teams

Many observers have seen that low-performing teams experience a common set of problems, including the following:

- Confusion about the team's objectives
- Ambiguity about team goals and how they will be achieved
- Missing handoffs or duplicating work between individuals who do not understand their unique roles or interdependencies
- Unclear expectations from the leader
- Lengthy decision-making cycles and an unclear authority for decisions
- Mismatched expectations for communication and information sharing
- Long and unproductive meetings
- An inability to successfully manage conflicts

self-directed work teams, virtual teams, and cross-functional teams. Each of these teams solves a unique set of contemporary challenges in organizations, but also presents unique difficulties to overcome.

Self-Directed Work Teams

Self-directed work teams are also frequently referred to as self-managed work teams. Self-directed teams have a long history, but their major rise to popularity came in the 1980s when economic cutbacks resulted in the loss of a middle management layer in many organizations, forcing companies to look to new ways of organizing work. The result was the pushing down of decision making into lower levels of the organization, often into teams (Orsburn & Moran, 2000). A self-directed work team is described as follows:

> A group of interdependent, highly trained employees who are responsible for managing themselves and the work they do. They set their own goals, in cooperation with management, and the team plans how to achieve those goals and how their work is to be accomplished. . . . Employees on a self-directed team handle a wide array of functions and work with a minimum of supervision. (Ray & Bronstein, 1995, pp. 21–22)

A common myth is that a self-directed team can do whatever it wants, and many managers and leaders fear that if given authority, productivity will suffer and laziness will become the norm (Hitchcock & Willard, 1995). In fact, self-directed teams have a wide variety of responsibilities, from goal setting, organizing work processes and schedules, sorting out roles and responsibilities, monitoring results, and taking action when results do not meet requirements. Some teams take on roles that were formerly the sole province of management, such as hiring team members and conducting performance evaluations.

Making the transition to self-directed teams usually challenges individual and cultural models of work, such as how decisions get made and who is ultimately responsible for productivity and performance. As a result, significant learning is required for managers and employees alike, which involves "learning how to behave under an empowered management philosophy including the roles and skills required, and the unlearning of old habits and behaviors (e.g., waiting for managers to solve problems)" (Druskat & Dahal, 2005, pp. 204–205). Employees must take ownership of team processes and be motivated to manage them as a group. Without significant learning, practice, and attention to team development, self-directed teams and leaders can quickly revert to "old" habits where leaders direct the team's actions and make its decisions. Management behavior is an important factor in the transition to self-directed work teams, and their attitudes and actions have been called "the single largest threat" (Ray & Bronstein, 1995, p. 215) to successful implementation. Managers must shift from "paternalistic" behaviors of monitoring and supervision to acting as a coach or mentor to the team (Yeatts & Hyten, 1998).

Self-directed work teams require significant leadership commitment, mutual trust between management and employees, acceptance of new and sometimes ambiguous roles, and willingness to invest in time and money for training and development of teams. Self-directed teams are also prone to special challenges, such as resistance from leadership, the need to manage conflict within the team, power and control, team decision making, and giving and receiving feedback. The most successful self-directed work teams also have a support structure that encourages their ongoing development and growth beyond the initial implementation period.

Virtual Teams

We have already noted how organizational teams are increasingly diverse and geographically distributed. These teams help organizations respond to the global customer environment and take advantage of expertise located throughout the world. Such teams are often referred to as virtual teams, defined as teams where members "work together through electronic means with minimal face-to-face interaction" (Malhotra, Majchrzak, & Rosen, 2007, p. 60). In a virtual team, team members from San Francisco, Denver, and London may all join a conference call and e-mail chat to solve a customer problem, perhaps pulling in an expert from Beijing when necessary. Virtual teams may hold few face-to-face meetings, conducting most team meetings through computer-mediated communications or other technologies. Thus, a distinguishing feature of a virtual team is the use of electronic tools to communicate and share information. This can involve not only very common and well-established technologies such as telephone conferences and e-mail, but many organizations increasingly use Internet-based chat and instant messages, social networking technologies, handheld communications devices, and Internet-based collaboration tools to facilitate easy and quick interaction among team members.

When members are not collocated, coordination of work across physical and time-zone boundaries is the central challenge. It is also a challenge to build and develop a team, to create "avenues and opportunities for team members to have the level and depth of dialogue necessary to create a shared future" but where "issues of cultural diversity, geographic distance and member isolation can increase the challenges to effective collaboration" (Holton, 2001, p. 36). It can be challenging for members to build trust or to get to know one another on a personal level through electronic technology. Many feel that e-mail creates easy opportunities for miscommunication and misunderstanding, increasing the potential for conflict that is difficult to resolve through the same mechanism.

Dyer et al. (2007) identify four problems that seem to trouble virtual teams more frequently than face-to-face teams:

- *Lack of trust and mutual understanding.* Members may represent different cultures and develop conflicts, mistrust, or stereotypes when other members enact different cultural preferences.
- *Violated expectations.* Members may find differences in the use of different technologies, the expression of emotion through technology, or the time it takes one member to respond to another's request.

- *Lack of training and effective use of communication technologies.* More effective virtual teams make use of available technologies and know how to apply them in the appropriate situation.
- *Lack of effective team leadership.* The authors note that leading a virtual team can require a significant investment of time. Malhotra et al. (2007) also identify special challenges of virtual team leaders, who must establish team trust, evaluate and measure progress, and ensure participation, all using distance technology.

To address these issues, some observers recommend several remedies (Connaughton & Daly, 2004), including creating opportunities to meet face-to-face to build relationships, creating opportunities for dialogue and "small talk" for team members to get to know one another on a personal level, holding team sessions to agree on team norms about the frequency and type of communications (such as frequency of and process for conducting meetings), and scheduling discussions or training sessions on cultural differences.

Cross-Functional Teams

Cross-functional teams are a response to the increasing complexity of operations in many organizations and the demand for rapid pace, focus, and problem solving (Parker, 1994). A cross-functional team is "a small collection of individuals from diverse functional specializations within the organization" (Webber, 2002, p. 201). Members are not usually part of the same department but represent varied departments, units, or geographies, and they are often brought together for a defined period to work on a specified project or problem. Team members usually report to a project team leader but also report to a functional unit "home" manager who directs their day-to-day work. An example of a cross-functional team would be a product development team where representatives from marketing, sales, customer service, finance, and product engineering all bring their unique experience to collaborate on a single team.

The same benefits of implementing cross-functional teams are also its major challenges. First, "functional diversity" of membership brings multiple perspectives together to enhance a team's knowledge and problem-solving ability (Webber, 2002), yet it also means that teams can have trouble communicating and finding common ground as team meetings become organizationally "multicultural" experiences (Proehl, 1996). Members may use different points of reference or vocabularies and exhibit different values. Second, cross-functional teams can have the benefit of including members who can be brought together for a short time to work on a project and then disband. Yet dedication of time can vary among organizational members, causing team conflicts and mismatched understandings of commitment to the team. This is "largely because the projects are not directly related to the members' immediate work, and members have many competing responsibilities and varying degrees of immediate management support for participating in organizational initiatives" (Proehl, 1996, p. 7). Third, having a single team leader who brings the team together can provide a single point of leadership, yet it can create confusion and frustration for organizational members who now find themselves with two managers who may have conflicting demands. This can create ambiguity regarding decision making, such as which manager controls performance evaluations and rewards such as compensation or pay increases.

Studies of cross-functional team success point to the need to address some of these common challenges early on in the formation of a cross-functional team. Leaders can develop a common team mission and identity in the early stages so that team members who represent multiple functional areas can feel a common sense of belonging, commitment, and accountability to the success of the cross-functional team. Parker (1994) specifically recommends clear, overarching team goals to reduce ambiguity and confusion about the team's authority and responsibility. Webber (2002) recommends both training for team leaders and that team leaders establish working relationships early with functional managers to explicitly negotiate time expectations for those members working on the team, and to agree on a performance appraisal and rewards process.

Team Development

Whether we are discussing a more traditional, intact, and collocated team, or one of the teams explored above, researchers have noted that most teams grow and develop in a common way.

One of the most well-known theories of group development comes from Tuckman (1965; Tuckman & Jensen, 1977), who proposed based on an extensive review of published studies that groups appear to experience a five-stage evolutionary process of development. Wheelan (2005) proposed a similar model with different labels. Table 11.2 reviews these two models of group development. Not all teams will develop according to these stages, and not all will move sequentially from stage to stage. Some teams may find themselves "stuck" in one stage, or they may revert back to a previous state. For example, if a team cannot resolve a team conflict, team members may become guarded and may exhibit more of the characteristics of the first stage. While these models are overly simplistic, they may be instructive for practitioners. For the change agent, being aware of stages of team development can help to pinpoint common team problems and suggest interventions to enhance the team's effectiveness and ability to develop to subsequent stages of productivity.

Team-Building Interventions

Interventions to enhance team effectiveness can come from two general philosophies. Some researchers find it useful to distinguish between *team development programs* and *team interventions* (Barner, 2006).

Team development programs proactively encourage teams to develop as healthier groups. These programs "employ a training approach to team-building that

Table 11.2   Stages of Team Development

Tuckman (1965); Tuckman and Jensen (1977)	Wheelan (2005)	Stage Characterized By:
Forming	Dependency and inclusion	Team members explore initial interactions with one another in an "orientation" period as they begin to build relationships. There is generally a low level of trust and high anxiety and confusion about the group's purpose and objectives. There are likely to be conversations about expectations, group rules, and structure. Communication may be guarded, exploratory, and cautious. Disagreement is rarely expressed. The group is generally highly dependent on the team leader, who is usually unchallenged, and members generally consent to what the leader says.
Storming	Counterdependency and fight	Members begin to express disagreements with one another and with the leader as members feel more comfortable and safe with the team. Emotions may run high as members have conflicts over goals, roles, or group values. Group cohesion may give way to subgroups or coalitions. Previously agreed-to group norms or rules may be broken. Members may try to negotiate the conflicts, work through them and move on to the next stage, or they may become mired in unhealthy conflict.
Norming	Trust and structure	The group attempts to manage some of its conflicts by coming to agreement on group norms, roles, goals, and more. There is increased cohesion and a return to the harmonious climate of the first stage, but with increased trust, cooperation, and commitment. The team generally begins to focus again on task achievement with less dependency on the leader. Conflict management techniques are now used effectively, and individuals feel free to express their opinions.

(Continued)

Table 11.2 (Continued)

Tuckman (1965); Tuckman and Jensen (1977)	Wheelan (2005)	Stage Characterized By:
Performing	Work	Team members find synergy and begin to find repeated and successful ways of interacting to achieve group goals. Team members have clarity and agreement on goals, roles, and working processes. The team begins to see a period of high productivity and accomplishment of their objectives as energy is devoted to work tasks. The team monitors its own results and evaluates its own effectiveness, discussing problems and identifying opportunities for improvement. Team leaders more frequently delegate or leave routine decisions to the group.
Adjourning	N/A	As the team's work is completed, the team may disband or members may leave.

relies heavily on the use of team exercises and simulations" (Barner, 2006, p. 48). A team development intervention might help a new team with start-up needs. For existing teams, it might help them to move from stage one to stage two of the models discussed in Table 11.2 by encouraging forthright communication and the healthy expression and management of disagreement. Team development programs often work with groups throughout the group process so that the team develops in a healthy way. In other words, a development intervention can be useful even when the team is not "at war, dysfunctional, incompetent, or distrustful" (Byrd, 2000, p. 157). They are often opportunities to allow healthy groups to develop even more effective patterns.

By contrast, team interventions "employ a problem-solving approach to team-building that helps established work groups identify and address obstacles and constraints to high performance" (Barner, 2006, p. 48). These are likely to be more reactive than proactive, designed to address a problem that a team is experiencing. For example, members on a team may experience role conflict that impedes their performance, and they may need an intervention to sort through the confusion. "To use a seagoing analogy," Barner (2006) writes, "team development programs take the form of redesigning boats when they are dry-docked, whereas team intervention engagements involve repairing leaky vessels while they are still at sea" (p. 49). These are likely to be situations in which a change agent is called in to correct an explicitly identified problem or barrier to the team's effectiveness. The team is often stuck and needs the assistance of a change agent to get unstuck.

Whether they address development of a healthy team or team problems, most of these interventions go by the general label *team building*. As we will refer to it here,

"Teambuilding is the activity of attempting to improve a work group's effectiveness at doing its work, maintaining the relationships of its members and the team's contributions to the wider organizational system" (Coghlan, 1994, p. 21).

Team building, however, has different meanings for different people. In some lay circles, team building has come to refer to fun, enjoyable, often relaxed activities in which team members may learn more about one another outside the work environment. To some, team building has come to mean any team-focused relationship-building event. Many consulting companies have been founded on this principle and now invite executives to learn scuba diving or sailing, or to work together to prepare a six-course meal with a top chef. Some clients request that OD practitioners build team-building activities into a meeting agenda, suggesting that the team meet for dinner, drinks, or an activity after the meeting. Such events are often enjoyable for the participants and usually build camaraderie. However, as Wheelan (2005) puts it, "Research does not suggest that rock climbing, whitewater rafting, blind trust walks, or playing basketball on donkeys increases productivity in any way" (p. 16).

Others may hold an image of a team-building session as a time for members to "sit around and criticize one another, delve into personal matters, or just express their feelings about all kinds of issues, many not related to work" (Dyer, 1994, p. 15). Activities such as these are less effective at some of the more challenging and pervasive problems that teams experience, such as resolving interpersonal and role conflicts, improving communication patterns, enhancing the team's decision-making ability, or correcting process confusion. It is this latter set of challenges to team effectiveness that better encompasses the issues to be addressed in a team-building intervention.

Team building has a negative connotation for some clients because it cannot be denied that team-building activities often fail to achieve their objectives. In fact, some researchers have found that team-building interventions have no resulting effect on team performance (Salas, Rozell, Mullen, & Driskell, 1999). Others have found that the team building–performance link is a highly complex one, in which the effect on team performance depends on the amount of time the team has been together, the amount of time the team spends working together, the duration of each unique task, and the timing of the intervention (Bradley, White, & Mennecke, 2003; Woolley, 1998). It may also be that team-building interventions appear to not have met expectations when we implement them as one-time "fix-all" efforts and not as a part of a longer term strategy (Boss, 1983). Building a high-performing team takes time. To think of a single team-building intervention as having "fixed" a team "conjures up pictures of OD consultants as magicians waving wands and curing all ills in the brief time that they have with the team—this is clearly naive" (Rushmer, 1997, p. 317).

Finally, Boss (1983) has observed a pattern of regression after team-building interventions, when team cohesion and unity, and energy for collaboration and trusting relationships, revert back to old traditions. This is especially true when there is little follow up after the intervention, no support structure for continuing the changes, no leadership support, and no associated changes in policies or processes. All of these postintervention factors should also be taken into account to ensure a successful team-building intervention.

As you might expect, team-building interventions start with a data gathering methodology (using one or more of the methods described in Chapter 7) to determine the focus area for the intervention. Two widely used data gathering methods specific to teams are the *team diagnostic survey* and the *team diagnostic meeting*. Team diagnostic surveys vary significantly but usually ask team members to individually rate the team on such items as "Members are clear about group goals," "Members are clear about their roles," "The group uses effective decision-making strategies," and "The group uses effective conflict management strategies" (Wheelan, 2005, pp. 49–51). Many practitioners design customized surveys of this sort, depending on the team's current needs. A more formally tested empirical team diagnostic instrument has been designed by Wageman, Hackman, and Lehman (2005) and consists of a 15- to 20-minute survey designed to assess such areas as team structure, goals, leadership, and cohesiveness. Use of a designed and tested instrument such as this one can increase validity and allow comparisons to other high-performing teams.

A second data gathering method, a team diagnostic meeting, allows the group itself to assess its own functioning, usually face-to-face. In an open environment of self-evaluation, with or without a facilitator, team members discuss the team's strengths and weaknesses, and they design their own action plans to address them, which may involve one or more team-building interventions. (Some possible diagnostic discussion questions are listed in Table 11.3.) In one variation of a diagnostic setting, team members write down the issues that inhibit the team's effectiveness, small subgroups sort the issues by theme, and the team discusses and prioritizes the problem areas, which are then the focus for problem-solving meetings on another occasion.

The chief advantage of this method is that the group itself owns and chooses its own categories of analysis without relying on the predefined categories of a survey. Use of data gathering or diagnostic methods such as these can help to narrow the team-building intervention to the highest priority areas of concern to the team. Once the data gathering or diagnostic activity is completed, a team-building intervention may be appropriate if the data show any of the signs listed in Table 11.4.

Table 11.3   Questions to Ask During a Team Diagnostic Meeting

- What are this team's strengths?
- How are we doing against our goals?
- What factors have contributed to our success?
- What is getting in the way of our goal achievement?
- How well do we solve problems?
- How well do we make decisions?
- How effective are our team meetings?
- How well do we understand our unique roles and responsibilities?
- How well do we collaborate in our work together?
- How well do we communicate with one another?
- How well do we work with other teams?
- How do we handle disagreement or conflict?
- How well do we work with the team leader?
- What problems should we be working to address?

Table 11.4 Signs That a Team Intervention Is Necessary

Dyer (1994, p. 79) lists 12 signs that a team intervention is warranted:

- Loss of production or unit output (productivity)
- Increase of grievances or complaints from the staff
- Evidence of conflicts or hostility among staff members
- Confusion about assignments, missed signals, and unclear relationships
- Decisions misunderstood or not carried through properly
- Apathy and general lack of interest or involvement of staff members
- Lack of initiation, imagination, innovation—actions taken for solving complex problems
- Ineffective staff meetings, low participation, minimal effective decisions
- Slow start-up of a new group that needs to develop quickly into a working team
- High dependency on or negative reactions to the manager (or team leader)
- Complaints from users or customers about quality of service
- Continued unaccounted increase of costs

There are a wide variety of team-building interventions, and most change agents are prone to highly adapt them based on the needs of the team. The next sections describe six common team-building interventions that relate to common needs of a high-performing team, such as team formation and change, job design and work process analysis, roles and responsibilities, and problem solving:

1. Team start-up and transition meetings

2. Confrontation meetings

3. Role negotiation and role analysis

4. Work redesign

5. Workout

6. Appreciative inquiry

Some of these interventions work well for new teams, while some work best for existing teams with work history. Table 11.5 compares these six team intervention approaches.

Team Start-Up and Transition Meetings

In many organizations, teams are frequently formed, and then they work, evolve, and disband, with team members moving on to other projects. This, in fact, is one of the major advantages of teams, because members' skills and experiences can be combined to tackle a problem or situation and then move on to

Table 11.5 A Comparison of Team Intervention Approaches

Intervention	New Teams	Existing Teams
Team start-up	X	
Confrontation meetings		X
Role negotiation and role analysis	X	X
Work redesign		X
Workout		X
Appreciative inquiry	X	X

another team and another problem (Katzenbach & Smith, 1993). Teams can struggle through the start-up process, however, often failing to devote the time and energy to forming the team effectively and instead the team will quickly jump in to performing work or solving problems. This is especially true for temporary or ad hoc teams who may see little need to invest time in the team's initial forming stages. Even when leaders transition or team members join (or leave) the team, there is a period of adjustment that will require attention to get the team back to its formerly productive ways. Team members may use the transition to stop and wonder whether the goals and processes that the team has depended on to date will remain in place. Roles may need to change as team membership changes. Without conscious attention to the initial stages of team formation, many teams will flounder for an extended period until they sort out the team's purpose, team member roles, and working relationships on their own through trial and error. During this time, without much attention to the team, team members can become disengaged and withdrawn, and productivity can suffer.

Team start-up (for new teams) or transition meeting interventions (in the case of a new leader) can both be effective interventions to start teams off quickly. West (2004) writes, "The beginning of a team's life has a significant influence on its later development and effectiveness, especially when crises occur. Start-up interventions can help create team ethos, determine clarity of direction, and shape team working practices" (p. 77). A well-structured team start-up and transition intervention can also do the following:

- Quickly establish agreements and norms so that the team can begin to function more quickly
- Provide opportunities to surface team member disagreements and misunderstandings earlier rather than later
- Clarify basic team functions such as goals and operating methods
- Allow team members to begin to develop interpersonal relationships
- Provide team members with clear and well-defined roles

Golembiewski (1979a) offers several instructive design guidelines for working with new groups or those in transition. Because the teams are new, start-up and transition intervention designs generally emphasize developing structure versus "unfreezing" groups out of any previous agreements. It may be necessary to design sessions that limit the amount of information that a new team tries to process at any one time, instead providing boundaries for discussions to avoid the team becoming overwhelmed. Frequent breaks away from team development or team building may be useful to allow the team to have a chance to work and experiment, and then return to the team development session with fresh knowledge.

A sample start-up or transition meeting outline is listed in Table 11.6.

Table 11.6   A Sample Start-Up or Transition Meeting Agenda

1. Introductions of each team member
   Career history and background, education, family, personal interests or hobbies

2. Talk with the leader
   The leader's vision of and expectations of the team
   Leadership style, "hot buttons," work preferences, values
   Personal, "getting to know you" interview with the leader
   Team member expectations and needs of the leader

3. Exploration of team charter, mission, and purpose

4. Exploration of team goals and objectives
   Priorities
   Timelines and milestones
   Metrics (type, number, frequency of updates, targets, communication of
      results)

5. Exploration of team member roles and responsibilities
   Team member roles, titles, job functions, interdependencies among members

6. Agreement on team norms and guidelines for work
   How will we make decisions?
   What will be our basic method for work (individual tasks, subcommittees,
      the whole group considers all topics)?
   How do we make sure that everyone gets a chance to discuss issues or raise
      concerns?
   How will we communicate and resolve differences?
   How will we ensure the completion of work? How will we change things
      that are not producing results? (Dyer, 1994, pp. 132–135)

7. Agreement on team meetings
   Expected attendance
   Frequency
   Length
   Location
   Usual topics
   Agenda

Confrontation Meetings

The confrontation meeting was first outlined by Beckhard (1967). It consists of a half-day to daylong session of any type of team (though it was first outlined as a session specifically for executive teams) and is in many respects a kind of team diagnostic meeting as described earlier. It is more effective with intact teams that have worked together for some period versus new teams that do not have an extended history. The name of the intervention might suggest that it is intended to address or expose team conflict, but what is "confronted" are the team's obstacles, broadly defined. In a confrontation meeting, the team examines its own effectiveness and health, and it develops action plans to address major areas of ineffectiveness and dissatisfaction. Beckhard writes that the confrontation meeting is appropriate for the following situations:

- There is a need for the total management group to examine its own workings.
- Very limited time is available for the activity.
- Top management wishes to improve the conditions quickly.
- There is enough cohesion in the top team to ensure follow-up.
- There is real commitment to resolving the issues on the part of top management.
- The organization is experiencing, or has recently experienced, some major change (Beckhard, 1967, p. 150).

Beckhard writes that "in periods of stress following major organizational changes, there tends to be much confusion and energy expended that negatively affects productivity and organization health" (1967, p. 153). The rapid nature of the confrontation meeting allows for an effective gathering and sharing of data without the extended time and expense of an organizationwide survey.

The confrontation meeting is structured in seven phases (Beckhard, 1967):

Phase 1: Climate setting (45 minutes to an hour). The session begins with the leader setting expectations to encourage an open and honest discussion.

Phase 2: Information collecting (1 hour). The group is divided into subgroups of seven to eight people, usually representing a broad cross-section of levels and functional specializations. Each subgroup lists obstacles to productive goal achievement and suggestions that would improve the organization.

Phase 3: Information sharing (1 hour). A representative from each subgroup reports back to the larger group. A facilitator begins to group the contributions into categories.

Phase 4: Priority setting and group action planning (75 minutes). Groups are re-formed into functional units, sitting with others in their normal work team. Each group prioritizes the problems that had been shared in phase 3 and identifies the issues that they believe should be given the most attention.

Phase 5: Organization action planning (1 to 2 hours). Subgroups share their priorities with the larger group.

Phase 6: Immediate follow up by top team (1 to 3 hours). The confrontation meeting ends and the top management group holds a private meeting to discuss the nominated priorities and to agree on what follow-up actions they will support. Within a few days they report back to the attendees on which actions they have selected.

Phase 7: Progress review (2 hours). A follow-up meeting is held with all attendees to review progress 4 to 6 weeks after the confrontation meeting.

The confrontation meeting can have the advantage of encouraging participation and ownership by team members. Beckhard notes that this approach can fail if team leaders do not listen to or accept input from team members, if they do not follow up on the team's priorities, or if they set overly aggressive goals that do not get met.

Role Negotiation and Role Analysis

Because team members are, by definition, interdependent with interrelating work activities, they can often find themselves in the frustrating position of not knowing how the various pieces of work fit together to achieve the overall team objectives. Whether team members have worked together at length or are just starting, member roles are a frequent area of confusion. Consider the following common situations:

- Members may not be clear about one another's assignments, so they do not know who to approach with a question or problem.
- There may be overlapping work, with multiple team members performing the same activities.
- There may be work necessary to accomplish that no team member is performing.
- There may be confusion about how the work contributes to the team's goals.
- The team may have evolved a new vision, purpose, or strategy, but old roles still remain.
- The team may have no process for assigning the work to a new team member.
- There may be frustrations about the equitable distribution of work (who gets the good assignments, who gets too many/too few assignments).
- The team leader may assign multiple people to similar activities, leading team members to wonder who is truly responsible for the task, or whether the tasks relate at all.

The result can be team members who fight for the same work while other work gets lost, and inevitable last-minute crises that come about because of the confusion (Dyer, 1994). These role-related challenges can be categorized into several types of role problems that often occur in teams (Adair, 1986):

1. *Role conflict* (one team member). Occurs when one team member holds two mutually incompatible roles. For example, a member leading a project team who is expected to discover the best possible solution but whose manager expects her to advocate a single solution at the same time.

2. *Role conflict* (multiple team members). Occurs when team members hold the same role, and these are in conflict with one another. An example might be two salespeople who are given the same territory with the same customers.

3. *Role incompatibility.* Occurs when there are incompatible expectations about a given role. For example, some may expect the operations manager to facilitate the meeting while other members expect him to quietly take notes.

4. *Role overload.* Describes the situation when a person has too many roles to fulfill, such as sitting on multiple committees and being expected to act as the liaison between all of them, or to participate on the project team and all subteams.

5. *Role underload.* When a role is not fully developed with enough significant work or responsibilities.

6. *Role ambiguity.* When the role owner or team members are unclear about the responsibilities of a given role.

Having well-written job descriptions can address some of these challenges but tends to still leave some role issues unresolved. A role negotiation exercise and a second related intervention called "responsibility charting" can help teams resolve the confusion, conflict, and frustration about roles.

Role Negotiation Exercise

The role negotiation exercise (also called role analysis technique) puts team members in the position of negotiating responsibilities among themselves without needing a leader to make the decision for them. As a result, it is highly participative and can build team consensus about responsibilities. It results in each member having a documented and agreed-upon role description, with an understanding of the preferences and needs of other team members. As an intervention, it is relatively simple to implement, can be done in a short time, and requires no special training of team members to carry out. The four steps of a role negotiation are these (Dayal & Thomas, 1968; Dyer, 1994; Golembiewski, 2000e; Harrison, 1972; West, 2004):

Step 1: Privately, each team member takes a piece of flip chart paper and writes down the activities and responsibilities of his or her role. "This means sharing all information about how the focal person understands the job—*what* is expected, *when* things are expected to be done, and *how* they are expected to be done" (Dyer, 1994, p. 120).

Step 2: Next, the completed flip charts are placed around a room and every team member reads each flip chart. Clarifying questions may be asked of the author about how that author has defined the role.

Step 3: Each team member writes a list on a separate piece of notebook paper with what he or she wants any other team member to do (a) more of, (b) less of, or (c) keep doing the same. Every team member comments on every other team member's role.

Step 4: The lists are sorted so that each team member has a list completed for his or her role (with each of the three categories listed in Step 3) by every other member. These may be written on flip charts and posted publicly for all to read or they may simply be handed out to each person. Team members can then meet in pairs or as a whole team to discuss their lists and negotiate what they would like each other to keep doing or to do differently. It is in this step where the value of the exercise becomes most meaningful, with members usually needing to compromise and be willing to change in at least some small degree. As Harrison (1972) puts it, "Unless a *quid pro quo* can be offered in return for a desired behavior change, there is little point in having a discussion about it" (p. 90). Members will thus learn how to express their own needs from one another and negotiate how or whether those needs can be fulfilled. Harrison also suggests that following a role negotiation exercise, team members try to keep to the negotiated agreements they have made for at least a short time, but that if they do not work, they should try to renegotiate them. Over time, he believes, the team will learn how to do this negotiation as part of its ongoing work activity.

Role negotiation requires an environment of openness and safety, comfort in expressing disagreement and getting beyond disagreement, the ability to express one's wants and needs, and mutual commitment to each other and to the group. Lest it sound too simple: The analysis, charting, and negotiation of member roles on a team is not simply a matter of documenting who will do what, as this process intervention may appear. Complex identity matters and political struggles are at play when members negotiate responsibilities. If I used to be responsible for reviewing all mechanical engineering designs for the company's products, and the team decides that everyone will share that action and I now will begin to work more closely with suppliers only on designs I reviewed, I may feel that I have lost a part of my professional identity. I may feel like I have been demoted or that I am no longer as significant a contributor as I once was. Consequently, change agents who implement role analysis and clarification interventions will be more successful if they are aware of and sensitive to the complexities of managing personal impacts and transitions.

Responsibility Charting

The responsibility charting technique (Beckhard & Harris, 1977) can help a team with its decision-making processes so that members understand who is responsible and involved with what actions and decisions. It can reduce conflict by specifying up front, before the situation occurs, what involvement is necessary in what ways by which team members. Like role negotiation, role analysis is deceptively simple: It consists of the development of a chart or grid on which are written the team's major activities and which members are given the responsibility of completing them. The simplicity of the design belies its power, since completing the chart can be a focal point to pull a group out of a conflict or confusion and surface unexamined difficulties. An example of a role analysis chart is provided in Table 11.7.

Team member names are listed at the top of the grid, and down the left-hand column are listed the team's major activities. One of the following letters is placed under each team member name, in the row for each activity, representing that team member's responsibility for the activity (or it may be left blank if the member is not involved):

- *R: Responsible.* This person is responsible for ensuring that this action is carried out.
- *A/V: Approval or veto.* This person has authority to approve or veto actions and decisions for this item.
- *S: Support.* This person supports the activity with time or other resources.
- *C: Consulted.* This person should be consulted or included in the action.
- *I: Informed.* This person should be communicated to or informed about the status of the activity.

Variations exist among practitioners in which letters should be included. Some, for example, call a role analysis chart a "RACI" chart, and leave out the *S*. Golembiewski (2000d) advocates adding a *D* (for example, *R-D* and *A-D*) to signify responsibility or authority for a decision, and *Imp* to signify responsibility for implementation.

Table 11.7 A Role Analysis Chart

Team Member / Activity	Member 1	Member 2	Member 3

Beckhard and Harris (1977) advocate a number of useful constraints or "rules" to the use of responsibility charts. First, they recommend that every activity line must have one and only one person responsible—only one *R*. If more than one person must be responsible, the activity should be segmented so that the boundary of each member's responsibility is documented clearly. Second, a large number of approvals— *As*—might be an indication that there are too many approvals, and team activity might be streamlined by reducing the number of necessary approvers. Similarly, having too many people consulted on an action may be unnecessarily involving team members and inviting input, which can lead to those consulted becoming surrogate or informal approvers, again slowing down team implementation.

Work Redesign

Hackman and Oldham (1980) describe work redesign as the answer to the question, "How can work be structured so that it is performed effectively and, at the same time, jobholders find the work personally rewarding and satisfying?" (p. 71). When jobs are designed well, people find them more motivating and contribute more effectively to the outcomes that the team seeks. Thus, work redesign can be both an individual intervention and an intervention into the effectiveness of a team.

Hackman and Oldham write that some tasks are best done by individuals, but that especially complex tasks are usually best performed by a team. This is true only if the team and task are well-designed. Yet the authors write that "it turns out that designing work for groups is *not* merely constructing a 'team version' of a good individual job design. . . . For groups, one must consider person-job, person-group, and group-job relationships, as well as how these components fit together" (p. 67).

The Hackman and Oldham model of work group effectiveness defines three criteria to look for in an effective work group. Team membership, goals, and individual jobs on a team can be assessed on these three dimensions.

1. *Level of effort brought to bear on the group task.* How well the group's task is designed will affect how much effort team members can or will put toward the task. Well-designed tasks have the following:
    a. *Skill variety.* Team members bring a number of their skills to bear on the task.
    b. *Task identity.* The work is a "whole and meaningful piece of work" (p. 171).
    c. *Task significance.* The work matters to others internal or external to the team.
    d. *Autonomy.* Team members have some freedom in designing the work, such as the order and priority of subtasks to be accomplished.
    e. *Feedback.* The team gets adequate and truthful information about its performance.

These five design criteria about the properties of the job itself can be diagnosed in a number of ways, including a Job Diagnostic Survey (JDS) created by Hackman and Oldham (1975). If any of them is significantly missing, there are likely to be motivational problems on the team toward the task, as team members are likely to see the work as less meaningful and personally satisfying.

2. *Amount of knowledge and skill applied to task work.* The composition of the group is an important design feature that will contribute to or inhibit a group's effectiveness. Team members must have appropriate competence to perform the skills and tasks needed by the team, and the team must have enough members to handle the amount of work needed but not so many that extra members actually contribute to a decline in the team's productivity. Team members should have the interpersonal skills to manage conflict and work with a wide variety of work styles and personalities. If team members are not trained for the tasks they are asked to perform, they will be frustrated and productivity will decline, and if the team has too many members, each member likely will not have a significant enough task to perform to find the task motivating.

3. *Appropriateness of group norms about performance processes.* This category concerns such items as team agreements about the consistent use of team processes, how the team will measure its progress, and how changes will be made when processes and results do not meet expectations. Teams must have enough standardization that they do not waste time continually deciding how routine tasks are to be performed, yet they must have enough flexibility to recognize when alterations of standard processes are needed.

> The challenge in designing a work group, then, is to help members develop norms that reinforce the use of strategies that are uniquely appropriate to the group task, and that are amenable to change when task requirements or constraints change. (Hackman & Oldham, 1980, p. 181)

Several principles can help change agents to work with teams to design tasks more effectively (Hackman & Oldham, 1980):

1. *Combining tasks.* Skill variety can be increased by combining work tasks so that team members do not always perform the same routine tasks over and over, but have an array of activities to reduce monotony and make use of different skills.

2. *Form natural work units.* Task identity and significance can be increased by forming work units so that the same person performs related activities. These might be organized any number of ways, for example, by geography, customer account, or industry.

3. *Establishing client relationships.* Work can be made more meaningful when team members have contact with their customers or clients. They begin to see the impact of their work on their customers, and they get direct feedback about how customers use their work and feel about it.

4. *Vertically loading the job.* Autonomy increases when jobs are vertically loaded, that is, when team members take a greater responsibility for both a larger number of process steps as well as the authority to decide when and how the work will be accomplished.

5. *Opening feedback channels.* Managers often have feedback or data about a team's performance that they do not share, for whatever reason. Making this information available to the team can increase motivation. For example, if a team has immediate access to a monthly customer survey, they can begin to see connections between that month's work and the customer satisfaction feedback.

Finally, Hackman and Oldham note that very little impact will be achieved to individual jobs and group performance if the group is not supported in the context of the whole organizational system. There should be an appropriate compensation and rewards system in place to recognize excellent performance, a training and education system that can help team members to learn effective interpersonal and task skills, and clear communication from management about the constraints on the group (such as budget or timelines).

Workout

Workout is a problem-solving methodology that was originally developed at General Electric but has now been adapted for use by teams in many organizations. General Motors has labeled the process a "GoFast," Unilever has called it a "Cleanout," and it goes by the name "Trailblazing" at Armstrong (Ulrich, Kerr, & Ashkenas, 2002, p. 286). The process is for use by single teams, cross-functional teams, or multiple functions. As originally designed, it can involve dozens or even hundreds of employees from across an entire company. For this reason, it can also be called a whole organization intervention, more examples of which are discussed in the next chapter. As described here, it is also appropriate for teams in a mini-Workout scenario, where team members use it as a problem-solving methodology for their own internal processes. On a team, a Workout can be a powerful intervention to encourage participation and willingness to initiate an organizational change.

The purpose of a Workout is to identify and eliminate unnecessary work, work that might be taking up extensive time or resources but that is adding little value, work that is bureaucratic in nature, or work not meeting expectations because of process errors or other deficiencies. In the Workout process, it is not solely the leader's responsibility to identify these team problems. Team members that actually do the work are considered to understand it best, so their input is most important. For example, a team member might identify two meetings that have the same agenda and only a few different participants and propose that these meetings be combined to save time and reduce duplication of effort. Another member might note that she is required to produce weekly reports that are only read rarely and suggest a different frequency for producing them. Team members both propose improvement opportunities and take responsibility for designing solutions and proposing changes to senior management.

As designed, the process is relatively simple:

Small groups of managers and employees, cross-functional or cross-level or both, address critical business issues, develop recommendations, and present them to a senior leader at a Town Meeting. After open dialogue, the leader makes "on-the-spot," yes-or-no decisions on those recommendations, empowers people to carry out the ones that are approved, and afterwards reviews progress regularly to make sure that results are actually achieved. (Ulrich et al., 2002, p. 23)

Planning the Workout session begins with the selection of an appropriate business problem, usually involving a process where results are unsatisfactory. Team members are selected who have a stake in the outcome and energy to contribute, and a Workout is planned for 1 to 3 days, during which the process will be redesigned or other changes will be proposed. Senior management support before the Workout session is necessary to ensure that they are open to the change and ready to listen carefully to team recommendations. With halfhearted management support, the team will not have backing later when there are inevitably obstacles to implementation.

The Workout session itself generally follows a five-step process (Ulrich et al., 2002):

1. *Introduction.* Participants learn about the purpose, goals, and structure of the Workout. All participants are encouraged to see the meeting as an opportunity to develop and implement a wide range of solutions, not as a chance to defend one's own function or territory.

2. *Brainstorming.* Small groups develop lists of ideas about what the Workout should accomplish.

3. *Gallery of ideas.* Groups identify their top ten best ideas and post them for others to read. The larger group reviews the ideas and votes on three to four to work on for the remainder of the Workout session.

4. *Action planning.* Teams are formed to expand on the ideas that were described, identifying actions that should be taken and changes that should be made. They identify costs and benefits for making the change and create a project plan and timeline for implementation of the initiative. A project sponsor and team leader are also identified. During a longer Workout session, a process might be redesigned on the spot at this stage.

5. *Town meeting.* The town meeting is the opportunity for Workout participants to present their ideas to senior management. Participants describe the change desired and potential costs, risks, and benefits to the organization of making the change. Senior leaders ask questions to clarify, challenge, and test the team's thinking and are asked to make a yes-or-no decision immediately. They may decide to delegate the decision or poll other managers in attendance. Initiatives that are agreed to are immediately sponsored and expected to begin implementation. Some Workout sessions end with the symbolic physical action of the senior leader(s) signing the flip charts or project plans to publicly demonstrate their commitment to the effort.

Following the Workout session, senior leaders check on the initiative progress on a regular basis. In the first days and weeks following the Workout, the high level of enthusiasm for the project can be supplanted by negativity and discouragement as the difficult change work begins. Leaders can help to encourage the implementation team to maintain energy and focus on the project.

Appreciative Inquiry

Most discussions of organizational effectiveness, including written works such as this one, contain an implicit medical model of organizational health. Problems are seen as deficiencies, illnesses, and cancers to be rooted out and eliminated. Our language is full of descriptions of issues, gaps, barriers, obstacles, snags, crises, errors, conflicts, and mistakes. Team meetings that direct attention to "what's going wrong here" create negative environments where people focus on harmful and destructive actions and relationships, and these conversations often create a cycle of depression, pessimism, and low energy. Organizational members can come to see the problems as insurmountable and hopeless. As members of a team continually examine what is wrong, this habit even seems to carry over to the implementation of any possible solution, as team members may point out weaknesses and faults with even the most promising changes. Energy wanes and morale suffers. It is no wonder that there are few to sign up for yet another problem-solving meeting.

Some authors suggest that more progress might be made in a team if change agents were to direct their attention to what is working and where things are going well instead. A recently popularized method of intervening in teams and organizations called *appreciative inquiry* (Cooperrider & Whitney, 2005; Srivastva, Cooperrider, & Associates, 1990) aims to do just that. Whereas ordinary problem-solving approaches follow a standard process of identifying problems, brainstorming possible causes and their negative effects, generating solutions, evaluating possible solutions, and implementing the ideal solution, the appreciative inquiry process begins with the team's strengths. By appreciating what is working well and where the team has found success, positive energy is released, and the team begins to gain a better understanding of its own valuable contributions. These conversations are naturally more enjoyable, encouraging, and upbeat. Cooperrider and Whitney (2001) write that "the seeds of change—that is, the things people think and talk about, the things people discover and learn, and the things that inform dialogue and inspire images of the future—are implicit in the very first questions we ask" (p. 20). Consider the different reactions a team might give to "what's going wrong in this team?" and the following alternative set of appreciative inquiry questions:

- Describe a time in your organization that you consider a high point experience, a time when you were most engaged and felt alive and vibrant.
- Without being modest, tell me what it is that you most value about yourself, your work, and your organization.
- What are the core factors that give life to your organization when it is at its best?
- Imagine your organization 10 years from now, when everything is just as you always wished it could be. What is different? How have you contributed to this dream organization? (Cooperrider & Whitney, 2005, p. 14)

The conversation that results from these questions creates an environment of openness, hope, and participation in creating a better team or organization. These questions also tend to free creative thinking and avoid allowing a group to get bogged down in the problems of the present.

Its creators see appreciative inquiry as philosophically in contrast with the traditional action research paradigm, where problems of the past are examined through disciplined data gathering and examination, and solutions are implemented and measured. It is based in the "power of the positive question" and that "human systems grow and construct their future realities in the direction of what they most persistently, actively and collectively ask questions about" (Ludema, Cooperrider, & Barrett, 2001, p. 191). It is thus highly consistent with the social construction model of organizational change discussed in Chapter 4, harnessing the power of language and communication in creating organizations and teams as they unfold and are always in-process. For the change agent, appreciative inquiry requires a shift in mind-set to "view organizations as living spiritual-social systems—mysteries of creation to be nurtured and affirmed, not mechanistic or scientific operations with problems to be solved" (Cooperrider & Whitney, 2005, p. 46). We are well-trained in rooting out problems and their solutions, but this new way of intervening also requires a new way of thinking, asking questions, and directing a team's energy.

The appreciative inquiry process consists of four steps or phases, called a "4-D cycle" (Cooperrider & Whitney, 2005):

1. *Discovery.* The discovery process consists of engaging the team and relevant stakeholders in a dialogue about strengths, best practices, accomplishments, and rewarding experiences. Topics are turned around from what is absent or not working to what the team would like to see happen more often and what is working well.

2. *Dream.* Participants look to the future to imagine how things could be, articulating and sharing their visions for the future.

3. *Design.* The team collaboratively constructs a vision for a new future and actions that move the team or organization to a desirable new point.

4. *Destiny.* Last, the discussion focuses less on action plans and spreadsheets and more on creating grassroots networks (including those beyond the team) of interested and committed parties who are empowered and who freely choose to take action on their own.

Several studies have attested to the positive outcomes that resulted from using an appreciative inquiry approach. In one review of the literature, Bushe and Kassam (2005) found that appreciative inquiry was most successful and transformative when it generated new knowledge, new ways of thinking about the organization, or new approaches to taking action. Barrett and Cooperrider (1990) present a compelling case study of change in a hotel management team where conflict and defensiveness were high. Problem-solving and conflict resolution efforts had stalled, and conflicts had become aggressively hostile and confrontational. Instead of focusing on the negativity of the past, the authors encouraged the group to begin to share their images for what might be different. They began to imagine a new hotel environment and to discuss changes to both the hotel and the team that would fit with their shared vision. Over time, personal conflicts waned as the group learned to resolve its ideational disagreements in favor of a shared future.

Some may find the appreciative inquiry approach naive, wondering how a team or organization could succeed if it failed to honestly admit to and examine its problems. Appreciative inquiry does not deny that problems exist, but it tries to reframe them into new subjects for dialogue. For example, one group of consultants worked closely with a customer service department at a major airline. Instead of focusing their attention on the problem of mishandled, lost, or late baggage (a problem they all agreed plagued the airline), the consultants helped them turn the discussion to developing an "exceptional arrival experience" for customers (Whitney & Trosten-Bloom, 2003, p. 134). The discussion then turned to exploring all of the multiple aspects of that experience instead of becoming mired on the baggage concerns, which were just a part of the larger topic. Interest and energy remained high, because the topic was attractive, it encouraged thought and participation, and it inspired dialogue about a new future.

Intergroup Interventions

To this point we have concentrated our attention on the development of a single team. As we know, however, teams do not exist in isolation. They usually interact with other teams inside and outside organizations. The East Coast production team works with the West Coast production team, the customer service team produces reports for the sales team, client management teams create contracts to hand off to internal project teams, and so on. During the course of their work, for various reasons teams can come into conflict with one another. They can develop rivalries and become competitive. Some interdepartmental competition may be beneficial; for example, when two sales teams each try to outperform the other, participants may be motivated to work harder and increase regional sales. When coordination is required and unhealthy conflict increases, however, performance can significantly decline. Organizations may consider these team conflicts unique, but in fact a long history of research in psychology and sociology demonstrates why and how social groups come into conflict and what can be done to resolve these disputes.

Why would teams experience conflict when they are ostensibly part of the same organization and dedicated to its larger purpose? There are so many reasons, in fact, that participants in one research study could identify as many as 250 unique types of intergroup conflict (Cargile, Bradac, & Cole, 2006) among collectives as large as nations and religious groups. Of the general categories that participants identified, several sources of intergroup conflict are especially germane to organizational environments:

- *Economic differences.* Competition over limited resources such as budgets and opportunities for promotion.
- *Beliefs.* Different cultural beliefs about how things should be done.
- *Past injustice.* A perception that one group has been mistreated by the other.
- *Egocentrism.* One group holds a feeling of superiority over other groups and resists them to maintain its group identity.
- *Communication.* Difficulties in exchanging information or holding dialogue with the other team.

It may also be the case that simply dividing up into groups and functions, with unique identities and team or department names, actually creates the seeds of intergroup conflict. In a classic series of studies in the 1950s, Sherif and colleagues (see Sherif & Sherif, 1979, for a summary) found ingroup/outgroup conflict to rapidly develop in children's groups almost from the moment teams were created. In similar studies, team members tended to favor their own team and hold negative feelings about members of other teams, even when there was no significant incentive for them to hold those feelings (West & Markiewicz, 2004). Over time, members come to perceive other teams as threats, perceptions that feed anxiety and hostility toward other teams. They begin to develop more cooperative and cohesive relationships with their own team members. Thus, there is some evidence that organizational structures themselves can contribute to conflict.

An us-versus-them mentality prevails when different teams with unique identities perceive their interests to be in conflict with those of another team. When the team feels a stronger team identity than a larger organizational identity, they can come to see other teams as competitors (van Knippenberg, 2003). Minor conflicts can spiral, reducing trust and cooperation between teams, and encouraging stereotyping of other teams' members. These findings are especially notable not only for typical organizational teams but also for increasingly prevalent situations such as mergers and acquisitions (which is discussed in more detail in the next chapter).

Some minor intergroup conflict is natural and likely, but when extreme symptoms are noticeable, an intervention may be recommended. When teams come into conflict and are unable, unwilling, or otherwise fail to resolve their conflicts, some of the following behavior patterns might become evident:

- Unit members avoid or withdraw from interactions with people from the other unit when they should be spending more working time together.
- The mutual product or end result desired by both units is delayed, diminished, blocked, or altered to the dissatisfaction or one or both parties.
- Needed services between units are not asked for.
- Services between units are not performed to the satisfaction of those units.
- Feelings of resentment or antagonism occur as a result of unit interactions.
- People feel frustrated, rejected, or misunderstood by those in the other unit with whom they must work.
- More time is spent in either avoiding or circumventing interaction with the other unit or internally complaining about the other unit than in working through mutual problems (Dyer, 1994, p. 144).

Such negative behavior patterns are far from inevitable, however, and research fortunately points to several interventions that can reduce it.

The overarching objective of an OD intervention in these circumstances is to reduce the interteam conflict by breaking down barriers between teams, encouraging the development of a shared identity and purpose, and improving cooperative processes. Researchers have demonstrated a reduction in interteam conflict through several means (summarized in Table 11.8):

1. *Increasing intergroup contact* (Dovidio, Gaertner, & Kawakami, 2003). More communication among group members alone is not sufficient to completely resolve intergroup disputes, especially those that are long-standing or particularly hostile. However, it is more likely when certain conditions are present, such as group members having equal status and a common goal. Particularly when team members establish friendly personal relationships through increased contact, tension is reduced and team members begin to associate those positive feelings to other members of the team as well.

2. *The implementation of a superordinate goal* (Johnson & Lewicki, 1969; Sherif, 1979). A superordinate goal is one that is "*urgent, compelling,* and highly appealing for *all* groups involved" (Sherif, 1979, p. 261) and is "beyond the resources and efforts of one group alone" to accomplish (Johnson & Lewicki, 1969, p. 10). That is, it is not enough for the goal to be simply shared—it must be one that each group could not reach if it were to try to do so alone. Conflict is reduced when teams come together in a cooperative context to reach a goal that is important to them, and when team members witness members of the other team working hard on an interdependent task. Superordinate goals are most likely to be effective means for reducing interteam conflict when they are initiated by a third party, not by one of the conflicting teams. Higher level managers and executives are often in a good position to do this.

3. *Recategorization* means developing a "common in-group identity" (West & Markiewicz, 2004, p. 62). This involves finding or highlighting the common identities that both teams share, for example, stressing how members are all part of the same organization.

4. *Finding a common enemy,* or an external threat to the well-being of both groups. Some have argued that the common-enemy approach only reduces conflict momentarily, and when the enemy is defeated, the intergroup conflict returns, because the groups never really resolved the underlying differences (Blake, Shepard, & Mouton, 1964). In organizational contexts, finding a common enemy is often a simple task. This might involve emphasizing how both teams are working for the same organization (the common identity approach suggested above) and against a common set of external competitors who are trying to lure business away from the organization.

5. *Exchanging team members.* Teams may develop a rotation program or invite members of other teams to observe or attend team meetings. This can increase understanding and appreciation of how other teams work, and can also provide opportunities for learning.

Table 11.8   Ways to Reduce Intergroup Conflict

1. Increase intergroup contact

2. A superordinate goal

3. Recategorization and developing a common in-group identity

4. Find a common enemy

5. Exchange team members

An Intervention to Resolve Intergroup Conflict

One widely used method for reducing interteam conflict was first reported by Blake and his associates (Blake et al., 1964; Blake, Mouton, & Sloma, 1965) and was initially designed to reduce very hostile union-management conflicts. The intervention consists of eight activities over a 2-day meeting of the members of both groups:

1. With support of the leaders of both groups, an outside consultant explains the purpose of the session. The session will not attempt to resolve specific process issues or disputes between the groups. Instead, the objective is increased understanding of the other and dedication to improving the relationship. All conflicts are not likely to be fully resolved by the end of the session, but the session should be a first step in the reduction of conflict and launch further work on the specific differences between the teams. Time: 30 minutes.

2. Next, each group meets separately to develop two lists. The first list is the team's description of how it sees itself, especially as the group relates to the other group. The second list is the team's description of the other group. The task, as Blake et al. (1964) put it, "is to describe the *character,* the quality, of the relationship; that is, typical behavior and attitudes" (p. 161). Most groups, the authors note, find it easier to create the latter list about the other group than the former list about themselves. Yet, the development of the group's self-image is an important step in the group examining its own motivations and actions as well. Group members begin to jointly confront the idea that they are a contributor to the relationship with the other. In one variation of this activity, Beckhard (1969) presents different topics for the two lists. On the first list, each group writes what it thinks of the other group, and on its second list, it writes what it thinks the other group will say about them. Time: up to 5 hours.

3. The lists are exchanged. Now each group has the other group's lists. Group A sees how Group B sees A, and how Group B sees itself. The two groups can now compare their self-images with how the other group sees them, and they can begin to point to areas of similarity and difference. Both groups may see Group A as comprised of skilled and talented content experts. But Group A may see Group B as "slow to act and

make decisions" whereas Group B may see itself as "deliberate, conscientious, and thoughtful in evaluating options prior to decisions." Time: up to 1 hour.

4. Each group has time to ask clarifying questions of the other group. The urge to deny the other group's interpretation will be strong, but members are all asked to seek understanding and elaboration of the images first. Time: up to 2 hours.

5. Groups return to their separate meeting rooms for a period of self-diagnosis and discovery. Each group is given two questions: "One, what is it we do . . . that has contributed to the image the other group has of us? Second, what is it in our *own* beliefs and actions that leads us to the conclusion we have reached about ourselves?" (Blake et al., 1965, p. 43). For example, Group B would try to examine why Group A sees it as slow to act. Now each group not only understands how each group sees the other, but each has begun to analyze its own contributions to the relationship and the source of misunderstandings or different interpretations. Time: up to 4 hours.

6. Each group exchanges its diagnostic lists with the other. A joint dialogue is then held in which members analyze diagnoses, share additional insights, and possibly reinterpret past actions. Team members may reach new points of understanding and agreement in order to resolve past differences, and they are also likely to discover deeply held differences that still remain. Time: up to 3 hours.

7. The groups develop a list of remaining key issues in the relationship to be resolved. These might involve changes to meeting structures to enhance communication, clarification of underlying value differences and a plan to find common ground, or a commitment to trust, respect, and openness in the relationship. Time: up to 2 hours.

8. The groups agree on a plan for next steps. This might involve the leaders or a task force comprised of members of both groups holding a series of meetings to resolve the issues. Time: up to 1 hour.

Variations on Intergroup Interventions

Dyer et al. (2007) present several variations of this intervention. In one variation, they invite Group A to hold its discussion of Group B in Group B's presence, though with the ground rule that Group B may only listen and observe the dialogue, followed by Group B holding the discussion with Group A listening. In this variation, both groups have the opportunity to hear the discussion firsthand rather than in list form, yet it can also be risky where the issues are especially contentious. In a second variation, the authors ask each group to meet separately, but to use an appreciative inquiry approach and to describe their ideal relationship with the other group. This design can have the advantage of encouraging members to consider a new vision and imagine an alternative to the current relationship. In a third approach to intergroup conflict, the authors use a task force team comprised of members that both teams find agreeable. The task force is given the responsibility of resolving some of the obstacles to working together. Issues might be resolved quickly in this design, but because all members are not involved, acceptance of the task force recommendations might be minimal. In all cases, the authors recommend that a structure be designed to resolve future disputes, perhaps through the use of a task force or review board that meets regularly to assess the team relationship.

In addition, there are times when a team may have relationships or conflicts with more than one other team, or a team may desire feedback on how it is perceived. In these cases, an intervention called an "organization mirror" (French & Bell, 1999) can be effective in introducing the focal team to issues in their relationships with multiple other teams. In this intervention, representatives from other groups are invited to participate in a dialogue about the focal team. Focal team members sit on the outside of a large circle, and representatives from other teams sit inside the circle. Guests discuss their perceptions of the focal team and the facilitator invites specific examples. Focal group members observe and take notes, and following the discussion subgroups are formed of team members and guests to work on the identified issues. This intervention can be an excellent way for a team to gain feedback on its performance and perceptions of its working relationships with other teams.

Finally, Alderfer (1977) has described an intervention called a "microcosm group—a structural innovation designed to increase information flow vertically and horizontally among differentiated units" (p. 194) of an organization. The group is a new group comprised of a sample of individuals from the entire organizational population. They might represent each of the company's six sales divisions, or they may come from each of the major departments in the organization. Alderfer describes how one microcosm group helped to design and interpret an organizationwide employee survey, and in another essay, how a microcosm group was used to improve race relations in a large organization (see Alderfer & Smith, 1982). Such groups break down the boundaries often created by different organizational structures and can help to solve some of the information and process problems that occur in this environment. One advantage of the microcosm group is that it brings together representatives from many groups, whereas many of the intergroup interventions described earlier only address conflicts between two groups.

Summary

Teams are the foundations of most organizations today, yet they can also be plagued by a consistent set of problems. Among their other attributes, high-performing teams have clear goals, with knowledgeable members who are mutually committed to the team's success and have well-defined individual roles. Unfortunately, this is not always the case. Teams can struggle with a number of common problems, including confusion about goals or roles, or conflict among members or between teams. Such problems are often symptoms that could be addressed with a team-building intervention to improve team effectiveness. Understanding how teams are structured and how they grow and develop can help a change agent design an appropriate intervention to improve their effectiveness. In this chapter, we addressed six common team interventions: team start-up and transition meetings, confrontation meetings, role analysis, work redesign, Workout, and appreciative inquiry. We also discussed interventions that can improve the effectiveness of relationship between teams, in particular, to resolve interteam conflicts. These are just a few of the interventions and their variations that can help to develop effective teams. If teams are indeed the backbone of successful organizational change, then interventions such as these are likely to become important for any change agent to master.

For Further Reading

Dyer, W. G. (1994). *Team building: Current issues and new alternatives* (3rd ed.). Reading: Addison-Wesley.

Dyer, W. G., Dyer, W. G., Jr., & Dyer, J. H. (2007). *Team building: Proven strategies for improving team performance* (4th ed.). San Francisco: Jossey-Bass.

Levi, D. (2001). *Group dynamics for teams* (2nd ed.). Thousand Oaks, CA: Sage.

West, M. A. (2004). *Effective teamwork: Practical lessons from organizational research* (2nd ed.). Malden, MA: Blackwell.

Wheelan, S. A. (2005). *Creating effective teams: A guide for members and their leaders* (2nd ed.). Thousand Oaks, CA: Sage.

Case Study 5: Solving Team Challenges at DocSystems Billing, Inc.

Read the DocSystems Billing case, including the briefing document and four scenes, and consider the following questions:

1. What problems exist in this organization? How do these problems differ based on the employees' roles? Why do employees object to Jim's proposed solution?

2. Make a recommendation to the client about what could be done next based on the data included. Summarize your observations for Jim, offer possible interpretations, and suggest an approach for next steps.

Briefing Document: DocSystems Billing, Inc.

About the Company

DocSystems Billing, Inc., processes insurance billing paperwork for a network of small health care clinics throughout the United States. Privately owned physician practices, as well as specialists such as cardiologists and physical therapists, contract with DocSystems to process the billing paperwork through the maze of health care insurance companies and networks. DocSystems charges either a flat fee for each bill they process or a percentage of the total, depending on the contract with the provider.

About the Call Center

- Forty full-time employees work at the on-site call center: 30 Medical Insurance Specialists (who handle cases of moderate complexity) and 10 Senior Insurance Consultants (who handle very complex cases). The senior consultants have usually worked up through the ranks, often first working on basic billing, then as medical insurance specialists. Most of them have a long tenure with DocSystems, ranging from 17 to 23 years.

- An additional 100 employees (called "Billing Specialists") work at an outsourced call center. DocSystems contracts out the initial processing of claims and basic computer input. The contract employees used to work at DocSystems until the outsourcing.

- The call center was outsourced a year ago to another organization. Almost all of the former DocSystems employees were offered jobs with the new company, but the pay and benefits were not comparable. Word has spread to the former colleagues who remain at DocSystems that the outsourcing company treats its employees poorly.

Call Center Reorganization

The remaining group of 40 employees was reorganized into two new teams, which was just completed about 3 months ago. Initially, there had been two managers—Alex managed the senior insurance consultants, and Dana managed the medical insurance specialists. Both reported to Jim, the senior director. In the new structure, Alex and Dana both manage 20 employees, with each managing half of the specialists and half of the consultants.

That meant that some of each group remained with their former manager, while some moved to a new manager. Senior management hoped that the integrated teams would start to share knowledge between more senior and more junior practitioners.

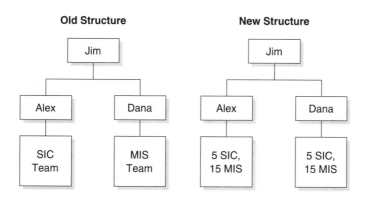

Roles and Work Process

Billing Specialist

The billing specialists do the initial computer input and handle the majority of the cases. Normally this occurs without any need for DocSystems intervention or assistance, but there are occasionally difficult issues that arise. For example, a cardiologist may have conducted a certain procedure that fits more than one category in the DocSystems database, and the billing specialist may be unsure how to categorize it accurately. A phone tree system has been set up between the outsourced organization and DocSystems so that the billing specialist can call any of the medical insurance specialists, who are required to be on call at least 4 to 5 hours during a typical 8-hour shift. The partners can also formally escalate cases by handing them off through the system for a medical insurance specialist to work.

Medical Insurance Specialists (MIS)

A similar process works for the medical insurance specialists. They are assigned insurance cases on a round-robin basis. They typically handle two types of cases: (1) any case that has been "kicked back" by the insurance companies for more information and (2) any case where the patient has filed a complaint, grievance, or appeal. Like the billing specialists, they work on the case to get it accurately processed and filed, and if they run into problems, they can call on their senior counterparts, the Senior Insurance Consultants, to ask a question. They also have the opportunity to formally escalate cases to have one of the senior insurance consultants handle the case if it seems too complicated.

Senior Insurance Consultants (SIC)

The senior insurance consultants handle anything and everything, but they usually work on only the most complex cases. They also answer questions from the medical insurance specialists. They usually get their work from formally escalated cases that the medical insurance specialists cannot handle on their own.

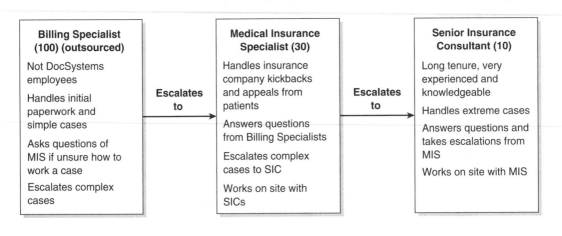

The DocSystems Case in Four Scenes

Central Characters

Jim: Senior Director, Customer Service, DocSystems

Dave: Organization Development Consultant, DocSystems

Rosie Jones: Medical Insurance Specialist, DocSystems

Carlos Chavez: Senior Insurance Consultant, DocSystems

Michelle: Senior Insurance Consultant and Carlos's colleague

Scene 1: The First Client Meeting

Dave and Jim sit at a large oval table in Jim's office, discussing the OD engagement and plans for the upcoming team meeting.

Jim: Thanks for meeting with me. I really need your help facilitating this team meeting.

Dave: No problem, I'm glad to help. Maybe you can start by telling me what you're trying to accomplish.

Jim:	Basically we're trying to redesign how the call center works. We have a few problems. The first problem relates to processing times. Our physician clients obviously want their payments as quickly as possible, so the billing specialists must work very rapidly to input the payment request to the insurance company. Also, our physicians want us to service their patient problems and appeals very quickly. Each role in the process is critical to getting the work done and processed as quickly as possible. Time is our number one success metric, and it's our number one failure right now.
Dave:	What are the results today?
Jim:	Right now we only have about 80% of our customers that say that they're satisfied with our services. From what I've read in our industry, that's at the very bottom. We're seriously in danger of losing customers if we can't speed up.
Dave:	Have you done any analysis of where the bottlenecks might be occurring?
Jim:	Yes. First, you should realize that the workload is tremendous. Each week, the billing specialists handle almost 2,000 claims in total. Our medical insurance specialists handle about 50 cases each per week, and the senior consultants about 10. It might not seem like a lot to handle only 10 or 50 cases per week, but some of the more complex cases can take 2 to 4 hours each to process. If we can't meet our time commitments, our clients and patients get frustrated. So we have metrics in place to monitor how well it's going. If a case takes more than 4 hours to process, it turns "red," which means that in our automated system, the case shows up on our urgent list. When a case turns red, we know from past data that it represents a customer that is dissatisfied, or it doesn't meet our service levels. The more red cases, the more likely we are to lose a customer or to lose money because we have to reimburse our clients when we don't meet our agreements with them.
Dave:	What about the outsourcing? Do you have contractual agreements with them on their own processing timelines?
Jim:	Yes, and actually, they're doing pretty well. We don't usually have too many problems with them. The real problem comes when the cases get escalated to us. We have far fewer cases to handle, yet since they're complex they tend to take longer. Some of our physicians have special service contracts with us where their requests and their patients get top priority. They pay extra for the service, and they expect higher service from us as a result. For our Platinum Tier physicians, we have an agreement that we will get back to them with a resolution to their problem within 2 to 3 hours.
Dave:	What is the cycle time today?
Jim:	It's 15 hours at the moment. In other words, they expect a resolution in less than half a day, and we get them an answer in two days.
Dave:	What do you think is causing the delay?

Jim: First, the cases are remaining with the medical insurance specialists for too long. Their cases turn red at a faster rate than anyone else's. It's the volume that's killing us. Each of them is forced to juggle 10 to 20 cases at a time. It's too much for them to take on, in addition to the calls that keep coming to them from the billing specialists.

Dave: Why don't they escalate to the senior insurance consultants?

Jim: They do, sometimes. But once they've started to work it, I guess they think they may as well finish it. We just need to hire more people, but we can't afford it right now.

Dave: Do you have any ideas about what could solve this problem?

Jim: Yes, and that's in part the reason I called to get your help. I want the 10 senior consultants, who are the most knowledgeable, to help the 30 medical insurance specialists with their caseloads. We want more collaboration on the teams. That's why I've scheduled the 2-day meeting that we talked about, and I'd like your help facilitating the team through a design session where we get their input and figure out how this new collaboration process will work.

Dave: I'm definitely willing to help facilitate the session, and I believe it's the right approach to involve them in the design. First, though, I think it would help me to understand their work better if I could see how they worked. Do you think that one of the medical specialists and one of the senior consultants would let me observe them for a few hours?

Jim: I'm sure they wouldn't mind at all. You should meet with Rosie and Carlos, who are our top performers. I'll send them an e-mail and ask if it would be OK if you contacted them and set up a time to talk. Rosie and Carlos will also be on our project design team, so it will be good for you to get to know them now.

Scene 2: Observation With Rosie Jones

Rosie Jones, a medical insurance specialist, looks up as Dave approaches her desk.

Dave: Hi, Rosie. I'm Dave.

Rosie: Nice to meet you. Please have a seat. I hope I can help you with your questions.

Dave: I appreciate you letting me observe. As I said when we arranged this, I really don't want to take up too much of your time. I'm just interested in learning more about what you do so we can figure this project out together. What are these monitors for?

[Dave points to the three computer monitors all located side by side on Rosie's desk.]

Rosie: This one is for my e-mail, this one is for the case database, and this one shows the calls that are currently waiting on hold.

Dave: And the one with the case database—what are the numbers and colors?

[Dave notices that the screen is full of line after line of case numbers, patient names, and insurance company names. About half are in black and about half are red. More than 30 cases are listed on the screen.]

Rosie: These are all of my open cases. The numbers represent the case numbers, and the red type means that the case is behind. This last column shows the status. So if you look, most of them either say "Waiting Patient," or "Waiting Physician." On those, I'm waiting for a return call. Some I could just close out now. So at the moment, there's not much I can do. Well, I guess on these last three I could get started on them. Let's see what they say.

[Rosie clicks on the screen and opens up one of the red cases.]

Rosie: This one says DED-1, which means "Denied for patient status." I'm not sure what happened, but it looks like we may have sent the case to the wrong insurance company, who denied the case and sent it back to us. This patient also has two health insurance companies to deal with. I'm going to have to call the physician.

[Dave looks at the screens, mesmerized by the amount of detail there is to monitor. Rosie is typing and clicking so quickly, Dave can't follow. Rosie marks the current case "Waiting Physician."]

Dave: It certainly seems that there's a lot going on at any one time. How often do you escalate cases?

Rosie: *[looks up quickly and stares at Dave]* I don't really need to. I know how to do my job. These are my cases, and I want to work them. Besides, we all know what happened to the billing specialists when they got outsourced. You think I want to give up my work and not be doing anything?

Dave: What do you think about the model that Jim is talking about, where the senior consultants would jump in and help out with your caseload when it's too much?

Rosie: *[forcefully]* You mean Big Brother watching over me?

Scene 3: Observation With Carlos Chavez

Later that same day, Dave arrives at his appointment with Carlos Chavez, a senior insurance consultant.

Dave: Thanks for letting me sit with you for a bit. How long have you been with DocSystems?

Carlos: *[pouring a cup of coffee]* It will be 19 years next month. I've done it all, from billing, to insurance, to management. I remember when we used to have only three insurance companies to deal with, and I knew the physicians personally. Now there are so many clients, patients, and insurance companies, it's really amazing.

[Carlos adds sugar and cream to his cup and they return to his desk, just a row of cubicles away from Rosie's. Like Rosie, Carlos has three monitors arranged in a semicircle on his desk, each showing the same information that Dave saw on Rosie's monitors.]

Dave: What kinds of cases do you tend to work on?

Carlos: Well, here's my list right now.

[Carlos points to the case monitor. There are just three cases showing, all listed in red type.]

Carlos: I have this one, which was escalated because the patient was so upset. She had three different physicians she was working with, and only two were part of our client list. The insurance company got confused and ended up paying too much, but we also ended up mistakenly billing the patient for the work of one of the physicians. You can see the case notes are three screens long.

[Carlos scrolls through the case record showing the extensive list of comments.]

Dave: Looks like there is indeed a lot to sort through. How many of these do you work at a time?

Carlos: *[putting his feet up on his desk]* Ah, it's not that bad. This is pretty typical, with about one new case per day. It will take a few hours to sort through, but mostly it's manageable, isn't it, Michelle?

[Carlos yells over his cubicle wall to a neighbor. Michelle stands up and introduces herself to Dave as a senior insurance consultant.]

Carlos: Michelle and I both left Alex's team to work for Dana. Well, I supposed we were technically forced to work for Dana. *[They laugh.]*

Michelle: Yeah, that's been a joy, hasn't it? If at first you don't succeed, reorganize to make sure you won't.

Carlos: *[turning to Dave, voice rising]* You know, we were put into our new team 3 months ago. Dana just had our first staff meeting on Thursday last week. She hadn't even called us to welcome us to her team.

[Michelle pulls out a sheet of paper filled with tally marks. At the top it reads, "Where's Dana?" There is a cartoon drawing of a person on top of a mountain with "Dana" written above it, and 15 stick figures at the bottom of the mountain with question marks over their heads.]

Dave: So until last week, you hadn't even spoken to your new manager?

Carlos: Whatever. It was much better on Alex's team, but hey, I figure the pay's the same whether I leave at 5:00 or 6:30, whether I have 3 cases or 30. We've had the standard 2% raise for the past 3 years, and it won't be any different this year.

Dave: What do you think about the model that Jim has proposed to the design team, where the senior consultants would help out on the medical insurance specialist caseload?

Carlos: I guess I understand where he's coming from. But I don't want to sit on the phone all day dealing with the same old patient status issues. Been there, done that. And I'm not about to take over the caseload for a lazy med specialist who just waits until the case gets old enough for me to work it for them.

Scene 4: The Design Session

It's 8:30 on Wednesday morning. Jim begins the design session meeting with a kick-off presentation. In attendance are Dave, Rosie, Carlos, and Alex (the manager of one of the call center groups).

Jim: I really appreciate everyone taking time out of their schedules to work on this program. I'm confident that we can come up with a good solution. You're among our top performers in the division, and you know best what will work and what won't work in our company.

Jim spends the first few hours of the meeting reviewing the importance of the call cycle times, showing the group charts with the data he has collected: customer satisfaction numbers (last year, year to date, last month), call answering times (in minutes, listed by month for the past 12 months), case volumes (number of new cases opened, number of cases closed for the past 12 months), and number of red cases (by month).

Next, Dave facilitates the group through an approach that Jim has suggested all along, where the senior insurance consultants would collaborate on cases with medical insurance specialists. In the new process, senior consultants would have a new job task of monitoring the current list of red cases and pulling them from the medical insurance specialists if they felt that they could work the case faster based on their knowledge and experience. The new process would require that all senior consultants monitor the list regularly and read through any new red cases.

Dave notes to himself that neither Rosie nor Carlos raised the objections they had shared with him privately, but instead both seem very energetic and willing to experiment with some changes. With confidence high, the group takes a lunch break. After lunch, Dave checks the agreement the team appears to have reached.

Dave: So, Carlos, what do you think of the solution we're proposing?

Carlos: It will never work.

Dave: Why?

Carlos: I don't know. I can just tell you right now, this will never work.

[The group looks silently at Dave.]

Dave: You seemed more confident this morning. What changed your mind?

Carlos: I was out at lunch talking with Michelle and a couple of other people on Dana's team. They hate the idea and think it's just more work for us, and a way for the medical insurance specialists to pawn off their tough cases. I mean, no offense to Rosie, she handles her own cases well. But why should we jump in? We have our own work to do. People are basically lazy, and unless you force them to work on the new cases, they aren't going to volunteer.

After an hour of discussion, the group makes little progress. The morning's agreement has dissolved. With only a few hours to go in the meeting, the attendees begin to abandon hope that they could reach a solution, and Jim intervenes.

Jim: Look, here's what I propose. Let's call it a day for now, and we can reconvene next week to talk about it more. Thanks for your input, everyone, I know that we can handle this. It's a tough situation but I appreciate your participation on this project. Dave, can you hang around for a few minutes?

[The group walks out quietly as Dave begins to stack up some of his papers.]

Jim: *[shaking his head]* I really thought we were headed toward a solution. *[raising his voice]* Why can't people just say what they think if they have a problem? Why did we have to go through all of this?

Dave: I know that you're frustrated, and I'm getting a bit frustrated myself. Clearly the team is frustrated. But I also have to remember that it's better that we find out their objections now rather than a month from now when we're wondering why the new model isn't working.

Jim: I'm at a loss. What do we do now?

Dave: I've listened carefully to the team today, and I'm also thinking about my meetings with Rosie and Carlos. I'm also thinking about the structure of the work and of the two teams at this point. Let's plan to meet at 8:00 on Friday morning. I'll prepare my thoughts about what I've heard so far and what I think we should do next.

Jim: Friday at 8 works for me. I'm anxious to get your perspective.

CHAPTER 12

Whole Organization and Multiple Organization Interventions

The acquisition of MPC, a small chemical manufacturing company, by ComChem, a well-established, older company in the same industry, presented many challenges to both organizational cultures. MPC had been a family-run business with just 25 employees, each of whom had developed strong ties to the husband and wife team founders. The company was well-integrated into the small local community, sponsoring little league teams and contributing financially to area charitable organizations. Employees were involved in most significant decisions, companywide formal and informal communication was frequent, and employees were highly valued and recognized for their contributions through an annual employee appreciation dinner. The environment was casual yet professional, and customers were loyal to the company, as it had served a specific niche in the market serving small local businesses. ComChem also began as a family-owned business, but in a large community serving a customer base of large corporations. Customer service was an important value held by ComChem employees. ComChem employees were treated well, with many perks and benefits available to them, such as a game room that employees were welcome to use at any time and free lunch catering.

After the acquisition deal was signed, executives of ComChem traveled to the MPC site frequently to help employees through the merger, though no one permanently relocated to work there. Some aspects of the transition were frustrating to MPC employees, such as the lack of information about goals, objectives, and the future direction of the organization, vague information about new product pricing, and confusion in job roles. Yet the frustration was short-lived because employees were told honestly that goals had not been determined, for example, and senior managers from both companies openly admitted that the work of integrating the two companies was tough. To thank employees for their patience during the difficult transition, they gave each employee a cash bonus, and they added a basketball court and other perks to the MPC site as a way of making employees feel welcome, valued, and equal to the "old" employees from ComChem. MPC employees saw proof that the values in the new organization were similar to what they were used to, as both customers and employees were treated well at ComChem (Shearer, Hames, & Runge, 2001).

- What factors do you think make a merger succeed or fail?

n this chapter, we will address some of the predominant organization development (OD) interventions that are designed to target changes in an entire organization or in more than one organization. Typically, such large organization interventions are designed to address issues that affect almost every member. Examples include such topics as the organization's strategy, structure, culture, organizational identity, future direction, interaction with its environment, relationship to other organizations such as suppliers and local or national governments, mergers and acquisitions, customer satisfaction, and product quality. This chapter describes the following commonly practiced large-scale interventions, those most frequently mentioned in surveys of OD practitioners (Covin, 1992; Massarik & Pei-Carpenter, 1992), overviews of the field (Bunker & Alban, 1997), and descriptions in the practitioner and academic literatures:

- Organizational culture assessment and change
- Organization design and structure
- Directional interventions: strategic planning and real time strategic change, scenario planning, and search conferences and future search
- Quality and productivity interventions: reengineering, Total Quality Management, and Six Sigma
- Mergers and acquisitions
- Transorganization or interorganization development

These "large-scale" interventions are done for a number of reasons. There are enormous pressures on organizations to reduce costs, increase productivity, speed up cycle time of product development, clarify direction, improve morale, and increase participation (Covin, 1992). Sometimes organizations approach large-scale interventions consciously and intentionally, such as when they develop a 3- to 5-year strategic plan, engage in a culture change initiative, or acquire/merge with another organization. Change may also be forced on the organization unintentionally due to economic, regulatory, or customer requirements; a competitor's new product that requires a company to quickly keep up; or changes that occur inside the organization such as an unexpected leadership departure (Cummings & Feyerherm, 1995). Organizations often choose a large-scale intervention when the task is complex or urgent, or when multiple people are required to accomplish it (Bunker & Alban, 1992).

Whatever the reason, "The purpose of an OD intervention in a large system is to make lasting change in the character and performance of an organization, a stand-alone business unit, or a large department" (Cummings & Feyerherm, 1995, p. 204). By "character," we mean that large-scale organizational interventions significantly affect integral aspects of the organization's functioning, structure, and processes (Ledford, Mohrman, Mohrman, & Lawler, 1989). Thus, large-scale interventions are visible, wide-ranging, and require significant commitment and attention of organizational leaders and members.

Characteristics of Contemporary Large-Scale Interventions

Three characteristics of contemporary large-scale interventions are (1) the involvement of a wide variety of participants, (2) greater timeline of the intervention, and (3) a change in the consultant's role. While these may not apply to every kind of large intervention or every application of a large-scale intervention for any individual client, they do indicate trends that seem to be taking hold among OD practitioners.

Participation. Large-scale interventions, particularly the directional interventions that we will discuss, now tend to include a greater variety of stakeholders than may have been true for interventions like these in the past. The early 1990s saw a shift in the use of whole organization interventions, which invited increased participation in formerly leadership-only decisions such as strategic planning and organizational design. The former "top-down" model of organizational change, where decisions were announced by top leaders who expected subordinates to accept them and carry them out, produced little buy-in from those lower in the hierarchy forced to adapt. To increase both the adoption rate and cycle time of change (and often to develop better decisions), many large-scale interventions began to involve multiple organizational levels (Bunker & Alban, 1992, 1997, 2006).

Large interventions now often involve sizable groups, with hundreds or even thousands of participants (for an example of a large group intervention with as many as 4,000 to 13,000 participants, see Lukensmeyer & Brigham, 2005), or even more in multiple organizations or where entire societies and nations are affected. In fact, even in a single global organization, an intervention that engages many thousands of employees is now commonplace. Including multiple levels and roles in the intervention can lead to better knowledge since problems can be examined from multiple angles, but it also allows participants to learn about the problems, perspectives, and challenges of organizational members they may never have met. In addition, internal and external boundaries have become blurred, as participants from outside the organization, such as suppliers or customers, may be included as well. Even though the groups are large and may initially sound unwieldy, large interventions are often structured using smaller subgroups for purposes of idea generation and dialogue.

Timeline. Despite the need for rapid change, many interventions that target a whole organization rarely consist of a single intervention activity; rather, they often involve multiple activities over a longer period (Covin, 1992, found that the timeline is often longer than a year). Thus, a small list of objectives may be tackled with several individual intervention activities designed to address them.

Practitioner Role. The practitioner's role has also changed, as many large-group interventions ask organizational members to take primary responsibility for generating and analyzing data, and the practitioner's role is "that of a community organizer who structures, encourages, and helps focus the issues" (Bunker & Alban, 1992, p. 581). Rather than the practitioner having responsibility for gathering and interpreting data, organizational members can generate their own data and then can be taught and assigned how to analyze and interpret it.

Thus, whole organization interventions can be quite large and complex. We begin with one of the most pervasive whole organization interventions—that of organizational culture assessment and change.

Organizational Culture Assessment and Change

As discussed in Chapter 2, organizational or corporate culture began to take hold among executives and change practitioners beginning in about the 1980s. Since that time, interest in cultural assessment and change has blossomed. Further unpacking the meaning of *culture* can be illuminating, because culture can refer to a wide variety of behaviors, actions, meanings, and symbols in organizations. Consider the following list of elements of organizational culture:

- *Language, metaphor, and jargon.* How organizational members speak to one another, using what terms. An example is whether organizational members are referred to as "associates" (some retail stores), "individual contributors" (some corporate environments), or "cast members" (such as at Disneyland). Organizational members develop specialized acronyms and terms that often only they understand.
- *Communication* (patterns and media). Who communicates to whom, on what topics, using what media. In some large organizations, the highest leaders send e-mail to all employees, while in others in-person communication is preferred. These choices can be situation- or topic-dependent as well.
- *Artifacts.* For example, pictures or posters on the wall, lobby decor, or dress style. Some organizations have explicit rules for who is permitted what sized office, with what furniture style, or even what model of phone or cell phone calling plan is authorized.
- *Stories, myths, and legends.* What stories from the past resonate with organizational members to recall lessons and learnings from positive or negative events. An organization that has undergone an especially traumatic event, such as a bankruptcy, is likely to have a set of stories and assumptions that are repeated to guide new decisions in order to avoid repeating historical mistakes.
- *Ceremonies, rites, and rituals.* These are formal and informal gatherings or recurring events in which a standard "script" seems to be followed. Examples include a corporate picnic or holiday party, initiation rites such as those in a fraternity or sorority, or even repetitive events such as annual sales conferences, staff meetings, or performance appraisals.

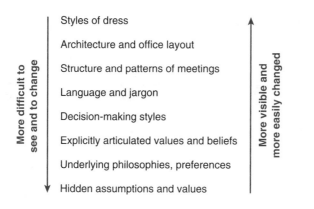

Figure 12.1 Organizational Culture

- *Values, ethics, and moral codes.* Doing what is "right" may mean doing it quickly in one organization or doing an exhaustive study of all possible options in another organization. Organizations have espoused values, those that they explicitly articulate, and hidden underlying values, those that guide decision making but about which organizational members are usually less conscious.
- *Decision-making style.* Including what information is needed before a decision is made, who is consulted, whether opinions are freely offered, who makes the final decision, and how it is communicated.

Elements of culture can be visible, such as styles of dress, office spaces, and language choices, and they can also be invisible or hidden, such as the organization's values, ethical beliefs, and preferences. The more deeply held the belief and more tacit the assumption, often the more difficult it is to change. Figure 12.1 illustrates these elements of culture.

Among experts on organizational culture, perspectives differ on how culture can or should be assessed. Edgar Schein (2006b), one of the most well-known authors on organizational culture, writes that "many organizations think that a general cultural assessment would be of value to them. Unless the culture assessment is tied to a change initiative, however, it is fairly useless" (p. 457).

Schein's culture assessment involves focus groups (detailed below) because groups and teams create culture, so he argues that the data used to understand the culture should also come from groups, not individual surveys. Schein's assessment of culture is qualitative, which has been the dominant way of studying culture. However, another well-respected set of authors on culture has found success with an Organizational Culture Assessment Instrument (OCAI) (Cameron & Quinn, 2006), a quantitative methodology where organizational members complete individual surveys to give change agents insight into the culture. By comparing organizations on dimensions such as internal versus external focus, and preferences for flexibility or control, the "competing values framework" (which is the basis for the OCAI; see Cameron & Freeman, 1991; Cameron & Quinn, 2006; Denison & Spreitzer, 1991) to organizational culture posits four idealized culture types:

- *Clan.* People strongly identify with the group, as in a family, placing a strong emphasis on the team and teamwork. Organizational members are loyal and friendly.
- *Adhocracy.* Innovation is prized, with organizational members having a large amount of independence and autonomy. The organization emphasizes developing cutting-edge products and services and leading the market.
- *Hierarchy.* Tradition and formality are dominant values. The emphasis is on stability, rules, and efficient processes.
- *Market.* Organizational members are competitive, hardworking, and demanding. Productivity and beating the competition are emphasized.

Organizations rarely fit one of these categories precisely; instead, they have elements of each cultural type to a greater or lesser degree. Culture may be a problem or need to be considered for change if elements of the culture or the environment are incongruent with one another (for example, if processes are formal as in a hierarchical culture but the external environment requires the innovation of an adhocracy culture). Thus, the OCAI can help change agents understand broad patterns of cultural values across the organization and open up conversations with organizational members about how the culture can be changed.

Schein (2004, 2006b) has developed a culture change process involving focus groups that are asked to define the culture and to determine how it should be changed. His process involves soliciting commitment from top leadership for the effort, and then beginning a series of focus groups that explore the elements of culture listed above (such as communication patterns, ceremonies, and artifacts). In Schein's process, subteams, often from different parts of the organization, are asked to do the following:

1. Describe the organization's existing culture, including specific examples of artifacts, rituals, and language.

2. Define the organization's explicitly articulated values.

3. Analyze whether the values fully explain the existence of the artifacts or whether there are underlying assumptions that amount to additional hidden cultural values.

4. Describe how the explicit or hidden values inhibit or strengthen how the organization achieves its goals.

5. Share any subcultural differences among the teams.

6. Discuss and come to agreement on action plans to change the negative cultural values.

Once changes to the culture have been identified, how are the new values actually introduced into the organization? Because cultures have tacit beliefs and values at their foundation, it is easy to fall into thinking that culture is inevitable, or that it is something that an organization "has" rather than something that people in the organization "do." In other words, each time we repeat a cultural value, we reinforce it even though we had a choice to do something different. A culture can be changed,

Schein (1990b, 2004) states, through actions that explicitly reinforce new cultural values and those that dismiss the old, beginning primarily with the most visible actions of leadership. Examples include the following:

- Leaders can hire new managers and employees into the organization, as well as promote those who model the new cultural values, and visibly reward them.
- Those who do not model new cultural values and behaviors can be punished or removed.
- Old artifacts, rituals, and ceremonies can be removed or discontinued, and they can be replaced by new ones.
- Leaders can take the opportunity to discuss the new cultural values at every opportunity, such as in staff meetings, employee e-mails, and one-on-one meetings.
- Leaders can model the new culture through their actions, explaining to employees why an action is being done (Deetz, Tracy, & Simpson, 2000).
- Leaders can tell stories of success or failure that relate to the new values.

There are a number of excellent cultural assessment methodologies, both quantitative and qualitative, that have been developed by scholars and OD practitioners. Regardless of the methodology chosen, it is important to be conscious of the reasons and uses of the assessment. It is tempting to ascribe all organizational problems to problems of "culture," which can be esoteric to many leaders, and unnecessarily broad for the change agent to diagnose when the problem can be defined more specifically.

Organization Design and Structure

Many organizations conduct a regular restructuring, giving employees new titles or job descriptions, or perhaps creating, combining, or dividing departments. These structural changes often fail to achieve their desired outcomes, which frequently occurs when organizations approach design activity as a knee-jerk reaction to other problems or alter the organizational structure without considering larger implications.

However, there are many times when organization design genuinely needs to be addressed. The organization may be a new division or may have grown substantially. The organization may have outgrown its previous model due to size or complexity. Other signs for concern exist when departmental barriers inhibit process effectiveness and the organization is no longer serving its customers well, or employees may be frustrated at the internal obstacles to getting their work done (Ashkenas, Ulrich, Jick, & Kerr, 2002).

Such challenges can be addressed when a design perspective (as opposed to a restructuring) is taken. The purpose of a design effort, according to Jay Galbraith (1977), one of the leading experts on organization design, is to develop consistency between the organization's strategy, goals, and structure:

Organization design is conceived to be a decision process to bring about a coherence between the goals or purposes for which the organization exists, the patterns of division of labor and interunit coordination and the people who will do the work. (p. 5)

This implies that the organization must be clear about its strategy, customers, and the processes by which the organization delivers value to customers. It may be the case that a strategic intervention is necessary first if the strategy cannot be clearly articulated. Indeed, Galbraith, Downey, and Kates (2002, p. 12) recommend that "the design process always begins with reviewing the strategy."

The terms *structure* and *design* are often used synonymously, but they are not. An organization's structure tends to refer to the ways in which boxes are drawn on organizational charts, whereas design refers to not only the structure but also other elements that support the structure. Design has five components, all of which must be in alignment and must support one another to produce a capable, effective organization (Galbraith, 1995; Galbraith et al., 2002). These five elements combine into what Galbraith terms the *star model,* depicted in Figure 12.2:

- *Strategy:* The organization's direction and long-term vision
- *Structure:* Roles, responsibilities, and relationships among functions
- *Processes and lateral capability:* Decision-making processes, integrative roles, and cross-functional collaboration mechanisms
- *Reward systems:* Compensation and recognition, goals and measurement systems
- *People practices:* Hiring, performance reviews, and training and development

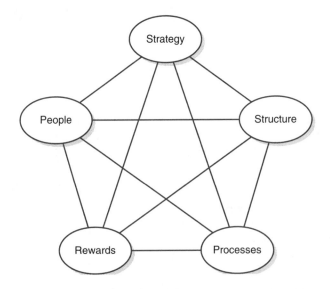

Figure 12.2 Star Model

SOURCE: Galbraith, J. R. (2002). *Designing Organizations: An Executive Guide to Strategy, Structure, and Process.* San Francisco: Jossey-Bass, p. 10. Reprinted with permission.

Each of these five components supports and must be in alignment with the other four. When any aspect of the star model is out of alignment with the rest of the model, the organization's performance suffers. If the strategy is not clear to employees, for example, individuals and teams will be confused about their purposes and overarching objectives. If reward systems do not explicitly articulate tangible and intangible recognition in support of the goals and objectives, the organization may be rewarding the wrong activities. Galbraith et al. (2002, p. 5) offer an instructive diagnostic chart to help identify areas of misalignment in the organization's design (see Figure 12.3).

Stanford (2005) suggests a five-phase process for an organizational design change:

1. *Preparing for change.* This includes assessing the current organizational structure, assessing the organization's strategy, and outlining objectives for a new design.

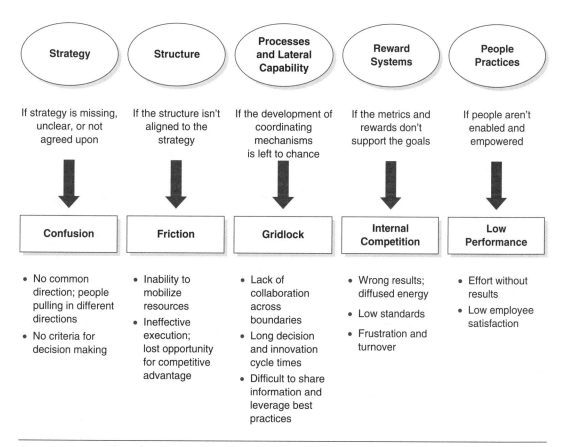

Figure 12.3 Unaligned Organization Design

SOURCE: Galbraith, J., Downey, D., & Kates, A. (2002). *Designing Dynamic Organizations: A Hands-On Guide for Leaders at All Levels.* New York: AMACOM, p. 5. Reprinted with permission.

2. *Choosing to redesign.* An organizational design change can be highly disruptive. Once word leaks that a new structure is imminent, employees may begin to feel anxiety over the transition to a new team, new manager, or new job. Gaining feedback from a large group of stakeholders on the criteria for a new design can help to assess the prospects for a successful transition (Galbraith et al., 2002).

3. *Creating the high-level design.* Developing alternative scenarios and evaluating them against tests such as those described below. This includes not only considering alternative structures, but how the structure will affect processes, rewards systems, metrics, people selection, and skill development.

4. *Handling the transition.* Communicating plans to employees and helping them through the transition.

5. *Reviewing the design.* Evaluating the results of the new structure, measuring outcomes, and making adaptations or any new changes.

Common Organizational Structures

Five common organizational structures include the functional, unit, matrix, network, and boundaryless or process structures. Each of these is described below in its purest form, with its advantages and disadvantages, though there are many variations and combinations of structures (Galbraith, 1995).

Functional Structure

The functional structure is arguably the most common and well-known hierarchical structure. In this design, divisions are organized by the type of work they do, so that divisions of marketing, finance, sales, manufacturing, product development, and so on are led by a single executive who reports to a chief executive officer, for example. Those who work in marketing work with other like-minded marketing professionals on marketing-related concerns, so its chief advantages lie in its ability to help divide labor and focus on narrow areas of specialty. It can also be a highly efficient structure. The marketing budget, when centralized in this manner, can be used for leverage to develop a contract with a single vendor for all printed brochures, for example. Standard practices can be developed for the department to reduce duplication of work (Galbraith, 1995). Figure 12.4 shows an example of a functional structure.

Disadvantages of the functional structure include interdepartmental coordination and complexity. Coordination between functions generally is expected to happen at higher management levels, which can slow down interdepartmental information sharing unless other lateral or horizontal capabilities are developed. When the organization becomes more complex, with multiple products, services, and markets, the demands placed on the functional structure can exceed the capacity of the system to cope with the decisions and information needed. Thus, the functional structure is best for smaller companies with fewer product lines that have a long life cycle (Galbraith, 1995). Because of this, many observers believe that the once-dominant functional structure has been outgrown, since in many (perhaps most) organizations, speed and fast product turnover have become the norm.

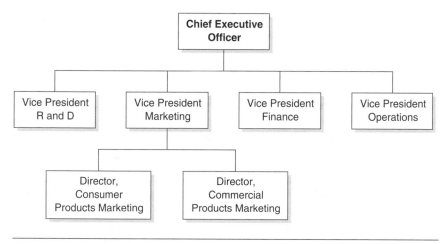

Figure 12.4 Functional Structure

Unit Structure

A unit structure is an alternative to a functional structure, and it divides responsibilities by the market, product, service, or geography that the unit serves. A financial services company might choose to organize by a unit structure, with divisions for auto loans, mortgage loans, retirement accounts, and banking. Instead of a single division to handle customer accounts, there might be separate loan officers, financial advisers, and processing and billing departments in each of those divisions. When implemented at its fullest, in a unit structure each unit has its own human resources, information technology, finance, sales, and marketing departments. With a unit structure, coordination and focus within a single unit is clear, since in the auto loan department, there are specialists who work solely on auto loans, and attention is not diverted to the special and unique challenges of mortgage loans. Figure 12.5 shows an example of a unit structure.

However, the unit structure can also lead to duplication of work and inefficiencies, since multiple departments may not be sharing skills and resources most effectively. (They may unnecessarily duplicate purchases of information technology, for example.) Because different divisions may operate independently, they may not share information or knowledge effectively. When those who do business with the company have a relationship with more than one division, they can be frustrated when they experience different policies and processes, such as billing and invoicing, or the lack of information

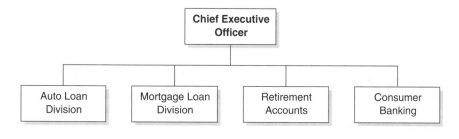

Figure 12.5 Unit Structure

sharing between divisions (the mortgage division may not share information with the auto loan division to streamline a consumer's loan application information).

Matrix Structure

Matrix organizational forms were first developed in the 1960s and 1970s as an attempt to address some of the disadvantages of the first two forms and to maximize their advantages. In a matrix form, the specialist functions and unit functions both exist, in some respects. Imagine a technology company that manufactures personal computers, printers, software, and handheld devices. If it operates in a matrix structure as depicted in Figure 12.6, it might have teams in each division with responsibility for engineering, marketing, and operations. Each of those latter functional groups would have a leader to oversee the company's overall strategy for that division. For example, the leader of marketing would be responsible for ensuring a consistent marketing strategy across all divisions, while the leader of the printer division would be responsible for the success of the company's printing products.

While Figure 12.6 depicts the most basic of matrix structures, organizations have evolved ever more complex versions in the decades since the matrix was originally popularized, particularly in organizations that do business globally and need a strong geographic dimension to their structure. Consider how Figure 12.6 might look if we added three geographic regions reporting to the CEO. Each of those geographic divisions might also have

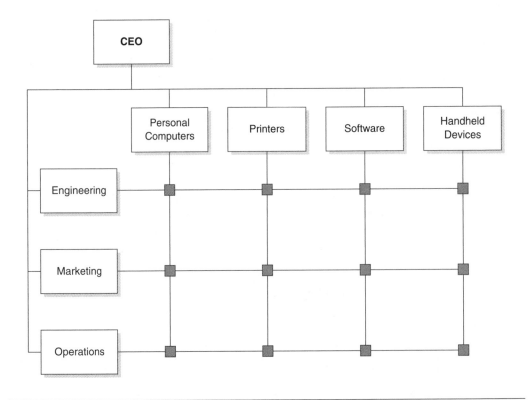

Figure 12.6   Matrix Structure

connections to the other lines of the business, to create a department responsible for marketing printers in Europe, or engineering software in Japan. Galbraith (2009) even explores what a four-dimensional matrix structure looks like, including a discussion of the challenges of planning, leadership, and human resources policies that these structures present.

Matrix organizations work especially well under three conditions (Davis & Lawrence, 1977): first, when there exist pressures for *multiple areas of focus,* such as when a group needs to focus on both technical expertise in a certain field and unique customer requirements of a given market. Second, matrix organizations work well when *the work is especially complex or interdependent* and additional coordination is required. When people are interdependent in multiple ways, a matrix may help to improve communication patterns. In the example above, information can be shared at both the product line and functional level. Finally, a matrix is appropriate when *resources need to be shared* for maximum efficiency. When skills are scarce and resources are at a premium, a matrix facilitates reassignment of the most scarce resources to the necessary areas. A marketing manager could move from personal computers to handheld devices, for example.

Matrix structures can be challenging to implement and can cause role conflict for the individual who can be caught between the demands of two managers. Decision processes can be complicated by seemingly needing approval of managers at many levels in order to proceed. The matrix structure can thus lead to power struggles among managers.

Network Structure

Like the matrix structure, the network structure dissolves the traditional hierarchical functional structure. Indeed, the network structure reduces the organization's functions down to its central competencies, and a network of suppliers and partners provides services that the organization does not consider central (or that are not cost-effective to perform internally) (Miles & Snow, 1992). In one type of network, organizations may design their own products internally, but may contract with an outside manufacturer and shipping company to build and deliver products to customers. They may work with local distributors or third-party providers who may sell directly to customers on behalf of the company, but these distributors are independent entities, not in-house sales agents. In some networked organizations, the "external" suppliers may be so tightly integrated with the organization's people, processes, and technology that the line between being internal and external to the organization is blurred. The organization may even ask outside suppliers, manufacturers, and distributors to integrate their own processes and technology on behalf of the company. The organization therefore becomes a "broker" of services among the various players (Miles & Snow, 1986). An example of this type of network is presented in Figure 12.7. Other types of networks exist as well (Miles & Snow, 1992).

Network organizations can be cost-effective and flexible, and they can focus the organization on its central purpose. They can also cause problems when the organization must rely on the performance (and organizational health) of an external company over which it may have little control. The transition from internal ownership to external control can also be challenging if organizational knowledge or processes are not robust enough to share effectively.

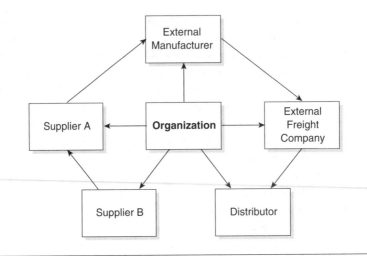

Figure 12.7   Network Structure

Boundaryless and Process Structure

Boundaryless and process designs became popularized in the 1990s as a way to structure an organization to achieve flexibility as a principal objective (Bahrami, 1992). This design emerged primarily in high-technology companies where creativity and innovation, along with rapid product development cycles and quick time to market, were necessary to remain competitive. The boundaryless design breaks down the traditional hierarchy and replaces it with cross-functional, often self-managed, teams that form and restructure as the business changes. Roles, titles, jobs, and teams are no longer rigidly built into the structure of the organization, but negotiated and flexible depending on the needs of the organization. The ability to rapidly form teams, set objectives, adapt to change, and build relationships are all key skills in the boundaryless organization.

One slightly more structured version of a boundaryless organization is to design by process steps. There may be a division focused on the process of gathering customer requirements and developing new products. Another division may be focused on creating customer demand and processing orders. A third may focus on manufacturing orders and delivering products to customers. A process leader may be in charge of each process step. Boundary-breaking designs like this one are good when rapid cycle time is necessary, since there are fewer boundaries to interrupt process flow and decisions to revise the process can be made at the local level. The work flow and each department's connections to the customer are much clearer to all organizational members. Galbraith (2002) notes that the process structure was once a popular organizational structure, but that the structure is less useful in organizations that have automated or outsourced many processes and thus do not have jobs assigned to them as the structure intends. Figure 12.8 shows an example of a boundaryless or process structure.

The task of leadership and management is particularly challenging in the boundaryless organization, as old ways of managing in the traditional hierarchy no longer apply. In an organization accustomed to traditional vertical decision-making authority, a boundaryless structure can be a foreign way of managing. Leadership now performs an integrative function (Shamir, 1999), managing tensions among

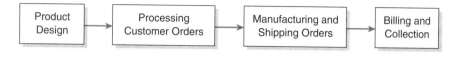

Figure 12.8   Boundaryless or Process Structure

authority, tasks, politics, and identities (Hirschhorn & Gilmore, 1992). Leaders in the boundaryless organization must help to form teams, negotiate between teams, sort through role conflicts, balance competing interests between groups, and encourage employees to maintain an organizational connection even while teams are being disbanded and reformed.

Lateral Capability

As you might have noticed, each structure has its advantages and disadvantages. What is appropriate for one organization, based on its strategy, may be inappropriate for another. In addition, every structure choice will solve some problems while it creates others. For example, the common functional structure, appropriate and effective for many organizations, can create challenges in sharing information across functions. In the geographic structure, a regional sales group can maintain a local focus on its customers, but it may have difficulty knowing how to solve a certain problem that, in fact, has already been solved in another region because of the challenge in sharing solutions across geographic boundaries.

To compensate for the flaws in a chosen structure, organization designers develop lateral capabilities, or horizontal mechanisms that enable the organization to enhance connections between groups or divisions created by the structure. Whereas the structure develops the vertical organization by creating departments and groups with common objectives, lateral practices help the organization share information across these boundaries.

Galbraith, Downey, and Kates (2002) describe five kinds of lateral capability. Some of these can occur naturally or informally, whereas others must be designed deliberately and typically more formally.

1. *Networks:* Networks can facilitate information sharing across department boundaries by exposing members of one group to those in another. Imagine making an acquaintance in another division at a training program or office party, then later needing a contact in that division to help solve a problem you are experiencing.

2. *Lateral processes:* A lateral process is a key organizational process that crosses major divisions. Consider a process such as new product design, which might involve employees from service, sales, marketing, operations, and research and development.

3. *Teams:* Cross-functional teams can be established in which members maintain relationships on the team as well as in their division. A product sales team, with representatives from each geography, can meet regularly to share best practices and solve problems they have in common related to selling a particular product.

4. *Integrative roles:* Integrative roles are formal positions with the responsibility to share information across the structure. A marketing liaison who works in customer support might gather all customer problems on a regular basis, meet with the marketing team, and then bring back information to customer support on upcoming product releases and marketing initiatives.

5. *Matrix structures:* We discussed the use of matrix structures above, but note that matrix structures are not only a structure but a lateral capability as well. By implementing structural relationships at multiple levels, the matrix structure attempts to compensate for maximizing one element of the structure (product) with another (geography). Thus, it formalizes information sharing across groups within the structure.

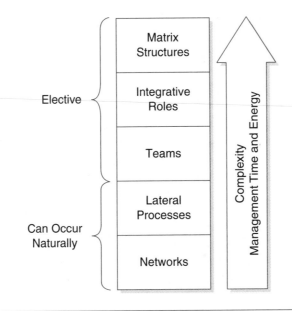

Figure 12.9 Continuum of Lateral Capability

SOURCE: Galbraith, J., Downey, D., & Kates, A. (2002). *Designing Dynamic Organizations: A Hands-On Guide for Leaders at All Levels.* New York: AMACOM, p. 137. Reprinted with permission.

Notice that as more sophisticated types of lateral capability are chosen, there is an associated cost in time, energy, and complexity. Which type of lateral capability to implement thus depends on the organization's needs.

Tests of a Good Design

Given the complexities and tradeoffs involved in selecting any of these organizational structures, what should a change agent consider when evaluating a proposed new design? Nadler and Tushman (1992) suggest that change agents evaluate the design's ability to contribute to the strategy and task needs of the organization while appropriately fitting with its social and cultural environment. Strategic factors include a design that does the following:

- Supports the implementation of strategy
- Facilitates the flow of work
- Permits effective managerial control
- Creates doable, measurable jobs

Social and cultural factors include examining how:

- Existing people will fit into the design.
- The design will affect power relationships among different groups.
- The design will fit with people's values and beliefs.
- The design will affect the tone and operating style of the organization.

Goold and Campbell (2002) list nine tests of whether an organization is well designed, propositions that can be used to appraise a design to see whether it is appropriate. They write that the first four of these tests of structure are for "fit" with organizational goals, strategies, skills, and plans. The final five are tests of good design, helping an organization achieve the right level of balance in processes, and may suggest modifications to the design to account for the unique challenges in any organization.

1. *The market advantage test.* Does the structure match how the organization intends to serve its markets? If the organization serves customer segments differently in different geographies, then having geographic divisions makes sense. No customer segment should be missed and no segment ideally should be served by multiple divisions in order to provide maximum focus.

2. *The parenting advantage test.* Parent organizations should organize in ways that allow them to provide the most value to the rest of the organization. If innovation is a key value of the parent company, has it organized in ways that maximize innovation throughout the organization?

3. *The people test.* The design should support the skills and energy of the people in the organization. If the design requires that the head of engineering also manage finances, and finding a single replacement for those dual specialized skills is unlikely if the current leader were to leave, the design may be risky. In addition, the design may be risky if it will frustrate valuable employees who may lose status in the new structure.

4. *The feasibility test.* Will the design require a major cultural shift, such as a matrix design in a culture very comfortable with rules and hierarchy? Will information technology systems require drastic, expensive changes to report performance by customer industry versus geography?

5. *The specialist cultures test.* Some organizational units maintain different subcultures for good reasons. A group focused on the company's core products may think of innovation as a gradual series of incremental improvements to existing products, but a new products division may need rapid innovation for products that have a short life cycle. Combining R&D from both divisions may result in a dangerous culture clash.

6. *The difficult-links test.* How will divisions in the new structure develop links between them, and who will have authority when conflicts arise? If six divisions each have separate training functions, how will they coordinate the use of instructional resources such as classrooms and trainers?

7. *The redundant hierarchy test.* To what extent are layers of management necessary to provide focus, direction, or coordination for the units in their scope? If the purpose and value of a level of management is the same as the ones below it, it may be unnecessary.

8. *The accountability test.* Does the design streamline control for a single unit, or is authority—and accountability—diffused among different units? Will it encourage units that cannot collaborate to blame one another for poor performance?

9. *The flexibility test.* How will the new organization react when a new product is to be designed? Is it clear how the organization would work if the strategy were to change? Does the design actually obstruct and confuse rather than streamline and clarify?

Few designs will achieve all of these criteria. Goold and Campbell (2002) recommend that design planning be an iterative process, and that as a design fails one test, it should be revised and run through the list of tests once more. That said, "There is no one best way to organize" (Galbraith, 1973, p. 2), so some tradeoffs are inevitable. Ideally, "If management can identify the negatives of its preferred option, the other policies around the star model can be designed to counter the negatives while achieving the positives" (Galbraith, 2002, p. 15). Being conscious of how the design addresses the strategy and working with the other elements of the star model to address the flaws with the design is the best advice.

Directional Interventions

In this section we will consider interventions that help organizational members understand and define what actions they should take to develop the organization for the future. They include (1) strategic planning and real-time strategic change, (2) scenario planning, and (3) search conferences and future search. Broadly speaking, while each has a similar general objective, in that they all help organizational members agree on and plan for the future, they differ in their outcomes and process.

Strategic Planning and Real-Time Strategic Change

There are dozens of definitions of strategic planning, and an equal number of writers who have recommendations about how to conduct it. Vaill (2000) defines strategic planning as follows:

> Planning for the fulfillment of the organization's fundamental purposes. It includes the process of establishing and clarifying purposes, deciding on the objectives whose attainment will help fulfill purposes, and determining the major means and "pathway" (strategies) through which these objectives will be pursued. (p. 965)

Strategic planning involves making decisions about the organization's purpose, products, vision, direction, and action plans. It also involves tradeoffs and choices about customers and markets, as well as introspective analysis about the organization's competitive advantage and challenges in its current environment (Porter, 1996).

Strategy also includes a discussion of mission (the purpose of the organization, including its products, markets, and customers) and goals and objectives (the targets, timelines, and methods by which the strategy will be translated into specific measurable activities). Strategies can be developed for almost any length of time—organizations often develop annual strategies as well as those for 3 to 5 years, or even 10 years or more, depending on the organization and its industry. Rapidly changing technology organizations may choose to develop a short-term plan of only a few years, whereas more established and less changing industries may choose longer time horizons.

Among management scholars, much has been written about the intricacies of strategy development. A perfect strategic plan, however, runs into challenges when the real work of implementation begins. Beer and Eisenstat (2000) write that there are six "silent killers" of strategy implementation, all of which relate centrally to the concerns of OD practitioners:

1. Top-down or laissez-faire senior management style

2. Unclear strategy and conflicting priorities

3. An ineffective senior management team

4. Poor vertical communication

5. Poor coordination across functions, businesses, or borders

6. Inadequate down-the-line leadership skills and development (p. 30)

Despite the potential for OD to address these implementation challenges, OD practitioners have historically not been deeply involved in the development of an organization's strategic plan, which has generally been a top management activity. This may be because of OD's intellectual history or reputation for a lack of business knowledge and the assumption by many executives that OD has little to offer the economic, financial, and marketing-oriented world of organizational strategy. The focus of the internal change agent, however, on the effective implementation of strategy can be a defining characteristic of successful strategic planning. Internal OD practitioners can contribute to the process of developing the strategy itself but also can make leaders aware of many additional concerns as they formulate the strategy, such as the following:

- How individuals and teams adapt to changes in strategic direction
- Implications of the strategy on organizational design
- How organizational processes support or hinder the strategy
- Elements of the organizational culture (language, rituals, etc.) that support or hinder the strategy
- How performance management and rewards systems relate to the strategy
- How strategic initiatives can be translated into goals
- Collaboration between departments to achieve strategic objectives

A Strategic Planning Case Study

Consider this example of a strategic planning process published by Beer and Eisenstat (1996). Alpha Technologies is a $1.7 billion technology company with offices throughout the world. It had been composed of a number of different units, gathered together over time through acquisitions and mergers, so that a central problem for leaders was developing an integrated strategy. In response, company leaders developed a strategic planning process that required in-depth analysis of competitors, market conditions, customer needs, and product lines. Executives consulted one another to develop these departmental strategies, but the company became increasingly anxious that implementing these strategies would prove too difficult to carry out effectively because of internal barriers to change.

A strategic human resources management (SHRM) process was created so that the internal dynamics of strategy implementation could be understood. A small employee team, made up of individuals one or two levels below the senior team, was appointed to gather data from the organization about the factors that would support or inhibit the organization's implementation of its strategy. Areas for analysis included anything from organizational practices and resources to management capabilities. In a 3-day session, the employee data gathering team returned to share the data with top leaders, who listened to the presentation of data and jointly diagnosed the results and planned actions to take based on the feedback. The team analyzed the organizational culture, satisfaction levels of stakeholders such as customers and employees, leadership effectiveness, career development and training, the organization's ability to undertake interdepartmental coordination, and more.

In one division in particular, some difficult and honest feedback was shared. The employee task force reported that while the division was currently successful, future threats could undermine success due to a number of interpersonal and internal factors. These included low morale, a top-down management style in the division, low cross-functional interaction between departments, and poor upward and downward communication. As a result, the president of the division agreed to make certain changes to his own behavior, cross-functional management teams were created, and the senior team worked on its own team functioning. Other departments made staffing or role changes. In still other cases, disagreements about the overall division direction and strategy surfaced. Task force members reported being anxious about sharing the data, but that once the issues were raised, they did not experience any retribution for honest feedback.

The process resulted in organizational members being allowed to "discuss the undiscussable" (Beer & Eisenstat, 1996, p. 608), though this remains a challenge outside of the SHRM process. A higher level of involvement of employees and connections to senior management has opened up avenues for feedback and participation. Top executives say that the development of the company's overall strategic agenda relies to a significant extent on the SHRM process. While the process continues to be refined and is far from perfect, "The strength of these interventions is that because they are highly structured and consultant led, they allow organizations composed of individuals who may not possess sophisticated inquiry skills to raise and address collectively difficult issues" (Beer & Eisenstat, 1996, p. 617).

The Integrated Strategic Change Process

While strategic planning and OD may not have a lengthy history, it is clear that opportunities abound for integration and that OD brings "subject matter expertise, process expertise, and intervention expertise" (Worley, Hitchin, & Ross, 1996, p. 10) to the strategy effort.

Worley et al. (1996) have developed a four-step strategic planning and implementation process designed specifically for OD practitioners to add significant value to the planning effort. They call the process *integrated strategic change* (ISC) and write that their approach considers strategy development in combination with the often more challenging issues of strategy implementation, such as organization design, employee motivation and skills, and collaboration and teamwork across the organization. In this process, the strategy does not stand alone, but it aligns the organization around the necessary means to make it effective through a change plan. The ISC process consists of these steps, with the first two comprising strategy development activities, and the next two comprising the change management activities to make the strategic plan effective:

1. *Strategic analysis.* The first step is to conduct a strategic analysis, which involves an assessment of the organization's readiness for strategic change, an understanding of the organization's values and priorities in creating a strategic plan, and a diagnosis of the organization's current strengths, weaknesses, opportunities, and threats (SWOT). It also includes a diagnosis of the organization's strategic orientation, including mission, goals, and core processes.

2. *Strategy making.* The next step is to formulate the strategy. This involves the organization's vision and strategic choices about the amount of change that will be proposed in the new strategy. Leaders analyze the organization's environment, performance, and core competencies to determine whether minimal revision of the strategy is appropriate or whether it needs more radical change. Decisions are made about adapting or improving existing processes, and about the future of the product portfolio, including areas to invest or reduce.

3. *Strategic change plan design.* The strategic change plan outlines not only the major activities that will be implemented or will change when the strategy is adopted but also the impact that the strategy will have on stakeholders inside and outside the organization.

4. *Strategic change plan implementation.* Leadership has a particularly important task in the implementation of the change plan. Leaders must communicate the vision and strategy, including the rationale for the change and how the leadership team arrived at major strategic decisions.

Real-Time Strategic Change

Real-time strategic change (Jacobs, 1994) is a related intervention that OD practitioners have developed that can increase the pace of change. It can be applied to a number of topic areas that require commitment throughout the organization, including organizational members' ownership of and follow-through on implementing a strategic plan (Dannemiller & Jacobs, 1992). While it is not explicitly a strategy development process, it can help organizations implement the strategic plan by increasing awareness and commitment to the plan and its foundations. Philosophically, it has much in common with the search conference methodology that we will discuss later in this chapter, but the objectives are slightly different.

In real-time strategic change, participants work on present-day concerns, or "real business issues, such as cost containment, product quality, and increased responsiveness and sensitivity to the marketplace needs of customers" (Dannemiller & Jacobs, 1992, p. 484). It can involve hundreds of members from throughout the organization who work together to solve problems and discuss opportunities facing the entire organization, not just on those facing their own group or department. "Real time" in this process means "the simultaneous planning and implementation of individual, group, and organization-wide changes" (Jacobs, 1994, p. 21). "Strategic change" means that organizational members will work together on important issues in the organization's internal and external environment, including "customer and supplier needs, competitors' strategies, industry trends, market challenges and opportunities" and more (Jacobs, 1994, p. 22). Participants discuss changes to the entire organization, including the implications of those changes internally. By involving a large group of employees in such strategic decision making, both problems and additional strategic opportunities can be known earlier. It works especially well in strategic planning situations when (Jacobs, 1994):

1. A leadership team has decided that its organization needs a new strategic direction based on drivers for change either from inside or outside their own organization;

2. A draft strategy has been developed by a leadership team prior to the event;

3. The leadership group is open to feedback on the strategy by participants, and to revising it based on this feedback; and

4. The participants in this event comprise the entire organization, or a critical mass of people from a larger organization (pp. 54–55).

Real-time strategic change events are generally structured over a 3-day period. The first day is focused on "building a common database of strategic information" (Jacobs, 1994, p. 56). Participants sit in "max-mix" groups (groups that represent a diverse set of functions, roles, and departments throughout the organization) and share an experience they have had in the organization over the past year that was exasperating or maddening, along with what the next year is expected to be like (both good and bad). Participants summarize the themes representing their current view of the organization and hear from leaders who talk honestly about their own views of the organization. With a commonly shared present state, organizational members learn more about the strategic plan from top leaders, asking questions to clarify their understanding. Next, customers or content experts may give presentations to expand the group's perspective. Participants explicitly discuss changes that they need to make or that other functions need to make for the strategy to be successful. Through processes of individual group discussion, posting themes, and voting, organizational members are drawn back and forth between their own small group contributions and the ideas and beliefs of the larger group. The conclusion of the event asks intact teams to work on action plans as a team to take feedback from other groups and to make decisions about how they can support the strategic plan, designing follow-up initiatives that they will commit to accomplishing. Jacobs (1994) states that the real-time strategic event combines dissatisfaction with a current state, a vision for the future, and action planning that can overcome resistance to change when a large group goes through the experience at the same time.

It is clear that as organizations follow the strategic planning process, OD practitioners can offer a significant contribution:

> By infusing strategic planning processes with the OD perspective, organizations can understand better when and how to make substantive changes in their strategic orientations. Without this integration, we fear organizations will continue to generate elegant strategies that fail to get implemented or effectively implement organizational changes that have but a tenuous relationship to firm performance. (Worley et al., 1996, pp. 153–154)

More and more, OD practitioners are developing skills in strategic planning. They have value to add to the development of strategic content by becoming experts in strategic planning processes, especially in the areas of implementation and change. The integrated strategic change process and real-time strategic change are two methodologies by which OD practitioners can accomplish this.

Scenario Planning

Scenario planning was developed as a management methodology in the late 1960s and 1970s at Royal Dutch/Shell company to better plan for the possible economic and oil demand conditions of the mid-1970s. By using a process of defining and elaborating on various alternative scenarios, they could prepare for what they saw as (and what turned out to be) an eventual oil crisis (Wack, 1985a, 1985b). As we have discussed, the contemporary environment is characterized by a rapid pace of change and a great deal of uncertainty, which has made scenario planning increasingly popular in the past 5 to 10 years. Globalization, increased competition, and economic changes have made a single predictable forecast almost impossible to create or for organizations to respond to. Scenario planning thus encourages organizations to consider several likely possible future states, to consider which of those is most likely, and then to develop plans and actions that could account for a number of possible future situations. In a highly uncertain environment, scenario planning helps to "inform decision making, learn through challenging the currently held mental models, enable organizational learning, and enable organizational agility" (Chermack & Lynham, 2002, p. 373).

An organization can benefit from scenario planning in many circumstances (Schoemaker, 1995):

- Uncertainty is high relative to managers' ability to predict or adjust.
- Too many costly surprises have occurred in the past.
- The company does not perceive or generate new opportunities.
- The quality of strategic thinking is low.
- The industry has experienced significant change or is about to.
- There are strong differences of opinion, with multiple opinions having merit (p. 27).

Similar to other methods of forecasting, scenario planning involves gathering data to forecast possible future conditions. However, "scenario planning simplifies the avalanche of data into a limited number of possible states" (Schoemaker, 1995, p. 26) that allow organizational members to consider and to address. Thus, it is in contrast with strategic planning, in which an organization develops its own plans for its future, and risk mitigation or contingency planning, in which an organization plans for a single future event that may or may not happen (for example, the computer backup system may crash). A scenario is also not a vision statement, which is an organization's desired future state, is based on its values, and is intended to energize and motivate organizational members.

Instead, scenario planning "embraces uncertainty by identifying those unknowns that matter most in shaping the future of a focal issue" (Steil & Gibbons-Carr, 2005, p. 17). Scenario planning works best when there are a number of possible options and there is a high level of uncertainty about which options are likely to pan out. City planners may be able to develop contingency plans if this year's rainfall amounts fail to fill the reservoir to capacity (rationing or price increases, for example). But will the city's infrastructure be robust enough to support the city's needs in 25 years? How will environmental conditions, upstream water usage, tax revenues, transportation, housing prices, interest rates, population increases or decreases, and water rights legislation all affect the future needs of the city? Moreover, which of those factors will be most important to take into consideration? While some data are likely to be available on many of these topics, it may not be possible to predict with certainty how those factors will interact to produce a single likely future state.

In a scenario planning process, detailed stories or narratives (scenarios) are developed that describe plausible future circumstances. "A scenario is a well-worked answer to the question: 'What can conceivably happen?' Or: 'What would happen if . . . ?'" (Lindgren & Bandhold, 2003, p. 21). Scenarios contain enough detail as to be conceivable and credible, and they should be written in a persuasive enough narrative that they help decision makers visualize the future and its impacts on the organization. Scenarios contain both dramatic imagination but also thought-provoking analysis. In the city planning example above, planners might construct a scenario of what the city looks like 25 years from now, imagining a dramatic increase in the population due to the growth and expansion of three of the area's major employers, all high-tech companies. Interest rates have remained steady, and the area's moderate climate and attractive business environment has brought 25,000 new residents to the community, putting a great strain on the city's infrastructure. A second scenario may predict the mergers of the area's three employers leading to job loss and residents moving away from the city to the south metro area where the employment climate is stable, implying that the city's water needs will also remain stable, providing an opportunity to sell excess capacity to surrounding communities. The two scenarios describe very different future states but also describe the conditions to be monitored that will affect the need to take action.

While there are many variations, one recommended scenario planning methodology consists broadly of four major activities (Ralston & Wilson, 2006):

1. *Getting started.* Before any scenarios are written, a scenario planning team should be formed (usually somewhere around a dozen members who have executive support) and the group must determine the time horizon to be discussed and the focal topic of interest. The group should agree on the process and outcomes of the effort.

2. *Laying the environmental-analysis foundation.* Group members gather quantitative data about facts and trends as well as qualitative data about views of the future from organizational members. At this stage, the group explores external factors such as demographic trends, social and environmental patterns, and other economic, political, and technological concerns.

3. *Creating the scenarios.* The factors discussed earlier are now analyzed and compared for their predictability and influence on the organization. Three to five story lines or scenarios are written that capture the majority of the extreme future alternatives. A table compares the scenarios across several variables of concern.

Good scenarios, according to Lindgren and Bandhold (2003), have the following seven characteristics:

- *Decision-making power.* The scenario provides enough detail that decisions can be made based on the scenario coming true.
- *Plausibility.* The scenario must be realistic and believable.
- *Alternatives.* Scenarios should imply options and choices, each of which could be a likely future state.
- *Consistency.* A scenario should be consistent in its own story. That is, to use the example above, proposing employment loss but income increases might need to have some explanation to make it consistent.
- *Differentiation.* Scenarios must be different enough from one another that they describe genuinely alternative situations (ideally they would be diametrically opposed).
- *Memorability.* Scenarios should be limited in number, and each should provide dramatic narrative for ease of recall.
- *Challenge.* The scenarios should confront what the organization currently believes about future events.

4. *Moving from scenarios to a decision.* The scenario planning group and the leadership team discuss implications of each scenario, including the opportunities and threats to the organization for each alternative. Current strategic decisions are tested and debated. The group makes decisions about what actions to take and agrees on metrics and processes for communicating and monitoring the actions.

While scenario planning is simple to explain in concept, it is very difficult to do and to facilitate (Ogilvy, 2002). Facilitating a team through a scenario planning exercise also requires a healthy team in which members have "patience, respect for others, a sense of humor, a reservoir of knowledge and experience, [and] the ability to listen closely to what others have to say" (Ogilvy, 2002, p. 180). A scenario planning intervention can involve not only creative thinking about uncertain and unknown events but also can require the ability to thoughtfully consider ideas and future events that are opposed to one another. Organizational members can have difficulty rationally considering a future in which, for example, the organization's products are obsolete or unnecessary. One purpose of scenario planning is to push these options as topics of discussion.

About scenario planning, Wack (1985a) concludes as follows:

> By presenting other ways of seeing the world, decision scenarios allow managers to break out of a one-eyed view. Scenarios give managers something very precious: the ability to reperceive reality. In a turbulent business environment, there is more to see than managers normally perceive. . . . It has been my repeated experience that the perceptions that emerge when the disciplined approach of scenario analysis is practiced are richer and often critical different from the previous implicit view. (p. 150)

Search Conferences and Future Search

Search conferences and future search conferences are related interventions during which a broad cross-section of stakeholders meet over a short period to develop agreements and action plans to move the organization to a desired future. These techniques have been pioneered and explained in detail by Emery and Purser (1996) and Weisbord and Janoff (2000; Weisbord, 1992), with others proposing additional variations on or applications of the same concept (Axelrod, 1992; Cahoon, 2000). While there are some differences between the two formats (particularly in how the conference planners deal with conflict; see Emery & Purser, 1996, p. 215), both intervention methodologies seek to encourage commitment to a common vision of the future and to develop energy to work on the action plans that will bring about that future in a highly participative environment. We will concentrate below on how future search conferences work.

Features of a Future Search Conference

Size, Length, and Subject. A future search conference is a 2½- to 3-day meeting (with a typical size of about 60 participants) to create action plans for an issue or concern that participants share. It is not a problem-solving conference, in the sense that it is not intended to get a group together to determine how to deal with the county's homeless population or how to reduce the cycle time for shipping of the company's most popular product (though those may be topics for action planning later). Instead, the topic is likely to be "a future search for ABC county" or "the future of ABC company," topics that tend to promote positive energy toward a desired future. It is also not a team-building meeting where members negotiate roles or work processes.

Attendance. The objective in inviting participants is to "get the whole system in the room." A broad cross-section of stakeholders is invited to participate. A conference to determine the future of a school district may invite administrators, students, parents, teachers, staff, business leaders, and elected and government officials (see Bailey & Dupre, 1992; Schweitz & Martens, 2005). Involving multiple stakeholder groups is an important feature of a search conference, for two reasons. First, involvement leads to better input and better decisions. When participants share what they know, every participant learns something about another stakeholder group (their opinions, goals, and problems) that they may not have realized when they examined the situation from their perspective. New relationships are built. Second, involvement means that implementation is more likely because solutions already have built-in commitment from people who developed them. Extensive "selling" is less necessary. "The mayor opens one door, the grass-roots activist another, the ordinary citizen still a third. Together, they make possible a range of commitments none could make alone" (Weisbord & Janoff, 2000, p. 66). Weisbord and Janoff (2000) recommend that 25 to 40% of the participants be from outside the organization. Most importantly, participants must care about the topic and have a stake in its outcome.

Data Gathering and Interpretation. The future search conference methodology approaches the task of data gathering and interpretation differently from the traditional role of the OD practitioner. Instead of the practitioner leading the data gathering and interpretation process, Weisbord remarks that "in search you have people interacting, collecting, and interpreting their own data" (Manning, 1994, p. 88). Participants may bring external data, but their own experiences tend to be the most powerful source of data. By conducting the data interpretation process themselves, participants take responsibility for managing their own content and group process, skills that will be important following the conference as groups take action without the aid of a consultant.

Exploring the Wider Context. The conference is designed for participants to hold a broad dialogue about their shared past and present before attempting to plan a future. In doing so, they learn how their past paths intertwine and interrelate and how they each have arrived at a particular interpretation of the present based on this foundation. With the wider context as a foundation, participants can have a dialogue about a future in which they also all will participate.

Structure. A future search conference involves few to no presentations, training, or speeches by top executives. Instead, it tends to follow this 3-day pattern (Weisbord & Janoff, 2000):

Day 1 (Afternoon)

The first theme for the afternoon is a focus on the past. Participants sit in heterogeneous groups, often with people whom they have never met. On long sheets of paper posted on the wall, participants write their experiences along 5- to 10-year time frames under three categories: "Personal," "Global," and a third focusing on the company, community, or the issue on which the conference is focused. Immediately, all participants are up and writing a sentence or two explaining, for example, what was happening in the company in the 1990s, in their personal life in the 1980s, and so on. All participants share something from their own experience. Back in their mixed groups, participants analyze common themes in the data and present their findings to one another. Then the topic immediately shifts to present trends that are affecting them. The activity is a "mind map," a large graphic display of trends and their relationships to one another. As the final activity of the day, participants vote on which of the top trends they believe are most influential. In a very short time, participants have established a shared past and conducted an analysis of current influential trends. Importantly, by completing a small task together, they have also learned something about collaborating and appreciating one another's perspectives.

Day 2 (Morning)

The next morning, participants are reseated into stakeholder groups (e.g., customers work with customers, suppliers with other suppliers). Now working with others with whom they share a common role, they analyze the influential trends from the previous day, and they share with the larger group what their individual stakeholder groups are currently doing with respect to the trends and what they would like to do in the future. Next, the same groups make two lists. The first list is their list of "prouds," or those things they are currently doing with respect to the organization or focal issue that they are proud of or that are working well. The second is a list of "sorries," those things they regret or that are not working well. By the end of the morning, the stakeholder groups have acknowledged their place in the system's success. Because each group has admitted to its regrets as well as acknowledged its successes, groups end up on equal footing and they notice the ways in which they are interrelated.

Day 2 (Afternoon)

In the afternoon, talk turns to the future, and participants are again reseated in diverse stakeholder groups. Each group has a single deliverable: a creative presentation of their desired state in 10 to 20 years, often putting themselves into the future and looking back on today with the "hindsight" of experience. The presentations take the form of "putting on a skit or a play or writing a poem or singing a song" (Manning, 1994, p. 89). Unleashing creative forces tends to free participants' energy from the discouraging issues and problems of the present. Participants often report that this was the most energizing, entertaining, and powerful part of the conference. After hearing each presentation, the groups develop lists of the common themes they heard, possible projects that could result, and any areas of disagreement that they have with the desired futures.

Day 3

The final day is devoted to developing agreements and action plans. The whole conference group reviews the lists of themes, projects, and disagreements from the previous day. Individuals and stakeholder groups face the reality of the choices they need to make about the future, and they may not be willing to support some of the identified alternatives. Such disagreements are not resolved during the conference but are placed on a list. The objective is to identify those actions, based on a common vision of the future, that groups can support. Once projects or themes are agreed to, stakeholder or ad hoc groups meet to develop short-term or long-term action plans. Participants develop postconference plans for communication and follow-up in meetings or through websites or newsletters.

Future search conferences following this structure have been sponsored in hundreds if not thousands of organizations around the world, in virtually every industry and organizational profile. In a short time, it can be an excellent intervention to encourage groups from multiple perspectives to develop a common vision of the future. Like most other interventions, it does not work well when skeptical participants or sponsors are coerced into participation, when there are significant differences in underlying values, or when mixed stakeholder groups are intentionally not included because they are distrusted.

Quality and Productivity Interventions

The three interventions in this section that address organizational quality and employee productivity arguably suffer more from a "fad" mentality than do most of the other interventions discussed in this book. Total Quality Management, reengineering, and Six Sigma have all had moments of popularity as well as moments where their techniques have been assailed in both the popular and academic press. None was, strictly speaking, developed as an organization development intervention in the same traditions as we have discussed, but because change agents are frequently involved in their application, it is important for most OD practitioners to be at least somewhat familiar with them.

Total Quality Management

Total Quality Management (TQM) developed as the earliest of these three approaches, gaining widespread attention in the 1980s as a response to the quality challenges to American manufacturing coming from Japan. TQM uses quality principles and tools to manage and improve processes through employee involvement in teams. Quality, in this respect, is not just the responsibility of manufacturing products that are error-free. Instead, quality is everywhere. "Total quality management can be defined as creating and implementing organizational architectures that motivate, support, and enable quality management in all the activities of the enterprise" (Heilpern & Nadler, 1992, p. 138). However, there is much variation in what TQM means and a number of highly specialized tools and techniques that many consider to be part of a TQM effort, including the following:

Practices such as benchmarking, continuous improvement, *Kaizen,* concurrent engineering, just-in-time, empowerment, *Poka-Yoke,* micro process control, cycle time, flexible manufacturing, lean production, customer focus, value added, suppliers as partners, cross-function networking, statistical process control, and total system control. Since TQM means so many different practices, TQM means different things to different consultants. (Boje, 1993, pp. 4–5)

TQM involves systems thinking (as we discussed in Chapter 4), where customers receive the output of the organization's inputs and process steps. In TQM, processes are systematically measured using statistical techniques, called *statistical process control* (SPC), to chart the accuracy and productivity of each process. Problems are examined and solved using specific analysis techniques. Not only does TQM require significant training for employees to learn these techniques, but it requires a cultural shift in many organizations to consider the impact of every process on customer quality, with every employee taking ownership and responsibility for quality. In addition, management processes, including measurement tools, rewards, and communications, are all impacted by the adoption of a TQM mentality. Effectively implementing a TQM program can take 5 to 7 years (Heilpern & Nadler, 1992).

TQM comprises five basic activities (Adams, 1992):

1. *Identify customers and what they value at all levels.* The top management team must support the quality effort in the organization and should meet regularly with top and potential customers to assess the organization's products and services. Moreover, TQM also emphasizes meeting the needs of internal customers, for those departments that serve others internal to the organization, such as finance or human resources.

2. *Identify products and services provided.* Customers should be asked which products or services they value, how they use those products or services, and what improvements would make the product or service even more valuable.

3. *Define processes.* Flowchart techniques are used to document the actual process in use today, with all its flaws, including rework, testing, and quality checks. Employee teams can document processes and point to common problem or errors in the process.

4. *Simplify the process.* Like quality circles, ad hoc cross-functional employee teams can take ownership for process improvement activities as those closest to the action. Unnecessary process activities can be combined with others or eliminated to streamline the number of steps required.

5. *Continuously improve.* Incremental process changes can be made regularly when data from SPC charts and root cause analysis tools prove that there is a fault in the process. SPC charts show the standard variations in the process so that when a process exceeds these levels, action can be taken to understand and correct where errors are occurring. Management must rely on data (such as quantitative charts) to make decisions rather than making decisions on a hunch or best guess.

Critics of TQM point to its high failure rate (about three-quarters of implementations fail to live up to their expectations, according to Spector & Beer, 1994), the wide gap between its "rhetoric and reality" (Zbaracki, 1998), and presumptive packaging as an employee involvement strategy masking a mechanism for management control (in the footsteps of Taylorism) through statistics (Boje & Winsor, 1993). Supporters, however, point to significant improvements in organizations that have used the TQM approach, documented in the annual Malcolm Baldrige Quality Award competition.

Reengineering

Hammer and Champy's (1993) book *Reengineering the Corporation* argued that management fads and quality efforts had done little to improve productivity and profitability in corporations. They pointed out that in most organizations, there exist tremendous inefficiencies caused by organizational structures that segment research and development, engineering, manufacturing, shipping, customer service, and more into distinct divisions that may each be successful but at the expense of another department. Rather than make small incremental changes to existing processes (such as small technology improvements that could save a few hours or dollars in manufacturing or shipping), companies could save more time and money by rethinking and restructuring entire operations. As an example, they pointed to a company that reengineered its credit processes so that instead of separate departments handling applications, credit checks, writing loans, and so on, one person would follow the request through the entire process. By involving fewer departments and giving one person the responsibility to manage the process, cycle time was reduced considerably. Hammer and Champy write that reengineering is not the same as automation, downsizing, or reorganizing; rather, it is a rebuilding process where entire organizational operations are created anew. The reengineering movement touched off by Hammer and Champy's book continues today, sometimes under the moniker of *business process reengineering* (or *redesign*) (BPR), though today it does often involve new technology and downsizing.

Reengineering efforts are comprised of a leader, a process owner, a reengineering team, and an overall reengineering steering committee and "czar" (who oversee all of the organization's reengineering efforts). The organization's major processes are defined and mapped to understand the work currently being done. Three criteria help the team determine which processes are ripe for reengineering: processes that are not working as they should, processes that affect the organization's customers, and processes that would have a high impact if redesigned. Once the organization has chosen a process to be reengineered, it is the responsibility of a reengineering team to remove barriers, create new process steps, develop new job roles, shift responsibilities, or consider any of a number of other possible changes. They consider how to implement core reengineering principles such as "as few people as possible should be involved in the performance of a process" (Hammer & Champy, 1993, p. 144).

The reengineering movement is related to and consistent with the widespread belief in OD to think both structurally and systemically about larger organizational processes and practices rather than improvements in a single department or system. However, there are also important value conflicts with OD. The primary values of reengineering tend to be about organizational profitability and process control rather than participation (Moosbruker & Loftin, 1998). Hammer and Champy (1993) note that two major flaws with most reengineering programs are that they let the corporate culture stall the effort and they fail to run the program from the top down, writing that "frontline employees and middle managers are unable to initiate and implement a successful reengineering effort" (p. 207). Consequently, when pushed through without involvement from those affected, many reengineering efforts have failed to manage major transitions. As an outcome, OD practitioners have found that reengineering efforts that have in the past resulted in downsizing, rightsizing, or other euphemistic terms for layoffs often color how organizational members approach reengineering interventions (Church, Burke, & Van Eynde, 1994), which has led to significant employee dissatisfaction. This has prompted many observers to call for integrating OD values and processes (such as participation, open communication, employee involvement, and shared leadership) with the potentially significant improvements gained through reengineering programs (Cheyunski & Millard, 1998; Moosbruker & Loftin, 1998).

Six Sigma

Six Sigma grew out of quality improvement initiatives at Motorola in the late 1980s, and it gained popular attention when Harry and Schroeder (2000) published a book by the same name. Motorola executives were convinced that they could develop higher quality products at a lower cost, a proposition that has been proven over and over through many Six Sigma projects. Within 4 years of implementing the Six Sigma program, the company calculated that it had saved $2.2 *billion* in productivity increases and cost reductions. It has been used by companies such as GE, AlliedSignal, Ford, Sony, and many more.

The term *six sigma* has two meanings. The first is as a statistical measure; the second is as a business process improvement initiative that uses statistical methods or strives for Six Sigma–level performance. As a statistical measure, six sigma (6σ) refers to the existence of fewer than 3.4 "defects" for every 1 million opportunities. Most processes operate at about a 3 or 4 sigma level, or approximately 10,000 to 60,000 errors for every million opportunities. For example, at 4σ (99% accuracy), the post office would misplace about 20,000 pieces of mail per hour. At 6σ, it would misplace *seven*.

Six Sigma also refers to projects that are undertaken to measure and improve an organization's processes. Six Sigma is also built into the infrastructure of the organization through the establishment of several important roles, called *champions, master black belts, black belts,* and *green belts.* Black belts and green belts lead improvement projects whereas champions and master black belts remove obstacles and provide support and mentoring. Black belts work with green belt team members to apply quality tools to specific problems to drive financial savings and productivity improvements directly to the organization's bottom line. The quality tools used in Six Sigma look much like those that have been around in other quality programs for years. The difference, according to Harry and Schroeder, is that Six Sigma stresses the application of these tools and diligently questions existing work processes to result in a dramatic, measurable impact to the bottom line.

To implement and sustain a Six Sigma program, Harry and Schroeder (2000) write that it takes three steps:

1. *An honest assessment of the organization's readiness to implement Six Sigma.* This includes an assessment of strategic direction, the chances of meeting financial and growth goals, and the organization's ability to adapt effectively and efficiently to new circumstances. Will the company culture (including executives, managers, and employees) expend the necessary energy and provide commitment?

2. *Willingness to expend the needed resources.* There are direct and indirect financial impacts to launching a Six Sigma program. Direct and indirect payroll costs include the number of people dedicated to the effort full-time and the time devoted by executives, team members, and process owners to measuring and improving processes. There are significant training costs as well.

3. *Reflection on the objectives, scope, and timeframe for the program.* This includes an assessment of what the organization wants to accomplish in which areas in what time period, and whether it is appropriate to implement a pilot program in one area, or in the entire organization at once.

Total Quality Management, reengineering, and Six Sigma all aim to improve customer satisfaction and productivity through process improvement efforts. With each program, critics have pointed out that its popularity has waned as improvements either failed to materialize or were short-lived. Yet most agree that this failure is not due to the programs themselves. Their failure, in many cases, has been due to practitioners' neglecting to think of the program as an organizational change intervention, with all of the associated cultural and stakeholder challenges as we have discussed in this book. In this respect, many observers believe that OD principles have much to offer the quality movement.

Mergers and Acquisitions

It has been estimated that anywhere from 50% to 75% of all mergers and acquisitions fail to achieve their financial or strategic objectives (Marks, 2002; Marks & Mirvis, 2001; Nahavandi & Malekzadeh, 1993). Despite the negative press of a low success rate, merger and acquisition activity increased substantially in the 1990s and 2000s (Daly, Pouder, & Kabanoff, 2004; Tetenbaum, 1999). The mergers of HP and Compaq, Daimler and Chrysler, and Exxon and Mobil all grabbed headlines, and each has faced its challenges.

Simulated experiments (see Weber & Camerer, 2003), empirical studies (see Daly et al., 2004), and case studies of mergers (see Horowitz et al., 2002) all attest to neglected cultural factors and incompatible cultures as primary reasons why mergers do not live up to their expectations. Almost 40 years ago, Blumberg and Wiener (1971) noticed that "the financial and economic components of mergers are part of a total mix of problems that includes such things as expectations about norm development, role changes, leadership style, decision-making processes, and goal orientation" (p. 87) but the latter categories rarely get the majority of the attention. It seems that not much has changed in this respect over time. Organizations tend to invest time, money, and energy in initial due diligence activities, such as assessing strategic fit, evaluating financial models, considering possible market and customer reactions, and contemplating product roadmaps, but tend to invest relatively little in understanding the merger's possible impact on people (Tetenbaum, 1999), unlike the rare example that opens this chapter. This has been true despite the fact that many executives increasingly recognize that successful merger and acquisition integration depends fundamentally on people (Cartwright & Cooper, 1993). Executives may examine the financial and strategic aspects of an acquisition because they may be less amenable to change, while culture and people issues are assumed to somehow fall into place.

In many mergers in today's knowledge and service economy, effectively integrating the acquiree's employees is as important as acquiring customers and intellectual property. Failing to appropriately integrate them often means that the most talented never identify with the target company and eventually leave—in fact, up to 75% of senior managers tend to leave within 3 years unless specific efforts are made to integrate them effectively (Tetenbaum, 1999). Despite the popular "120-day plans" or "business as usual" mantras, mergers cause significant disruption. The political reality can quickly become apparent—even the dominant focus of attention—as employees and managers in both organizations begin to jockey for new roles and opportunities in the new structure. As employees worry about their job security, whether they will have the skills to be successful in the new company, whether compensation and benefits will be comparable, and whether they will feel comfortable with the new corporate identity, productivity and morale often suffer serious declines (Holbeche, 2006).

When two organizations come together, culture clashes can occur on a variety of dimensions, such as whether the two companies match or differ with respect to the following:

- Consensus decision making or autonomous decision making
- Risk taking or risk averse
- Formal or informal
- Emphasis on rapid agreement or on thorough analysis
- Emphasis on standard rules or on flexibility
- Emphasis on centralized corporate control or on regional control
- Hierarchical or egalitarian structures
- Long-term orientation or short-term orientation
- Preference for face-to-face or for e-mail communication

Successfully integrating two cultures requires significant work even before merger and acquisition agreements are signed. In each phase of the merger and acquisition process, leaders should devote some attention to cultural issues.

1. *Precontract stage.* In the precontract stage, "human due diligence" (Harding & Rouse, 2007) requires cultural assessments of both the acquiring company and the company being acquired. As Deetz et al. (2000) write, "before an organization should even consider merging with another, it should take stock of its own corporate philosophies, goals, and visions" (p. 175). Knowing one's own culture will help to identify blind spots or potential problem areas in an acquisition. Likewise, the acquiring company should know what strengths and weaknesses exist in the target company's culture. For example, an organization with a strong culture for innovation and problem solving, where organizational members distrust solutions not invented by members of the organization, may have trouble merging with another like-minded culture if organizational members distrust the newcomers. Harding and Rouse (2007) also recommend evaluating the top management's structure and function, and management and decision-making processes, and to examine the skills and capabilities of the target organization's top teams and individuals. These facts can aid in determining whether the acquisition is a good idea at all. Some organizations that take cultural due diligence seriously actually walk away from acquisition deals when their assessment indicates that the integration would be so difficult and argumentative due to cultural factors it would not be worth it (Tetenbaum, 1999). This level of assessment can be difficult, especially for confidentiality reasons, because the OD practitioners or human resources department are often left out of the early stages of negotiation and due diligence.

Transition to the new culture begins the moment the deal is announced. Executives, managers, and the integration team should be prepared for and plan for employee responses to the shock of the acquisition announcement. Communication plans should include the delivery of messages in person (Deetz et al., 2000), frank discussion of the challenges of integration (Marks & Mirvis, 2001), two-way dialogue to allow employees to express their own concerns and ideas, and education about the acquiring company to ease the transition to a new cultural and organizational identity.

2. *Postcontract, "combination phase."* Once the merger or acquisition is announced and employees of both organizations can begin discussing it in the open, they can further explore cultural attributes of both organizations and develop what Trompenaars and Prud'homme (2004) call a "cultural gap analysis." An integration team can be the focal point for such an effort.

Many authors recommend that effective merger integration should be handled by an integration team formed by executives, managers, and employees of both companies. The job of the integration team will be to handle the daily decisions and actions needed to effectively bring both organizations together, and it should be managed by a respected leader who can resolve conflicts among integration subteams. Tetenbaum (1999) also recommends that the integration team have a cultural leader who has strong skills and a high level of knowledge of organizational culture.

The level or type of acculturation should be an explicit topic of dialogue, however difficult it may be for the team to discuss. Nahavandi and Malekzadeh (1993) write of four acculturation scenarios:

- *Assimilation.* This occurs when the acquired company relinquishes its cultural practices and adopts those of the acquiring company.
- *Integration.* The acquired company and acquiring company both retain and also both relinquish aspects of their cultural identities, perhaps sharing cultural elements between them.

- *Separation.* The acquired company retains most of its original cultural attributes, frequently remaining as a division or stand-alone part of the acquiring company.
- *Deculturation.* The acquired company gives up its cultural attributes but is unwilling to adopt those of the acquiring company, usually leading to dissolution of the old organization.

They write that in acquisitions of stronger cultures, integration and separation are more effective strategies, but assimilation or deculturation are likely to be more successful when acquiring a weak culture. Often, integration teams claim to be doing a cultural integration out of respect for the target company, when their actions point to a cultural assimilation strategy. In addition, employees of the target company may be unwilling to abandon their previous culture, no matter how much the integration team would like them to do so. Cartwright and Cooper (1993) write that "many mergers and acquisitions fail, or develop often avoidable problems from the outset, because one of the parties does not recognize, share, or accept the other's perception of the marriage terms" (p. 65). Honest conclusions and communications about the acculturation scenario will help the integration team make appropriate integration decisions and will help the team maintain credibility with employees of both organizations.

3. *Postcombination.* Once the two organizations are legally combined, it is common for the integration team to quietly disband, declare the organizations integrated, and ask members to return to their former jobs. As Buono (2003) notes, "pre-combination transition planning teams continue to be disbanded too early" and "far too many organizations continue to treat the merger and acquisition process as an engineering exercise . . . rather than a far more chaotic set of events that readily affect people's lives and future prospects" (p. 91). This may be because many observers note that a long, drawn-out integration is likely to result in long-term ambiguity and confusion. This is unfortunate, however, because this is where the cultural integration work truly begins, as new teams need guidance and support in team formation activities and learning to cope with the cultural challenges ahead. Such integration work can take up to 2 years or longer, depending on the size and difficulty of the acquisition, and without an integration team to provide resources and attention to integration activities and challenges, managers have few avenues for support. Research suggests that leadership turnover will increase threefold after an acquisition, complicating the continuity often needed in a turbulent circumstance (Krug, 2009).

Several activities can help to make transitions easier. For example, communications should continue following the effective acquisition date to support employees in their adoption of the new culture, continuing to provide education on the organizational vision, strategies, and goals. To help organizational members learn to work more effectively together, Tetenbaum (1999) recommends that a superordinate goal be established that requires employees from both organizations to collaborate.

Successfully integrating two cultures requires significant attention and dedicated resources. Cultural analysis of both the acquired and acquiring companies in the early stages of the combination can provide valuable information about the subjects in the integration that are likely to be contentious and most challenging. It is likely that regardless of the acculturation strategy, because there are so many cultural attributes of any organization (as well as its myriad subcultures) cultural conflict is probably unavoidable. It is possible, however, to be attuned to the dimensions and degrees of cultural difference so that potential conflicts can be better understood, and managers and employees can be prepared for what to do when it happens.

In the postcombination phase, attention must be given to how the merger evolves at the team and department level for the organization to achieve the value desired from the combination. Galpin and Herndon (2008) report the results of a study of executives from 21 different industries who had experienced a merger or acquisition. Almost half of respondents (49%) reported that their organization was in need of "merger repair—that is, my company has several operational, productivity, service, and/or performance issues resulting from poorly conducted M&A integration efforts" (p. 7). This research suggests that continual monitoring and adjustment following the close of the combination is a key competency in achieving a successful merger or acquisition. Indeed, Barkema and Schijven (2008) note that "acquirers are typically unable to optimally integrate acquisitions the first time around" (p. 702) and that "restructuring plays an important role in more fully realizing the potential of the firm's acquisitions" (p. 715), suggesting that organization design work early in the process and in the years following the acquisition is also important (Jasinski, 2010). While we continue to learn more about effective actions in the postcombination phase, it is likely that this phase continues for a longer period and requires more conscious attention than it often receives.

Transorganization or Interorganization Development

A special circumstance in organization development describes the application of OD concepts to situations in which multiple organizations join together in networks or collaborative relationships with a shared purpose (Cummings, 1984). They are referred to as transorganizational systems, or "meta-organizations" (Ahrne & Brunsson, 2008). Many observers have noted that these kinds of relationships are increasing in frequency, but that the field of organization development has been slow to understand the unique challenges involved in these relationships (Clarke, 2005; Cummings, 1984). Ahrne and Brunsson (2008) estimate that there are upwards of 200,000 meta-organizations in Europe alone.

Multiple organizations may enter together into interorganizational relationships (also called transorganizational systems) "to exchange or pool their resources, or they may decide to work together toward some common and mutually agreed upon end, or they may collaboratively produce a new product or service" (Alter & Hage, 1993, p. 2). Sometimes these multiple organization systems arise to address problems and challenges that none could solve independently, perhaps because each did not have the resources to solve the problem or because the organizations are interdependent and must cooperate to solve it (Chisholm, 2000). Examples of these multiple organization relationships include the following:

- Joint ventures for new products or services
- Consortia to develop industry standards
- Production networks

- Public-private partnerships, such as those in education or health care
- Co-ops or purchasing networks
- Trade agreements, associations, or unions
- Joint research and development consortia
- Lobbying associations of for-profit and not-for-profit organizations

Each of these types of transorganizational system (TS) differs in how it is organized. For example, in the development of a joint venture, two or three organizations may meet periodically to determine who will handle which responsibility and how they will work together to meet each organization's objective. Perhaps one may do research and development while the other does manufacturing. In other situations, such as in a trade association or industry standards consortia, there may be yet another new organization formed with representatives from each of the participating organizations. (The United Nations would be such an example.) In still other situations, organizations may participate in name alone, or they may have only an economic relationship such as in a purchasing network.

Chisholm (2008) describes a system that developed in Romania in the 1990s called the Collaborative Alliance for Romanian Orphans. Hundreds of organizations from around the world joined in a consortium to provide relief to an estimated 140,000 orphans left in state institutions. They shared the goals of providing emergency relief, improving the health care system, and in a short time trained hundreds of medical professionals and cared for tens of thousands of children.

Transorganizational systems develop in a three-step process of identification, convention, and organization (Cummings, 1984). Each of these stages presents unique topics of concern:

1. *Identification.* The focus is on the reason for forming the TS, as well as finding and inviting members who have a stake in the issue or concern to participate. Because different groups will see the problem differently, they may have different ideas about the problem's scope and boundaries, so identifying relevant members and establishing the scope of the relationship can be difficult.

2. *Convention.* This second stage consists of soliciting input on each member's perception of the problem, members' objectives and motivations to join, and developing a commitment to taking action to address the issue.

3. *Organization.* Members explore and agree on the desired future they would like to see, including actions each would agree to take to reach that future. Some have used the search conference methodology described earlier to do so (Clarke, 2005; Trist, 1985). Participants develop working arrangements on topics such as communication preferences, norms of participation, decision making, leadership, and structure. For example, what decisions and actions can the TS take on behalf of its members without explicit permission?

From one perspective, problems in these relationships can be addressed with a number of the strategies described in Chapter 11 on single-group interventions, such as new team formation activities and team-building interventions. However, transorganizational systems also have special characteristics that make the application of traditional OD interventions particularly challenging and in many cases demand a different approach, for example:

1. *Hierarchy and structure* are different in transorganizational systems from that in typical organizations. In many cases, group members participate on equal footing with no hierarchical relationship between them, and no higher level "manager" to resolve disputes. Members must conduct their own activities in a self-regulating fashion (Chisholm, 2000). Some have suggested that transorganizational systems are "underorganized" (Brown, 1980; Cummings, 1984), meaning that participants are only loosely tied to one another, with vaguely defined purposes and few or no policies or formal procedures. In these situations, change strategies should "increase organization of the system" (Brown, 1980, p. 190) such as "increasing shared norms and values, and designing structures, roles, and technologies to create predictability and regularity" (Cummings, 1984, p. 399).

2. *Membership relationships* are unique compared with most organizations in which employees all have the same relationship (or similar relationships) to the organization. Membership in a transorganizational system can be voluntary, as in the case of cooperative production network or international political body, in which case participation and engagement of all members is a primary concern. In these cases, it helps to know members' motivations for participating and individual members' goals and objectives. Different members may have different objectives and desires for the system, some of which may conflict. Participation can also be involuntary or mandated by regulation or law, where conflict may be more apparent (Cummings, 1984). In both cases, members of the transorganizational system also are members of their "home" organization, and often must report back to them or get official permission from them to act on the home organization's behalf. Consequently, negotiations and agreements often involve several rounds of discussion. Change agents working with these systems can help to define decision processes so that members are clear about what levels of agreement are required.

3. *Trust and collaboration* are special concerns in transorganizational systems (Vangen & Huxham, 2003), and political issues are likely and can be highly charged. For example, competitors may decide to cooperatively join together and come to agreement on joint industry standards because the market demands it, but each has a separate interest in its own success. Members may suspect other members' motives and hidden agendas for their choices, contributions, or opinions. Lobbying, vote-trading, power struggles, and coalitions are likely results. Vangen and Huxham (2003) write that trust and collaboration can be developed in these systems through a gradual cyclical process of trust building, taking risks, managing power imbalances and dynamics, and achieving modest incremental successes as a foundation for further trust. They also note that it may not be possible to build a highly trusting relationship in these systems, and that the system must learn how to manage with this situation.

Summary

In this chapter, we have discussed a number of large-scale intervention techniques directed at changing the character and performance of whole systems. In this category of interventions, changes have been made in recent years to design interventions that involve a broad number and type of stakeholders, "getting the whole system in the room" to encourage increased participation and commitment to organizational change. This has been true whether the target is a single strategic planning session in one organization or a search conference involving thousands of citizens in multiple nations. Because of their subject matter and magnitude, large-scale interventions can be among the most difficult to execute effectively. However, if success in the contemporary organizational environment means being successful at large-scale change, such interventions are likely to be the hallmark of any successful organization.

For Further Reading

Large-Group Interventions

Bunker, B. B., & Alban, B. T. (1997). *Large group interventions: Engaging the whole system for rapid change.* San Francisco: Jossey-Bass.

Mohrman, A. M., Jr., Mohrman, S. A., Ledford, G. E., Jr., Cummings, T. G., Lawler, E. E., III, & associates (Eds.). (1989). *Large-scale organizational change.* San Francisco: Jossey-Bass.

Organizational Culture

Cameron, K. S., & Quinn, R. E. (2006). *Diagnosing and changing organizational culture: Based on the competing values framework* (Rev. ed.). San Francisco: Jossey-Bass.

Schein, E. H. (2004). *Organizational culture and leadership* (3rd ed.). San Francisco: Jossey-Bass.

Organization Design and Structure

Galbraith, J. R. (1995). *Designing organizations: An executive briefing on strategy, structure, and process.* San Francisco: Jossey-Bass.

Galbraith, J., Downey, D., & Kates, A. (2002). *Designing dynamic organizations: A hands-on guide for leaders at all levels.* New York: AMACOM.

Strategic Planning and Real-Time Strategic Change

Jacobs, R. W. (1994). *Real time strategic change.* San Francisco: Berrett-Koehler.

Worley, C. G., Hitchin, D. E., & Ross, W. L. (1996). *Integrated strategic change: How OD builds competitive advantage.* Reading, MA: Addison-Wesley.

Scenario Planning

Ralston, B., & Wilson, I. (2006). *The scenario planning handbook.* Mason, OH: Texere.

Schwartz, P. (1996). *The art of the long view.* New York: Doubleday.

Search Conferences and Future Search

Emery, M., & Purser, R. E. (1996). *The search conference: A powerful method for planning organizational change and community action.* San Francisco: Jossey-Bass.

Weisbord, M. R., & Janoff, S. (2000). *Future search: An action guide to finding common ground in organizations and communities* (2nd ed.). San Francisco: Berrett-Koehler.

Quality and Productivity Interventions

Hammer, M., & Champy, J. (1993). *Reengineering the corporation.* New York: HarperCollins.

Harry, M., & Schroeder, R. (2000). *Six Sigma: The breakthrough management strategy revolutionizing the world's top corporations.* New York: Currency.

Mergers and Acquisitions

Nahavandi, A., & Malekzadeh, A. R. (1993). *Organizational culture in the management of mergers.* Westport, CT: Quorum Books.

Transorganization or Interorganization Development

Chisholm, R. F. (2008). Developing interorganizational networks. In T. G. Cummings (Ed.), *Handbook of organization development* (pp. 629–650). Thousand Oaks, CA: Sage.

Cummings, T. G. (1984). Transorganizational development. *Research in Organizational Behavior, 6,* 367–422.

Case Study 6: Reorganizing Human Resources at ASP Software

Read the ASP Software case and consider the following questions:

1. How does the client feel about how the change has been managed at this point? How do you think the management team or employees feel?

2. What has Susan done well in managing the change to this point? What could she have been done differently?

3. What intervention strategy and intervention activities would you recommend to Susan? Are there individual interventions covered in Chapter 10 that might be appropriate to support managers and employees in this change? How would you structure them? What roles would Susan, the management team, and the consultant play?

Nathan Miller's phone buzzed on his desk in his home office.

"Hi, Nathan? This is Susan McNulty, from ASP Software, I'm the vice president of human resources here. I got your name from Joan Orman at Kendall Consulting."

Nathan smiled. Joan had been a talented coworker during his time at Kendall several years ago. He had since received many referrals from her for his growing organization development practice. "Of course—what can I do for you?" Nathan inquired. ASP was a familiar company to Nathan. It was a large employer in the area, a high-tech organization in a community without many technology companies. ASP built software products for Fortune 500 companies, employing about 750 software engineers in product development and 500 sales executives. Including the other support functions needed to make the company run (marketing, HR, finance, and so on), it employed almost 1,500 people in the region.

"Well, we're reorganizing our human resources department here at ASP, and I was asking Joan whether she knew of anyone who might be able to help us with a team-building exercise, and your name came up. Do you think you might be able to do that for us?"

"Well," Nathan paused. "I might be able to help you with some ideas—team building could be a possibility, or there are other initiatives we could work on as well. Can you tell me a little about what you're trying to do there at ASP? Perhaps give me some of the context?"

"Sure," Susan said. "We're changing our model from a functional model to a full client management services model. Of course, that model requires a lot of teamwork, and we've also had a small reduction in staff, so...." She paused for emphasis.

Nathan listened. He wasn't sure what a "full client management services model" meant, but it was clearly important to Susan.

Susan continued. "So, with this new focus on teams, it seemed important to our change team that we conduct a team-building activity. I was hoping that maybe we could meet in person and I could describe our model and we could talk about how you might be able to help us? Say, Tuesday at 2:30?"

"That sounds fine. I know right where your headquarters are located. Should I stop in the lobby and ask for you?" Nathan asked.

"That's fine. I'll see you then."

"I'm so glad you could make it. It's nice to meet you in person." Susan welcomed Nathan to ASP software headquarters, a four-story building located just outside downtown. The building was a standard glass-and-steel box, with a shiny chrome ASP logo featured prominently in the marble-floored lobby. The lobby was a busy place as employees and visitors were constantly coming and going. Nathan wore a visitor's badge and had been waiting in the lobby until Susan came down to greet him.

On the fourth floor, Susan and Nathan sat down in a conference room. It was a large, mahogany table surrounded by 12 leather chairs. On the wall he noticed a cherry wood–framed print of mountain climbers. At the bottom read "Teamwork: Giving a helping hand makes all the difference." Another showed a kayaker paddling down a river, with the text "Goals: Effort is nothing without a vision." Also in the room were a video-conferencing unit and a recessed screen that appeared via remote control. Track lighting provided spotlights on the framed prints.

"Thanks for inviting me. It sounds like you have an interesting and challenging change underway," Nathan said.

"Oh, yes, I think so. I'm really pleased that the management team has adopted this new structure. I think it will improve our productivity and reputation as an HR team," Susan said.

"So you said that you're changing models? Can you tell me what that means?" Nathan inquired.

"Sure." She handed Nathan an organizational chart.

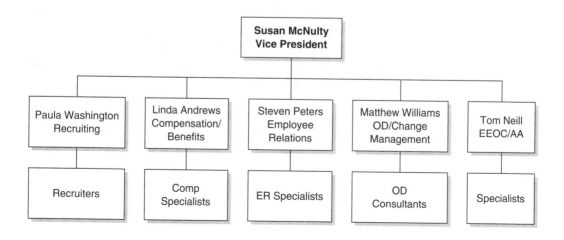

"This chart shows how we are currently organized, by HR function. I have five managers on my team, and each has a separate function. Paula is in charge of our recruiting function, and she supervises all of our talent acquisition work. She has five recruiters working for her. Her recruiters work with managers to open jobs; they search for candidates, conduct preliminary interviews, and process job offers. Linda has compensation, benefits, and rewards. That includes stock grants, executive compensation, and job leveling, plus any other compensation studies that our executive team requests. Linda currently has two compensation specialists reporting to her. Steven Peters has eight employee relations specialists—they do most of the day-to-day work with the management teams they support, to help them conduct performance reviews and to deal with employee complaints and problems. Matthew is our organization development and change management expert, and he has four OD consultants working for him. They work on various projects, but they generally advise the management teams they work with, facilitate meetings, and develop and conduct training. Finally, Tom has our EEOC responsibilities, including legal reporting and compliance, but also investigations of complaints such as harassment or mistreatment of employees. He has three investigation specialists who do data analysis and reporting."

"That sounds like a common organizational structure for a human resources department, in my experience," Nathan said. "What prompted a change?"

"Well," Susan started, "our internal client managers—the internal 'customers' of our department—haven't been very happy with the service they've been receiving from the HR department. One of the company's biggest challenges is recruiting—we have about 200 new positions a year to recruit. Combining those jobs with positions that we need to fill as a result of turnover means that each of our recruiters is handling two dozen positions at any given time. That has led to some frustration from the ASP management team. A manager will need to hire someone, and he'll have to call one person in Paula's organization to get the position opened, then deal with a person on Linda's team to figure out what the compensation level should be, and neither of those people is the person that the manager typically works with on employee relations issues from Steven's team. That can cause some problems on its own, but what really has frustrated them is that the next time he has to hire someone, he'll have to call Paula again, and might be assigned a different recruiter. It's a trend that we see in many companies today—our managers are looking for one person to call to handle all of their HR services. And we really need to open positions, interview candidates, and get job offers out much more quickly than we are today. It's a tight market out there for the best people."

Susan continued. "At the same time, most of the management team really isn't involved with the strategic aspects of the business, designing HR programs that make the most sense with where the business is going. In the software industry, we must move very quickly, and we're constantly looking for new talent and examining different ways to compensate them to maximize loyalty, retention, and productivity. I've been involved with our corporate strategic direction, but the rest of the HR team has been oriented toward the day-to-day activities instead of the bigger picture, so they're not adding as much value as they could."

"That sounds like a common complaint," Nathan said. "What kinds of changes are you going to make?"

"Here's the new organizational chart." Susan handed Nathan another sheet.

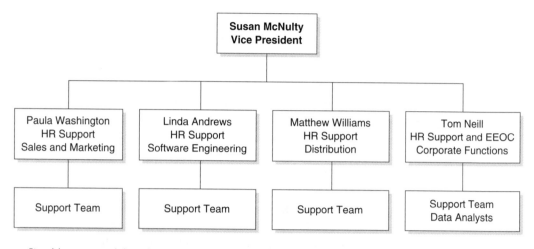

"In this new model, we've organized teams to serve the various internal departments that run the ASP software business—we call them our internal 'customers.' So for example, Paula will now support only the sales and marketing team, and she will be supported by a team that will consist of four team members, called 'generalists,' who will all support various assigned members of the management team in sales and marketing. The advantage is that Paula will now be the central point of contact for our VP of sales and marketing, and she will be much more involved in developing and understanding sales and marketing strategy, so that our human resources strategies—compensation, hiring, change management—will all be aligned with the sales strategy. Linda will do the same thing with software engineering. Matthew will support our distribution function. In this way, we'll be much more client-focused, and we will be much more strategic and responsive to the business. Once a new employee is hired, that person will work with one HR generalist throughout his or her career at ASP, in career planning, compensation, etc. I also asked Tom to keep the EEOC function with two data analysts since that was his expertise and it didn't make sense to combine with the other functions, but he'll also take on a support role for all corporate functions, like finance and legal."

"Has this been announced formally?" Nathan asked.

"Mostly. We had our first meeting last week. We told them that some changes were coming, and most people were aware of it generally but not the specifics. Today we had the second meeting where I published the chart with the names in the positions," Susan answered.

Nathan noticed that the new organizational chart contained fewer boxes. "You had mentioned a staffing reduction?" he asked.

"You're paying attention," Susan said. "At the same time as we discussed this model, we determined that our expenses were about 10% more than we could afford, so we had to reduce our total headcount by 4 positions. Those will come from several areas, including two employee relations specialists, one EEOC data analyst and one recruiter," Susan said.

Nathan did the math quickly in his head. There was one position unaccounted for. "I only get 22 people when you used to have 27. Am I missing one position?" Nathan asked.

"Good observation." Susan smiled. "I haven't published it yet or announced it because I still need to formalize it, but I've asked Steven Peters to take on the role of director of HR operations. The four members of the management team will all report directly to Steven, and he will be responsible for the day-to-day operations of the HR organization. My role will change slightly, since I've been asked by our CEO, David Kaufman, to take on several additional responsibilities and to assist him with special customer calls. While I will have the same title, I won't have time to sort out the daily problems, so I've invited Steven to take on this new responsibility. It's a good development opportunity for him, and it saves me time. We have another meeting with the whole organization on Monday, and I'll share Steven's new role with them at that time."

"Do you have a sense for how people feel about this change generally? Both on the management team and among the support teams?" Nathan asked.

"On the management team I think there's a bit of relief, since they knew I was going to reduce it by one position and the four that are left are settling into their new roles. They know that they have jobs, although they don't know yet about Steven's promotion. Among the generalists I think there's a range of opinions. There is a lot of anxiety about the staffing reduction, and I'm not sure that people have gotten over that yet. The old teams were pretty tight, and I think that some people are looking forward to their new roles while others are wondering about their new team members or their new manager. Some of them, particularly the ones that used to be recruiters, are looking forward to expanded roles that will give them more access to their client managers. Others, such as the employee relations specialists, are not looking forward to the recruiting responsibility."

"Have the employee relations specialists ever done recruiting before?" Nathan inquired.

"One or two used to do that in a previous company. But most of them haven't, so they will probably need some training initially. I'm willing to let them have that time to adjust and learn," Susan said.

"Anything else? Who else might be especially happy or unhappy with this change?" Nathan probed.

"Among the employee relations specialists, Steven was a very popular manager. Matthew has had a couple of run-ins with one of the ER specialists we have assigned to his group—that relationship has been contentious in the past, but it was the only spot to put that one individual, so we had to deal with it. I think Matthew will be very professional about it," Susan added.

"Tell me about the relationship that Steven has had with his peers," Nathan inquired.

"Steven has been very popular as a team member and as a leader in his own group, there's no question. I don't think there are any issues there." Susan shook her head. "But it will be a slight change to those who don't know him well, like the recruiters or the compensation specialists. It might be hard for his former team members to relate to him in a different way. But Steven is popular and he projects a very pleasant charisma, so I know he'll quickly take over the leadership position."

"What measures of success are you looking for?" Nathan asked.

"We've always measured the effectiveness of our recruiters in several ways: number of qualified candidates presented to management, and in cycle time of open position to acceptance of offer. We'll continue to measure our generalists in that way, which I think makes some of them a bit anxious since they're not used to recruiting. Right now it takes us about 77 days to open a position, find candidates, interview them, and get a job offer out. I'm looking for our generalists to move twice as quickly as that. That means each generalist will have a quota of jobs to fill and will be measured on time to fill those positions. But generally I'm looking for more satisfied internal clients and fewer complaints. We should also be able to do more with less since each person will have direct responsibility for their internal clients—they won't need to go from team to team to get the job done."

"How about for my work—are there any specific outcomes you're looking for?" Nathan wondered.

"Not exactly—I'm looking for your guidance about how to proceed. What we need to do is to get beyond this change as quickly as possible so that we're starting to show real results to our internal client managers. I think people are still pretty upset about losing some of their coworkers, and the rumors have been running rampant for the past several weeks. We stopped some of that with the meeting last week and this week, by sharing our plans and showing them the organizational chart. But we've lost a lot of time in getting to this point and now we need to move quickly to get people into their new teams and to start recruiting immediately," Susan stressed.

"You had mentioned initially that you were looking for a team-building activity?" Nathan asked, remembering their phone conversation.

"Yes. With these new teams, only a few of them have worked together before closely. This will require a new kind of coordination among the team members—instead of doing their own thing and managing their own projects, they'll be part of a team to support each business function. They'll still have their own responsibilities, but they will need to share information, determine a strategy and direction, and take on new and unfamiliar responsibilities. I'm thinking that some kind of team-building activity would be really helpful to them—they could get to know each other better, perhaps in a social setting. The other thing I was thinking since we talked on the phone is doing a personality test like the Myers-Briggs or another assessment so that people could examine each other's working style? I just don't know where to start."

The conversation began to die down, and Susan posed the final question.

"So after all of that, do you think you can help us?" Susan inquired.

"I think there are a couple of things that come to mind that could help make this transition smoother," Nathan said. "Why don't I put together a proposal for how I think things could proceed, and we can take it from there?"

"I would really appreciate that. You come highly recommended and I appreciate your insights and guidance," Susan said. "I look forward to reading your proposal."

SOURCE: Anderson, D. L. (2005a), Reorganizing Human Resources at ASP Software. In J. Keyton & P. Shockley-Zalabak (Eds.), *Case Studies for Organizational Communication* (2nd ed., pp. 167–175). Los Angeles: Roxbury. Reprinted with permission.

Case Study 7: The Future of the Crossroads Center

Read the Crossroads Center case and answer the following questions:

- How would you summarize the current situation at the Crossroads Center?
- What is the client looking to accomplish? What challenges exist for the client in accomplishing his objectives?
- How would you design a future search conference, strategic planning session, or scenario planning engagement for the client? Choose one of these and develop an agenda to present to the client, describing the purpose, goals, objectives, and structure for the session based on the descriptions presented in Chapter 12 and in the supplemental readings suggested at the end of the chapter.

The Crossroads Center was founded 16 years ago as a nonprofit drug and alcohol treatment center for adults and adolescents. The center is located in a quiet rural area about an hour from a major urban center. It consists of six separate cream-colored buildings that encircle a large park, walking paths, and a duck pond. Except for a small, almost hidden sign on the main building, most community members cannot distinguish the center from any other set of office buildings or detached apartment units located in the sleepy town.

The center has two segments that operate differently depending on the patient's age. The first is an adult treatment facility, where treatment primarily consists of support provided by psychologists and licensed therapists. Adults who enroll at the center usually find out about it through their health insurance provider, which pays 100% of the center's fees for up to 30 days of inpatient treatment and 30 outpatient visits. The center's staff can support up to 120 adults at any given time.

The second part of the center is an adolescent residential treatment facility, where patients live together in the facility and are supported by a network of clinical psychologists, physicians, nurses, addiction counselors, and therapists. The center also provides staffed teachers who also provide educational assistance while the patients live at the center, which can last for up to 8 weeks depending on a patient's needs. The residential center is much more expensive to operate, given the additional staff and housing needs, so there are typically just 30 to 40 patients living at the center at any point in time. The funding sources for the adolescent treatment facility include insurance as well, but also funding from grants and foundations, as well as federal and state programs.

Darrin Spoldi was appointed director of the center almost 3 years ago. During his short tenure, the center received three new grants from nationwide foundations and increased by one-third the number of patients that the center has reached. Darrin called Lisa Rodriguez last week with an urgent request. The center was at risk due to a new law, and he needed some advice to avoid the worst-case scenario.

"I'm really glad that you're here," Darrin said, as he and Lisa walked along the sidewalk path outside the center. "We're in a desperate situation, and if we don't do something soon, we may not be able to keep the center open."

"You sounded very concerned when we spoke last week," Lisa admitted. "But I had thought when we spoke a few months ago that things were going so well."

"Exactly," Darrin said quietly, looking down at the weeds on the edge of the sidewalk. "I had just gotten a major grant and our funding seemed more solid than at any point during my time here. Ironic, as it turns out. Things were sailing smoothly until just recently. In fact, just a few weeks ago we concluded our yearlong study on adolescent recidivism since we hired the additional therapist staff."

"Recidivism? What's that?" Lisa asked.

"It's our return rate. We follow up with our patients after they leave the center to see how they are doing and whether they are able to maintain the skills they learn during their time here or whether they need to return to a center for additional treatment. We found out that our patients have the lowest rates of return to drug and alcohol abuse among centers like ours in this region. In fact, the rate has improved by about 15% over a few years ago."

"To what do you attribute this result?" Lisa wondered.

"There's no question. It's both our teachers and our therapists," Darrin said confidently. "Patient after patient in the study we did reported that they had incredible support from the therapists, and having the teachers here on staff kept them focused on their studies, so that when they returned to school they had little difficulty assimilating. About a year and a half ago we added three new therapists to the staff, and the change was incredible. I know how good our work is here. I've worked in treatment facilities like this throughout my career, and this is the most successful model I've seen."

"Tell me about what's causing your concern for the center," Lisa asked.

"Don't misunderstand. I might sound calm now, but I suppose I'm just numb from thinking about this. It's not just a 'concern.' This is the biggest crisis I've faced in my career," Darrin said. "You might have heard about the changes that the state legislature just made to the social services budget for this fiscal year. Well, the budget for social services includes a set of regulations requiring that treatment facilities that receive state funding have a certain percentage of their staff hold medical degrees from an accredited medical school. I guess the regulations were intended to address the large number of facilities that are run primarily by lower-skilled technicians, with few medical professionals actually administering services. Last year's controversy regarding abuse in nursing home facilities prompted a number of community groups to call for additional regulations. The result, though, is that even facilities like ours face the same criteria. In any case, the law was just recently signed by the governor, and facilities have just 6 months to comply with the law or to forfeit all state funding, retroactive to the signing date of the legislation."

"What does that mean for Crossroads?" Lisa asked.

"In other words, the center will continue to receive state funding for the next 6 months, but if we cannot comply with the law in that time period, we need to return 6 months' worth of funding to the state," Darrin said.

"What would it take to comply?"

"Currently, the center's staff of teachers and therapists put the staff below the required threshold to receive funding. Most of them have advanced academic degrees, but they are not medical practitioners according to the legal definition. We would have no problem if we just let our teachers and therapists go," Darrin said. "But they are critical members of our staff, and as I said, our patients give them a great deal of credit for their treatment. I just don't think that is an acceptable solution. Another possibility would be to refuse the state funding, but then trying to operate with our remaining funds would be impossible. With money coming just from the federal government and from our grants, we would not only have to have a layoff of staff, we'd have to reduce the number of patients we serve by about two thirds, and we would turn away a lot of people who need our help. I've done a lot of thinking about this in the last several weeks, and I haven't been able to come up with a solution that is acceptable to anyone."

"Does the community understand what's happening to the center and what might happen if it closed?"

"We have purposely maintained a low profile in the community for the last several years. Before I arrived, it's my understanding that there was a call among the county supervisors for the center to close or move, and we did not have a lot of support. I don't know what all of the issues are, but there is some animosity among the board of directors toward the county board of supervisors. Nothing came of it, obviously, and the board of directors recommended that I not spend a lot of time in the community for a while until things settled down. I'm not sure how many community leaders even know how we've contributed to the community by treating our own local adults and adolescents," Darrin concluded.

"What have you done so far?" Lisa asked.

"A few weeks ago we had a small meeting of the top administrators, about eight of us. We just talked in circles, bouncing back and forth between trying to figure out how to continue to operate without state funding or trying to meet the state's requirements and maintain our current funding. We didn't come to any conclusions, but we agreed to meet again this week. I do have to say, though, that the staff has been great about this. Morale is high, and our administrators are highly involved and motivated to find a solution. I've worked with other groups that would have given up or quit, but this group is participative, engaged, and smart. They're keeping each other going," Darrin said.

"Let me summarize. A highly successful local center is going to close because of a state law that holds unintended consequences, and the closure will affect a large number of patients, staff, and community members. It seems to me that there are a lot of groups who have a stake in this center being successful and continuing to operate. There are the patients and staff, obviously, but also the patients' families, the grants and foundations that contribute to your success, the community, even the state legislature," Lisa concluded.

"You've got it," Darrin said quietly.

Lisa continued, "You have a lot on your shoulders here. I can see that it's affecting you a great deal personally. What do you think of bringing together a larger group to help you decide what to do? We could keep it to your staff, or we could invite members of these other groups."

"It sounds like a good idea," Darrin agreed. "And at this point I'm at a loss about what to do next, so I'll take any suggestions. Tell me more. Who would we invite? How long would it take, and how would it be structured?"

"Let me think more about that. I can get you a proposal quickly and we can get started as soon as possible," Lisa said.

"For the first time in a few weeks, I'm starting to feel hope," Darrin smiled. "I'm looking forward to your proposal."

CHAPTER 13

Sustaining Change, Evaluating, and Ending an Engagement

Consultants conducted a comprehensive organization development intervention with the employees and management team of the Communications and Electrical division of the city of San Diego, California, in order to improve productivity and employee satisfaction. Each of the city's work groups attended team-building sessions in which they participated in problem-solving exercises and clarified team members' roles. Top managers received one-on-one coaching on problem solving, and managers attended training courses to learn how to be more effective in managing meetings, evaluating employee performance, and more. The consultants offered observations to teams on team decision making, problem solving, group dynamics, and communication. When the interventions were concluded, the consultants evaluated the results, comparing this division to similar divisions within and outside the city. They gathered quantitative measures of employee productivity; they conducted an employee survey; they gathered employee data on absences and turnover; and they solicited citizen feedback on satisfaction with the department. Compared to the situation before the interventions, costs were lower, employee efficiency significantly increased, and job satisfaction increased. "Those who invest time, energy, and money to accomplish certain goals via an OD project can never know whether those goals have been reached unless they make some effort to evaluate the project" (Paul & Gross, 1981, p. 77).

- When concluding an organization development engagement, what do you think it would be important to evaluate to assess the success of the effort?

I n the previous three chapters we discussed a number of individual-, team-, and organization-level interventions that can be used to implement change. In this chapter, we will discuss what happens after those changes are made. What other supporting systems, processes, or changes can be put into place so that the change persists and is long-lasting and effective? Moreover, how do clients and change agents know whether the interventions to implement change made a difference at all? To answer these questions we will address what experts recommend about effective ways to sustain and evaluate change.

The final stage in our model of the organization development (OD) process is concerned with ending engagements, or the process of separating from and exiting the client's environment. Even internal consultants who continue to work for the organization after the engagement is done need to concern themselves with successfully transitioning ownership of the process back to the client and explicitly calling the engagement to a close.

Sustaining Change After the Intervention

Interventions such as those described in the previous three chapters all describe methods to achieve personal change (such as learning how to become a more effective manager), team change (new roles on a team), and organizational change (a new structure for a division). Lest anyone get too confident in the achievements that have been made to this point, many observers warn of the difficulties to come. "Now your troubles begin," write Senge et al. (1999):

> As your original "seedlings" begin taking root, they come into contact with new features of their environment, such as predators, rivals, and other life-forms that will resist the presence of a new entity. Your task is now to sustain life, not just over a few months, but over a period of years. (p. 240)

Indeed, once people try out changes like these, they may find them exceedingly difficult to maintain. For example, the new team roles may not feel as comfortable as the old roles, and members may long for the past despite the fact that the old roles did not work well. The new structure for the division might cause confusion and mistakes as people wonder who is responsible for which decisions. It might feel awkward initially to communicate differently with a coworker. In such cases, there is the likelihood of a relapse to how things used to be done before the intervention. Relapse is a possibility for several reasons.

First, we are often motivated to maintain a change when a change agent, manager, or external consultant is watching. When observers leave, we often slip back into the comfort of the old way. Leaders may support the change because they feel compelled to follow the recommendations of the change agent, but then they fail to continue to work on the change when the engagement concludes.

Second, the change is often a more difficult state, requiring more conscious energy, emotion, or attention, and we may have dedicated our attention to it when we were asked to, but cannot keep up that level of energy:

Work group members have to change individual behaviors and habits and stick with those changes. This requires ongoing focus, attention, and discipline on their part because of the challenge of maintaining new behaviors in the face of ongoing work challenges. (Longenecker & Rieman, 2007, p. 7)

Daily struggles with workload and the psychological demands of maintaining conscious attention to the change can require enough dedication that the demands of personal, team, and organizational changes can be too much to maintain.

Third, organizational members may naturally be unskilled initially as they adapt to the new way. Education may be required, and it can take weeks or months to achieve results as people continue to learn. Without the patience to push through the natural and awkward phases of trial and error and the inevitable initial mistakes, many organizational members claim that the change has failed, and return to the old way.

Fourth, systemic organizational forces such as rewards or cultural values, expectations, and beliefs may be too powerful to overcome, and they may inhibit members from fully adopting the change. A manager who receives coaching to become more assertive in selling his ideas may become pushed back into old habits when his next performance review calls him "confrontational." A leader who chooses to involve others in the department in high-level decisions may reverse that approach when she is passed over for a promotion and labeled a weak decision maker. Mounting internal complaints may force the finance department to continue producing customized reports that they had eliminated in a process improvement effort. Other organizational members or other systems, structures, and processes may provide intractable barriers to change.

What is required are methods for sustaining and stabilizing the gains that have been achieved, for working through the barriers to maintaining change, and for pushing through the difficult initial stages of change so that it lasts. The challenge is to develop techniques for making the "new way" stick. To sustain change, most experts recommend that the change become "institutionalized." Change has been institutionalized when organizational members no longer think of the change program as a special initiative or project. "In the final analysis," Kotter (1996) writes, "change sticks only when it becomes 'the way we do things around here,' when it seeps into the very bloodstream of the work unit or corporate body" (p. 14). You may recall the phrase "the way we do things around here" as one definition of organizational culture. In other words, the change program is most effectively institutionalized when it becomes part of the culture, or an integral part of the ordinary practices, programs, values, and beliefs of organizational members. Depending on the number of organizational members involved and the magnitude of the change, this can be a substantial endeavor, one that can take years to fully mature. Many writers emphasize "anchoring" the change, forcing it to become irreversibly "hardwired" into the organization. This approach helps to sustain change, but it may have its disadvantages.

Work too hard at stability, and complacency and stubborn adherence to the new status quo may become the rule, which can inhibit future change attempts. (The same change agents who are frustrated with organizational members' earlier resistance to change are often those same change agents that later want organizational members to stick unyieldingly with the new way.) Too much stability can be harmful, as can too much change. In other words, "The routinization of current practices may block other potentially more significant developments. A desire to sustain current methods may prevent staff from acquiring new skills and experience, thus reducing morale and damaging performance" (Buchanan et al., 2005, p. 191). There is a constant tension between stability and change in organizations, with both offering opportunities for and threats to the organization's long-term survival. Too much routine—sticking with values, ideas, methods, or practices that no longer work—is dangerous to adaptation, but too much change can mean low productivity, frustration, and confusion.

Lawler and Worley (2006) write that the hallmark of successful contemporary organizations is no longer their ability to make changes stick:

> Creating a stable organization to perform in a complex and rapidly changing environment is following a recipe for failure. The primary drivers of organizational effectiveness are fluid and dynamic; so too must be the primary elements and processes of strategy and organization. (p. 18)

The solution may not be to try to "refreeze" the organization as Lewin's classic model and others would suggest, but instead to develop organizations that can learn how to change. Practices that encourage evaluation and adaptation can be more effective in the long term. After all,

> The purpose of change is to create an asset that did not exist before—a learning organization capable of adapting to a changing competitive environment. The organization has to know how to continually monitor its behavior—in effect, to learn how to learn. (Beer, Eisenstat, & Spector, 1990, p. 164)

The objective is to develop practices that support the desired direction and remove barriers to the change, and to implement opportunities for regular evaluation and renewal that encourage appropriate and necessary alterations but avoid stagnation.

Mechanisms to Sustain Change

Beckhard and Harris (1977) recommend seven practices that can encourage regular maintenance and renewal of a change. They write that these practices can help leaders understand the effectiveness of the change and also provide opportunities for information sharing about the change among members who may only see a certain aspect of the change given the limited view they may have in their individual roles. Most of these recommendations are directed toward team and organizational change, not personal change, but can be adapted to individuals:

1. *Periodic team meetings.* Perhaps the most fundamental mechanism for sustaining change is a regular meeting during which team members can come together to share results, perspectives, and opinions about how the change is operating. Beckhard

and Harris (1977) write that such meetings invite "members to think through what they have done and what has happened since the last meeting and where they are going in the next intermediate period" (p. 101) in order to encourage members to think about the change as an ongoing process rather than a discrete event.

2. *Organization sensing meetings.* Especially for large-scale organizational changes, it is useful for top leaders to hear directly from organizational members about how the change is working. Sensing meetings are a process whereby the top leader may meet with groups of employees from various departments throughout the organization. These can be mixed groups of a random sample of employees, or they can be comprised of employees with a similar level or role. Provided that these are information-gathering meetings and not used to penalize or discipline anyone, they can be valuable ways of minimizing hierarchy and clarifying the change for both leaders and employees.

3. *Periodic intergroup meetings.* Particularly in intergroup changes where new roles, processes, or relationships are developed, a regular meeting among members of the groups involved can serve as a point to renew and evaluate the changes that have been made.

4. *Renewal conferences.* A renewal conference is a specific event, often held off-site, where organizational leaders or members meet to evaluate and discuss the change. Beckhard and Harris (1977) note that many organizations hold these off-site events annually during a strategic planning cycle to evaluate changes in the market or organizational environment, consider the organization's response, and plan for the future. These can also be effective at a department or team level.

5. *Goal-directed performance review.* Performance reviews evaluate departments and individuals against specific measurable goals. "If an effective, goal-directed planning process is in place, one generally finds that the organization is alive, energized, and relatively clear about its priorities," write Beckhard and Harris (1977, p. 103). Having clear and consistent goals, with rewards to support them, provides unambiguous support for the desired change. Documenting these goals and expected results in performance plans helps organizational members to focus on the activities that matter most in support of the change.

6. *Periodic visits from outside consultants.* A return visit from the change agent who helped to implement the change can encourage the organization to take an objective look at its progress:

> We have found that insisting on such review visits for at least a year or so after a major change "forces" the organization leadership to have follow-up meetings. It forces them to look at the promises they made at the last meeting, to review progress, and to do some conscious thinking about priority planning for the future. (Beckhard & Harris, 1977, pp. 103–104)

A return visit from a change agent can prompt reflection on what has changed (or not) since the last meeting.

7. *Rewards.* Despite the best of intentions and regular reviews, a change will not be sustained if organizational members are rewarded or recognized (promoted, compensated, or even simply complimented) for doing something that is in opposition to the change. Recognition systems should be carefully analyzed for the activities and values that they support, and rewards should be put into place that "provide recognition to the people who maintain the new and different ways of doing things, especially when under pressure" (Jackson, 2006, p. 184). Burke (1993) agrees:

> Formally and publicly recognizing people for having helped to move the organization in the change direction not only will serve to reinforce and stabilize the new behaviors but will send a clear signal as well to others in the organization as to what the "right" behaviors are. (p. 154)

To this list, Armenakis, Harris, and Feild (1999) have also proposed seven practices that change agents can use to institutionalize change:

1. *Active participation.* Giving organizational members the opportunity to influence the change as it takes shape, through participative decision-making practices or learning by practice and observation, can encourage adoption of the change and ownership of its implementation.

2. *Persuasive communication.* Regular communication about the status of the change, repetition of its rationale and purpose, and motivation to continue it can encourage hesitant organizational members and reinforce the change message.

3. *Management of internal/external information.* Survey data, benchmarking metrics, and other sources of data can reinforce the need for the change and increase confidence in the organization's approach.

4. *Human resources management practices.* This includes not only rewards as mentioned above but also other human resources practices such as employee selection, performance appraisals, and training and development activities that can each support the change.

5. *Diffusion practices.* When changes are piloted in one area of the organization and then implemented in another, employees from the pilot division can help spread the message about the change to other divisions.

6. *Rites and ceremonies.* Activities such as employee meetings, leadership conferences, retirement parties, and recognition ceremonies can provide opportunities to symbolically reinforce the change. Armenakis et al. (1999) describe one organization that issued new badges to employees with motivational messages at a top leadership meeting to explain a new joint venture.

7. *Formalization activities.* Other changes in organizational structure, policies, and practices may be necessary to support the change and eliminate inconsistencies or barriers to adoption of the change.

These mechanisms need not be last-minute decisions after an intervention is carried out. They can be built into the intervention planning process and carefully considered as changes are debated so that all of the organization's systems, structures, processes, and cultural beliefs work seamlessly toward the same desired outcome. The most successful organizations, according to Lawler and Worley (2006), will learn not only how to master these practices, but to encourage the next change to take shape as well. "This means creating an organization that encourages experimentation, learns about new practices and technologies, monitors the environment, assesses performance, and is committed to continuously improving performance" (p. 21). This view of sustaining change is less about institutionalizing and stabilizing practices, and more about learning how to change effectively as a regular part of organizational life.

Evaluation

The word *evaluation* can bring up negative connotations for many people, perhaps rooted in poor current or past experiences with getting feedback: teachers and red pens slashing through a student's essay, or a manager's judgment about an employee's annual progress against performance goals. It is among the final stages of the organization development engagement, and is also frequently omitted. Practitioners and clients may be unsure about what or how to evaluate the effort, but such information can be invaluable to the client and practitioner personally as well as to the organization as it considers how the OD engagement made an impact. "The question that the consultant must answer is, 'Has the intervention in organization X made a difference?'" (Randolph & Elloy, 1989, p. 634). A deceptively simple question, it is also fraught with challenges.

Challenges to Evaluation

Many practitioners and change agents fail to evaluate because of the many challenges and barriers to conducting an effective and thorough evaluation. As Burke (1993) puts it,

> The evaluation process of OD practice can be compared to an annual physical examination—everyone agrees that it should be done, but no one, except a highly motivated researcher, wants to go to the trouble and expense of making it happen. (p. 168)

In fact, only relatively recently have OD practitioners pushed to evaluate their efforts. In the 1970s, practitioners lamented that they did not know enough about how to evaluate OD and that few practitioners conducted formal evaluations of their OD programs. A barrage of articles and meta-analyses appeared in which academic researchers were trying to figure out whether OD actually made a difference (see Armenakis, Feild, & Holley, 1976; Morrison, 1978; Porras & Berg, 1978a, 1978b). Most recommended increasing rigor for evaluative studies. While later analyses in the 1980s pointed to improvements in OD evaluation methodology and frequency (Vicars & Hartke, 1984), conducting an evaluation remains a challenge today.

The following are some of the largest barriers to evaluation (see Martineau & Preskill, 2002):

- *Takes resources.* After a lengthy cycle of contracting, data gathering, data analysis, planning, and conducting interventions, many practitioners and clients are unwilling to commit the resources to evaluation. It takes the time of organizational members to gather and analyze data, to participate in interviews, or to respond to a survey.
- *Fear of the results.* The client may fear that resources were dedicated to producing nothing at all, or possibly that the situation has even deteriorated. The change agent may fear negative feedback or the possibility of developing a professional reputation for managing engagements that did not obtain desired results.
- *Takes energy.* Many clients and change agents would rather commit energy to producing change than to evaluating it. Occasionally the change agent is the only party interested in the results and may have difficulty persuading the client to expend the necessary energy to gather the data.
- *Accepted proof.* The client or change agent may have accepted that the intervention worked, from past experience or reports from others, and they may find no need to conduct an evaluation themselves.
- *Unsure what to evaluate.* Without a clear goal set during the contracting phase, clients and change agents may be unsure about what to evaluate. Some outcomes, such as "improved conflict management" or "better team meetings," may be vague or difficult to evaluate.
- *Seen as optional.* Evaluation is often seen as a "nice to have" step in the process rather than a requirement.
- *Practitioner training.* Many practitioners are not formally trained in evaluation methods. Some evaluation methodologies require statistical knowledge or a background in qualitative data analysis that practitioners may not have.
- *Research design and practice.* Early in the history of OD, social science preferences for quantitative, experimental research designs made it difficult to find true experimental groups so that variables could be isolated and assessed. This view has changed considerably since the 1970s, but it explains some of the lack of OD evaluation conducted in earlier years.

A further difficulty to conducting an evaluation of an OD effort is that organizational interventions are complex and it may not be possible to establish conclusively whether the organization's results are due directly to the specific activities of the OD program. Armenakis et al. (1976) noted that many practitioners found methodological challenges to evaluating OD efforts, such as the difficulty of assessing what constituted an improvement, the lack of true comparison groups, controlling for outside influences, and time lags that may mean years between intervention and results.

Reasons to Evaluate

Despite these challenges, there are many good reasons to evaluate an organization development engagement:

1. *Evaluation provides focus.* "An evaluation forces the definition of the change objectives, . . . clarification of the change outcomes that are expected [and] clarification of how these change outcomes are to be measured" (Burke, 1993, p. 171). Being disciplined about evaluation will prompt the client and change agent to return to the original objectives of the engagement, to be specific about what outcomes were desired, and to document whether those objectives were achieved.

2. *Evaluation results may facilitate support.* Clients can have increased confidence that the OD effort was worthwhile and may be more likely to support such efforts in the future. Change agents can retain evaluation results (with permission) in a "success stories" file as part of a professional portfolio of successful engagements.

3. *Results provide feedback for change.* "An evaluation facilitates planning for next steps and stages of organizational improvement and development" (Burke, 1993, p. 171). An evaluation can uncover barriers to change and the results can point to future possibilities for improvement.

4. *Client and change agent growth.* Evaluation helps the change agent to understand the aspects of the intervention strategy that did or did not work as anticipated. The change agent can learn from this experience and potentially correct it next time, whether it is in the client's organization or in another engagement.

In several respects, evaluation may be best seen not as part of the ending of an engagement, but as a transition to a new beginning. In Figure 5.2, the OD process listed in Chapter 5, an arrow connects the final stage of the model to entry, symbolizing the recursive and continuing process of improvement work. McLean, Sullivan, and Rothwell (1995) refer to evaluation as being both formative and summative; that is, it is formative when it is conducted during the intervention or looking forward to future interventions and it is summative when it looks back to address how effective the intervention was. Evaluation can be seen as another data gathering step that can then be developed into another contract, fed back to the client, and used for development of another intervention strategy.

What to Evaluate

Evaluation can offer insights into both the organization's processes and the outcomes or results of the intervention. In addition, the OD engagement itself can be a target for evaluation. Porras and Berg (1978b) have developed an extensive set of process and outcome variables that practitioners can consider as they decide what to evaluate in any given engagement (see Figures 13.1 and 13.2).

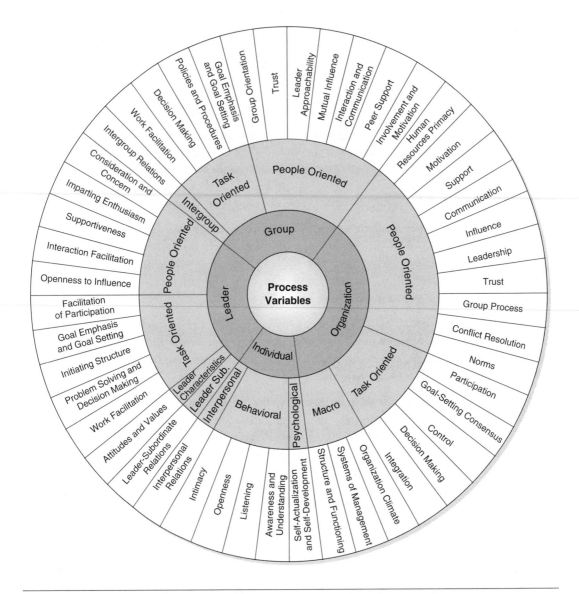

Figure 13.1   Process Variables in Organization Development Evaluation

SOURCE: Porras, J. I., & Berg, P. O. (1978). The Impact of Organization Development. *Academy of Management Review,* *3,* 249–266. Reprinted with permission.

Process variables evaluation consists of how the intervention may have changed behavioral, people, and task processes. These consist of subjects such as motivation, conflict resolution, decision making, group trust, and participation. Process variables also consist of areas such as whether organizational members are completing the necessary activities they need to complete and whether employees are properly trained. Improving these areas may be the objective of any given intervention, but the overall outcome objective is usually an organizational result. In other words, the longer term objective of a team-building activity would be improved team functioning with an end result of a more productive, effective team. Process variables contribute to outcome variables.

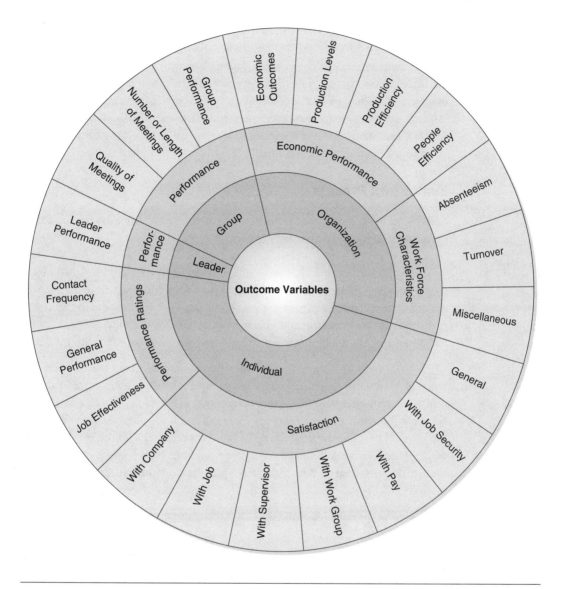

Figure 13.2   Outcomes Variables in Organization Development Evaluation

SOURCE: Porras, J. I., & Berg, P. O. (1978). The Impact of Organization Development. *Academy of Management Review, 3*, 249–266. Reprinted with permission.

Outcome variables usually concern organizational level outputs such as productivity, customer satisfaction, costs, revenue, quality, cycle time, and employee turnover. Many OD efforts work directly on process variables, but most clients are interested in outcome variables as results. Measuring both process and outcome variables may help to show the logical link between the OD effort and some impact (even if tentative) on the organization's results. In addition, measurement of this kind can demonstrate other changes, both beneficial and negative, even if they were unintended. These results can provide input to other possible interventions.

The OD engagement itself can be a topic for evaluation. Clients and practitioners can evaluate how well the OD process was followed, including client and practitioner satisfaction with contracting, data gathering, data analysis, feedback, and the intervention strategy. Practitioners can evaluate how well they adhered to or modeled OD values. Holbeche (2006) recommends evaluating learning: "What new learning and knowledge have been embedded in the organization and how?" (p. 427). The change agent-client relationship itself can also be a topic for evaluation (see the next section on separation).

Evaluation Process

The process of evaluation is not significantly different from developing a data gathering strategy as discussed in Chapter 7:

1. First, the client and change agent should meet to restate the original objectives of the engagement and to decide what data would best illustrate the changes desired at the personal, team, or organization level. They may choose to evaluate at each level, as some recommend (Livingston, 2006). They should also discuss for what purpose they are evaluating the results and what will be done with the data.

2. Next, determine the form the evaluation should take, and whether the data will be gathered through interviews, focus groups, surveys, or another method. Will it be a series of interviews with team members, will it be an organizationwide survey, or will it consist of gathering last quarter's employee turnover data? Which of these would best illustrate the effects of the OD program? Will the client be satisfied with qualitative data showing employee opinions from interviews, or is quantitative data necessary? Which process variables and outcome variables are of interest?

3. Collect the data, following the recommendations for effective data collection listed in Chapter 7.

4. The client and change agent should meet to evaluate the results and to plan next steps, if any. Some clients will want a final written report showing the objectives of the engagement, the activities conducted, and the end result (Stroh & Johnson, 2006). It may be advisable to be cautious about making sweeping claims about causation in any final report or interpretation, however tempting it may be.

Ethics of Evaluation

Evaluation prompts ethical concerns similar to the data gathering and diagnosis phase of the OD process. The biggest potential ethical challenge in the evaluation phase is to misinterpretation and misrepresentation of data (White & Wooten, 1985). This may occur somewhat innocently by both change agent and client, both of whom may badly wish for the data to show that the engagement made a difference. They may choose to only gather or report on the data that show a change, and to ignore the data that show negative results. Issues of anonymity for those that participate in interviews apply at the evaluation data gathering phase, as employees may fear retribution if it is revealed that they do not see significant change, do not support the change effort, or are not doing what is required for the change to be successful.

Ending an Engagement: Separation and Exit

To paraphrase a popular saying, "All (good) engagements must come to an end." Consulting engagements are by definition temporary relationships, and the project at some point must be turned over to the client. Attention to the ending process is necessary because "too many OD projects may linger unproductively or may end abruptly and without adequate follow up" (Van Eron & Burke, 1995, p. 395). Even if the client identifies additional work or a second project, in which case the client-consultant relationship may continue, the present engagement as it had been defined during the contracting phase comes to an end. Just as the contracting phase sets the tone for how the consulting relationship will evolve, so too does the process of ending an engagement set the tone for the transition to a second engagement. Skillfully and ethically ending engagements is an important competency for an OD professional.

Endings can be initiated by clients, by consultants, or by mutual agreement. Ideally, engagements end by mutual agreement, but there may be reasons for either the change agent or client to end the engagement earlier. The moment to end the engagement may be obvious to both parties if goals have been reached and agreements of the original contract have been met. At other times, endings may need to be provoked and initiated, especially if the engagement is not progressing well. Among the telltale signs that an engagement might need to come to an end are the following:

- The client keeps putting things off.
- Agreements are made and forgotten (by either side).
- The consultant appears to have a higher emotional stake in the outcomes than the client does.
- The client is doing better and really doesn't need outside help (Weisbord, 1973/1994, p. 412).

Endings should be done explicitly and with planning rather than allowing an engagement to fade away without attention. Long delays or awkward extensions of unproductive engagements do a disservice to both the client and change agent, which is why Weisbord (1973/1994) notes that "I welcome ending a contract explicitly by having it tested and found wanting. Better a clean death than lingering agony" (p. 412). As Weisbord alludes, too often endings happen without planning or forethought. Client and change agent run out of topics for the weekly project status meeting. The client lacks information or motivation to take another action and tells the change agent to wait for a few weeks until the situation becomes clearer. Eventually, both client and change agent find other projects or priorities and the engagement fades away.

Instead, change agents and clients can benefit from an explicit ending process by scheduling an ending feedback meeting. An ending meeting invites clients and change agents to articulate a number of subjects related to the engagement and intervention:

- What did we learn about the OD process?
- What did we learn from the consultant-client relationship?
- What was the initial presenting problem and did that change as we did further investigation?
- Would the client engage with the practitioner again?
- To what extent has the client learned how to solve problems like these alone?
- What were the most successful aspects of the engagement?
- What were the most challenging?
- What would we have done differently?
- What should we consider doing next time if we are faced with this problem again?

Clients and practitioners can also give each other feedback on strengths and opportunities for improvement: what each did that may have been particularly helpful to the success of the relationship and the engagement or specific things that may have created barriers to improvement. Postconsultation transition plans should also be discussed at the ending meeting so it is clear whether and how the change agent may be further involved with the client's organization. For example, the change agent may stop attending team meetings or may only attend once per month. These changes should be discussed so that the team is aware of the change and not surprised when the change agent abruptly fails to attend. Another topic for the postconsultation separation meeting concerns how the client may wish to follow-up or contact the change agent for another engagement.

Ethics of Endings

Ethical concerns can enter into the separation process, both when the act of separation is excessively delayed and when it happens too quickly. Extending an engagement for too long can be ethically questionable. As White and Wooten (1985) write,

> As the change effort progresses through the continuation/maintenance stage reducing dependency is a difficult issue for most change agents to encounter. It involves reduction of effort and withholding of change agent services from the client system. Of specific ethical interest is the issue of the change agent continuing the intensity of a helping relationship or services. (p. 161)

Separation may be ethically necessary to reduce dependency on the change agent and to avoid the change agent's (especially for external consultants) continuing to accept payment if the contracted services have been completed or if the client is no longer benefiting. Moreover, the longer the change agent participates in the client system, the more he or she may "go native" or become such a part of the system that objectivity is lost and separation is psychologically difficult on both change agent and client. In such cases the change agent can become dependent (psychologically and financially) on the client.

Ending an engagement too early can also be ethically questionable, as it can mean leaving the client in a poor position to manage the change alone. Change agents who may feel that the client is not making enough progress or that the relationship is poor may look for reasons and ways to exit when things get difficult. The opposite can also occur, when a change agent may believe erroneously that the client is ready to assume the reins alone. Here,

> Of specific difficulty is the assessment of organizational capability to carry through the long-term aspects of a change effort, including the necessary processes to diagnose and solve problems. Improper assessment of client system health can lead to premature exit on the part of the change agent. (White & Wooten, 1985, p. 162)

An honest assessment of the motivation of the change agent and client to end the engagement is important to ensuring that it ends ethically.

Summary

The final stages of the organization development process involve developing a process to sustain the change, evaluating the change, and exiting the engagement. Each of these steps involves the change agent gradually developing opportunities for the organization to maintain the momentum that ideally was achieved during the intervention process and to assume full ownership of the change process so that the change agent can separate from the environment. Sustaining change involves creating systems, structures, or processes so that relapse to the "old ways" of doing things is prevented. Barriers to implementing the change need to be understood and removed, and periodic opportunities to discuss, review, assess, and renew the change need to be put into place. Evaluating the engagement involves assessing the process and outcomes that the intervention strategy attempted to address, and it is best thought of as another data gathering stage that both looks back on what was achieved and looks forward to gather feedback that can lead to new interventions or future changes.

Last, all engagements come to an end. Ending meetings can provide an explicit opportunity to assess the engagement and discuss what was learned and accomplished. Ethically separating with integrity involves assessing one's motivation for ending to ensure that it happens neither before the client is truly ready (to avoid leaving the client without skills to appropriately manage the change) nor too late so that it lingers and encourages change agent or client to become dependent on the other.

For Further Reading

Buchanan, D., Fitzgerald, L., Ketley, D., Gollop, R., Jones, J. L., Lamont, S. S., et al. (2005). No going back: A review of the literature on sustaining organizational change. *International Journal of Management Reviews, 7*(3), 189–205.

Livingston, R. E. (2006). Evaluation and termination phase. In B. B. Jones & R. Brazzel (Eds.), *The NTL handbook of organization development and change: Principles, practices, and perspectives* (pp. 231–245). San Francisco: Pfeiffer.

Porras, J. I., & Berg, P. O. (1978). The impact of organization development. *Academy of Management Review, 3,* 249–266.

Van Eron, A., & Burke, W. W. (1995). Separation. In W. Rothwell, R. Sullivan, & G. N. McLean (Eds.), *Practicing organization development: A guide for consultants* (pp. 395–418). San Diego: Pfeiffer.

CHAPTER 14

The Future of Organization Development

Throughout this book we have seen examples of organization development (OD) interventions in action with individuals, teams, and whole organizations, and you have had the opportunity to apply these new skills through several case studies that represent how organizations face the challenges of change. Organizations today are facing increasing pressures in a challenging environment. This environment makes the interventions to achieve change discussed in previous chapters even more relevant.

In this chapter we will address a few of these challenges to organizations, from pressures that exist within and outside the organization, and we will address how OD concepts are relevant to helping organizations through these challenges. We will also review the current state of OD theory and practice, what challenges lie ahead for the field, and what the field can do to respond.

The next sections review four major challenges that organizations face today and relate the relevance of OD to each:

- Increasing complexity of change
- Globalization
- Changing workforce demographics
- Changes in the nature of work

Increasing Complexity of Change

The first trend is increasing change and the complexity of change. Organizations face incredible pressure to quickly change in a complex and increasingly global environment. It is not just that the amount of change has increased over the past

5 to 10 years, but the speed of change has become even more noticeable. As Friedman (2007) writes,

> The experiences of the high-tech companies in the last few decades that failed to navigate the rapid changes brought about in their marketplace . . . may be a warning to all the businesses, institutions, and nation-states that are now facing these inevitable, even predictable changes, but lack the leadership, flexibility, and imagination to adapt—not because they are not smart or aware, but because the speed of change is simply overwhelming them. (p. 49)

Indeed, the changes that organizations are making are more complex than ever. Many scholars note that the majority of these large-scale change initiatives fail to achieve their desired results, placing even more pressure on executives to search for the next major innovation that will help the organization become more competitive (Holbeche, 2006).

To touch on just two of these major areas of change, outsourcing and offshoring are perhaps the two most obvious examples of major changes that affect almost every large organization. In fact,

> Depending on whom you ask, anywhere from one-half to two-thirds of all Fortune 500 companies are already outsourcing and offshoring to China, India, and other countries. If companies are not already [doing so] chances are they're either looking into it or their financial department is asking why they are not. (Kehal & Singh, 2006, p. vii)

Early outsourcing involved relatively simple decisions such as the outsourcing of janitorial services or copy machine maintenance, but in the 1980s a more complex, second generation of outsourcing decisions came into play as more companies outsourced their information technology and non–core manufacturing processes. Now, even some parts of the organization previously thought to be "immune" to outsourcing are now being outsourced. Outsourcing is not isolated just to IT or payroll; human resources and even legal departments are being outsourced. CAT scans completed in a Vail, Colorado, hospital may now be read and interpreted by a radiologist overseas (Friedman, 2007). Product engineering, marketing, and public relations are all facing outsourcing to some degree (see De Vita & Wang, 2006, for a review of the history of outsourcing).

From an OD perspective, this is significant because familiar ways of working and our commonly held assumptions about work are rapidly disappearing. Organizational boundaries are dissolving. Organizations are now better thought of as loosely coupled systems where suppliers are given unprecedented access and insight into organizational strategies, technologies, proprietary intellectual property, and work sites. This creates such complexity that some scholars are questioning our old assumptions about the very definition of organization. Outsourcing of this magnitude has enormous implications on a system as new processes must be developed and handed over, and staffing changes often accompany the change to justify the financial costs. Even though some employees usually stay behind to manage the outsourced relationship, it takes a Herculean effort to get attention, engagement, and motivation to make the change effective. Moreover, old teams are broken up and new teams are formed, requiring attention to team transitions and coping with the loss of friends and former colleagues.

In the face of overwhelming and complex change and high expectations for productivity, the role of the human resources and OD practitioner is more relevant than ever. Consider the tremendous impact on people in this context. OD consultants understand the human dynamics of change and are attuned to the social costs and benefits of organizational challenges. "In a world where change is constant, for organizations to be adaptive decisions must be pushed down the hierarchy and members must be aligned around the same strategic goals. OD practitioners know how to do this" (Bradford & Burke, 2005, p. 196). As improvements are needed to processes, and outsourcing arrangements mean new ways of working, skilled OD consultants provide a valuable service. They facilitate work redesign sessions and they encourage leaders to follow appropriate communication and change management practices. As organizations cope with increased expectations and as they struggle to define their futures, OD practitioners can help to structure the kinds of interventions discussed in Chapters 10, 11, and 12 to improve the effectiveness of individuals and groups. Recall Weisbord's imperative to get the "whole system in the room"—employees, management, customers, suppliers, and the community—in sessions such as future search conferences where a collaborative process increases the likelihood of successful implementation of change.

Globalization

As organizations move toward offshoring parts of their operations outside the United States, or open subsidiaries in other countries, more people are facing being a member of a team with someone residing on another continent. As Friedman (2007) writes in his book, *The World Is Flat,*

> It is now possible for more people than ever to collaborate and compete in real time with more people on more different kinds of work from more different corners of the planet and on a more equal footing than at any previous time in the history of the world. (p. 8)

He goes on to emphasize the importance of jobs in the future that "will involve collaborating with others or orchestrating collaboration within and between companies, especially those employing diverse workforces from around the world" (p. 285).

OD practitioners are still coming to terms with global cultural differences and how organizational members react differently to different types of interventions. Several studies have compared different countries on six dimensions of national culture first explored by Hofstede (2001) and later expanded by Hofstede, Hofstede, and Minkov (2010): power distance, uncertainty avoidance, individualism-collectivism, masculinity-femininity, long-term orientation, and indulgence-restraint. The first four of these dimensions appeared in Hofstede's seminal work *Culture's Consequences,* and the final two were added based on subsequent research. Figure 14.1 summarizes these four dimensions.

Power Distance: How power in institutions and organizations is distributed

Low Power Distance	High Power Distance
"There will be less emotional resistance to change, higher levels of risk taking, and less emphasis on hierarchical structures" (Yaeger, Head, & Sorensen, 2006, p. 48).	Employees will do what is asked and will not take risks. Hierarchical decision making and communication flow patterns dominate. Change will be communicated from the top when appropriate and necessary.

Uncertainty Avoidance: How a society feels about uncertain or ambiguous situations

Weak Uncertainty Avoidance	Strong Uncertainty Avoidance
Organizations will tolerate ambiguous situations, unknown variables, and unclear information. Members expect unpredictable situations to arise and will not be threatened by needing to adjust.	Organizations will adopt formal rules and policies and expect detailed risk mitigation plans in the event of a problem. Change is threatening and will likely prompt a high degree of resistance.

Individualism Versus Collectivism

Individualism	Collectivism
The self is the basic unit. Employees prefer to work and be managed and rewarded as individuals. Sacrifice for the benefit of the collective is less persuasive.	The group is the basic unit. Employers may provide for employees as they would family members. Employees may work against their own self-interest if all will benefit.

Masculinity Versus Femininity

Masculinity	Femininity
The organization is a competitive environment where performance and action are the central objectives. Rewards, status, and achievement are highly important, and work fits centrally into this culture.	Organizations promote cooperative and collaborative environments. The culture may value thought and planning before action. Spiritual achievement is more valued than economic achievement, and work fits less centrally into the lifestyle.

Short-Term Versus Long-Term Orientation

Short-Term Orientation	Long-Term Orientation
The focus is on immediate profits, short-term gain, and rapid achievement of results. There is a greater tendency to spend versus save. People are highly concerned with status. What is "right" is always right, regardless of situation.	The focus is on later profits, competitive positioning, and sustained results. There is a greater tendency to save for later versus spend now. People are more concerned with social inequality than current status. What is "right" varies by circumstance and is not universally applicable.

Indulgence Versus Restraint

Indulgent	Restrained
A high degree of importance is placed on friendship, networks, leisure time, and enjoying life. There is less emphasis on moral discipline. Maintaining societal order is not a high priority.	A lower degree of importance is placed on friendship, networks, and leisure time. There is a higher emphasis on moral discipline and a high importance is placed on maintaining social order.

Figure 14.1   Six Dimensions of Culture

Jaeger (1986) has argued that while the translation is not perfect, OD's values can be related to Hofstede's dimensions of culture. He noted that OD could be considered low power distance, low uncertainty avoidance, feminine (low masculinity), and equally individual and collective. Jaeger found that by comparing OD's ratings on the Hofstede scale with those of different nations, we can better understand the likely degree of cultural fit of OD interventions and national culture. Likewise, Fagenson-Eland, Ensher, and Burke (2004) found that attributes of national culture, such as the culture's preferences for individualism or collectivism, centralized power or egalitarian participation, affected practitioners' preferences for certain interventions. Yaeger, Head, and Sorensen (2006) agreed, finding that OD is more compatible with low power difference and low uncertainty avoidance cultures that tend to match OD's interest in collaborative, equitable, and participative environments, and that OD seems to be less compatible in high power distance, high uncertainty avoidance, and high masculinity cultures that tend to emphasize hierarchy, control, and structure.

The values of several nations appear to match well with those of OD, such as Denmark, Norway, and Sweden. Sorensen and Head (1995) noted that in Denmark, OD interventions are used extensively, with the most frequently used including such interventions as survey feedback, team building, role analysis, and confrontation meetings.

Cultural values in Germany, Great Britain, and the United States appear to provide moderate consistency with OD's values:

> The U.S. and Great Britain are high on individualism and masculinity, and low on power distance and uncertainty avoidance. Group-based activities can easily meet with resistance. . . . Germany is moderate on power distance and uncertainty avoidance, and high on individualism and masculinity. This means that some of the more "democratic" based processes might require extra effort. (Yaeger et al., 2006, p. 67)

Structural approaches seem to work well in Germany, though there has been a great deal of criticism of OD's theoretical roots (Pieper, 1995).

OD's values also seem to be inconsistent with those in several countries. In Italy, for example, Boss and Mariono (1987) found that "Italian culture is not conducive to dealing with emotionally charged issues in a group context" (p. 246), which might be the objective of an organization mirror or confrontation meeting intervention. They found that team-building interventions focused on tasks were more effective than those that focused on interpersonal concerns. In China, role negotiation, confrontation meetings, third-party consultation, and organization mirror interventions were all judged by executives to be unacceptable interventions in that culture (Head, Gong, Ma, Sorensen, & Yaeger, 2006).

OD practitioners will need to continue to build their awareness of how different interventions can be adapted to different cultures. At the very minimum, practitioners today must "be aware of their own cultural value orientation, the value orientation of organization development, and the value orientation of the culture in which they are working" (Yaeger et al., 2006, pp. 77–78). This is just part of the complexity of global OD, however. Most research to this point has concentrated on single cultures and their adaptations of OD interventions. We know little about how OD interventions may need to be adapted and conducted with a global team comprised of members from many different countries. The new global team will complicate the applicability of different intervention strategies.

Changing Workforce Demographics

A fourth major trend affecting organizations today relates to the changing diversity of the workplace. You may have heard about the workforce demographic trends starting to hit society, and many of them are indeed staggering. Slowing population growth rates, an increasing proportion of older workers, and a diverse and global workforce are all converging to change the face of the workforce. By 2016, the U.S. Department of Labor reports, the number of workers from 55 to 64 will increase by more than 7 million, and the number of 35- to 44-year-olds will decrease. The percentage of workers 65 or older will increase by 84% ("Labor Force," 2007). Adapting the organization to these demographic changes and being at the forefront of these trends is critical.

Most demographers believe when the first baby boomers begin to retire in substantial numbers, the number of new workers may not be enough to replace them. This has serious implications for the health care system as most of us already experience, but consider some of the additional implications. Some analysts predict significant labor shortages even in the next several years, and that in the next 30 years, there will only be half the workers available to fill the jobs needed ("Fast Forward," 2003). Where will that knowledge go and where will the skills come from?

HR practitioners and OD consultants can develop programs to account for these changes, such as the mentoring or coaching programs discussed in Chapter 10. Many organizations are developing coaching programs where older workers share their knowledge and experience with the next generation. Others are developing part-time or consulting arrangements for what some call the "new retirement." Still other organizations are working closely with universities to hire graduates with skills they need, while others are investing in job training for new hires.

In addition, with the changing demographics of the workforce comes different work relationships and ways to manage. Some researchers have noted that those belonging to Generation X (those born roughly between 1963 and 1977) and Generation Y (those born after 1978) hold different attitudes about work than those in earlier generations, necessitating new organizational policies and management practices. Baby boomers (those born from 1945 to 1963) now represent 45% of the workforce, whereas Generation X represents 30% and Generation Y represents 15%. In other words, Generations X and Y together are as large a population today as the baby boomers, and they likely will become the majority in the next several years.

However, most organizational policies and management practices have been created to manage, develop, attract, and retain workers in ways that no longer fit the needs, expectations, and desires of these new generations. With baby boomers retiring in record numbers (consider that more than 50% of the federal workforce is now eligible for retirement according to Ludwick, 2007), if organizations are to successfully attract and retain the new generations of employees, they will need to make significant changes to compete for talent (O'Bannon, 2001). Examining the expectations and relationships to work and management for Generations X and Y can illuminate what these changes might be. Figure 14.2 explores the similarities and differences between Generations X and Y on a number of work-relevant dimensions.

Characteristic	Generation X	Generation Y
Birth Years	Between 1963 and 1977	After 1978
Attitudes toward work	Independent, free agent mentality toward work Desires to keep skills current Strives for work-life balance Willing to forgo some financial gains and status for personal time Technologically literate	More open than Gen X to leaving if work requirements not met Desires challenging work Wants to meet personal goals Wants flexibility in work Wants to know why before tackling the job Continually wired and connected to digital media
Attitudes toward management	Would rather be left alone to complete tasks Would prefer to learn just-in-time as needed Low confidence in leaders and organizations	Prefers a participative style of management Wants to participate in decision making Desires immediate feedback about performance Respects ability and skills over rank

Figure 14.2 Generation X and Generation Y in the Workplace

At work, Generation X has widely been portrayed as lazy, "slackers," disloyal, and uncommitted, but Tulgan (2000) emphasizes that such stereotypes are inaccurate and arise from conflicts they experience with poor management. In his interviews with Xers, Tulgan (2000) writes that four themes consistently emerge:

Belonging (is this a team where I can make a meaningful contribution?), learning (do I have access to information?), entrepreneurship (is there room in my work to define problems, develop solutions at my own pace, and produce results?), [and] security (am I able to monitor the success rate of my performance, my status at work, and the return on my investment?). (p. 33)

They value flexibility at work to the point that they will leave for jobs elsewhere when better opportunities present themselves, not expecting lifelong employment with a single company. Thus, they view themselves as "free agents" with the right to move as necessary to make best use of their skills in the right environment. They also value their family and free time and strive for a healthy balance with work. Financial gains are important, but Gen Xers are willing to earn less in order to maintain personal time.

Generations X and Y share many similarities but also important differences. For example, while they were both raised close to technology, Generation Y employees tend to be much more advanced with their knowledge of technology, spending 6 hours per day, on average, online (Eisner, 2005), and taking those skills to the workplace where they multitask at their desks and in meetings. They prize ability and skill development (rather than rank and job titles) and often seek out opportunities for learning. At work, they ask questions frequently with curiosity and a learning approach to their jobs, which can be perceived by their managers as threatening or challenging (Kehrli & Sopp, 2006). They dislike micromanagement yet value access to a manager who can provide immediate feedback and information as necessary.

A number of management practices are implicated in the expectations and work preferences of Generations X and Y. Both generations are likely to hold less loyalty to their employer than those of previous generations, moving on quickly to new jobs when opportunities arise and the current job is no longer satisfying. Consequently, adapting management styles to their needs will encourage stronger relationships to the organization. Minimally, the work environment should be flexible and ideally virtual, making use of both generations' technological literacy. Organizationwide communications can be sent through technology with the ability to be downloaded to portable media devices. Training can be delivered through these same methods in short packets of information that can be learned quickly. Managers should design jobs that provide challenge, opportunities to genuinely contribute (rather than put in time or "pay dues"), opportunities to participate in decision making, and opportunities to learn. Managers can follow up with employees by inviting text messages with status updates on projects (Kehrli & Sopp, 2006). Some have noted that despite these management challenges, employees from Generation Y may be easier to manage than those of Generation X. "Gen Y tends to value teamwork and fairness and is likely to be more positive than Gen X on a range of workplace issues including work-life balance, performance reviews, and availability of supervisors" (Eisner, 2005, p. 9). Rewards such as additional time off can be valuable retention mechanisms.

To cite a final example of the changes in workforce demographics, based on the 2010 census, the Census Bureau estimated that half of the nation's population growth since 1990 was due to immigration. There is increasing diversity in the U.S. workplace and an increasing trend toward global teams and virtual teams. Local and global workforce diversity must prompt organizations to take seriously the need for training and dialogue to develop understanding among people of different backgrounds. Diverse organizations contain the seeds of diverse ideas, and when these ideas have an opportunity to be surfaced and are considered seriously, the organization has a greater likelihood of developing more innovative solutions. An organization that does not reflect these population trends or does not take them seriously is not likely to succeed for long. It also magnifies the complexities of working in a team environment. OD practitioners who understand the complexities of global teaming (recall our discussions of team effectiveness in Chapter 11) are helping to design team interventions to maximize team effectiveness and helping teams become explicit about their roles and assumptions about how they work.

Changing Nature of Work

A third major trend is influenced by these changing workforce demographics. Work itself is changing. The 40-hour work week, with a 30-year career in one job for a single organization and a gold watch as a gift on retirement, is the exception rather than the rule. Most people now have multiple careers, with little need for a long-term tie to one organization—mirroring the loyalty that organizations often have for employees. Years of workplace downsizing and ever-reducing benefits have created what one study calls a "simmering malaise" ("Fast Forward," 2003), noting that when the economy improves, anger and dissatisfaction remain among employees still on the job. As Holbeche (2006) puts it, "This erosion of trust has undermined the basis of both commitment to the organization and higher levels of motivation" (p. 15).

As we discussed in Chapter 2, the new term for this is *employee engagement,* and some studies show disconcerting trends. Almost half of all Americans can be described as disengaged in their work; that is, they are not described as willing to put in discretionary effort to go above and beyond to perform at a high level (Saks, 2006). The solution is not simply to pay people more or find ways to make them "happy." Researchers are finding that those factors seem to play a less important role than ever in engagement, particularly among newer generations. As one set of researchers put it,

> Employees are emotionally and cognitively engaged when they know what is expected of them, have what they need to do their work, have opportunities to feel an impact and fulfillment in their work, perceive that they are part of something significant with coworkers whom they trust, and have chances to improve and develop. (Harter, Schmidt, & Hayes, 2002, p. 269)

What people report seeking in a job are accountability, autonomy, strong leadership, a sense of control, and opportunities for development. This is the reason why some believe that engagement is the highest in the nonprofit sector. A sense of a larger mission and passion for work is what many people desire.

Because of these desires to find a workplace that matches their own schedules and values, people are making new choices, redefining the very meaning of work and career. Consider just two ways that this is happening:

1. Almost 16 million Americans, or "about 1 in 9 workers" according to the Bureau of Labor Statistics (Hipple, 2010, p. 17), are self-employed, and four in five organizations report using freelancers to do work ("Fast Forward," 2003). It is now frequently difficult to tell the difference between an employee and a contractor in many organizations. Microsoft, for example, has such a volume of current and past contract employees that contractors at one point developed an online forum community devoted to those that have "orange badges" (special colored badges that distinguish contract from noncontract employees). Holbeche (2006) writes, "In some businesses, managing contractors and consultants is increasingly the norm rather than the exception" (p. 43). Many workers choose to work for themselves, setting their own hours and choosing their own work locations.

2. More people are making the choice to work part-time, work flexible hours, or telecommute. About 12% of all full-time employees did some work at home according to a recent report ("Work-at-home patterns by occupation," 2009), and more than 33 million employees telecommute at least once a month (Hodges, 2009). Technology changes now allow some employees to work from anywhere, making the term *telecommuting* somewhat outdated (Regenold, 2009). As more employees work at a distance from one another, team dynamics change. In fact,

global and virtual teaming has already become the norm: Virtual teams exist in more than half of all large companies (Martins, Gilson, & Maynard, 2004).

Consider the implications of these trends on working conditions and collaboration. With more fluid boundaries of organizational membership and greater physical distance comes an increase in social isolation in the workplace (Richardson, 2008). With increasingly mobile employees, changing teams and managers, and a decreasing loyalty and engagement in work, organizations have no choice but to learn and adopt some of the fundamental values of OD to survive. While it may be a start to develop part-time work arrangements or telecommuting policies, there are fundamental values changes needed as well. If organizations are to survive, their basic leadership and management values must change. This is where the values of OD work collide with some commonly held management practices (recall our discussion of OD values in Chapter 3). Hierarchical command and control management must give way to participative management and teamwork, competition must give way to collaboration, and the growth and development of the individual must be taken into account. Many organizations are rethinking their tall hierarchies, seeking new ways of designing organizations for involvement, participation, and empowerment.

OD practitioners have several ways that they can help in the current environment. They can coach managers and leaders (Chapter 10) to help them learn new ways of managing in the current environment. They can develop employee participation programs that will grow and develop the skills of individuals, engage them in their work, and create passion for the organization. They can help design new structures and enhance them with effective lateral coordination mechanisms (Chapter 12). They can confront leaders with hard truths, addressing systemic conflicts and creating cultures of collaboration (through effective feedback mechanisms as described in Chapter 10 or cultural change as illustrated in Chapter 12).

OD and Technology

OD has been influenced by technological developments in many areas such as data gathering in employee surveys and 360 feedback; employee development such as training, distance coaching, and mentoring; and OD work methods themselves, through virtual work and distance communications (Church, Gilbert, Oliver, Paquet, & Surface, 2002; Tippins, 2002). OD practitioners commonly administer employee surveys using electronic and Web-based methods, and they frequently use Internet-based assessment tools in 360 feedback and individual instruments. Virtual coaching and mentoring at a distance are now commonplace. Church et al. (2002) describe an intervention at PepsiCo in which career development and individual performance tools were implemented through an internal website. A new culture of individual growth and development was created in which individuals had access unlike ever before to a wealth of personal development and career resources.

As organizations change their uses of technology, OD practitioners will need to continue to evolve methods for using technology to conduct OD interventions with virtual teams and at a distance. Familiar OD "technologies" such as whiteboards and flip charts can be enhanced with social networking and distance collaboration tools, and more clients will expect OD practitioners to be adaptable to the needs of virtual teams (Church et al., 2002). The success of such efforts likely will depend heavily on the organization's familiarity with technology. Practitioners will need to be educated on how organizational members use technology, when and why they might reject an intervention using technology, and what tradeoffs exist in conducting interventions virtually versus face-to-face.

As people change and teams form, work, and dissolve, OD practitioners who understand the dynamics of teamwork and the uncertainty in changing social relationships facilitate the healthy start-up of new teams through transition meetings and team-building activities (Chapter 11). Left to their own trial and error, sorting through interpersonal issues on their own, a new team can take months to develop their work processes or understand roles and relationships. With the help of an OD consultant, this time can be cut significantly, and employees tend to have a greater tie to the team with greater engagement and satisfaction.

The Current State of OD: Strengths, Weaknesses, and Opportunities

As several authors have put the situation recently, organization development finds itself at a "crossroads" (Worley & Feyerherm, 2003, p. 97). From one perspective, Worley and Feyerherm argue, the central aim of OD initiatives to assist leaders in implementing change has never been a higher priority for executives. From another perspective, the traditional work and values of OD appear to lack the urgency needed by executives today. Despite the relevance of OD to address the challenges of the current environment, OD practice has not responded quickly enough to meet contemporary demands.

Several studies have been done recently of OD practitioners and executives to determine the strengths, weaknesses, and potential opportunities for OD to add more value to organizations. Wirtenberg and her associates (Wirtenberg, Abrams, & Ott, 2004; Wirtenberg, Lipsky, Abrams, Conway, & Slepian, 2007) reported on research conducted by the Global Committee on the Future of Organization Development, a consortium sponsored by major professional associations involved in OD.

Strengths of OD Practice Today

Among the strengths of OD today mentioned by practitioners were the following:

- The systemic orientation that practitioners bring
- Their ability to assist in managing change
- The techniques and processes they use (i.e., supporting teamwork and leadership development)
- Humanistic values that underlie OD practice (Wirtenberg et al., 2007, p. 12)

In addition, Worley and Feyerherm (2003), in an in-depth set of interviews with OD practitioners, found that the practitioners attributed their success to several skills and abilities, including broad education, training, experience, interpersonal skills, and a clear knowledge of self.

Weaknesses in OD Practice Today

Nonetheless, despite these strengths, business leaders often do not select an OD practitioner when faced with implementing a major change (Wirtenberg et al., 2007). Studies of practitioners and executives report several weaknesses with how OD is practiced today:

- Different practitioners define and practice OD differently. Intervention typologies are inconsistent and the boundaries are fluid between OD and other fields such as organizational behavior, management, and psychology (Worley & Feyerherm, 2003).
- OD practitioners have a tendency to rapidly adopt the latest intervention techniques and technologies, perhaps without fully considering their use or impact. Some practitioners "expressed concern that OD was jumping on bandwagons and in doing so risked its identity" (Worley & Feyerherm, 2003, p. 112).
- OD values are challenged by prevailing business-oriented values of efficiency, profitability, and productivity, which are rising above OD's historical values of humanism, participation, and democracy. As a result, OD practitioners struggle with how to reconcile situations in which these values conflict with each other.
- There is not a consistent set of skills and competencies required to be an OD practitioner, and a single certification path does not exist.
- While practitioners find themselves facilitating meetings, conducting Myers-Briggs sessions, coaching individuals, and resolving conflicts, these are not systemic change activities (Burke & Bradford, 2005).
- Departments of organization development in most companies are hidden within human resources departments, blunting their influence (Burke & Bradford, 2005).

Opportunities for OD to Add More Value

Organization development can continue its evolution and better adapt to the needs of contemporary organizational challenges if it makes several changes. Greiner and Cummings (2005) review OD's history and current practice and draw a parallel between an earlier crisis in OD and today. They show that in the 1970s, when OD narrowed its focus, it was initially unable to adapt to the changing conditions in many organizations and lost support among managers and executives. While the field eventually responded, the current state of OD points to six new red flags that they believe point to OD's lack of relevance today and point to future opportunities for OD to create "integrative solutions to the major issues facing tomorrow's organizations" (Greiner & Cummings, 2005, p. 108):

- Neglected involvement in top-management decision making
- Neglected involvement in strategy formulation
- Neglected involvement in mergers and acquisitions
- Neglected involvement in globalization
- Neglected involvement in alliances and virtual organizations
- Neglected involvement in corporate governance and personal integrity

Researchers and practitioners have noted several other ways that OD practitioners can enhance their practice and add more value. Improvements in leadership will be a constant need, so one trend will be "building leadership capacity now and for the future" (Wirtenberg et al., 2007, p. 15). Part of this building capacity will involve helping leaders with the complexity of managing change in a global environment. Practitioners and researchers know that not all processes for managing change and not all OD interventions work equally well in all cultures. "Global organization development practitioners have the discerning ability to encounter and overcome cross-culture complexities while accomplishing successful global organization development work" (Yaeger et al., 2006, p. 134).

Business skills will be highly important. Many OD practitioners lack deep business training, and thus lack background knowledge of finance, customers and market needs, competitive opportunities and threats, and more. As a result, they may not be aware enough of the business context for a change to be able to speak credibly with a client or potential client in the client's language, linking OD outcomes with business needs and results. Increasing business knowledge and developing interventions that address contemporary business issues will increase the value that the OD practitioner can provide, such as "effectively addressing organizational culture during organizational realignments, industry consolidations and mergers and acquisitions (M&A's)" (Wirtenberg et al., 2007, p. 15).

Adapting OD to the needs of the organization will require delivering value on a shorter time scale and learning how to balance classic techniques with new interventions, and to "rely a lot less on techniques and jumping on the latest fad" (Worley & Feyerherm, 2003, p. 104). This may involve practitioners learning how to adapt OD values to contemporary needs rather than insist on a set of humanistic values as appropriate in every situation. The question is whether the field can remain relevant to contemporary organizations and at the same time to keep a core set of concepts and values that practitioners share. OD's emphasis on its humanistic values (those explored in Chapter 3) may contradict some of the changes that practitioners are asked to implement. The field must struggle with the issue of how practitioners should balance the need to assist clients in making difficult business decisions (such as outsourcing, layoffs, and site closures) with OD's presumption that organizational members should be involved and participate in decisions that affect them.

Just as contemporary organizations struggle with issues of the pace of change, increasing technology, a global and demographically diverse workforce, and changes in work practices and values, so must OD change its own practices to model these new ways of operating for our clients. Stubborn adherence to old practices and values will not bring our clients along; it will instead further alienate the field from today's reality. At the same time, OD practices, techniques, and values remain relevant to the needs of contemporary workers. The field's current challenge is how to adapt its practices without abandoning its core precepts.

Summary

The nature of the organization is changing at the same time that the workforce and the nature of work itself are changing. The four intertwined trends described in this chapter are creating an environment that organizations must understand and address if they are to find the path to future sustainability. The new environment requires complex thinking, creativity, and attention to the human dynamics of organizations. As a result, this is a particularly relevant and necessary time to have the skills of a human resources or OD professional, given these challenges. These are not just skills needed by those formally designated with "OD consultant" titles. The skills of OD apply to managers, project managers, and team members.

OD is an optimistic field driven by possibility that a positive future lies ahead, and that change can be effectively accomplished through the appropriate application of social science theory to organizational practice. It is this optimism that brings many OD practitioners into the field and encourages their ongoing work to help individuals, groups, and whole organizations continue to change and grow. As the world changes and develops, new and multifaceted thorny issues will continue to present themselves, and the field of OD will continue to adapt and grow to find new ways of addressing our new problems.

For Further Reading

Bradford, D. L., & Burke, W. W. (Eds.). (2005). *Reinventing organization development*. San Francisco: Pfeiffer.

Sorensen, P. F., Jr., Head, T. C., Mathys, N. J., Preston, J., & Cooperrider, D. (Eds.). (1995). *Global and international organization development*. Champaign, IL: Stipes.

Wirtenberg, J., Lipsky, D., Abrams, L., Conway, M., & Slepian, J. (2007). The future of organization development: Enabling sustainable business performance through people. *Organization Development Journal, 25*(2), 11–22.

Worley, C. G., & Feyerherm, A. E. (2003). Reflections on the future of organization development. *Journal of Applied Behavioral Science, 39*, 97–115.

Yaeger, T. F., Head, T. C., & Sorensen, P. F. (2006). *Global organization development: Managing unprecedented change*. Greenwich, CT: Information Age.

References

Adair, J. E. (1986). *Effective teambuilding.* Aldershot, UK: Gower.

Adams, M. (1992). TQM: OD's role in implementing value-based strategies. In C. N. Jackson & M. R. Manning (Eds.), *Organization development annual: Intervening in client organizations* (Vol. 4, pp. 168–181). Alexandria, VA: American Society for Training and Development.

Ahrne, G., & Brunsson, N. (2008). *Meta-organizations.* Cheltenham, UK: Edward Elgar.

Alderfer, C. P. (1977). Improving organizational communication through long-term group intervention. *Journal of Applied Behavioral Science, 13,* 193–210.

Alderfer, C. P., & Smith, K. K. (1982). Studying intergroup relations embedded in organizations. *Administrative Science Quarterly, 27,* 35–65.

Alter, C., & Hage, J. (1993). *Organizations working together.* Newbury Park, CA: Sage.

Anderson, D. L. (2004). The textualizing functions of writing for organizational change. *Journal of Business and Technical Communication, 18,* 141–164.

Anderson, D. L. (2005a). Reorganizing human resources at ASP software. In J. Keyton & P. Shockley-Zalabak (Eds.), *Case studies for organizational communication* (2nd ed., pp. 167–175). Los Angeles: Roxbury.

Anderson, D. L. (2005b). "What you'll say is. . .": Represented voice in organizational change discourse. *Journal of Organizational Change Management, 18*(1), 63–77.

Antonioni, D. (1996). Designing an effective 360-degree appraisal feedback process. *Organizational Dynamics, 25*(2), 24–38.

Argyris, C. (1957). *Personality and organization.* New York: Harper & Brothers.

Argyris, C. (1970). *Intervention theory and method: A behavioral science view.* Reading, MA: Addison-Wesley.

Argyris, C., & Schön, D. (1978). *Organizational learning.* London: Addison-Wesley.

Argyris, C., & Schön, D. A. (1996). *Organizational learning II: Theory, method, and practice.* Reading, MA: Addison-Wesley.

Armenakis, A. A., Feild, H. S., & Holley, W. H. (1976). Guidelines for overcoming empirically identified evaluation problems of organizational development change agents. *Human Relations, 29,* 1147–1161.

Armenakis, A. A., Harris, S. G., & Feild, H. S. (1999). Making change permanent: A model of institutionalizing change interventions. *Research in Organizational Change and Development, 12,* 97–128.

Armenakis, A. A., Harris, S. G., & Mossholder, K. W. (1993). Creating readiness for organizational change. *Human Relations, 46,* 681–703.

Arnold, J. (2001). Careers and career management. In N. Anderson, D. S. Ones, H. K. Sinangil, & C. Viswesvaran (Eds.), *Handbook of industrial, work, and organizational psychology* (Vol. 2, pp. 115–132). London: Sage.

Arthur, M. B., & Rousseau, D. M. (Eds.). (1996). *The boundaryless career.* New York: Oxford.

Ashkenas, R., Ulrich, D., Jick, T., & Kerr, S. (2002). *The boundaryless organization: Breaking the chains of organizational structure* (Rev. ed.). San Francisco: Jossey-Bass.

Axelrod, D. (1992). Getting everyone involved: How one organization involved its employees, supervisors, and managers in redesigning the organization. *Journal of Applied Behavioral Science, 28,* 499–509.

Babbie, E. (1992). *The practice of social research* (6th ed.). Belmont, CA: Wadsworth.

Bahrami, H. (1992). The emerging flexible organization: Perspectives from Silicon Valley. *California Management Review, 34,* 33–52.

Bailey, D., & Dupre, S. (1992). The future search conference as a vehicle for educational change: A shared vision for Will Rogers middle school, Sacramento, California. *Journal of Applied Behavioral Science, 28,* 510–519.

Barkema, H. G., & Schijven, M. (2008). Toward unlocking the full potential of acquisitions: The role of organizational restructuring. *Academy of Management Journal, 51*(4), 696–722.

Barner, R. (2006). Managing complex team interventions. *Team Performance Management, 12,* 44–54.

Barrett, F. J., & Cooperrider, D. L. (1990). Generative metaphor intervention: A new approach for working with systems divided by conflict and caught in defensive perception. *Journal of Applied Behavioral Science, 26,* 219–239.

Barrett, F. J., Thomas, G. F., & Hocevar, S. P. (1995). The central role of discourse in large-scale change: A social construction perspective. *Journal of Applied Behavioral Science, 31,* 352–372.

Bartee, E. M., & Cheyunski, F. (1977). A methodology for process-oriented organizational diagnosis. *Journal of Applied Behavioral Science, 13,* 53–68.

Bartunek, J. M., & Louis, M. R. (1988). The interplay of organization development and organizational transformation. *Research in Organizational Change and Development, 2,* 97–134.

Bartunek, J. M., & Moch, M. K. (1987). First-order, second-order, and third-order change and organization development interventions: A cognitive approach. *Journal of Applied Behavioral Science, 23,* 483–500.

Bass, M. J., Buck, C., Turner, L., Dickie, G., Pratt, G., & Robinson, H.C. (1986). The physician's actions and the outcome of illness in family practice. *Journal of Family Practice, 23*(1), 43–47.

Beckhard, R. (1967). The confrontation meeting. *Harvard Business Review, 45*(2), 149–155.

Beckhard, R. (1969). *Organization development: Strategies and models.* Reading, MA: Addison-Wesley.

Beckhard, R., & Harris, R. (1977). *Organizational transitions.* Reading, MA: Addison-Wesley.

Beckhard, R., & Harris, R. (1987). *Organizational transitions* (2nd ed.). Reading, MA: Addison-Wesley.

Beeby, M., & Simpson, P. (1998). Barriers, boundaries and leaks in an organization development intervention. *Leadership & Organization Development Journal, 19,* 353–361.

Beer, M. (1980). *Organization change and development: A systems view.* Santa Monica, CA: Goodyear.

Beer, M., & Eisenstat, R. A. (1996). Developing an organization capable of implementing strategy and learning. *Human Relations, 49,* 597–619.

Beer, M., & Eisenstat, R. A. (2000). The six silent killers of strategy implementation and learning. *MIT Sloan Management Review, 41,* 29–40.

Benne, K. D. (1964). History of the T-group in the laboratory setting. In L. P. Bradford, J. R. Gibb, & K. D. Benne (Eds.), *T-group theory and laboratory method* (pp. 80–135). New York: Wiley.

Benson, G. S., & Lawler, E. E. (2003). Employee involvement: Utilization, impacts, and future prospects. In D. Holman, T. D. Wall, C. W. Clegg, P. Sparrow, & A. Howard (Eds.), *The new workplace: A guide to the human impact of modern working practices* (pp. 155–173). Chichester, UK: Wiley.

Benson, J. K. (1977). Organizations: A dialectical view. *Administrative Science Quarterly, 22,* 1–21.

Berger, P., & Luckmann, T. (1967). *The social construction of reality.* New York: Anchor.

Bergquist, W. (1993). *The postmodern organization: Mastering the art of irreversible change.* San Francisco: Jossey-Bass.

Bertlanffy, L. V. (1968). *General system theory: Foundations, development, applications.* New York: George Braziller.

Birnbaum, R. (1984). The effects of a neutral third party on academic bargaining relationships and campus climate. *Journal of Higher Education, 55,* 719–734.

Black, T. G., & Westwood, M. J. (2004). Evaluating the development of a multidisciplinary leadership team in a cancer-center. *Leadership & Organization Development Journal, 25,* 577–591.

Blake, R. R., & Mouton, J. S. (1964). *The managerial grid.* Houston, TX: Gulf.

Blake, R. R., & Mouton, J. S. (1968). *Corporate excellence through grid organization development.* Houston: Gulf.

Blake, R. R., & Mouton, J. S. (1978). *The new managerial grid.* Houston, TX: Gulf.

Blake, R. R., Mouton, J. S., & Sloma, R. L. (1965). The union-management intergroup laboratory: Strategy for resolving intergroup conflict. *Journal of Applied Behavioral Science, 1,* 25–57.

Blake, R. R., Shepard, H. A., & Mouton, J. S. (1964). *Managing intergroup conflict in industry.* Houston TX: Gulf.

Block, P. (2000). *Flawless consulting: A guide to getting your expertise used* (2nd ed.). New York: Jossey-Bass.

Block, P. (2001). Twelve questions to the most frequently asked answers. In P. Block (Ed.), *The flawless consulting fieldbook and companion* (pp. 393–403). San Francisco: Jossey-Bass.

Block, P. (2008). *Community: The structure of belonging.* San Francisco: Barrett-Koehler.

Blue Sky Productions. (1996). *Discovering community* [Videocassette]. Philadelphia: Author.

Blumberg, A., & Wiener, W. (1971). One from two: Facilitating an organizational merger. *Journal of Applied Behavioral Science, 7,* 87–102.

Boje, D. M. (1993). Editorial: Post-TQM. *Journal of Organizational Change Management, 6,* 4–8.

Boje, D. M., & Winsor, R. D. (1993). The resurrection of Taylorism: Total quality management's hidden agenda. *Journal of Organizational Change Management, 6,* 57–70.

Boss, R. W. (1983). Team building and the problem of regression: The personal management interview as an intervention. *Journal of Applied Behavioral Science, 19,* 67–83.

Boss, R. W. (2000). The psychological contract. In R. T. Golembiewski (Ed.), *Handbook of organizational consultation* (2nd ed., pp. 119–128). New York: Marcel Dekker.

Boss, R. W., & Mariono, M. V. (1987). Organization development in Italy. *Group & Organization Studies, 12,* 245–256.

Bowers, D. G., Franklin, J. L., & Pecorella, P. A. (1975). Matching problems, precursors, and interventions in OD: A systemic approach. *Journal of Applied Behavioral Science, 11,* 391–409.

Bradford, D. L., & Burke, W. W. (2005). The future of OD? In D. L. Bradford & W. W. Burke (Eds.), *Reinventing organization development* (pp. 195–214). San Francisco: Pfeiffer.

Bradford, L. P. (1974). *National training laboratories: Its history, 1947–1970.* Bethel, ME: National Training Laboratory.

Bradford, L. P., Gibb, J. R., & Benne, K. D. (Eds.). (1964). *T-group theory and laboratory method.* New York: Wiley.

Bradley, J., White, B. J., & Mennecke, B. E. (2003). Teams and tasks: A temporal framework for the effects of interpersonal interventions on team performance. *Small Group Research, 34,* 353–387.

Bridges, W. (1980). *Transitions.* Reading, MA: Addison-Wesley.

Brink, T. L. (1993). Metaphor as data in the study of organizations. *Journal of Management Inquiry, 2,* 366–371.

Brown, L. D. (1980). Planned change in underorganized systems. In T. G. Cummings (Ed.), *Systems theory for organization development* (pp. 181–203). Chichester, UK: Wiley.

Brutus, S., Fleenor, J. W., & London, M. (1998). Elements of effective 360-degree feedback. In W. W. Tornow, M. London, & CCL Associates (Eds.), *Maximizing the value of 360-degree feedback* (pp. 11–27). San Francisco: Jossey-Bass.

Buchanan, D., Fitzgerald, L., Ketley, D., Gollop, R., Jones, J. L., Lamont, S. S., et al. (2005). No going back: A review of the literature on sustaining organizational change. *International Journal of Management Reviews, 7*(3), 189–205.

Bunker, B. B., & Alban, B. T. (1992). Conclusion: What makes large group interventions effective? *Journal of Applied Behavioral Science, 28,* 579–591.

Bunker, B. B., & Alban, B. T. (1997). *Large group interventions: Engaging the whole system for rapid change.* San Francisco: Jossey-Bass.

Bunker, B. B., & Alban, B. T. (2006). Large group methods: Developments and trends. In B. B. Jones & M. Brazzel (Eds.), *The NTL handbook of organization development and change* (pp. 287–301). San Francisco: Pfeiffer.

Bunker, B. B., Alban, B. T., & Lewicki, R. J. (2005). Ideas in currency and OD practice: Has the well gone dry? In D. L. Bradford & W. W. Burke (Eds.), *Reinventing organization development* (pp. 163–194). San Francisco: Pfeiffer.

Buono, A. F. (2003). SEAM-less post-merger integration strategies: A cause for concern. *Journal of Organizational Change Management, 16*(1), 90–98.

Burke, W. W. (1977). Changing trends in organization development. In W. W. Burke (Ed.), *Current issues and strategies in organization development* (pp. 22–52). New York: Human Sciences Press.

Burke, W. W. (1992). Metaphors to consult by. *Group & Organization Management, 17,* 255–259.

Burke, W. W. (1993). *Organization development: A process of learning and changing* (2nd ed.). Reading, MA: Addison-Wesley.

Burke, W. W. (1994). Diagnostic models for organization development. In A. Howard & Associates (Eds.), *Diagnosis for organizational change: Methods and models* (pp. 53–84). New York: Guilford.

Burke, W. W. (2002). *Organization change: Theory and practice.* Thousand Oaks, CA: Sage.

Burke, W. W. (2004). Internal organization development practitioners: Where do they belong? *Journal of Applied Behavioral Science, 40,* 423–431.

Burke, W. W. (2008). A contemporary view of organization development. In T. G. Cummings (Ed.), *Handbook of organization development* (pp. 13–38). Thousand Oaks, CA: Sage.

Burke, W. W., & Bradford, D. L. (2005). The crisis in OD. In D. L. Bradford & W. W. Burke (Eds.), *Reinventing organization development* (pp. 7–14). San Francisco: Pfeiffer.

Burke, W. W., & Litwin, G. H. (1992). A causal model of organizational performance and change. *Journal of Management, 18,* 532–545.

Bushe, G. R., & Kassam, A. F. (2005). When is appreciative inquiry transformational? A meta-case analysis. *Journal of Applied Behavioral Science, 41,* 161–181.

Bushe, G. B., & Marshak, R. J. (2009). Revisioning organization development: Diagnostic and dialogic premises and patterns of practice. *The Journal of Applied Behavioral Science, 45*(3), 348–368.

Buzaglo, G., & Wheelan, S. A. (1999). Facilitating work team effectiveness: Case studies from Central America. *Small Group Research, 30,* 108–129.

Byrd, R. E. (2000). Team building and its risks. In R. T. Golembiewski (Ed.), *Handbook of organizational consultation* (2nd ed., pp. 157–161). New York: Marcel Dekker.

Cahoon, A. R. (2000). Using the search conference technique for team socialization and strategic planning. In R. T. Golembiewski (Ed.), *Handbook of organizational consultation* (2nd ed., pp. 163–167). New York: Marcel Dekker.

Cameron, K. S., & Freeman, S. J. (1991). Cultural congruence, strength, and type: Relationships to effectiveness. *Research in Organizational Change and Development, 5,* 23–58.

Cameron, K. S., & Quinn, R. E. (2006). *Diagnosing and changing organizational culture: Based on the competing values framework* (Rev. ed.). San Francisco: Jossey-Bass.

Cameron, K. S., & Whetten, D. A. (1981). Perceptions of organizational effectiveness of organizational life cycles. *Administrative Science Quarterly, 26,* 525–544.

Carey, A., & Varney, G. H. (1983). Which skills spell success in OD? *Training and Development Journal, 37*(4), 38–40.

Cargile, A. C., Bradac, J. J., & Cole, T. (2006). Theories of intergroup conflict: A report of lay attributions. *Journal of Language and Social Psychology, 25,* 47–63.

Carlson, J. G. (1985). Recent assessments of the Myers-Briggs type indicator. *Journal of Personality Assessment, 49,* 356–365.

Carlson, J. G. (1989). Affirmative: In support of researching the Myers-Briggs type indicator. *Journal of Counseling and Development, 67,* 484–486.

Cartwright, S., & Cooper, C. L. (1993). The role of culture compatibility in successful organizational marriage. *Academy of Management Executive, 7,* 57–70.

Cash, W. B., & Minter, R. L. (1979). Consulting approaches: Two basic styles. *Training and Development Journal, 33*(9), 26–28.

Chapman, J. A. (2002). A framework for transformational change in organisations. *Leadership & Organization Development Journal, 23,* 16–25.

Chermack, T. J., & Lynham, S. A. (2002). Definitions and outcome variables of scenario planning. *Human Resource Development Review, 1,* 366–383.

Cheyunski, F., & Millard, J. (1998). Accelerated business transformation and the role of the organization architect. *Journal of Applied Behavioral Science, 34,* 268–285.

Chin, R., & Benne, K. D. (1976). General strategies for effecting changes in human systems. In W. G. Bennis, K. D. Benne, R. Chin, & K. E. Corey (Eds.), *The planning of change* (3rd ed., pp. 22–45). New York: Holt, Rinehart, & Winston.

Chisholm, R. F. (2000). Using large system designs and action research to develop interorganizational networks. In R. T. Golembiewski (Ed.), *Handbook of organizational consultation* (2nd ed., pp. 197–211). New York: Marcel Dekker.

Chisholm, R. F. (2008). Developing interorganizational networks. In T. G. Cummings (Ed.), *Handbook of organization development* (pp. 629–650). Thousand Oaks, CA: Sage.

Church, A. H., & Bracken, D. W. (1997). Advancing the state of the art of 360-degree feedback. *Group & Organization Management, 22,* 149–161.

Church, A. H., Burke, W. W., & Van Eynde, D. F. (1994). Values, motives, and interventions of organization development practitioners. *Group & Organization Management, 19,* 5–50.

Church, A. H., Gilbert, M., Oliver, D. H., Paquet, K., & Surface, C. (2002). The role of technology in organization development and change. *Advances in Developing Human Resources, 4,* 493–511.

Church, A. H., Hurley, R. F., & Burke, W. W. (1992). Evolution or revolution in the values of organization development: Commentary on the state of the field. *Journal of Organizational Change Management, 5,* 6–23.

Clark, P. A. (1972). *Action research and organizational change.* London: Harper & Row.

Clarke, N. (2005). Transorganization development for network building. *Journal of Applied Behavioral Science, 41,* 30–46.

Clinebell, S., & Stecher, M. (2003). Teaching teams to be teams: An exercise using the Myers-Briggs type indicator and the five-factor personality traits. *Journal of Management Education, 27,* 362–383.

Coe, C. K. (1992). The MBTI: Potential uses and misuses in personnel administration. *Public Personnel Management, 21,* 511–522.

Coghlan, D. (1994). Managing organization change through teams and groups. *Leadership & Organization Development Journal, 15*(2), 18–23.

Coghlan, D., & Brannick, T. (2001). *Doing action research in your own organization.* London: Sage.

Cole, R. E. (1999). *Managing quality fads: How American business learned to play the quality game.* New York: Oxford.

Connaughton, S. L., & Daly, J. A. (2004). Leading from afar: Strategies for effectively leading virtual teams. In S. H. Godar & S. P. Ferris (Eds.), *Virtual and collaborative teams: Process, technologies and practice* (pp. 49–75). Hershey, PA: Idea Group.

Cooperrider, D. L., & Whitney, D. (2001). A positive revolution in change. In D. L. Cooperrider, P. Sorenson, D. Whitney, & T. Yeager (Eds.), *Appreciative inquiry: An emerging direction for organization development* (pp. 9–29). Champaign, IL: Stipes.

Cooperrider, D. L., & Whitney, D. (2005). *Appreciative inquiry: A positive revolution in change.* San Francisco: Barrett-Koehler.

Coram, R., & Burnes, B. (2001). Managing organisational change in the public sector. *International Journal of Public Sector Management, 14,* 94–110.

Corporate culture. (1980, Oct. 27). *BusinessWeek,* pp. 148–151, 154, 158, 160.

Cotton, J. L. (1993). *Employee involvement: Methods for improving performance and work attitudes.* Newbury Park, CA: Sage.

Covin, T. J. (1992). Common intervention strategies for large-scale change. *Leadership & Organization Development Journal, 13*(4), 27–32.

Cummings, T. G. (1984). Transorganizational development. *Research in Organizational Behavior, 6,* 367–422.

Cummings, T. G., & Feyerherm, A. E. (1995). Interventions in large systems. In W. Rothwell, R. Sullivan, & G. N. McLean (Eds.), *Practicing organization development: A guide for consultants* (pp. 203–234). San Diego: Pfeiffer.

Cummings, T. G., & Worley, C. G. (2001). *Essentials of organization development and change* (7th ed.). Cincinnati, OH: South-Western College Publishing.

Cunningham, J. B. (1993). *Action research and organizational development.* Westport, CT: Praeger.

Daly, J. P., Pouder, R. W., & Kabanoff, B. (2004). The effects of initial differences in firms' espoused values on their postmerger performance. *Journal of Applied Behavioral Science, 40,* 323–343.

Dannemiller, K. D., & Jacobs, R. W. (1992). Changing the way organizations change: A revolution of common sense. *Journal of Applied Behavioral Science, 28,* 480–498.

Davis, S. M., & Lawrence, P. R. (1977). *Matrix.* Reading, MA: Addison-Wesley.

Dayal, I., & Thomas, J. M. (1968). Operation KPE: Developing a new organization. *Journal of Applied Behavioral Science, 4,* 473–506.

Deal, T. E., & Kennedy, A. A. (1982). *Corporate cultures: The rites and rituals of corporate life.* Reading, MA: Addison-Wesley.

Deetz, S. (1985). Ethical considerations in cultural research in organizations. In P. J. Frost, L. F. Moore, M. R. Louis, C. C. Lundberg, & J. Martin (Eds.), *Organizational culture* (pp. 253–269). Beverly Hills, CA: Sage.

Deetz, S. A., Tracy, S. J., & Simpson, J. L. (2000). *Leading organizations through transition: Communication and cultural change.* Thousand Oaks, CA: Sage.

Denison, D. R., & Spreitzer, G. M. (1991). Organizational culture and organizational development: A competing values approach. *Research in Organizational Change and Development, 5,* 1–21.

De Vita, G., & Wang, C. L. (2006). Development of outsourcing theory and practice: A taxonomy of outsourcing generations. In H. Kehal & V. P. Singh (Eds.), *Outsourcing and offshoring in the 21st century: A socio-economic perspective* (pp. 1–17). Hershey, PA: Idea Group.

Dodgson, M. (1993). Organizational learning: A review of some literatures. *Organization Studies, 14,* 375–394.

Dovidio, J. F., Gaertner, S. L., & Kawakami, K. (2003). Intergroup contact: The past, present, and the future. *Group Processes & Intergroup Relations, 6,* 5–21.

Druskat, V. U., & Dahal, D. (2005). Leadership and self-managing teams: Leading a team that manages itself. In L. L. Neider & C. A. Schriesheim (Eds.), *Understanding teams* (pp. 197–233). Greenwich, CT: Information Age.

Dyer, W. G. (1981). Selecting an intervention for organization change. *Training and Development Journal, 36,* 62–68.

Dyer, W. G. (1994). *Team building: Current issues and new alternatives* (3rd ed.). Reading, MA: Addison-Wesley.

Dyer, W. G., Dyer, W. G., Jr., & Dyer, J. H. (2007). *Team building: Proven strategies for improving team performance* (4th ed.). San Francisco: Jossey-Bass.

Eaton, J., & Brown, D. (2002). Coaching for a change at Vodaphone. *Career Development International, 7*(5), 284–287.

Egan, T. M. (2002). Organization development: An examination of definitions and dependent variables. *Organization Development Journal, 20*(2), 59–71.

Eisenberg, E. M., & Riley, P. (2001). Organizational culture. In F. M. Jablin & L. L. Putnam (Eds.), *The new handbook of organizational communication* (pp. 291–322). Thousand Oaks, CA: Sage.

Eisner, S. P. (2005). Managing Generation Y. *SAM: Advanced Management Journal* (Autumn), pp. 4–15.

Ellet, W. (2007). *The case study handbook: How to read, discuss, and write persuasively about cases.* Boston: Harvard Business School Press.

Emery, M., & Purser, R. E. (1996). *The search conference: A powerful method for planning organizational change and community action.* San Francisco: Jossey-Bass.

Ennis, S., Goodman, R., Hodgetts, W., Hunt, J., Mansfield, R., Otto, J., & Stern, L. (2007). The competencies of the expert executive coach. In J. M. Hunt & J. R. Weinstraub (Eds.), *The coaching organization* (pp. 223–231). Thousand Oaks, CA: Sage.

Esper, J. L. (1990). Organizational change and development: Core practitioner competencies and future trends. *Advances in Organization Development, 1,* 277–314.

Eubanks, J. L., Marshall, J. B., & O'Driscoll, M. P. (1990). A competency model for OD practitioners. *Training and Development Journal, 44*(11), 85–90.

Eubanks, J., O'Driscoll, M., Hayward, G., Daniels, J., & Connor, S. (1990). Behavioral competency requirements for organization development practitioners. *Journal of Organizational Behavior Management, 11,* 77–97.

Fagenson-Eland, E., Ensher, E. A., & Burke, W. W. (2004). Organization development and change interventions: A seven-nation comparison. *Journal of Applied Behavioral Science, 40,* 432–464.

Falletta, S. V., & Combs, W. (2002). Surveys as a tool for organization development and change. In J. Waclawski & A. H. Church (Eds.), *Organization development: A data-driven approach to organizational change* (pp. 78–102). San Francisco: Jossey-Bass.

Farquhar, K. (2005). Intervention phase. In B. B. Jones & M. Brazzel (Eds.), *The NTL handbook of organization development and change* (pp. 212–230). San Francisco: Pfeiffer.

Fast forward: 25 trends that will change the way you do business. (2003). *Workforce Management, 81*(June), pp. 43–56.

Fink, A. (2002). *The survey kit* (2nd ed.). Thousand Oaks, CA: Sage.

Fink, A. (2005). *How to conduct surveys* (3rd ed.). Thousand Oaks, CA: Sage.

Ford, J. D. (1999). Organizational change as shifting conversations. *Journal of Organizational Change Management, 12,* 480–500.

Ford, J. D., & Ford, L. W. (1995). The role of conversations in producing intentional change in organizations. *Academy of Management Review, 20,* 541–570.

Ford, J. D., & Ford, L. W. (2008). Conversational profiles: A tool for altering the conversational patterns of change managers. *The Journal of Applied Behavioral Science, 44*(4), 445–467.

Ford, M. W., & Evans, J. R. (2001). Baldrige assessment and organizational learning: The need for change management. *Quality Management Journal, 8*(3), 9–25.

Franklin, J. (1995). Assessment and feedback. In W. Rothwell, R. Sullivan, & G. N. McLean (Eds.), *Practicing organization development: A guide for consultants* (pp. 139–169). San Diego: Pfeiffer.

Frantilla, A. (1998). *Social science in the public interest: A fiftieth-year history of the Institute for Social Research.* Ann Arbor: Bentley Historical Library, University of Michigan.

Freedman, A. M. (2006). Action research: Origins and applications for ODC practitioners. In B. B. Jones & M. Brazzel (Eds.), *The NTL handbook of organization development and change* (pp. 83–103). San Francisco: Pfeiffer.

Freedman, A. M., & Zackrison, R. E. (2001). *Finding your way in the consulting jungle: A guidebook for organization development practitioners.* San Francisco: Jossey-Bass/Pfeiffer.

Freeman, C. A. (1995). The seven deadly sins of OD consulting: Pitfalls to avoid in the consulting practice. *OD Practitioner, 27*(2&3), 26–30.

French, W. (1969). Organization development objectives, assumptions and strategies. *California Management Review, 12*(2), 23–34.

French, W. L., & Bell, C. H. (1999). *Organization development* (6th ed.). Englewood Cliffs, NJ: Prentice Hall.

Friedlander, F. (1976). OD reaches adolescence: An exploration of its underlying values. *Journal of Applied Behavioral Science, 12,* 7–21.

Friedman, T. L. (2007). *The world is flat.* New York: Farrar, Straus, and Giroux.

Gade, P. J., & Perry, E. L. (2003). Changing the newsroom culture: A four-year case study of organizational development at the *St. Louis Post-Dispatch. Journalism and Mass Communication Quarterly, 80,* 327–347.

Galbraith, J. R. (1973). *Designing complex organizations.* Reading, MA: Addison-Wesley.

Galbraith, J. R. (1977). *Organization design.* Reading, MA: Addison-Wesley.

Galbraith, J. R. (1995). *Designing organizations: An executive briefing on strategy, structure, and process.* San Francisco: Jossey-Bass.

Galbraith, J. R. (2002). *Designing organizations: An executive guide to strategy, structure, and process.* San Francisco: Jossey-Bass.

Galbraith, J. R. (2009). *Designing matrix organizations that actually work.* San Francisco: Jossey-Bass.

Galbraith, J., Downey, D., & Kates, A. (2002). *Designing dynamic organizations: A hands-on guide for leaders at all levels.* New York: AMACOM.

Gallagher, C. A., Joseph, L. E., & Park, M. V. (2002). Implementing organizational change. In J. Waclawski & A. H. Church (Eds.), *Organization development: A data-driven approach to organizational change* (pp. 12–42). San Francisco: Jossey-Bass.

Gallant, S. M., & Rios, D. (2006). Entry and contracting phase. In B. B. Jones & M. Brazzel (Eds.), *The NTL handbook of organization development and change* (pp. 177–191). San Francisco: Pfeiffer.

Galpin, T., & Herndon, M. (2008). Merger repair: When M&As go wrong. *Journal of Business Strategy, 29*(1), 4–12.

Gauthier, R., & Giber, D. (2006). Coaching business leaders. In M. Goldsmith & L. Lyons (Eds.), *Coaching for leadership* (2nd ed., pp. 116–125). San Francisco: Pfeiffer.

Geirland, J., & Maniker-Leiter, M. (1995). Five lessons for internal organization development consultants. *OD Practitioner, 27*(2&3), 44–48.

Gellermann, W., Frankel, M. S., & Ladenson, R. F. (1990). *Values and ethics in organization and human systems development: Responding to dilemmas in professional life.* San Francisco: Jossey-Bass.

George, J. M., & Jones, G. R. (2001). Towards a process model of individual change in organizations. *Human Relations, 54,* 419–444.

Glidewell, J. C. (1959). The entry problem in consultation. *Journal of Social Issues, 15*(2), 51–59.

Goffee, R., & Jones, G. (2005). Managing authenticity. *Harvard Business Review, 83*(12), 86–94.

Goldsmith, M., & Lyons, L. (Eds.). (2006). *Coaching for leadership* (2nd ed.). San Francisco: Pfeiffer.

Golembiewski, R. T. (1979a). *Approaches to planned change* (Part 1). New York: Marcel Dekker.

Golembiewski, R. T. (1979b). *Approaches to planned change* (Part 2). New York: Marcel Dekker.

Golembiewski, R. T. (2000a). Features of energizing data. In R. T. Golembiewski (Ed.), *Handbook of organizational consultation* (2nd ed., pp. 409–411). New York: Marcel Dekker.

Golembiewski, R. T. (2000b). The intervenor's world: Overall features and special traps. In R. T. Golembiewski (Ed.), *Handbook of organizational consultation* (2nd ed., pp. 549–554). New York: Marcel Dekker.

Golembiewski, R. T. (2000c). Model this, model that: Consultants can't do without them. In R. T. Golembiewski (Ed.), *Handbook of organizational consultation* (2nd ed., pp. 453–456). New York: Marcel Dekker.

Golembiewski, R. T. (2000d). Role analysis technique. In R. T. Golembiewski (Ed.), *Handbook of organizational consultation* (2nd ed., pp. 507–508). New York: Marcel Dekker.

Golembiewski, R. T. (2000e). Role negotiation as a controlling design. In R. T. Golembiewski (Ed.), *Handbook of organizational consultation* (2nd ed., pp. 509–511). New York: Marcel Dekker.

Gooding, A. D. (2003). Life coaching is not psychotherapy: There is a difference. *Annals of the American Psychotherapy Association, 6*(3), 36–37.

Goold, M., & Campbell, A. (2002). Do you have a well-designed organization? *Harvard Business Review, 80*(3), 117–124.

Greenwood, D. J., & Levin, M. (1998). *Introduction to action research: Social research for social change.* Thousand Oaks, CA: Sage.

Greiner, L. E., & Cummings, T. G. (2005). OD: Wanted more alive than dead! In D. L. Bradford & W. W. Burke (Eds.), *Reinventing organization development* (pp. 87–112). San Francisco: Pfeiffer.

Grodzki, L., & Allen, W. (2005). *The business and practice of coaching.* New York: W. W. Norton.

Gutteridge, T. G., Leibowitz, Z. B., & Shore, J. E. (1993). *Organizational career development.* San Francisco: Jossey-Bass.

Hackman, J. R., & Oldham, G. R. (1975). Development of the job diagnostic survey. *Journal of Applied Psychology, 60,* 159–170.

Hackman, J. R., & Oldham, G. R. (1980). *Work redesign.* Reading, MA: Addison-Wesley.

Hall, D. T. (1986). Breaking career routines: Midcareer choice and identity development. In D. T. Hall & associates (Eds.), *Career development in organizations* (pp. 120–159). San Francisco: Jossey-Bass.

Hammer, M., & Champy, J. (1993). *Reengineering the corporation.* New York: HarperCollins.

Hanson, P. G., & Lubin, B. (1995). *Answers to questions most frequently asked about organization development.* Thousand Oaks, CA: Sage.

Harding, D., & Rouse, T. (2007). Human due diligence. *Harvard Business Review, 85*(4), 124–131.

Harrison, M. I. (1987). *Diagnosing organizations: Methods, models, and processes.* Newbury Park, CA: Sage.

Harrison, M. I. (1994). *Diagnosing organizations: Methods, models, and processes* (2nd ed.). Newbury Park, CA: Sage.

Harrison, M. I., & Shirom, A. (1999). *Organizational diagnosis and assessment: Bridging theory and practice.* Thousand Oaks, CA: Sage.

Harrison, R. (1970). Choosing the depth of organizational intervention. *Journal of Applied Behavioral Science, 6,* 181–202.

Harrison, R. (1972). Role negotiation: A tough-minded approach to team development. In W. W. Burke & H. A. Hornstein (Eds.), *The social technology of organization development* (pp. 84–96). Fairfax, VA: NTL Learning Resources Corp.

Harry, M., & Schroeder, R. (2000). *Six sigma: The breakthrough management strategy revolutionizing the world's top corporations.* New York: Currency.

Harter, J. K., Schmidt, F. L., & Hayes, T. L. (2002). Business-unit-level relationship between employee satisfaction, employee engagement, and business outcomes: A meta-analysis. *Journal of Applied Psychology, 87,* 268–279.

Harvey, J. B. (1974). Organization development as a religious movement. *OD Practitioner, 3,* 4–5.

Head, T., Armstrong, T., & Preston, J. (1996). The role of graduate education in becoming a competent organization development practitioner. *OD Practitioner, 28* (1&2), 52–60.

Head, T. C., Gong, C., Ma, C., Sorensen, P. F., Jr., & Yaeger, T. (2006). Chinese executives' assessment of organization development interventions. *Organization Development Journal, 24,* 28–40.

Hedge, J. W., & Pulakos, E. D. (2002a). Grappling with implementation: Some preliminary thoughts and relevant research. In J. W. Hedge & E. D. Pulakos (Eds.), *Implementing organizational interventions: Steps, processes, and best practices* (pp. 1–11). San Francisco: Jossey-Bass.

Hedge, J. W., & Pulakos, E. D. (Eds.). (2002b). *Implementing organizational interventions: Steps, processes, and best practices.* San Francisco: Jossey-Bass.

Heilpern, J. D., & Nadler, D. A. (1992). Implementing total quality management: A process of cultural change. In D. A. Nadler, M. S. Gerstein, R. B. Shaw, & associates (Eds.), *Organizational architecture* (pp. 137–154). San Francisco: Jossey-Bass.

Heron, J., & Reason, P. (2001). The practice of co-operative inquiry: Research "with" rather than "on" people. In P. Reason & H. Bradbury (Eds.), *Handbook of action research: Participative inquiry and practice* (pp. 179–188). London: Sage.

Herzberg, F. (1993). Introduction to the Transaction edition. In F. Herzberg, B. Mausner, & B. B. Snyderman, *The motivation to work* (pp. xi–xviii). New Brunswick, NJ: Transaction.

Herzberg, F., Mausner, B., & Snyderman, B. B. (1959). *The motivation to work.* New York: Wiley.

Hipple, S. F. (2010). Self-employment in the United States. *Monthly Labor Review, 133*(9), 17–32.

Hirsch, J. I. (1987). *The history of the national training laboratories, 1947–1986.* New York: Peter Lang.

Hirschhorn, L., & Gilmore, T. (1992). The new boundaries of the "boundaryless" company. *Harvard Business Review, 70,* 104–115.

Hitchcock, D., & Willard, M. (1995). *Why teams fail and what you can do about it: Essential tools for anyone implementing self-directed work teams.* Chicago: Irwin.

Hodges, J. (2009, Dec. 31). Office (and beanbag) sharing among strangers. *Wall Street Journal,* p. D3.

Hoffman, E. (2002). *Psychological testing at work.* New York: McGraw-Hill.

Hofstede, G. (2001). *Culture's consequences.* Thousand Oaks, CA: Sage.

Hofstede, G., Hofstede, G. J., & Minkov, M. (2010). *Cultures and organizations: Software of the mind.* New York: McGraw-Hill.

Holbeche, L. (2006). *Understanding change.* Amsterdam: Elsevier.

Holland, J. L. (1985). *The vocational preference inventory.* Odessa, FL: Psychological Assessment Resources.

Holland, J. L. (1996). Exploring careers with a typology: What we have learned and some new directions. *American Psychologist, 51,* 397–406.

Holland, J. L. (1997). *Making vocational choices* (3rd ed.). Odessa, FL: Psychological Assessment Resources.

Holt, D. T., Armenakis, A. A., Feild, H. S., & Harris, S. G. (2007). Readiness for organizational change: The systematic development of a scale. *Journal of Applied Behavioral Science, 43,* 232–255.

Holton, J. A. (2001). Building trust and collaboration in a virtual team. *Team Performance Management, 3/4,* 36–47.

Horowitz, F. M., Anderssen, K., Bezuidenhout, A., Cohen, S., Kirsten, F., Mosoeunyane, K., et al. (2002). Due diligence neglected: Managing human resources and organizational culture in mergers and acquisitions. *South African Journal of Business Management, 33,* 1–10.

Hosking, D. M., & McNamee, S. (Eds.). (2006). *The social construction of organization.* Herndon, VA: Copenhagen Business School Press.

Hudson, F. M. (1999). *The handbook of coaching.* San Francisco: Jossey-Bass.

Hultman, K. (2002). *Balancing individual and organizational values: Walking the tightrope to success.* San Francisco: Jossey-Bass.

Hunt, J. M., & Weintraub, J. R. (2002). *The coaching manager: Developing top talent in business.* Thousand Oaks, CA: Sage.

Isabella, L. A. (1992). Managing the challenges of trigger events: The mindsets governing adaptation to change. *Business Horizons, 35*(5), 59–66.

Jackson, C. N., & Manning, M. R. (1992). Anatomy of an OD intervention. In C. N. Jackson & M. R. Manning (Eds.), *Organization development annual, vol. IV: Intervening in client organizations* (pp. 5–15). Alexandria, VA: American Society for Training and Development (ASTD).

Jackson, J. C. (2006). *Organization development.* Lanham, MD: University Press.

Jacobs, C. D., & Heracleous, L. T. (2006). Constructing shared understanding: The role of embodied metaphors in organization development. *The Journal of Applied Behavioral Science, 42,* 207–226.

Jacobs, R. W. (1994). *Real time strategic change.* San Francisco: Berrett-Koehler.

Jaeger, A. M. (1986). Organization development and national culture: Where's the fit? *Academy of Management Review, 11,* 178–190.

Jasinski, T. J. (2010). How MetLife balances effective organization design with the need for speed in postacquisition integration. *Global Business and Organizational Excellence, 29*(3), 6–16.

Johns, G. (1993). Constraints on the adoption of psychology-based personnel practices: Lessons from organizational innovation. *Personnel Psychology, 46,* 569–592.

Johnson, D. W., & Lewicki, R. J. (1969). The initiation of superordinate goals. *Journal of Applied Behavioral Science, 5,* 9–24.

Jones, M. O. (1996). *Studying organizational symbolism.* Thousand Oaks, CA: Sage.

Kaarst-Brown, M. L. (1999). Five symbolic roles of the external consultant: Integrating change, power, and symbolism. *Journal of Organizational Change Management, 12,* 540–561.

Kahn, W. A. (2004). Facilitating and undermining organizational change: A case study. *Journal of Applied Behavioral Science, 40,* 7–30.

Kahnweiler, W. M. (2002). Process consultation: A cornerstone of organization development practice. In J. Waclawski & A. H. Church (Eds.), *Organization development: A data-driven approach to organizational change* (pp. 149–163). San Francisco: Jossey-Bass.

Kanter, R. M., Stein, B. A., & Jick, T. D. (1992). *The challenge of organizational change.* New York: The Free Press.

Kaplan, R. E. (1978). Stages in developing a consulting relation: A case study of a long beginning. *The Journal of Applied Behavioral Science, 14,* 43–60.

Kaplan, R. S., & Norton, D. P. (2001). *The strategy-focused organization.* Boston: Harvard Business School Press.

Kast, F. E., & Rosenzweig, J. E. (1972). General systems theory: Applications for organization and management. *Academy of Management Journal, 15,* 447–465.

Katz, D., & Kahn, R. L. (1966). *The social psychology of organizations.* New York: Wiley.

Katzenbach, J. R., & Smith, D. K. (1993). *The wisdom of teams: Creating the high-performance organization.* Boston: Harvard Business School Press.

Kegan, R., & Lahey, L. L. (2001). *How the way we talk can change the way we work.* San Francisco: Jossey-Bass.

Kehal, H., & Singh, V. P. (Eds.). (2006). *Outsourcing and offshoring in the 21st century: A socioeconomic perspective.* Hershey, PA: Idea Group.

Kehrli, S., & Sopp, T. (2006, May). Managing Generation Y. *HR Magazine,* 113–119.

Keirsey, D., & Bates, M. (1984). *Please understand me: Character & temperament types* (5th ed.). Del Mar, CA: Prometheus Nemesis.

Kilburg, R. R. (1996). Toward a conceptual understanding and definition of executive coaching. *Consulting Psychology Journal, 48,* 134–144.

Kilmann, R. H., & Mitroff, I. I. (1979). Problem defining and the consulting/intervention process. *California Management Review, 21*(3), 26–33.

Kindler, H. S. (1979). Two planning strategies: Incremental change and transformational change. *Group and Organization Studies, 4,* 476–484.

Kleiner, A. (1996). *The age of heretics: Heroes, outlaws, and the forerunners of corporate change.* New York: Doubleday.

Kotter, J. P. (1996). *Leading change.* Boston: Harvard Business School Press.

Krug, J. A. (2009). Brain drain: Why top management bolts after M&As. *Journal of Business Strategy, 30*(6), 4–14.

Kuhnert, K. W. (1993). Survey/feedback as art and science. In R. T. Golembiewski (Ed.), *Handbook of organizational consultation* (pp. 459–465). New York: Marcel Dekker.

Labor force. (2007). *Occupational Outlook Quarterly* (Fall), pp. 40–47.

Laker, D. R., & Laker, R. (2007). The five-year resume: A career planning exercise. *Journal of Management Education, 31,* 128–141.

Larson, C. E., & LaFasto, F. M. J. (1989). *TeamWork: What must go right/What can go wrong.* Newbury Park, CA: Sage.

Lawler, E. E., III, Nadler, D. A., & Cammann, C. (Eds.). (1980). *Organizational assessment: Perspectives on the measurement of organizational behavior and the quality of work life.* New York: Wiley.

Lawler, E. E., III, & Worley, C. G. (2006). *Built to change.* San Francisco: Jossey-Bass.

Ledford, G. E., Jr., Mohrman, S. A., Mohrman, A. M., Jr., & Lawler, E. E., III. (1989). The phenomenon of large-scale change. In A. M. Morhman Jr., S. A. Mohrman, G. E. Ledford Jr., T. G. Cummings, & E. E. Lawler III, & associates (Eds.), *Large-scale organizational change* (pp. 1–31). San Francisco: Jossey-Bass.

Lepsinger, R., & Lucia, A. D. (1997). *The art and science of 360 feedback.* San Francisco: Pfeiffer.

Levi, D. (2001). *Group dynamics for teams* (2nd ed.). Thousand Oaks, CA: Sage.

Levinson, H. (1994). The practitioner as diagnostic instrument. In A. Howard & associates (Eds.), *Diagnosis for organizational change: Methods and models* (pp. 27–52). New York: Guilford.

Levinson, H. (1996). Executive coaching. *Consulting Psychology Journal, 48,* 115–123.

Levitt, B., & March, J. G. (1988). Organizational learning. *Annual Review of Sociology, 14,* 319–340.

Lewin, K. (1951). *Field theory in social science.* New York: Harper & Brothers.

Likert, R. (1961). *New patterns of management.* New York: McGraw-Hill.

Likert, R. (1967). *The human organization.* New York: McGraw-Hill.

Lindgren, M., & Bandhold, H. (2003). *Scenario planning: The link between future and strategy.* Hampshire, UK: Palgrave Macmillan.

Lippitt, R. (1949). *Training in community relations: A research exploration toward new group skills.* New York: Harper & Brothers.

Lippitt, R. (1959). Dimensions of the consultant's job. *Journal of Social Issues, 15*(2), 5–12.

Livingston, R. E. (2006). Evaluation and termination phase. In B. B. Jones & R. Brazzel (Eds.), *The NTL handbook of organization development and change: Principles, practices, and perspectives* (pp. 231–245). San Francisco: Pfeiffer.

Lofland, J., & Lofland, L. H. (1995). *Analyzing social settings* (3rd ed.). Belmont, CA: Wadsworth.

London, M., Smither, J. W., & Adsit, D. J. (1997). Accountability: The Achilles' heel of multisource feedback. *Group & Organization Management, 22,* 162–184.

London, M., & Stumpf, S. A. (1986). Individual and organizational career development in changing times. In D. T. Hall & associates (Eds.), *Career development in organizations* (pp. 21–49). San Francisco: Jossey-Bass.

Longenecker, C. O., & Rieman, M. L. (2007). Making organizational change stick: Leadership reality checks. *Development and Learning in Organizations, 21,* 7–10.

Ludema, J. D., Cooperrider, D. L., & Barrett, F. J. (2001). Appreciative inquiry: The power of the unconditional positive question. In P. Reason & H. Bradbury (Eds.), *Handbook of action research: Participative inquiry and practice* (pp. 189–199). London: Sage.

Ludwick, P. (2007, January/February). The boomers are already gone. *Journal of Housing & Community Development,* pp. 22–26.

Lukensmeyer, C. J., & Brigham, S. (2005). Taking democracy to scale: Large scale interventions—for citizens. *Journal of Applied Behavioral Science, 41,* 47–60.

Luthans, F., & Peterson, S. J. (2001). Employee engagement and manager self-efficacy: Implications for managerial effectiveness and development. *Journal of Management Development, 21,* 376–387.

Lyons, L. S. (2006). The accomplished leader. In M. Goldsmith & L. S. Lyons (Eds.), *Coaching for leadership* (2nd ed., pp. 3–16). San Francisco: Pfeiffer.

MacGregor, D. (1960). *The human side of enterprise.* New York: McGraw-Hill.

MacLennan, N. (1995). *Coaching and mentoring.* Hampshire, UK: Gower.

Malhotra, A., Majchrzak, A., & Rosen, B. (2007). Leading virtual teams. *Academy of Management Perspectives, 21,* 60–70.

Manchus, G., III. (1983). Employer-employee based quality circles in Japan: Human resource policy implication for American firms. *Academy of Management Review, 8,* 255–261.

Mann, F. C. (1957). Studying and creating change: A means to understanding social organization. In C. M. Arensberg et al. (Eds.), *Research in industrial human relations* (pp. 146–167). New York: Harper & Brothers.

Manning, M. R. (1994). Future search and the discovery of common ground: An interview with Marvin R. Weisbord. In C. N. Jackson & M. R. Manning (Eds.), *Organization development annual 5: Evaluating organization development interventions* (pp. 85–104). Alexandria, VA: American Society for Training and Development.

Manzini, A. O. (1988). *Organizational diagnosis: A practical approach to company problem solving and growth.* New York: AMACOM.

March, J. G. (1994). *A primer on decision making: How decisions happen.* New York: The Free Press.

Margulies, N., & Raia, A. P. (1972). *Organizational development: Values, process, and technology.* New York: McGraw-Hill.

Margulies, N., & Raia, A. (1990). The significance of core values on the theory and practice of organizational development. In F. Massarik (Ed.), *Advances in organization development* (Vol. 1, pp. 27–41). Norwood, NJ: Ablex.

Marks, M. L. (2002). Mergers and acquisitions. In J. Waclawski & A. H. Church (Eds.), *Organization development: A data-driven approach to organizational change* (pp. 43–77). San Francisco: Jossey-Bass.

Marks, M. L., & Mirvis, P. H. (2001). Making mergers and acquisitions work: Strategic and psychological preparation. *Academy of Management Executive, 15,* 80–92.

Marshak, R. J. (2006). Organization development as a profession and a field. In B. B. Jones & R. Brazzel (Eds.), *The NTL handbook of organization development and change: Principles, practices, and perspectives* (pp. 13–27). San Francisco: Pfeiffer.

Marshall, C., & Rossman, G. B. (1989). *Designing qualitative research.* Newbury Park, CA: Sage.

Martin, J. (1985). Can organizational culture be managed? In P. J. Frost, L. F. Moore, M. R. Louis, C. C. Lundberg, & J. Martin (Eds.), *Organizational culture* (pp. 95–98). Beverly Hills, CA: Sage.

Martineau, J. W., & Preskill, H. (2002). Evaluating the impact of organization development interventions. In J. Waclawski & A. H. Church (Eds.), *Organization development: A data-driven approach to organizational change* (pp. 286–301). San Francisco: Jossey-Bass.

Martins, L. L., Gilson, L. L., & Maynard, M. T. (2004). Virtual teams: What do we know and where do we go from here? *Journal of Management, 30,* 805–835.

Massarik, F., & Pei-Carpenter, M. (2002). *Organization development and consulting: Perspectives and foundations.* San Francisco: Jossey-Bass.

Mayhew, E. (2006). Organizational change processes. In B. B. Jones & M. Brazzel (Eds.), *The NTL handbook of organization development and change* (pp. 104–120). San Francisco: Pfeiffer.

McCaulley, M. H. (2000). Myers-Briggs type indicator: A bridge between counseling and consulting. *Consulting Psychology Journal, 52,* 117–132.

McLachlin, R. D. (1999). Factors for consulting engagement success. *Management Decision, 37,* 394–402.

McLean, G. N. (2006). *Organization development: Principles, processes, performance.* San Francisco: Berrett-Koehler.

McLean, G. N., & Sullivan, R. L. (2000). Essential competencies for internal and external OD consultants. In R. T. Golembiewski (Ed.), *Handbook of organizational consultation* (2nd ed., pp. 749–753). New York: Marcel Dekker.

McLean, G. N., Sullivan, R., & Rothwell, W. J. (1995). Evaluation. In W. Rothwell, R. Sullivan, & G. N. McLean (Eds.), *Practicing organization development: A guide for consultants* (pp. 311–368). San Diego: Pfeiffer.

Megginson, D., & Clutterbuck, D. (2005). *Techniques for coaching and mentoring.* Amsterdam: Elsevier.

Meglino, B. M., & Mobley, W. H. (1977). Minimizing risk in organization development interventions. *Personnel, 54*(6), 23–31.

Miles, R. E., & Snow, C. C. (1986). Organizations: New concepts for new forms. *California Management Review, 28,* 62–73.

Miles, R. E., & Snow, C. C. (1992). Causes of failure in network organizations. *California Management Review, 34,* 53–72.

Milstein, M. M., & Smith, D. (1979). The shifting nature of OD contracts: A case study. *Journal of Applied Behavioral Science, 15,* 179–191.

Mirvis, P. H. (1988). Organization development: Part I—An evolutionary perspective. *Research in Organizational Change and Development, 2,* 1–57.

Moates, K. N., Armenakis, A. A., Gregory, B. T., Albritton, M. D., & Feild, H. S. (2005). Achieving content representativeness in organizational diagnosis. *Action Research, 3,* 403–416.

Morhman, A. M., Jr., Morhman, S. A., Ledford, G. E., Jr., Cummings, T. G., Lawler, E. E., III, & associates (Eds.). (1989). *Large-scale organizational change.* San Francisco: Jossey-Bass.

Mohrman, S. A., Mohrman, A. M., Jr., & Ledford, G. E., Jr. (1989). Interventions that change organizations. In A. M. Morhman Jr., S. A. Mohrman, G. E. Ledford Jr., T. G. Cummings, E. E. Lawler III, & associates (Eds.), *Large-scale organizational change* (pp. 145–153). San Francisco: Jossey-Bass.

Moosbruker, J. B., & Loftin, R. D. (1998). Business process redesign and organization development: Enhancing success by removing the barriers. *Journal of Applied Behavioral Science, 34,* 286–304.

Morrison, P. (1978). Evaluation in OD: A review and an assessment. *Group & Organization Studies, 3,* 42–70.

Nadler, D. (1977). *Feedback and organization development: Using data-based methods.* Reading, MA: Addison-Wesley.

Nadler, D. (1981). Managing organizational change: An integrative perspective. *Journal of Applied Behavioral Science, 17,* 191–211.

Nadler, D. A. (1980). Role of models in organizational assessment. In E. E. Lawler III, D. A. Nadler, & C. Cammann (Eds.), *Organizational assessment: Perspectives on the measurement of organizational behavior and the quality of work life* (pp. 119–131). New York: Wiley.

Nadler, D. A., & Pecorella, P. A. (1975). Differential effects of multiple interventions in an organization. *Journal of Applied Behavioral Science, 11,* 348–366.

Nadler, D. A., & Tushman, M. L. (1983). A general diagnostic model for organizational behavior: Applying a congruence perspective. In J. R. Hackman, E. E. Lawler III, & L. W. Porter (Eds.), *Perspectives on behavior in organizations* (2nd ed., pp. 112–124). New York: McGraw-Hill.

Nadler, D. A., & Tushman, M. L. (1992). Designing organizations that have good fit: A framework for understanding new architectures. In D. A Nadler, M. S. Gerstein, R. B. Shaw, & associates (Eds.), *Organizational architecture: Designs for changing organizations* (pp. 39–56). San Francisco: Jossey-Bass.

Nahavandi, A., & Malekzadeh, A. R. (1993). *Organizational culture in the management of mergers.* Westport, CT: Quorum Books.

Neumann, J. (1989). Why people don't participate in organizational change. In W. A. Pasmore & R. W. Woodman (Eds.), *Research in organization change and development, 3* (pp. 181–212). Greenwich, CT: JAI Press.

Nicoll, D. (1998). Is OD meant to be relevant? Part III. *OD Practitioner, 30*(4), 3–8.

Niles, S. G. (2005). *Career development interventions in the 21st century.* Upper Saddle River, NJ: Pearson.

Noolan, J. A. C. (2006). Organization diagnosis phase. In B. B. Jones & M. Brazzel (Eds.), *The NTL handbook of organization development and change* (pp. 192–211). San Francisco: Pfeiffer.

Normann, R. (1985). Developing capabilities for organizational learning. In J. M. Pennings & associates (Eds.), *Organizational strategy and change* (pp. 217–248). San Francisco: Jossey-Bass.

O'Bannon, G. (2001). Managing our future: The Generation X factor. *Public Personnel Management, 30,* 95–109.

O'Brien, G. (2002). Participation as the key to successful change—a public sector case study. *Leadership & Organization Development Journal, 23,* 442–455.

O'Connell, J. (2001). Getting real. In P. Block, *The flawless consulting fieldbook and companion: A guide to understanding your expertise* (pp. 273–285). San Francisco: Jossey-Bass/Pfeiffer.

O'Driscoll, M. P., & Eubanks, J. L. (1992). Consultant and client perceptions of consultant competencies: Implications for OD consulting. *Organization Development Journal, 10*(4), 53–59.

O'Driscoll, M. P., & Eubanks, J. L. (1993). Behavioral competencies, goal setting, and OD practitioner effectiveness. *Group & Organization Management, 18,* 308–327.

Ogilvy, J. A. (2002). *Creating better futures: Scenario planning as a tool for a better tomorrow.* New York: Oxford University Press.

Olson, E. E., & Eoyang, G. H. (2001). *Facilitating organization change: Lessons from complexity science.* San Francisco: Jossey-Bass/Pfeiffer.

O'Reilly, B., & Furth, J. (1994, October 17). 360 feedback can change your life. *Fortune, 130*(8), 93–100.

Orenstein, R. L. (2002). Executive coaching: It's not just about the executive. *Journal of Applied Behavioral Science, 38,* 355–374.

Orsburn, J. D., & Moran, L. (2000). *The new self-directed work teams: Mastering the challenge* (2nd ed.). New York: McGraw-Hill.

O'Toole, J. (1995). *Leading change: Overcoming the ideology of comfort and the tyranny of custom.* San Francisco: Jossey-Bass.

Ott, J. S. (1989). *The organizational culture perspective.* Pacific Grove, CA: Brooks/Cole.

Ouchi, W. G. (1981). *Theory Z: How American business can meet the Japanese challenge.* Reading, MA: Addison-Wesley.

Parker, G. M. (1994). *Cross-functional teams.* San Francisco: Jossey-Bass.

Pasmore, W. A., & Fagans, M. R. (1992). Participation, individual development, and organizational change: A review and synthesis. *Journal of Management, 18,* 375–397.

Paul, C. F., & Gross, A. C. (1981). Increasing productivity and morale in a municipality: Effects of organization development. *Journal of Applied Behavioral Science, 17,* 59–78.

Peters, T. J., & Waterman, R. H., Jr. (1982). *In search of excellence: Lessons from America's best companies.* New York: Harper & Row.

Pfeiffer, J. W., & Ballew, A. C. (1987). *Using instruments in human resource development.* San Diego: University Associates.

Pieper, R. (1995). Organization development in West Germany. In P. F. Sorensen Jr., T. C. Head, N. J. Mathys, J. Preston, & D. Cooperrider (Eds.), *Global and international organization development* (pp. 115–132). Champaign, IL: Stipes.

Pittenger, D. J. (2005). Cautionary comments regarding the Myers-Briggs type indicator. *Consulting Psychology Journal, 57,* 210–221.

Porras, J. I., & Berg, P. O. (1978a). Evaluation methodology in organization development: An analysis and critique. *Journal of Applied Behavioral Science, 14,* 151–173.

Porras, J. I., & Berg, P. O. (1978b). The impact of organization development. *Academy of Management Review, 3,* 249–266.

Porter, M. (1996). What is strategy? *Harvard Business Review, 74*(6), 61–78.

Prasad, P., Pringle, P. K., & Konrad, A. M. (2006). Examining the contours of workplace diversity: Concepts, contexts and challenges. In A. M. Korad, P. Prasad, & J. K. Pringle (Eds.), *Handbook of workplace diversity* (pp. 1–22). London: Sage.

Proehl, R. A. (1996). Enhancing the effectiveness of cross-functional teams. *Leadership & Organization Development Journal, 17,* 3–10.

Putnam, L. L. (1983). The interpretive perspective: An alternative to functionalism. In L. L. Putnam & M. E. Pacanowsky (Eds.), *Communication and organizations: An interpretive approach* (pp. 31–53). Beverly Hills, CA: Sage.

Ralston, B., & Wilson, I. (2006). *The scenario planning handbook.* Mason, OH: Texere.

Randolph, W. A., & Elloy, D. F. (1989). How can OD consultants and researchers assess gamma change? A comparison of two analytical approaches. *Journal of Management, 15,* 633–648.

Ray, D., & Bronstein, H. (1995). *Teaming up: Making the transition to a self-directed, team-based organization.* New York: McGraw-Hill.

Reason, P., & Bradbury, H. (2001). Introduction: Inquiry and participation in search of a world worthy of human aspiration. In P. Reason & H. Bradbury (Eds.), *Handbook of action research: Participative inquiry and practice* (pp. 1–14). London: Sage.

Reddy, W. B. (1994). *Intervention skills: Process consultation for small groups and teams.* San Francisco: Jossey-Bass.

Regenold, S. (2009, Feb. 5). Working away. *New York Times,* p. D1, D4.

Richardson, C. (2008). Working alone: The erosion of solidarity in today's workplace. *New Labor Forum, 17*(3), 69–78.

Roethlisberger, F. J., & Dickson, W. J. (1939). *Management and the worker.* Cambridge, MA: Harvard University Press.

Rokeach, M. (1968). *Beliefs, attitudes and values: A theory of organization and change.* San Francisco: Jossey-Bass.

Rokeach, M. (1973). *The nature of human values.* New York: The Free Press.

Roth, G., & Kleiner, A. (1998). Developing organizational memory through learning histories. *Organizational Dynamics, 27*(2), 43–60.

Rushmer, R. (1997). What happens to the team during teambuilding? Examining the change process that helps to build a team. *Journal of Management Development, 16,* 316–327.

Sackmann, S. A., Eggenhofer-Rehart, P. M., & Friesl, M. (2009). Sustainable change: Long-term efforts toward developing a learning organization. *The Journal of Applied Behavioral Science, 45*(4), 521–549.

Saks, A. M. (2006). Antecedents and consequences of employee engagement. *Journal of Managerial Psychology, 21,* 600–619.

Salas, E., Rozell, D., Mullen, B., & Driskell, J. E. (1999). The effect of team building on performance: An integration. *Small Group Research, 30,* 309–329.

Sashkin, M., & Burke, W. W. (1987). Organization development in the 1980's. *Journal of Management, 13,* 393–417.

Schein, E. H. (1969). *Process consultation: Its role in organization development.* Reading, MA: Addison-Wesley.

Schein, E. H. (1978). *Career dynamics: Managing individual and organizational needs.* Reading, MA: Addison-Wesley.

Schein, E. H. (1987). *Process consultation* (Vol. 2). Reading, MA: Addison-Wesley.

Schein, E. H. (1990a). Back to the future: Recapturing the OD vision. In F. Massarik (Ed.), *Advances in organization development* (Vol. 1, pp. 13–26). Norwood, NJ: Ablex.

Schein, E. H. (1990b). Organizational culture. *American Psychologist, 45,* 109–119.

Schein, E. H. (1997). The concept of "client" from a process consulting perspective: A guide for change agents. *Journal of Organizational Change Management, 10,* 202–216.

Schein, E. H. (1999). *Process consultation revisited.* Reading, MA: Addison-Wesley.

Schein, E. H. (2004). *Organizational culture and leadership* (3rd ed.). San Francisco: Jossey-Bass.

Schein, E. H. (2006a). Coaching and consultation revisited: Are they the same? In M. Goldsmith & L. Lyons (Eds.), *Coaching for leadership* (2nd ed., pp. 17–25). San Francisco: Pfeiffer.

Schein, E. (2006b). Culture assessment as an OD intervention. In B. B. Jones & M. Brazzel (Eds.), *The NTL handbook of organization development and change* (pp. 456–465). San Francisco: Pfeiffer.

Schmuck, R. A., Runkel, P. J., & Langmeyer, D. (1969). Improving organizational problem solving in a school faculty. *Journal of Applied Behavioral Science, 5,* 455–482.

Schoemaker, P. J. H. (1995). Scenario planning: A tool for strategic thinking. *Sloan Management Review, 36*(2), 25–40.

Schwartz, P. (1996). *The art of the long view.* New York: Doubleday.

Schweitz, R., & Martens, K. (Eds.). (2005). *Future search in school district change.* Lanham, MD: ScarecrowEducation.

Scott, B. (2000). *Consulting on the inside: An internal consultant's guide to living and working inside organizations.* Alexandria, VA: American Society for Training & Development (ASTD).

Seidman, I. (2006). *Interviewing as qualitative research* (3rd ed.). New York: Teachers College.

Senge, P., Kleiner, A., Roberts, C., Ross, R., Roth, G., & Smith, B. (1999). *The dance of change.* New York: Doubleday.

Senge, P. M. (1990). *The fifth discipline.* New York: Doubleday/Currency.

Seo, M., Putnam, L. L., & Bartunek, J. M. (2004). Dualities and tensions of planned organizational change. In M. S. Poole & A. H. Van den Ven (Eds.), *Handbook of organizational change and innovation* (pp. 73–107). Cary, NC: Oxford University Press.

Shamir, B. (1999). Leadership in boundaryless organizations: Dispensible or indispensable? *European Journal of Work and Organizational Psychology, 8,* 49–71.

Shaw, P. (1997). Intervening in the shadow systems of organizations: Consulting from a complexity perspective. *Journal of Organizational Change Management, 10,* 235–250.

Shearer, C. S., Hames, D. S., & Runge, J. B. (2001). How CEOs influence organizational culture following acquisitions. *Leadership & Organization Development Journal, 22,* 105–113.

Sherif, M. (1979). Superordinate goals in the reduction of intergroup conflict: An experimental evaluation. In W. G. Austin & S. Worchel (Eds.), *The social psychology of intergroup relations* (pp. 257–261). Belmont, CA: Wadsworth.

Sherif, M., & Sherif, C. W. (1979). Research on intergroup relations. In W. G. Austin & S. Worchel (Eds.), *The social psychology of intergroup relations* (pp. 7–18). Belmont, CA: Wadsworth.

Silverman, S. B., Pogson, C. E., & Cober, A. B. (2005). When employees at work don't get it: A model for enhancing individual employee change in response to performance feedback. *Academy of Management Executive, 19,* 135–147.

Skelley, B. D. (1989). Workplace democracy and OD: Philosophical and practical connections. *Public Administration Quarterly, 13,* 176–195.

Smircich, L. (1985). Is the concept of culture a paradigm for understanding organizations and ourselves? In P. J. Frost, L. F. Moore, M. R. Louis, C. C. Lundberg, & J. Martin (Eds.), *Organizational culture* (pp. 55–72). Beverly Hills, CA: Sage.

Smith, F. J. (2003). *Organizational surveys: The diagnosis and betterment of organizations through their members.* Mahwah, NJ: Lawrence Erlbaum.

Smithson, J. (2000). Using and analysing focus groups: Limitations and possibilities. *International Journal of Social Research Methodology, 3,* 103–119.

Sorensen, P. F., Jr., & Head, T. C. (1995). Organization development in Denmark. In P. F. Sorensen, Jr., T. C. Head, N. J. Mathys, J. Preston, & D. Cooperrider (Eds.), *Global and international organization development* (pp. 48–64). Champaign, IL: Stipes.

Sorensen, P. F., Jr., Head, T. C., Mathys, N. J., Preston, J., & Cooperrider, D. (Eds.). (1995). *Global and international organization development.* Champaign, IL: Stipes.

Spector, B., & Beer, M. (1994). Beyond TQM programmes. *Journal of Organizational Change Management, 7,* 63–70.

Spradley, J. P. (1979). *The ethnographic interview.* New York: Holt, Rinehart, & Winston.

Srivastva, S., Cooperrider, D. L., & associates (Eds). (1990). *Appreciative management and leadership.* San Francisco: Jossey-Bass.

Stanford, N. (2005). *Organization design: The collaborative approach.* Amsterdam: Elsevier.

Steil, G., Jr., & Gibbons-Carr, M. (2005). Large group scenario planning: Scenario planning with the whole system in the room. *Journal of Applied Behavioral Science, 41,* 15–29.

Stewart, M., Brown, J. B., Donner, A., McWhinney, I. R., Oates, J., Weston, W. W., et al. (2000). The impact of patient-centered care on outcomes. *Journal of Family Practice, 49*(9), 796–804.

Stone, F. M. (2004). *The mentoring advantage.* Chicago: Dearborn.

Stone, F. M. (2007). *Coaching, counseling, and mentoring* (2nd ed.). New York: AMACOM.

Stroh, L. K., & Johnson, H. H. (2006). *The basic principles of effective consulting.* Mahwah, NJ: Lawrence Erlbaum.

Sullivan, R., & Sullivan, K. (1995). Essential competencies for internal and external OD consultants. In W. Rothwell, R. Sullivan, & G. N. McLean (Eds.), *Practicing organization development: A guide for consultants* (pp. 535–549). San Diego: Pfeiffer.

Sullivan, S. E. (1999). The changing nature of careers: A review and research agenda. *Journal of Management, 25*, 457–484.

Swanson, R. A. (2007). *Analysis for improving performance* (2nd ed.). San Francisco: Berrett-Koehler.

Swanson, R. A., & Zuber, J. A. (1996). A case study of a failed organization development intervention rooted in the employee survey process. *Performance Improvement Quarterly, 9*(2), 42–56.

Tannenbaum, R., & Davis, S. A. (1969). Values, man, and organizations. *Industrial Management Review, 10*(2), 67–86.

Tetenbaum, T. J. (1999). Beating the odds of merger & acquisition failure: Seven key practices that improve the change for expected integration and synergies. *Organizational Dynamics, 28*, 22–35.

Thompson, P. C. (1982). *Quality circles: How to make them work in America.* New York: AMACOM.

Thorne, K. (2004). *Coaching for change: Practical strategies for transforming performance.* London: Kogan Page.

Tietze, S., Cohen, L., & Musson, G. (2003). *Understanding organizations through language.* London: Sage.

Tippins, N. T. (2002). Organization development and IT: Practicing OD in the virtual world. In J. Waclawski & A. H. Church (Eds.), *Organization development: A data-driven approach to organizational change* (pp. 245–265). San Francisco: Jossey-Bass.

Trist, E. (1985). Intervention strategies for interorganizational domains. In R. Tannenbaum, N. Margulies, F. Massarik, & associates (Eds.), *Human systems development* (pp. 167–197). San Francisco: Jossey-Bass.

Trompenaars, F., & Prud'homme, P. (2004). *Managing change across corporate cultures.* Chichester, UK: Capstone.

Tuckman, B. (1965). Developmental sequences in small groups. *Psychological Bulletin, 63*, 384–99.

Tuckman, B., & Jensen, M. (1977). Stages of small group development revisited. *Group and Organization Studies, 2*, 419–427.

Tueke, P. (2005). The architecture of participation. In S. Schuman (Ed.), *The IAF handbook of group facilitation* (pp. 73–88). San Francisco: Jossey-Bass.

Tulgan, B. (2000). *Managing Generation X.* New York: W. W. Norton.

Ulrich, D., Kerr, S., & Ashkenas, R. (2002). *The GE work-out.* New York: McGraw-Hill.

Vaill, P. (2000). Strategic planning. In R. T. Golembiewski (Ed.), *Handbook of organizational consultation* (2nd ed., pp. 965–971). New York: Marcel Dekker.

Van Eron, A., & Burke, W. W. (1995). Separation. In W. Rothwell, R. Sullivan, & G. N. McLean (Eds.), *Practicing organization development: A guide for consultants* (pp. 395–418). San Diego: Pfeiffer.

Vangen, S., & Huxham, C. (2003). Nurturing collaborative relations: Building trust in interorganizational collaboration. *Journal of Applied Behavioral Science, 39*, 5–31.

van Knippenberg, D. (2003). Intergroup relations in organizations. In M. A. West, D. Tjosvold, & K. G. Smith (Eds.), *International handbook of organizational teamwork and cooperative working* (pp. 381–399). West Sussex, UK: Wiley.

Varney, G. H. (1980). Developing OD competencies. *Training and Development Journal, 34*(4), 30–35.

Vicars, W. M., & Hartke, D. D. (1984). Evaluating OD evaluations: A status report. *Group & Organization Studies, 9*, 177–188.

Wack, P. (1985a). Scenarios: Shooting the rapids. *Harvard Business Review, 63*(6), 139–150.

Wack, P. (1985b). Scenarios: Unchartered waters ahead. *Harvard Business Review, 63*(5), 73–89.

Waclawski, J., & Rogelberg, S. G. (2002). Interviews and focus groups: Quintessential organization development techniques. In J. Waclawski & A. H. Church (Eds.), *Organization development: A data-driven approach to organizational change* (pp. 103–126). San Francisco: Jossey-Bass.

Wade, H. (2004). Managerial growth: A coaching case study. *Industrial and Commercial Training, 36,* 73–78.

Wageman, R., Hackman, J. R., & Lehman, E. (2005). Team diagnostic survey. *Journal of Applied Behavioral Science, 41,* 373–398.

Walter, G. A. (1985). Culture collisions in mergers and acquisitions. In P. J. Frost, L. F. Moore, M. R. Louis, C. C. Lundberg, & J. Martin (Eds.), *Organizational culture* (pp. 301–314). Beverly Hills, CA: Sage.

Warrick, D. D., & Donovan, T. (1979). Surveying organization development skills. *Training and Development Journal, 33*(9), 22–25.

Watzlawick, P., Weakland, J., & Fisch, R. (1974). *Change: Principles of problem formation and problem resolution.* New York: W. W. Norton.

Webb, E., & Weick, K. E. (1979). Unobtrusive measures in organizational theory: A reminder. *Administrative Science Quarterly, 24,* 650–659.

Webb, E. J., Campbell, D. T., Schwartz, R. D., & Sechrest, L. (1966). *Unobtrusive measures: Nonreactive research in the social sciences.* Chicago: Rand McNally.

Webber, S. S. (2002). Leadership and trust facilitating cross-functional team success. *Journal of Management Development, 21,* 201–214.

Weber, R. A., & Camerer, C. F. (2003). Cultural conflict and merger failure: An experimental approach. *Management Science, 29,* 400–415.

Weick, K. E. (1979). *The social psychology of organizing* (2nd ed.). New York: McGraw-Hill.

Weick, K. E. (1995). *Sensemaking in organizations.* Thousand Oaks, CA: Sage.

Weick, K. E. (2000). Emergent change as a universal in organizations. In M. Beer & N. Nohria (Eds.), *Breaking the code of change* (pp. 223–241). Boston: Harvard University Press.

Weick, K. E., & Ashford, S. J. (2001). Learning in organizations. In F. Jablin & L. L. Putnam (Eds.), *The new handbook of organizational communication* (pp. 704–731). Thousand Oaks, CA: Sage.

Weick, K. E., & Quinn, R. E. (1999). Organizational change and development. *Annual Review of Psychology, 50,* 361–386.

Weisbord, M. R. (1976). Organizational diagnosis: Six places to look for trouble with or without a theory. *Group & Organization Studies, 1,* 430–447.

Weisbord, M. R. (1992). *Discovering common ground.* San Francisco: Berrett-Koehler.

Weisbord, M. R. (1994). The organization development contract. In W. L. French, C. H. Bell Jr., & R. A. Zawacki (Eds.), *Organization development and transformation: Managing effective change* (4th ed., pp. 406–412). Burr Ridge, IL: Irwin. (Reprinted from *OD Practitioner, 5*(2), 1973, 1–4)

Weisbord, M. R., & Janoff, S. (2000). *Future search: An action guide to finding common ground in organizations and communities* (2nd ed.). San Francisco: Berrett-Koehler.

West, M. A. (2004). *Effective teamwork: Practical lessons from organizational research* (2nd ed.). Malden, MA: Blackwell.

West, M. A., & Markiewicz, L. (2004). *Building team-based working: A practical guide to organizational transformation.* Malden, MA: BPS Blackwell.

What makes a small group tick. (1955, Aug. 13). *BusinessWeek,* pp. 40–45.

Wheelan, S. A. (2005). *Creating effective teams: A guide for members and their leaders* (2nd ed.). Thousand Oaks, CA: Sage.

White, L. P., & Wooten, K. C. (1983). Ethical dilemmas in various stages of organizational development. *Academy of Management Review, 8,* 690–697.

White, L. P., & Wooten, K. C. (1985). *Professional ethics and practice in organizational development*. New York: Praeger.

Whiting, V. R., & de Janasz, S. C. (2004). Mentoring in the 21st century: Using the Internet to build skills and networks. *Journal of Management Education, 28,* 275–293.

Whitney, D., & Trosten-Bloom, A. (2003). *The power of appreciative inquiry: A practical guide to positive change.* San Francisco: Berrett-Koehler.

Wilhelm, W. E., Damodaran, P., & Li, J. (2003). Prescribing the content and timing of product upgrades. *IIE Transactions, 35,* 647–663.

Wirtenberg, J., Abrams, L., & Ott, C. (2004). Assessing the field of organization development. *Journal of Applied Behavioral Science, 40,* 465–479.

Wirtenberg, J., Lipsky, D., Abrams, L., Conway, M., & Slepian, J. (2007). The future of organization development: Enabling sustainable business performance through people. *Organization Development Journal, 25*(2), 11–22.

Witherspoon, R., & White, R. P. (1996). Executive coaching: A continuum of roles. *Consulting Psychology Journal, 48,* 124–133.

Wolf, W. B. (1958). Organizational constructs—An approach to understanding organizations. *Academy of Management Journal, 1,* 7–15.

Woodman, R. W., & Pasmore, W. A. (2002). The heart of it all: Group- and team-based interventions in organization development. In J. Waclawski & A. H. Church (Eds.), *Organization development: A data-driven approach to organizational change* (pp. 164–176). San Francisco: Jossey-Bass.

Woolley, A. W. (1998). Effects of intervention content and timing on group task performance. *Journal of Applied Behavioral Science, 34,* 30–46.

Wooten, K. C., & White, L. P. (1999). Linking OD's philosophy with justice theory: Postmodern implications. *Journal of Organizational Change Management, 12,* 7–20.

Work-at-home patterns by occupation. (2009, March). *Issues in Labor Statistics,* Summary 09-02. Washington, DC: U.S. Department of Labor, Bureau of Labor Statistics.

Worley, C., & Varney, G. (1998, Winter). A search for a common body of knowledge for master's level organization development and change programs. *Academy of Management ODC Newsletter,* pp. 1–4.

Worley, C. G., & Feyerherm, A. E. (2003). Reflections on the future of organization development. *Journal of Applied Behavioral Science, 39,* 97–115.

Worley, C. G., Hitchin, D. E., & Ross, W. L. (1996). *Integrated strategic change: How OD builds competitive advantage.* Reading, MA: Addison-Wesley.

Yaeger, T. F., Head, T. C., & Sorensen, P. F. (2006). *Global organization development: Managing unprecedented change.* Greenwich, CT: Information Age.

Yeatts, D. E., & Hyten, C. (1998). *High-performing self-managed work teams.* Thousand Oaks, CA: Sage.

Zbaracki, M. J. (1998). The rhetoric and reality of total quality management. *Administrative Science Quarterly, 43,* 602–636.

Zorn, T. E., Christensen, L. T., & Cheney, G. (1999). *Do we really want constant change?* San Francisco: Berrett-Koehler.

Author Index

Subject Index

About the Author

Donald L. Anderson, PhD, University of Colorado, teaches organization development and design in the program in organizational and professional communication at the University of Denver. He is a practicing organization development consultant and has consulted internally and externally to a wide variety of organizations, including Fortune 500 corporations, small businesses, and educational institutions. His studies of organizational discourse and change have been published in journals such as the *Journal of Organizational Change Management* and the *Journal of Business and Technical Communication*. He is also the editor of the text *Cases and Exercises in Organization Development & Change* (Sage Publications, 2012). He is a member of the Academy of Management.